I0810221

PACIFIC JEWELRY AND ADORNMENT

PACIFIC JEWELRY AND ADORNMENT

ROGER NEICH AND FULI PEREIRA
PHOTOGRAPHS BY KRZYSZTOF PFEIFFER

University of Hawai'i Press
Honolulu

Copyright © Auckland War Memorial Museum, 2004
Copyright © David Bateman Ltd, 2004

All rights reserved. No part of this publication may be reproduced, stored in a retrieval system or transmitted in any form or by any means, electronic, mechanical, photocopying, recording or otherwise without the prior written permission from the publisher.

First published 2004 in New Zealand by David Bateman Ltd, 30 Tarndale Grove, Albany, Auckland, New Zealand

Published in North America by University of Hawai'i Press, 2840 Kolowalu Street, Honolulu, Hawai'i 96822

Library of Congress Cataloging-in-Publication Data

Neich, Roger.
Pacific jewelry and adornment from the collections of Auckland Museum / Roger Neich and Pandora Fulimalo Pereira ; photographs by Krzysztof Pfeiffer.
p. cm.
Includes bibliographical references and index.
ISBN 0-8248-2882-8 (alk. paper)
1. Jewelry--Oceania--Catalogs. 2. Ethnic jewelry--Oceania--Catalogs.
3. Jewelry--New Zealand--Auckland--Catalogs. 4. Auckland Institute and Museum--Catalogs. I. Pereira, Pandora Fulimalo. II. Pfeiffer, Krzysztof. III. Title.
NK7389.9.A1N45 2004
739.27'0995'0749324--dc22
200400110

Design www.inhousedesign.co.nz
Editorial services Jeanette Cook
Printed in China through Colorcraft Ltd, HK

CONTENTS

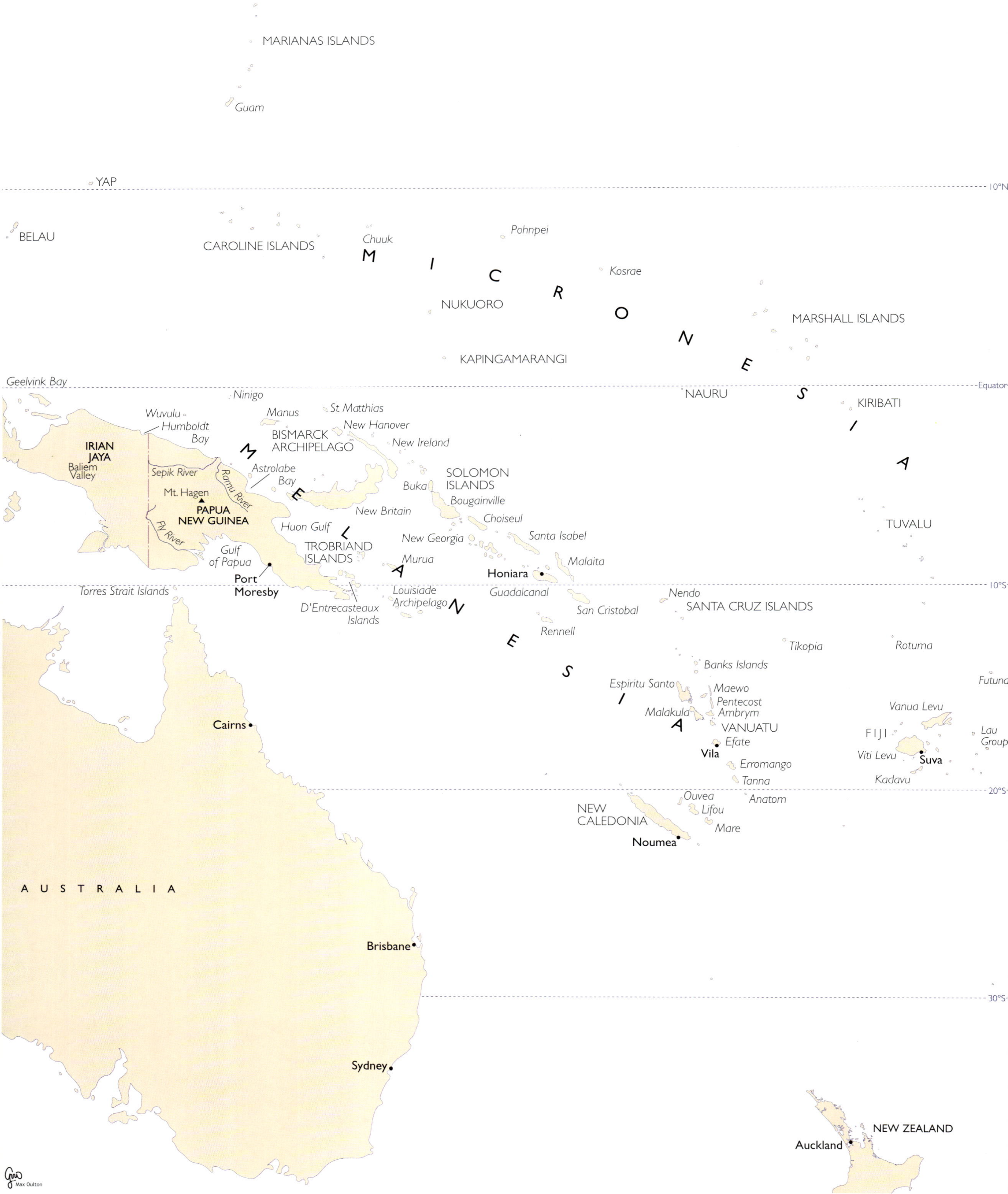

MARIANAS ISLANDS
Guam
YAP
10°N
BELAU
CAROLINE ISLANDS
Chuuk
Pohnpei
Kosrae
M I C R O N E S I A
NUKUORO
KAPINGAMARANGI
MARSHALL ISLANDS
Geelvink Bay
Equator
Ninigo
NAURU
KIRIBATI
Manus
St. Matthias
Wuvulu
Humboldt Bay
New Hanover
BISMARCK ARCHIPELAGO
New Ireland
IRIAN JAYA
Baliem Valley
M E L A N E S I A
Sepik River
Ramu River
Astrolabe Bay
SOLOMON ISLANDS
Buka
Mt. Hagen
Bougainville
PAPUA NEW GUINEA
New Britain
Choiseul
TUVALU
Fly River
Huon Gulf
New Georgia
Santa Isabel
TROBRIAND ISLANDS
Gulf of Papua
Murua
Malaita
Port Moresby
Honiara
Torres Strait Islands
Louisiade Archipelago
Guadalcanal
10°S
Nendo
SANTA CRUZ ISLANDS
D'Entrecasteaux Islands
San Cristobal
Rennell
Tikopia
Rotuma
Banks Islands
Futuna
Espiritu Santo
Maewo
Pentecost
Ambrym
Malakula
VANUATU
Vanua Levu
FIJI
Lau Group
Efate
Vila
Viti Levu
Suva
Erromango
Tanna
Kadavu
Anatom
20°S
Ouvea
Lifou
NEW CALEDONIA
Mare
Noumea
A U S T R A L I A
Cairns
Brisbane
30°S
Sydney
NEW ZEALAND
Auckland
Max Oulton

MAP OF THE PACIFIC

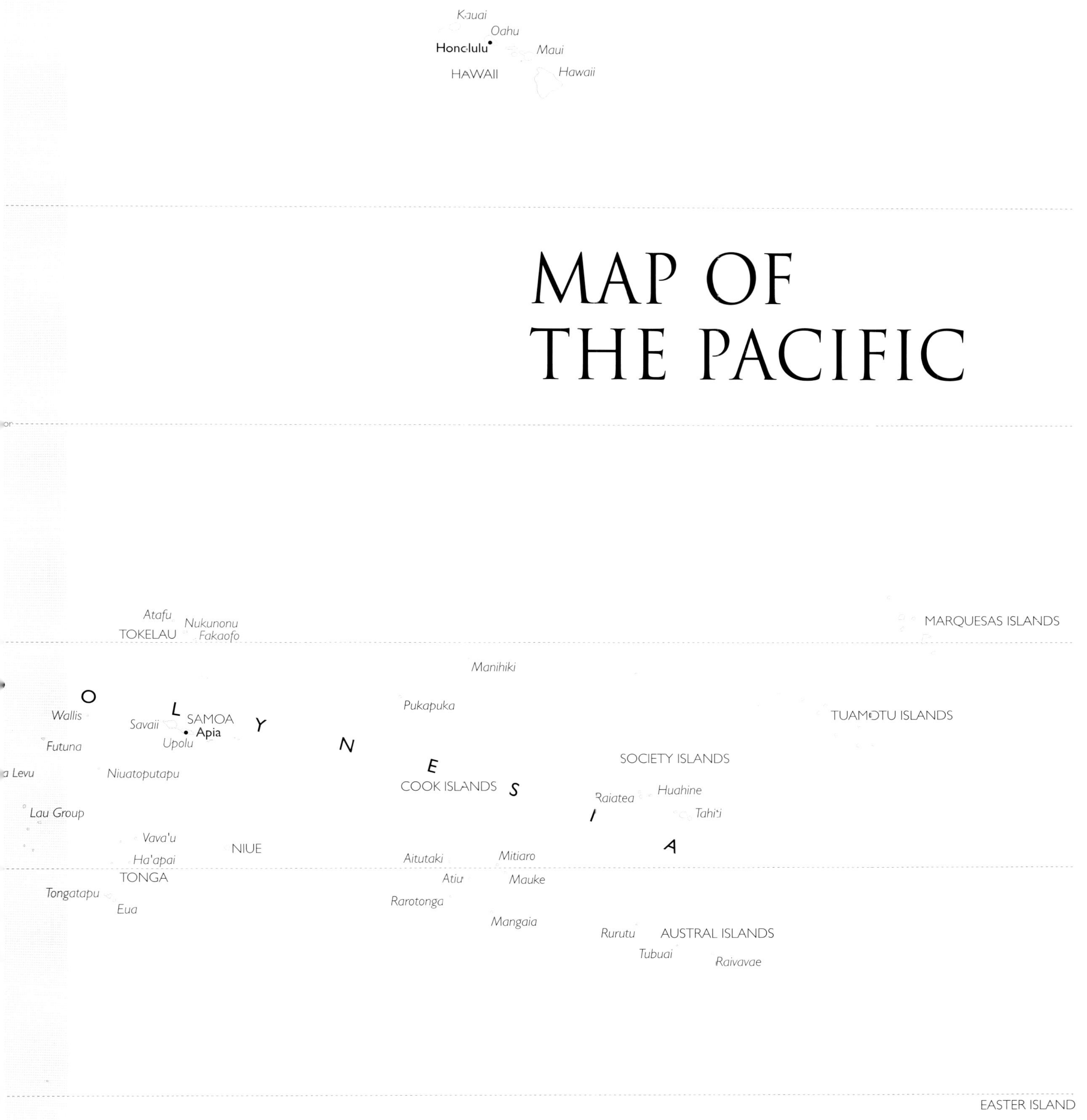

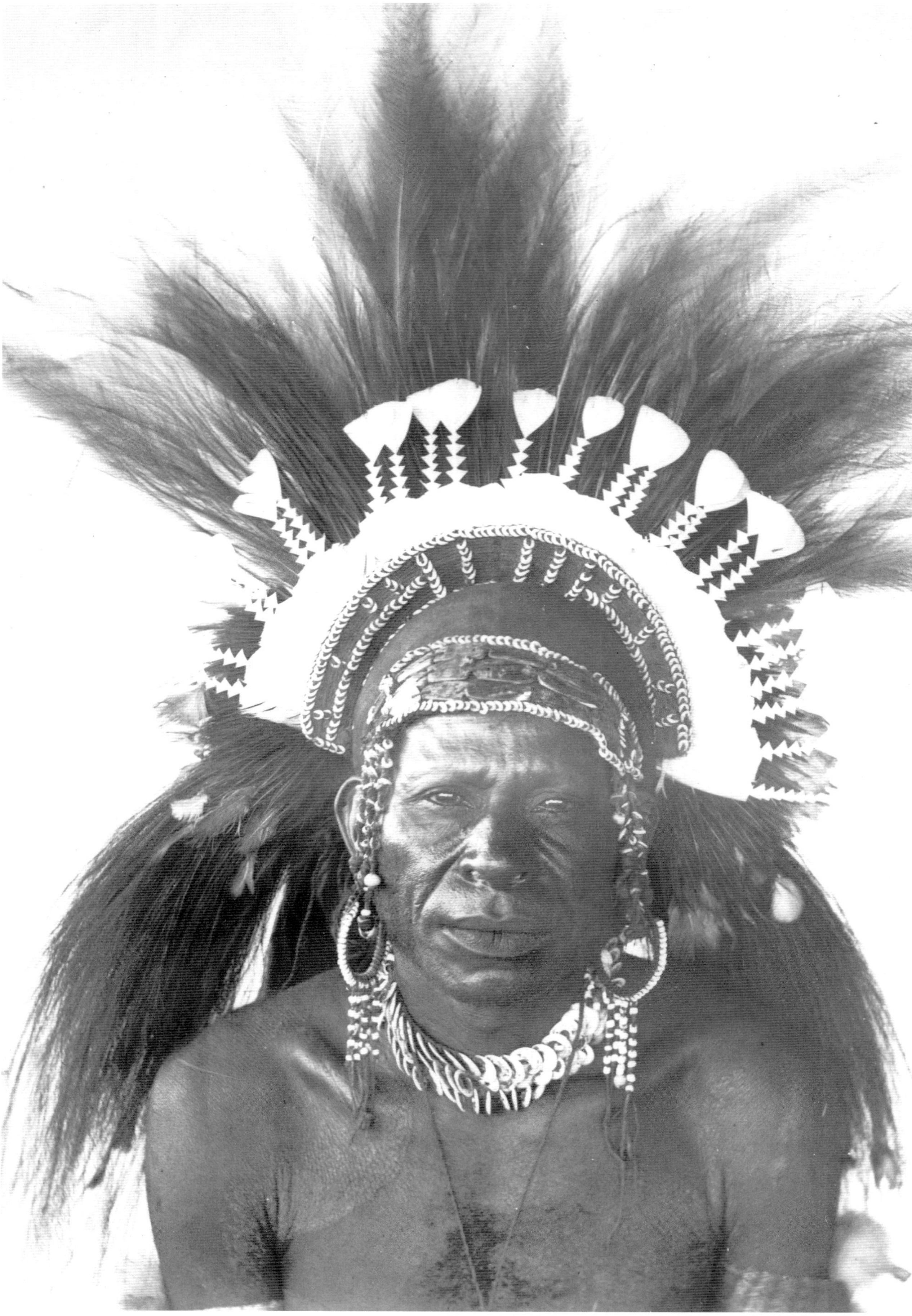

INTRODUCTORY ESSAY

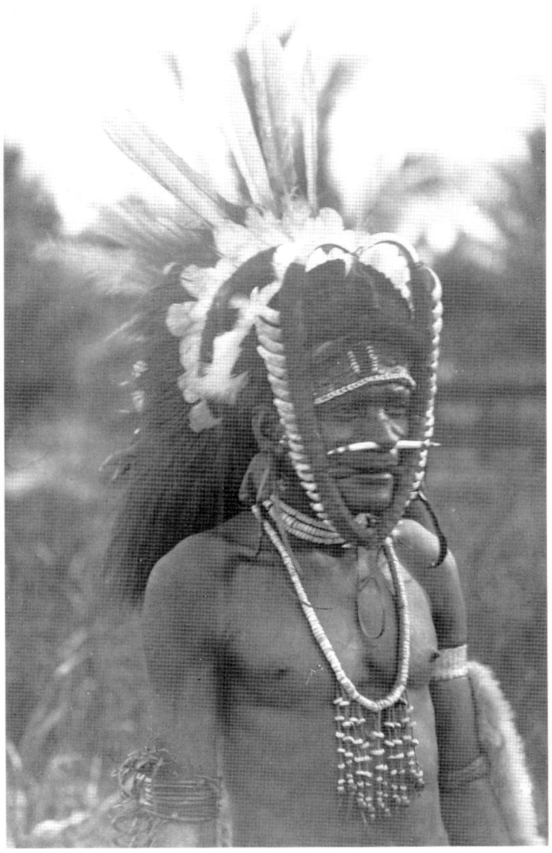

opposite and above: **Two Sets of Self-Decoration, Wanigela, Collingwood Bay, Oro Province, Papua New Guinea, Between 1901 and 1911**

These men, both from Wanigela, are wearing different sets of head-dresses and ornaments, probably relating to differences in age, status and clan affiliation. The man above holds his gibigibi *(boar-tusk face ornament) in his teeth, as it would be worn into battle, and has a bone nose pin through his nasal septum and an elaborate shell disc necklace. Both men wear the same type of forehead* nanemo *of* Spondylus *shell pieces and bunches of cassowary plumes at the back of their heads, but the feather plumes of their head-dresses have been treated very differently. A third type of head-dress worn by these men consisted of an array of hornbills' beaks that was reserved for men who had killed an enemy.*

Photos: Percy Money, Auckland Museum 97/53

PACIFIC DIVERSITY

Over the last several thousand years throughout the widespread island environments of the Pacific Ocean, the people of Oceania have developed a broad diversity of cultures. This long history has seen different groups of peoples moving into every area of the Pacific, meeting new and challenging environments. Some places, especially in the islands about the New Guinea mainland, had already been reached and occupied by people more than 40,000 years ago. Later arrivals had to adjust to living with or beside these earlier settlers. But as later explorers and settlers moved further out into the open Pacific, they found themselves to be the first humans in a pristine world.

Out of these ancient cultures in these new environments, the cultures of the Pacific as we know them today have evolved. From the high mountain valleys of New Guinea to the low coral atolls and the remotest specks of Micronesia and Polynesia, this diversity is expressed in language, song, dance, mythology, religion, family organisation, costume, architecture, canoe design and village life. Many of these cultures were in frequent contact with each other, sharing their ideas through exchange networks, trade, warfare and marriage. Others were more isolated, especially as long-distance ocean voyaging declined. However, underlying this diversity there is a basic unity of Pacific cultures that distinguishes them from other cultures of the world. This book celebrates this diversity and unity by presenting a wide and rich range of Pacific jewellery and body adornment.

Sadly, for much of this traditional jewellery, reliable and detailed information about its specific purposes and the cultural messages that it conveyed was not recorded at the time these items were still being made and worn. In those areas of the Pacific where fashions have changed and the old lifeways have become obsolete, most of this knowledge has been lost among the people themselves. In areas where the indigenous cultures are still strong, much can still be learnt from the people who live with this jewellery. In general we have more information about jewellery in Melanesia than in Polynesia and Micronesia, mainly because European contact occurred later in Melanesia and therefore more was recorded by ethnographers. Now, we have to rely on whatever written records are available and combine this with observation of the present role of jewellery in Pacific cultures. Perhaps most importantly, we must also try to recover as much empathy and understanding as possible by examining and enjoying the marvellous examples of Pacific jewellery that have been assembled in museum collections.

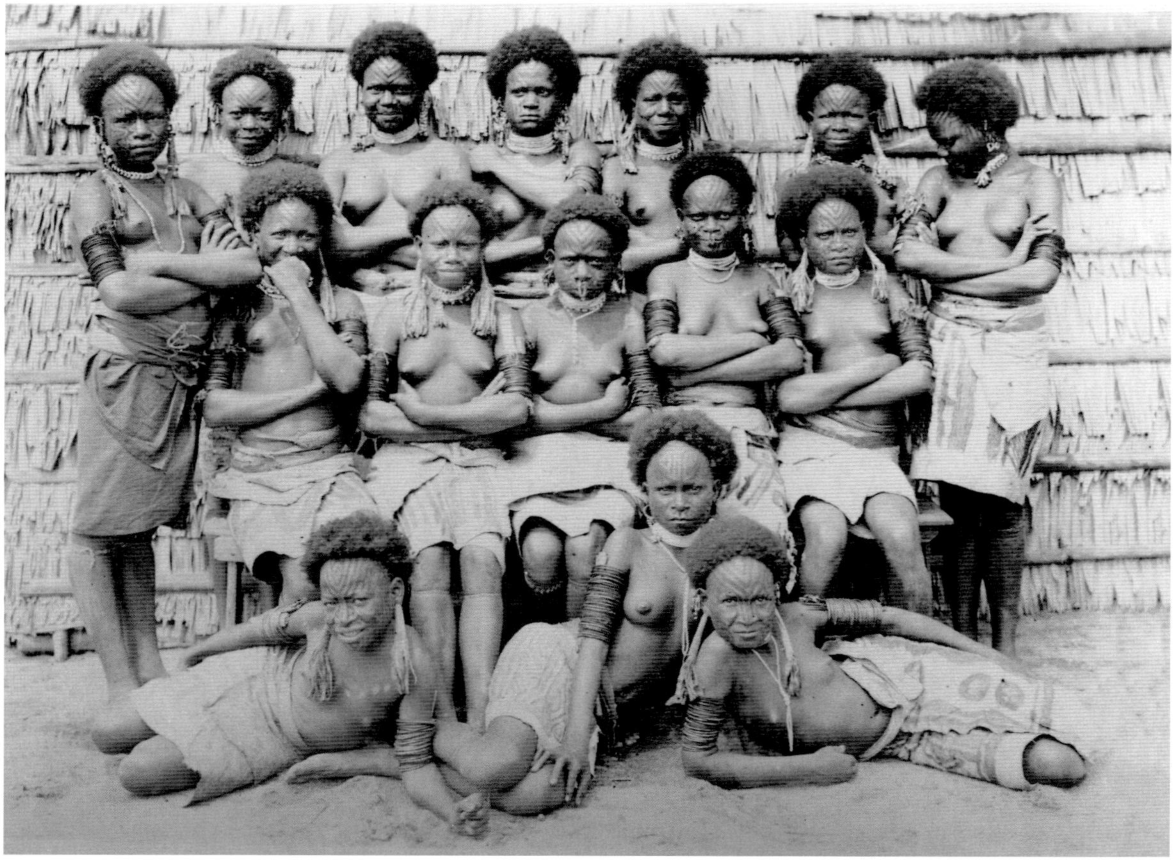

YOUNG GIRLS RECENTLY EMERGED FROM SECLUSION AFTER TATTOOING, WANIGELA, COLLINGWOOD BAY, ORO PROVINCE, PAPUA NEW GUINEA, BETWEEN 1901 AND 1911

When a group of Wanigela girls reached the age of puberty, they were given facial tattoos with designs that relate to motifs also applied to locally made pots and barkcloth. A skilled woman carried out the tattoo operation during three weeks of seclusion in her house, followed by three months of food restrictions. This group, with their new tattoos and wide range of ornaments including ear strings, nose rings, necklaces and arm bands, are now considered to be adults.

Photo: Percy Money, Auckland Museum 97/53, C41089

PACIFIC CULTURAL ORIGINS

ALL OF THE indigenous cultures of the Pacific have their origins back in the mainland of east and south-east Asia and the islands close to the Asian continent. Archaeology has shown that by at least 40,000 years ago, perhaps even 60,000 years ago, people of Asian origin had reached what are now New Guinea and Australia and the so-called Near Oceania islands of the Bismarck Archipelago and the Solomon islands. By 30,000 years ago, some of the New Guinea highland valleys had been occupied.

These population movements occurred mostly in periods of low sea level during the glacial advances of the Pleistocene period when New Guinea and Australia were sometimes joined by land bridges. However, the islands of Near Oceania were apparently never joined to this large land mass.

By the mid-Holocene period of about 10,000 years ago, the descendants of these people living about the coasts had developed a complex shell-working technology focused on shell fishhooks and shell adze blades. With this technology, they also produced the earliest known Pacific jewellery, which included *Trochus* shell arm rings, *Conus* shell ground discs, presumably designed to be worn about the body, and shell beads, presumably for stringing into necklaces and attaching to other body ornaments. Obviously, they applied an aesthetic sensibility to decorating their bodies, even though virtually nothing is now known about the ideas informing this aesthetic.

Within the islands of Near Oceania over this long time-depth period of 30,000 to 40,000 years, a tremendous cultural and linguistic diversity came into

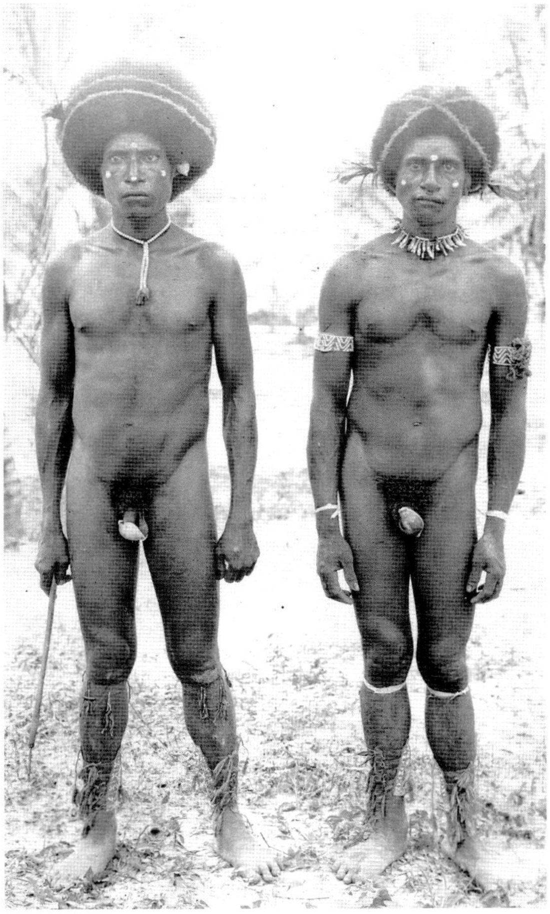

Young Men of Pak Island, Admiralty Islands, Bismarck Archipelago, 1920s

Photographed by Patrol Officer James Adams Wilkes at Pak Island to the east of Manus Island, these young Admiralty Islands men are wearing their full ceremonial dress of wigs, djamé *(penis shells), necklaces, arm bands, wrist cords and leg cords. Wigs are not otherwise recorded for the Admiralty Islands; but* Ovula ovum *shells, often incised with geometric designs, were worn on the penis for a range of special occasions, which usually included the energetic dance intended to demonstrate their phallic athleticism.*

Photo: James Adams Wilkes, Auckland Museum

being. Small scattered populations spoke several hundred distinct Papuan or non-Austronesian languages and became adapted to a multitude of different highland, coastal and small island environments. Their shell, stone, wood and fibre technologies became more sophisticated, eventually forming the foundation for the cultures that still exist today in these regions, alongside the later Austronesian arrivals. Jewellery made by the nineteenth century descendants of these pre-Austronesian Papuan-speaking peoples can give at least a sense and feeling for the sort of body jewellery created and worn by these ancient Pacific pioneers.

Beyond the islands of Near Oceania, human settlement did not begin until about 3,500 years ago, very soon after the Lapita cultural complex had developed, probably somewhere in the area of the Bismarck Archipelago. Lapita culture was based on large coastal lagoon and off-shore island villages, the raising of pigs, dogs and chickens, building oceanic voyaging canoes, making pottery both plain and dentate-stamped with repeating patterns, and the use of Austronesian languages. Constituting the most widespread language grouping of the pre-modern world, Austronesian languages are spoken as far west as Madagascar, through most of island South-east Asia, including aboriginal Taiwan, certain areas of New Guinea and the 'old Melanesia' of Near Oceania, and out into the wider Pacific as far east as Easter Island/Rapanui. The Oceanic branch of Austronesian languages includes all of the languages spoken in Polynesia and most of those in Micronesia, apart from some languages brought into Micronesia by settlers coming directly from Asian islands in the west.

Very rapidly, this Lapita culture and its Austronesian language spread through the use of sophisticated outrigger sailing canoes beyond Near Oceania, firstly down the chain of the large Solomon Islands populated by pre-Austronesian peoples, then out into the uninhabited islands of the further Pacific. Almost simultaneously, one branch moved south down through Vanuatu to New Caledonia while another went south-east to the Santa Cruz Islands.

Within another hundred or so years, from either Santa Cruz or northern Vanuatu, Lapita culture had reached Fiji by crossing a huge water gap of more than 800 kilometres. Then from Fiji there was a very rapid expansion of Lapita culture into Tonga and Samoa so that by 3000 years ago Austronesian-speaking Lapita peoples had extensively occupied this central area of the Pacific, including Futuna and Uvea. Further expansion stalled in this area for the ensuing 1000 years and it was here that Lapita culture was transformed into what we now recognise as Polynesian. This ancestral Polynesian culture included the beginnings of ranked societies, marked especially by the exchange of shell valuables, that would later develop into the hierarchical and chiefly cultures of Tonga, Tahiti, Hawai'i and New Zealand. Pottery types, adze forms and jewellery styles all show the continuity of eastern Lapita culture into ancestral Polynesian culture.

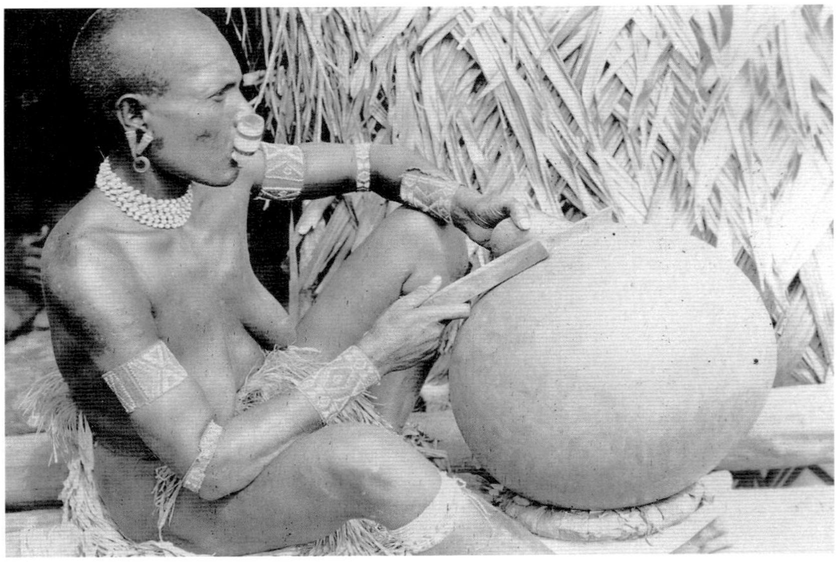

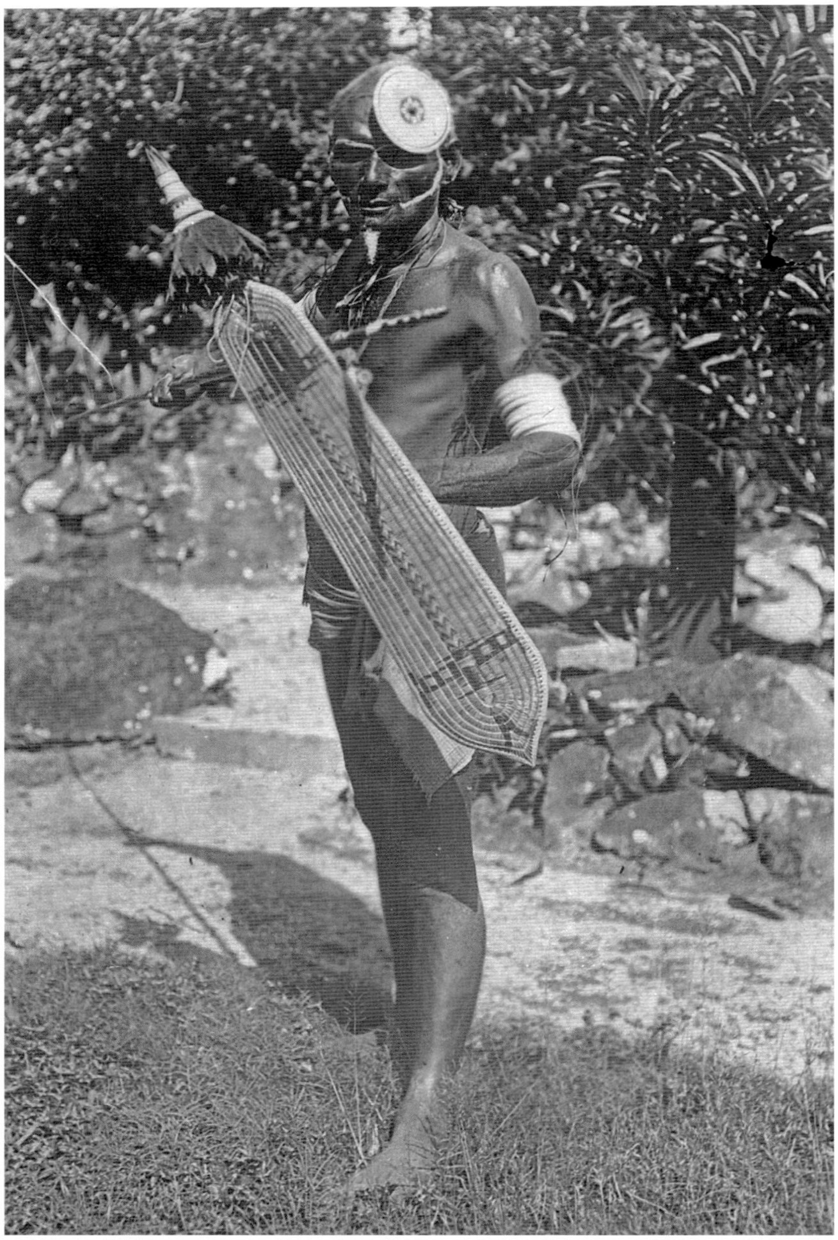

Woman Making Pottery, M'Buke Island, Admiralty Islands, Papua New Guinea, 1920s

M'Buke Island, south of Manus Island, was one of the three main areas in the Admiralty Islands, along with Timoenai on the south coast and Hus off the north coast, where earthenware cooking and water storage pots were made, for both local use and trade. This woman is using a small wooden beater on the outside and a smooth stone on the inside in a paddle-and-anvil technique to shape the wide bowl form of a sago cooking pot. She works while smoking her pipe and wearing her full complement of turtle-shell ear rings, beaded necklace, arm bands and leg bands.

Photo: James Adams Wilkes, Auckland Museum

Warrior Wearing A *Kapkap*, Simbo, Western Solomon Islands, 1920s

Men in most areas of the Solomon Islands wore kapkap *forehead ornaments for going into battle and for dancing at festivals as a symbol of their wealth.* Kapkaps *made in the northwestern islands of Choiseul, New Georgia and nearby Simbo often feature a small anthropomorphic figure in the centre of the turtle shell fretwork. In addition to his* kapkap, *this man wears clam shell arm rings. He carries his wickerwork fighting shield, which is decorated with a plume of feathers on a conical addition at the top.*

Photo: Clifford Collinson, Postcard, Accession Number 12/59, Auckland Museum

From this 'Polynesian homeland', the first Hawaiki, Polynesian explorers moved out north, east and south to reach all the island groups of Eastern Polynesia as far as the Society Islands, the Marquesas, the Tuamotu Islands, Hawai'i, Easter Island and New Zealand. The Polynesian outliers of the Solomons-Vanuatu-New Caledonia region all seem to have populations derived from Samoa and Futuna. This final expansion of the Lapita descendants was virtually completed by about 1000 AD, or perhaps about 1200 AD in New Zealand, and from that time on the Polynesian societies of each of these island groups have been developing their own distinctive brand of Polynesian culture. Jewellery and types of personal ornaments such as whale tooth pendants, bone necklace units and shell pendants underwent gradual changes that eventually produced jewellery and ornaments distinctive of each Polynesian group.

The material culture of the Lapita peoples included a wider range of jewellery and body ornament than any of the earlier peoples of Near Oceania although there was probably some interchange and borrowing of ideas between these cultures. Early Lapita jewellery was concentrated on shell rings used in various combinations, shell arm rings, composite bracelets, and necklaces of shell beads and drilled shell discs. In each of the island groups of 'new Melanesia', Polynesia and Micronesia, this common heritage of Lapita jewellery was diversified and developed to meet the needs and desires of the new cultures in their new environments.

In the north-western Pacific, the low coral atolls, raised *makatea* limestone islands and high volcanic islands of Micronesia were populated by peoples speaking two major subgroups of the Austronesian language family—Oceanic and Western Malayo-Polynesian. This mixture probably reflects the arrival of several different population movements into the area, some coming directly from the islands of south-east Asia into western Micronesia and some coming from the Lapita-derived Oceanic cultures. The evidence of historical linguistics suggests that the Oceanic cultures came from different areas and at different times, comprising one movement from the Solomons-Vanuatu region and another from the Bismarck Archipelago into Yap. In the 'Yapese empire', dating from about 1200 AD and extending through fourteen Carolinian atolls reaching 1,200 kilometres east of Yap, tributes of woven cloth, mats, plaited rope and shell valuables flowed into the superior lineages of Yap from the atolls. These shell valuables and currency items were often incorporated into personal jewellery that became heirlooms among the Yapese aristocracy. The Polynesian outliers of Nukuoro and Kapingamarangi south of the Caroline chain were probably settled from Tuvalu.

Back in 'old Melanesia', the pre-Lapita peoples had continued to develop and innovate their own jewellery repertoire through the centuries. Consequently, the recent and present heritage of Pacific jewellery embodies all of these influences from 40,000 years of human creative artistic endeavour, distinguished by patient persistence and quiet innovation.

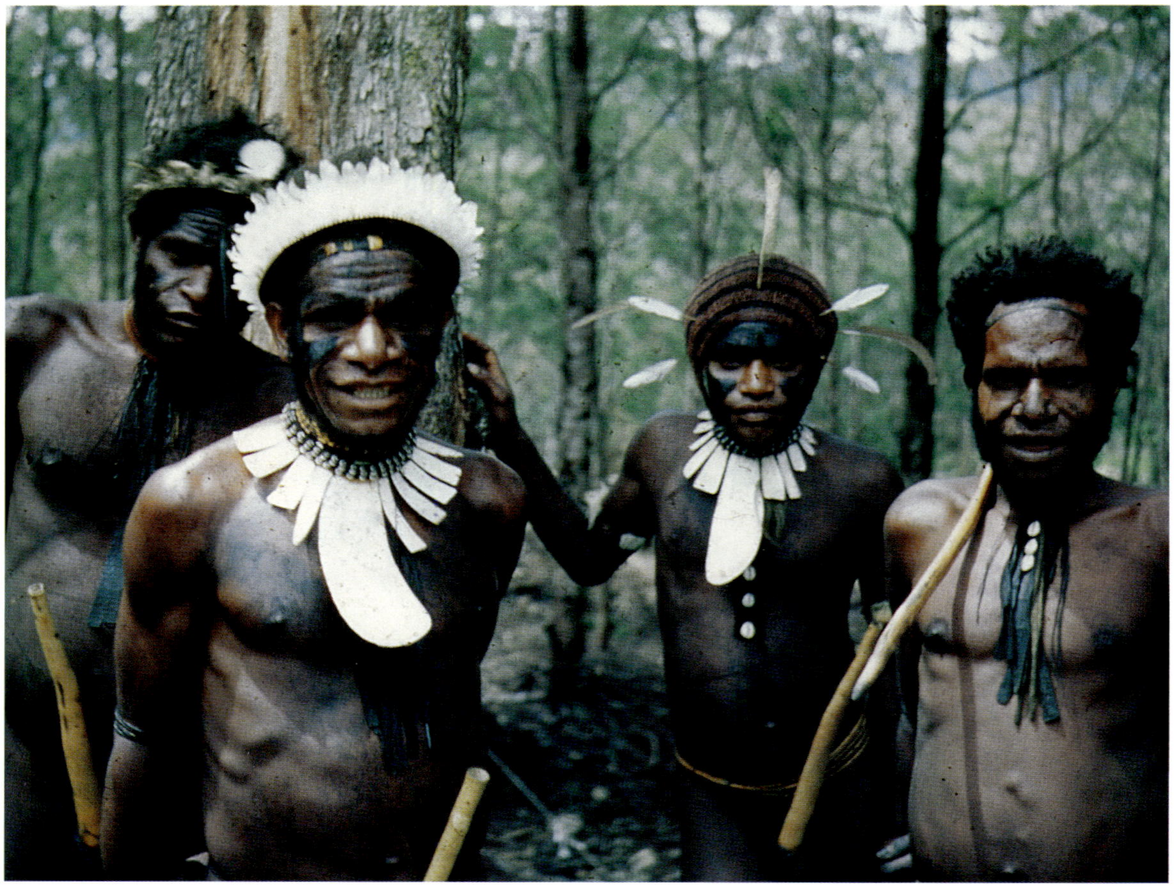

YOUNG MEN OF THE DANI PEOPLE, BALIEM VALLEY, WEST IRIAN, 1950S

Intently interested in the missionary photographer, these young Dani men in their usual daily attire wear a range of ornaments. This includes white feathers on their head-dresses, necklaces of seeds and beetle wing cases, with pendants of shell pieces and cowries traded up from the coast around their necks. All wear long straight penis gourds, grown to that shape by weighting the growing gourd with a stone. This straight gourd is characteristic of the Dani men although some have a wardrobe of different shapes and sizes. Other highland groups chose penis gourds of different shapes.

Photo: Russell Bond, Auckland Museum CT2993

JEWELLERY AND POWER

MOST PACIFIC PEOPLES believe in a vital spiritual energy, a life force that animates the universe. The very materials as well as the designs and patterns that people wore on their bodies focused this energy and helped to give them some control over its power. Within each Pacific culture, these concepts were understood and conveyed in culturally specific ways, as diverse as the hundreds of distinct cultures that developed in the islands of the wide Pacific Ocean.

All items of jewellery made by Pacific peoples exemplify culturally specific shapes and carry designs and patterns, either built into the structure of the object or added through colour and additional materials. By the nature of the materials and their techniques, most of these patterns are geometric, but figurative and naturalistic designs do appear, particularly in more recent works. Geometric designs convey cultural values and concepts at a deep subtle level, while figurative designs work at an obvious superficial level more accessible to those from outside the culture. Key values of balance, symmetry, exchange and reciprocity, nurture of growth, and replication for the benefit of future generations inform these geometric designs. Both consciously and unconsciously, these designs restate and reinforce these values in the daily lives of the people.

Traditional jewellery in the Pacific serves many more purposes than simple decoration. Where jewellery stops and costume begins is usually an irrelevant question in the Pacific. But for this exploration, our concentration is on detachable items that were added to costume elements or to the body directly for extra

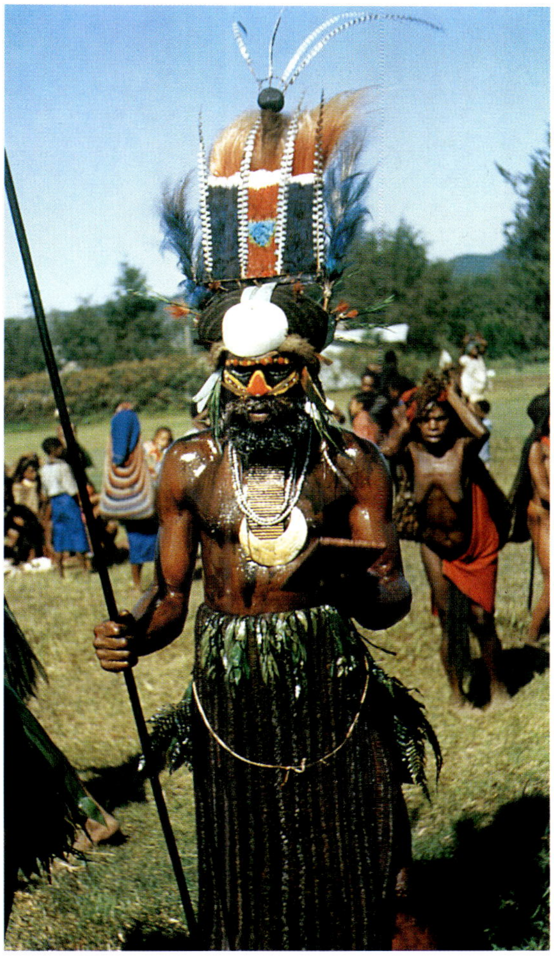

Man Of The Melpa People, Mount Hagen Area, Western Highlands, Papua New Guinea, 1963

This man's koi wal *head-dress consisting of a plaque of bird of paradise feathers, especially the highly valued King of Saxony bird plumes, denotes that he is a donor at a* moka, *a pig and pearl shell exchange festival. The* koi wal *is supported on a netted wig with a bailer shell frontal ornament. Around his neck hangs a pearl shell crescent and a long string of bamboo* omaak *sticks indicating that he has participated in many* moka *pig exchanges. His heavy dark netted* mbal omb *apron, which sways in unison with those of the other dancers in a long line, is also a sign of his donor status.*

Photo: Mrs A. Grace-Jones, Auckland Museum CT2264

effect beyond the needs of bodily modesty or comfort. This approach rules out the permanent adornments of patterned scarring or cicatrisation and tattoo, which are certainly very important forms of bodily enhancement in many parts of the Pacific.

Although they are also detachable from the person, the rich and diverse heritage of masks in the Melanesian areas of the Pacific is also ruled out of this survey on the grounds that masks are intended to disguise the individual wearer while creating the semblance of another being—either mythological, ancestral or human, or the embodiment of natural or spiritual forces. The use of masks never developed in Micronesia, except for one type in the Mortlock Islands; nor did it develop in Polynesia, except for a short experiment in copying Papua New Guinea masks that had been introduced into Rarotonga and Mangaia by returning Cook Island missionaries at the end of the nineteenth century.

An argument might be proposed that the wigs, feathers, shell ornaments and body paint of the New Guinea highlanders included here with other jewellery also go some way to disguise the individual and submerge him as simply a member of a social category. This especially applies to the self-decoration worn by a group as co-ordinated sets conveying specific messages to the viewers and participants at large gatherings such as Hagen *moka* and Enga *tee* exchanges, pig-killing festivals, compensation payments and fertility cult ceremonies. However, different compositions of this self-decoration are employed to denote individuals as donors, donors' wives, helpers, cult followers, mourners, warriors and so on. Individuals also manipulate the deeper cultural connotations of their self-decoration to emphasise different cultural values and concepts such as confidence, aggression, hostility, grief, fertility, prosperity, group solidarity and communion with ancestors.

Therefore ultimately, jewellery enhances the self-esteem and reflects the social position of the individual who wears it, despite some academic controversies about the role and status of the individual self in the context of Pacific cultures. Underlining the individual significance of Pacific jewellery is the fact that in many cultures of the Pacific, their jewellery is one of the very few personal possessions allowed to them, even to the extent that it was often buried with the individual to travel with his spirit to the afterworld.

Pacific peoples decorate and enhance their bodies to convey a wide range of messages to their fellows and to the outside world. Jewellery may serve as both physical and symbolic protection, as a way of displaying wealth and status, and as a means of projecting the personal, social and/or ethnic identity of the wearer. Nevertheless, as well as serving these symbolic/communicative and utilitarian purposes, most Pacific body decoration was also created with a strong aesthetic intention. Indeed, it is this aesthetic impact that provides and enhances the power of jewellery to carry out these other functions. But Pacific jewellery was not always intended to be beautiful; some was intended to shock, to frighten or to repel, but all of it was created to be worn and to be viewed by other people.

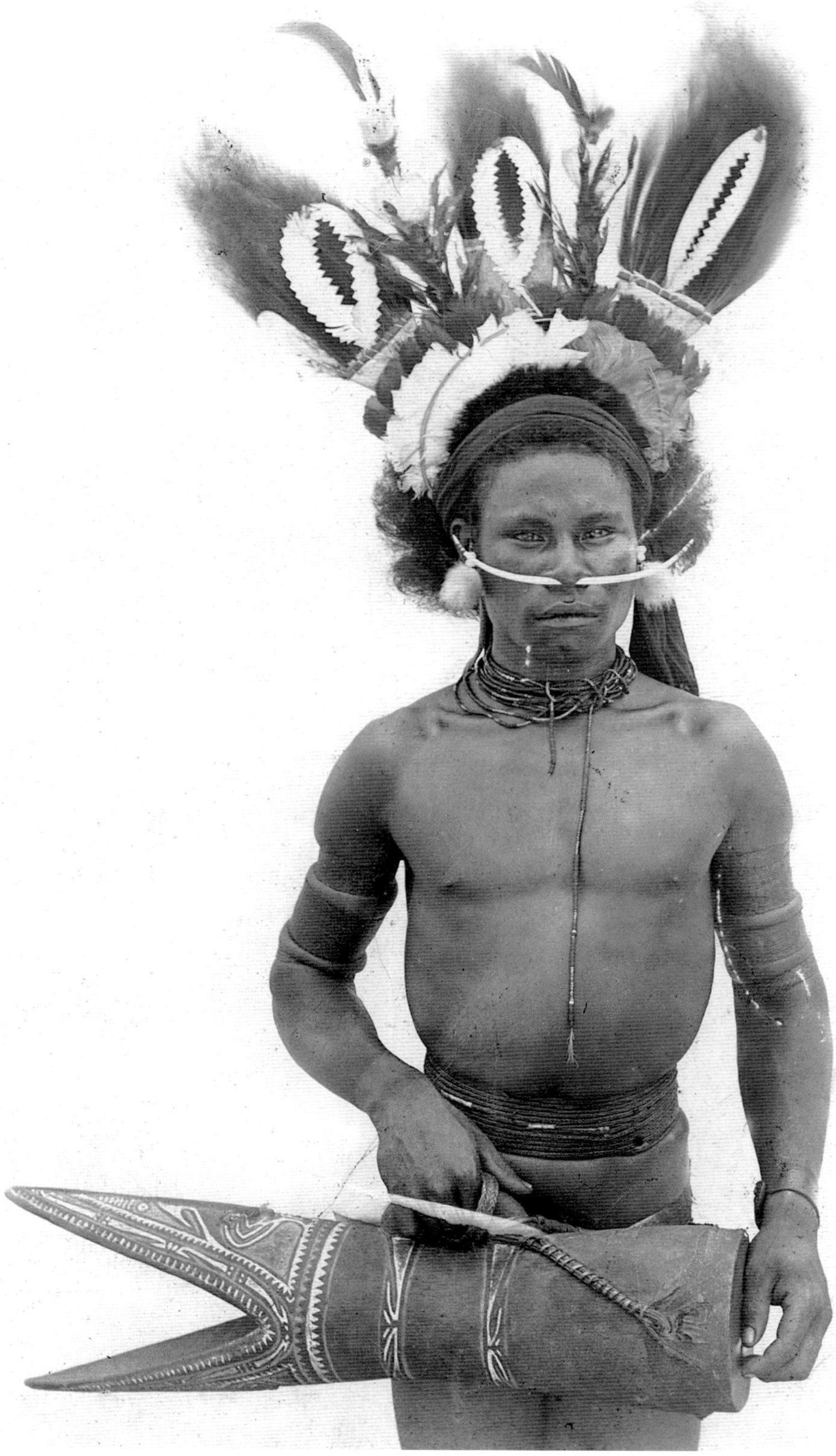

Young Male Dancer, Hanuabada Village, Port Moresby, Papua New Guinea, Between 1901 and 1911

This young Motu man is dressed for a special dance usually performed in connection with a feast at which the sponsor distributed large amounts of food to the guests to signify his wealth and social standing. The young men of the sponsor's lineage group would decorate themselves and perform these dances to support their leader. The head-dress includes bird of paradise plumes probably obtained by trade from his inland Koiari neighbours. A long, curved bone nose pin is decorated with fibre tassels and fibre bands constrict his arms and waist in typical Motu style. The lime-inlaid patterns of his dance drum indicate that it has been traded from the Elema or Namau people of the Gulf of Papua, probably during the annual hiri *trade expeditions when the Motu took pots to the Gulf to exchange for canoe hulls and sago.*

Photo: Percy Money, Auckland Museum 97/53

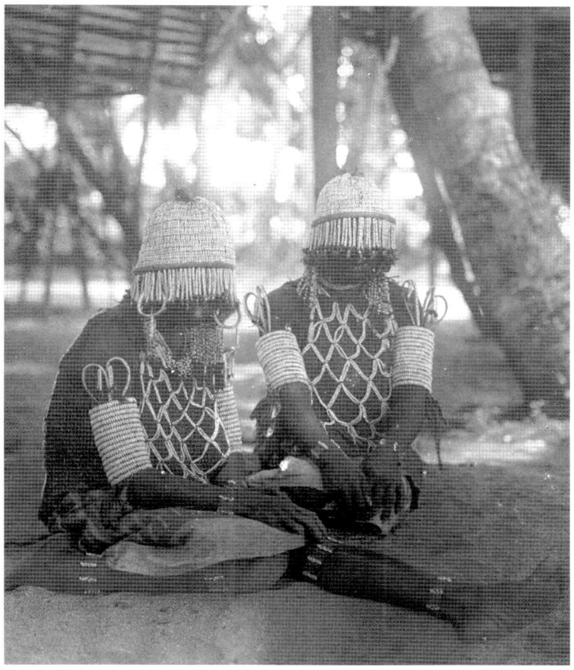

Widows In Mourning, Wanigela Village, Collingwood Bay, Oro Province, Papua New Guinea, Between 1901 and 1911

These two women are the widows of one man who has died within the previous year. Widows in this area clipped their hair short and covered themselves in white mud, and went into seclusion for at least a year. When they had to leave their house, they crawled along under a cover of barkcloth so that nobody could see their faces. While in seclusion, the widow made a mourning dress consisting of a wig, armlets and openwork bodice or blouse of white Coix lachryma-jobi *(Job's tears) seeds. After their period of seclusion had ended with a large feast, the widows always wore their mourning dress in public.*

Photo: Percy Money, Auckland Museum 97/53

THE MESSAGE OF THE MATERIALS

IN THE PACIFIC islands, almost any material was potentially useful for making jewellery. There was only one major absence and that was metal, which Pacific island cultures did not know of or use until after early Asian or later European contact. Whatever came to hand in the environment could have its value, beauty and power revealed or increased by the skill of the craftsperson. Other materials not present in the immediate environment had to be obtained by trade or by travel to other areas. These were often certain shells not available in the waters of home, animal products such as feathers, fur and teeth that came from animals restricted to certain environments, special stones found only in limited geological situations, and plant materials such as seeds, nuts and fibres growing only in particular forests or on particular islands.

The more common among these materials include coral, jade, slate, bone, palm wood, bamboo, human hair, human teeth, shark teeth, whale teeth, porpoise teeth, flying-fox teeth, cuscus teeth, dog teeth, boar tusks, fish teeth, fish vertebrae, *Nautilus* shells, turtle shells, pearl shells, marsupial fur, flying-fox fur, coconut shells, glass trade-beads, *Spondylus* shells, *Nassa* shells, *Ovula* shells, oyster shells, cowrie shells, *Cassis* shells, *Conus* shells, *Tridacna* giant clam shells both modern and fossilised, *Trochus* shells, frigate bird feathers, bird of paradise feathers, cassowary feathers, *Abrus* seeds, *Coix lachryma-jobi* seeds, everlasting daisies, orchid stems, *Pangium edule* nuts, *Parinarium* seeds and beetle carapaces. Probably one of the strangest materials for ornaments were the small live parrots and other colourful birds that were worn through their perforated earlobes by some New Zealand Maori men. But the list is almost endless.

The gathering of these materials or the travels to obtain them sometimes involved considerable physical effort and even danger. Hostile neighbours, unpredictable trading partners, treacherous coral reefs and the hazards of open sea travel in small canoes contributed to an increase in the intrinsic value of these materials, even before they reached the hands of the craftsperson. In the field of jewellery, as in so many other aspects of Pacific life, the gathering and preparation of certain materials was the domain of either men or women. Men usually made the long and dangerous trading expeditions while women worked closer to home, gathering on the reefs and foraging in the bush for the required materials.

Shells such as *Conus* and the big *Melo* 'bailer' shells used for breastplates were traded hundreds of miles from the coasts of New Guinea through many, often hostile, hands to reach the central highlands. Drilled red shell discs were favoured in much of the shell money and ornament current in Micronesia and northern Melanesia, but the *Spondylus* and *Chama pacifica* shells needed were rare and difficult to obtain because of their deep-water habitat. Consequently, centres for processing these shells into discs became concentrated in areas where the shells were more accessible, namely around Truk (Chuuk) in Micronesia, the Massim district of south-east Papua New Guinea, northern New Ireland, some of the islands of Kiribati, and around the coasts of Malaita.

In much of Melanesia, the gathering of *Tridacna* (giant clam) and *Conus* shells for the manufacture of arm rings was definitely the province of men. For the clam shells, it involved the physically demanding and dangerous work of gathering the heavy shells from the lagoon or, in the Solomon Islands, prising out fossil clam shells with their favoured yellow colouration from certain fossil coral reef deposits high in the hills. Similarly, gathering *Conus* shells by diving from canoes in the lagoon was men's work, apparently because fishing from canoes and diving for fish was universally considered men's work across the Pacific, while women gathered marine foods from the reefs, mud flats and streams by wading and hand picking.

Pearl shell is another much sought material of high value almost universally across the Pacific, perhaps because, in addition to its aesthetic appeal, it does not occur widely in every Pacific atoll lagoon. In the Caroline Islands of Micronesia, pearl shell is more abundant in the eastern islands; so it circulated as currency and tribute to Yap, where it became 'women's money' and was also transformed into jewellery that often became heirlooms.

Egg-cowries were imported from Vava'u in Tonga across 600 kilometres of open ocean in large double canoes to Fiji where they were called *bulileka* and regarded as fertility symbols. These were worn rarely in necklaces; more often they were used paired or singly as a throat pendant on a tight black neck cord worn by women dancers. Similarly, teeth from sperm whales stranded in Tonga were transported by Tongan sailors to Fiji where they were shaped into necklaces and breastplates, apparently by resident Tongan and Samoan craftsmen. Tongan sailors also carried the treasured red feathers of the Fijian lory and parrot to Samoa where they were incorporated into valuable fine mats and other ornaments.

Probably the most constant material elements in jewellery made in north-eastern New Guinea and the Bismarck Archipelago are the small white cowrie-like *Nassa* shells. Their most intensive use was in the *diwarra* or *tambu* shell currency of eastern New Britain, the Duke of York Islands and southern New Ireland, but their use as a component of jewellery is much more widespread. However, *diwarra* as a currency is so famous that some of the aura of monetary value carries over into the jewellery. As *diwarra*, the back of the shell was broken away and they were strung spaced slightly apart on stiff rattan, so that any desired length could be broken off. For use in jewellery, the back was also usually broken away or chipped into two holes but the shell was attached by fibre stitching.

The abundant mangrove swamps at the north-west end of the Gazelle Peninsula of New Britain were a major source of *Nassa* shells. After the north-west monsoon subsided in the spring, the Nakanai men of this district went out to collect the shells in palm leaves or bamboo containers. The harvest of live shellfish was stored in their dwelling houses, where they were prepared to endure the stink of decay in anticipation of the wealth to come. When the changing monsoon brought calm seas, canoe traders came along the coast from

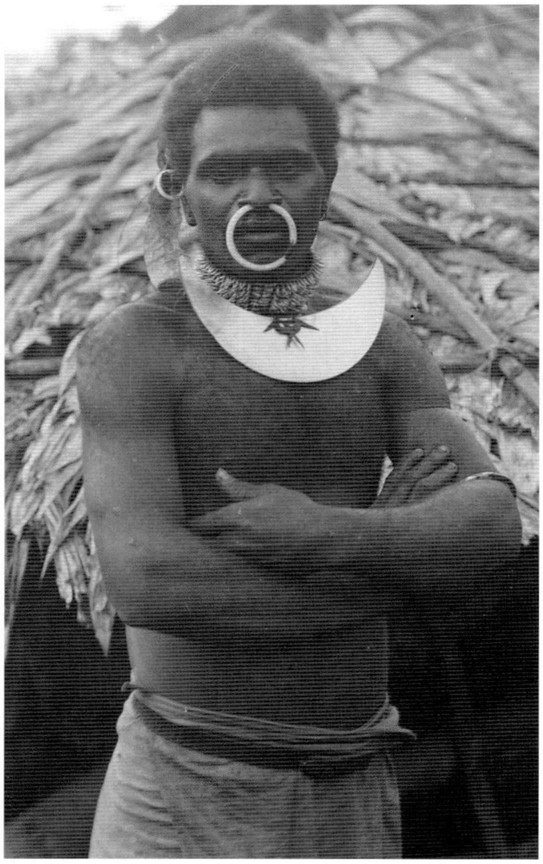

Young Man With Ornaments, Qarea, West Coast of Malaita, Solomon Islands, 1906

Qarea was a mission settlement with a small school, founded in the 1890s by Solomon Islanders who had returned from indentured labouring in Queensland and Fiji. To protect themselves from attack by inland bushmen, they built a coral block fort under the direction of their chief Konae. This young man is one of Konae's followers. After his time abroad, he has resumed the wearing of traditional Malaita valuable ornaments including his pearl shell crescent with turtle shell overlay, a boar tusk nose ring and necklace of mammal teeth on a fibre backing.

Photo: John Watt Beattie, Auckland Museum 6299

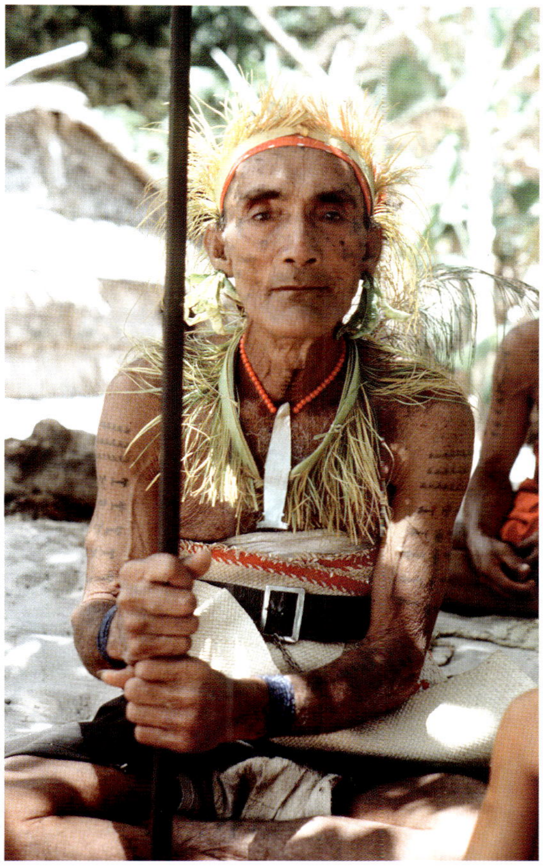

Elder of Tikopia, Polynesian Outlier, Solomon Islands, 1973

Pa Mangai, a Tikopian elder, sits in formal dress of fine plaited waist mat over a plain loincloth of beaten barkcloth. In addition to his traditional tattoo patterns, his most prominent ornament is a pearl shell neck pendant in the form of a trolling fishhook lure. This is suspended from a string of red glass trade-beads. Colourful, stripped plant leaf fibre decorations adorn his head and neck and are attached through his pierced earlobes. His cross-legged poise reflects the dignity expected of a Polynesian elder in this hierarchical society.

Photo: M. Pendergrast, Auckland Museum CT 3943

the north to exchange goods for the *Nassa* shells. This trading took place in an atmosphere of distrust and suspicion, sometimes even out at sea from canoe to canoe. The raw *Nassa* shells were processed back at the traders' home villages, where they were buried, bleached or scoured to produce the desired whiteness.

For the New Zealand Maori, *pounamu* (nephrite jade) became the ultimate material of prestige weapons, tools and jewellery. But its source was limited to three main geological localities in remote western areas of the South Island. Sea travel to these sources was almost impossible along the rough weather coast of south Westland, so all the jade had to be carried out on the backs of men and women over the high passes of the Southern Alps. People using these trails had to brave ice and snow and freezing rivers, dressed only in flax cloaks and plaited sandals, using rope ladders to negotiate some cliffs, and reed rafts to cross the larger rivers. Several definite jade trade routes led out to villages on the southern and eastern coasts of the South Island, which served as manufacturing and distribution centres for the wider jade trade to the rest of the country, reaching 1800 kilometres northwards. Aside from its intrinsic qualities of hardness and beauty, it is therefore no wonder that jade became so valuable and treasured in Maori culture.

Linguistic evidence suggests that dogs were first introduced into the islands of Melanesia by early human settlers, probably by some of the first Austronesian speakers to reach the Bismarck Archipelago. Then later Lapita migrants took the dog with them down through Melanesia and out into Polynesia. But it was in mainland New Guinea, the Bismarck Archipelago and the Solomon Islands that dogs' teeth assumed such a central role in currency and ornament. Dogs were never very numerous in these areas and as only the canines and those teeth behind the canines were used, making a maximum of four teeth per dog, their scarcity ensured their value.

Sometimes the teeth were extracted after the death or 'sacrifice' of the dog, but one account describes how the live dog was buried in the sand up to its neck so that the teeth could be extracted. In many of these islands, dog teeth were drilled and strung solely as currency, which was of higher value than other animal teeth or shell currencies. But even when incorporated as pattern elements into jewellery, they still retained much of their monetary value. Jewellery made with dog teeth frequently served as bride price and as special currency for other situations. Many thousands of dog teeth were in circulation in these areas as currency and ornament into the first half of the twentieth century. In view of their limited supply, these large numbers give a vivid indication of the time depth of dog teeth jewellery traditions.

Somewhat comparable to the role of dog teeth in currency and ornament is the place accorded to boar tusks, but with some significant differences. In much the same areas, especially north-eastern New Guinea and the Bismarck Archipelago, normal boar tusks were incorporated in jewellery and sometimes also had a monetary value. Pigs were highly treasured in all of Melanesia, to the extent that piglets might be suckled by the woman who cared for them or in

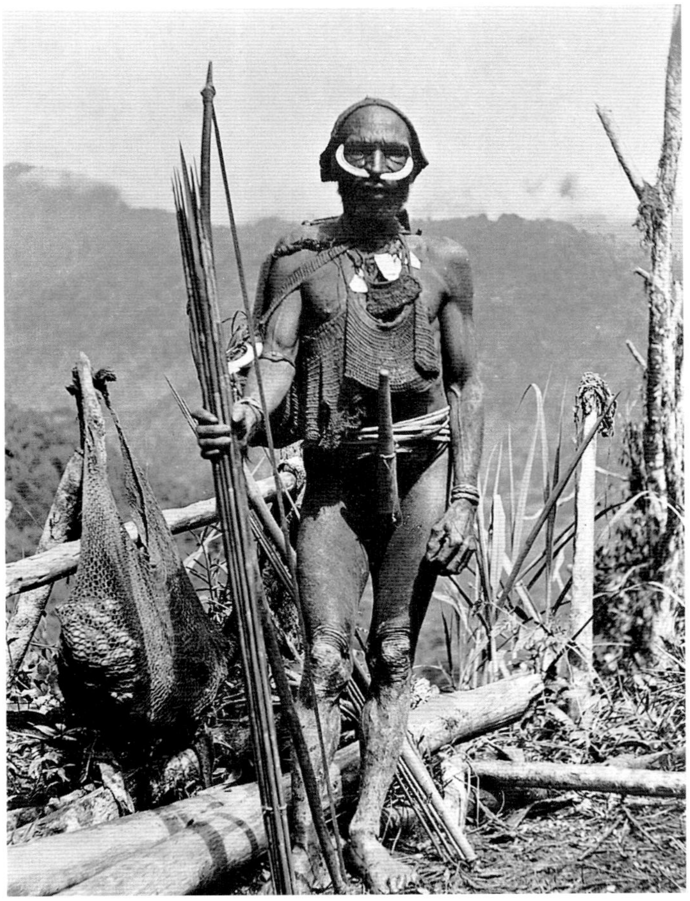

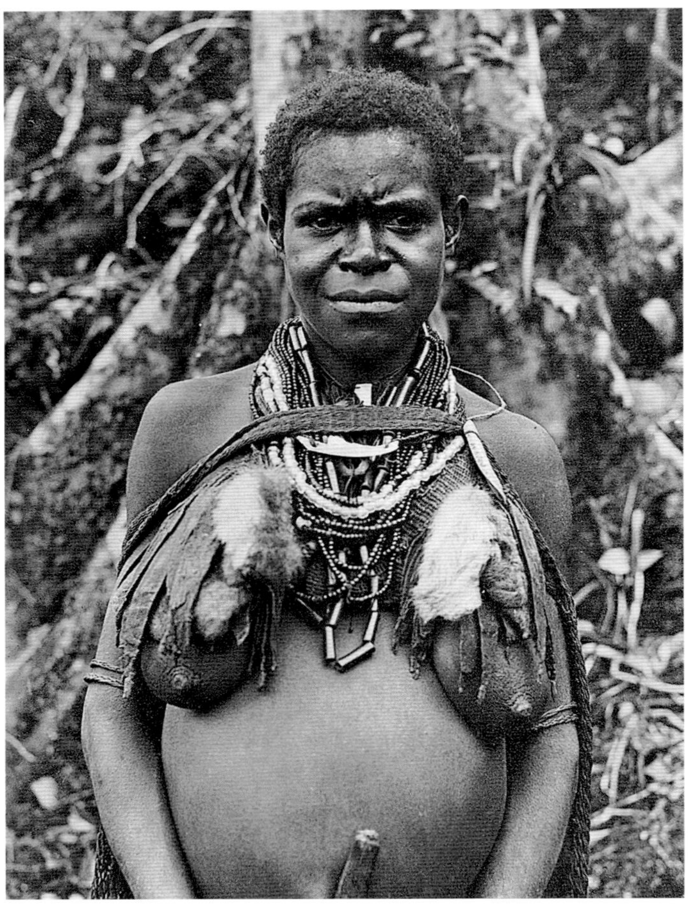

Man And Woman Of The Amungme Tribe, Utakwa River, Southern West Irian, 1913

These are some of the first New Guinea highlanders to be contacted by Europeans. They are members of the Amungme tribe who came down from the central highlands to meet the expedition led by Alexander Wollaston that was attempting to reach the snow-covered mountains of then Dutch New Guinea. The man wears a penis gourd, curved boar-tusks through his nasal septum, and fragments of shell traded in from the coast. The young woman wears a variety of necklaces strung with seeds and reed sections and marsupial fur, all gathered from her local environment.

Photos: Alexander Wollaston and Cecil Boden Kloss, Album 162, Auckland Museum

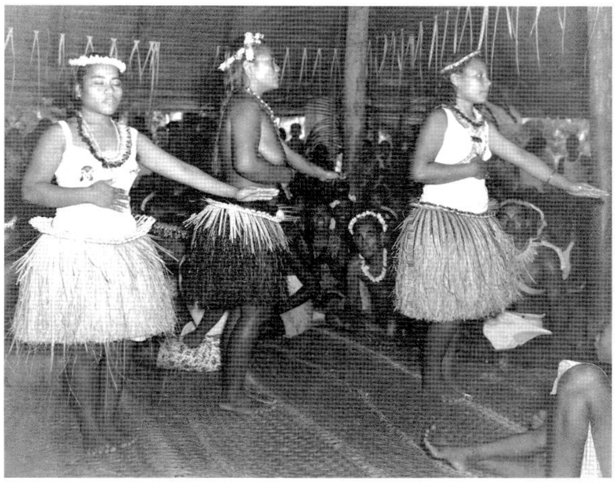

Young Women Dancing In *Maneaba*, Kiribati, 1940

The maneaba, *meeting house, is the central hub of the community. It is here that weighty political, economic and social issues are deliberated upon, but it is also where the community holds ceremonies and festivities, and dance is a major aspect of any celebration. Children are taught to dance from a very early age. These three young women wear typical dance attire. On their heads they have floral and pandanus wreaths, around their necks hang plaited pandanus ornaments and shell necklaces, and one wears a pair of sashes,* ririko, *criss-crossed around her upper body. Over their skirts,* takai *or* kakoko, *they are wearing important ornamental belts.*

Photo: Major Holland, Auckland Museum

Santa Cruz a favourite boar might have its ear pierced so that it could wear a shell ear ring or a piece of red cloth. In Vanuatu, especially in the northern islands, pigs with tusks that have grown into a full circle or even into a double circle are especially valuable for men wanting to move up a level in the graded societies, or *suque*. The upper canines of the boar are knocked out so that the lower tusks can grow around in a circle and back through the jawbone. As the tusks grow, the boar has to be fed by hand. At the grade-taking ceremonies, the aspirant kills his own and loaned pigs and takes on new ornaments as insignia to mark his new status and rank. The curled tusks of the dead pigs may also be worn later as ornaments.

To the south in New Caledonia and the Loyalty Islands, twisted cords of reddish brown flying-fox fur and various-sized beads of dull green jade, actually serpentine, assumed special values as part of currency items. Serpentine could be found at several sources in New Caledonia but the main supply came from the island of Ouen, near present day Noumea. From this importance, their employment as jewellery items, usually in the form of necklaces, is not unexpected.

People were attracted to these jewellery materials by their obvious physical properties of colour, shape, texture, hardness, or flexibility for pleasant swaying movement. Lines of New Guinea highlanders advancing en masse with their magnificent bird of paradise plume head-dresses waving in unison are an unforgettable sight. The sensual appeal of the shapes and textures of polished jade or large voluptuous cowrie shells was well recognised in many Pacific cultures. For some jewellery, hardness and strength of materials were appreciated, as in the case of heirloom items that passed down through the generations for hundreds of years, gaining a patina and softness of texture from rubbing gently upon human skin that bespoke of the honoured ancestors who had worn it in the past. For those entrusted with the custody and care of heirloom jewellery, the privilege of wearing it brought the ancestors into close contact and focused their power on the living descendants. For other jewellery, fragility and ephemeral beauty were more important, as in the case of rare and valuable feathers, precious shells and flowers.

In addition to these qualities, pleasant scents and sounds made during movement were sometimes important reasons for choice of materials. Thus fresh flowers, fragrant grasses and herbs were added to body decoration as much for their aroma as for their pleasing appearance. I still remember from 30 years ago the young rubbish collectors in the streets of Rabaul on the Gazelle Peninsula wearing huge bright red flowers in their hair as they ran alongside the collecting truck. Some Polynesian people especially were fastidious about the scent of their bodies, modifying it with specially chosen flowers and herbs, in addition to the scent of frangipani or sandalwood in the coconut oil on their bodies. Some jewellery was intended to make pleasant or rhythmic sounds as well as having a pleasant appearance. Obvious examples of this are leg rattles made of dog teeth in Hawai'i and *Pangium* seeds in New Guinea. More subtle is the pleasure that a woman of Puluwat in the Caroline Islands remembered from her childhood of the light tinkling sound of her mother's large turtle-shell ear rings as she moved about the house in the soft pink light of dawn.

Glass trade-beads have become an important and ubiquitous element of Pacific jewellery ever since the first arrival of Asian and European outsiders. They can be regarded as raw material since they were obtained ready-made in bulk by purchase or trade. Without any further processing, they were ready for the craftswomen to string or stitch them into whatever patterns were relevant to the local culture. Some very ancient beads found their way into the western fringes of the Pacific through Indonesia into western New Guinea and through the Philippine Islands into Micronesia. Old trade beads are usually seen as isolated single specimens incorporated into otherwise traditional jewellery. They could be strung among drilled shell discs or inlaid in gum or resin.

However, the majority of glass trade-beads seen in museum collections of Pacific jewellery were brought in by European traders in the nineteenth century. In many areas they completely replaced traditional drilled shell discs and shell beads as ornament and decoration in costume, as witnessed in the bead aprons and arm bands of the Admiralty Islands and the belts of the Solomon Islands. Glass beads on horsehair became a very popular decoration for clubs and for the body in Fiji, while in Tonga they were attached to the delicate decorations of fine combs. But glass beads never displaced the currency value of drilled shell discs in native economies of the Pacific. Cheap, brightly coloured glass beads and tubes are still being brought into some islands today, usually direct from Indonesia, Taiwan or South-east Asia, by Asian businessmen.

Beyond all these physical qualities of jewellery materials, some materials were sought and treasured because of their symbolic and associational properties and their links with ancestors and gods. Boar tusks carried some of the associations of fierceness and aggression seen in wild male pigs; hence they became appropriate body ornament for male warriors. In Samoa, large white *Ovula* cowrie shells are called *pule* and were used to decorate kava bowl cords, the prows and sterns of important canoes, and the costumes of important people. *Pule* also means the government in power and hence *pule* shells had a connotation of authority in Samoa.

Human hair was plaited into the cords of necklaces, belts and ornaments in parts of Micronesia and Polynesia, especially in Kiribati, Hawai'i and Niue for example, and carried very special connotations. In these societies with their strong reverence for ancestors, the use of human hair from the sacred head of a person in heirloom jewellery and body adornment emphasised the reality of its ancestral connection. In New Zealand, *pounamu* jade was regarded as the fish of Ngahue, a mythological ancestor who discovered the islands of New Zealand and returned to the Maori homeland of Hawaiki to guide his people back to his amazing new land. Precisely because of their foreign origin and new bright colours, glass trade-beads carried connotations of modernity, often accentuated by the addition of imported red cloth and the use of new imported commercial dyes.

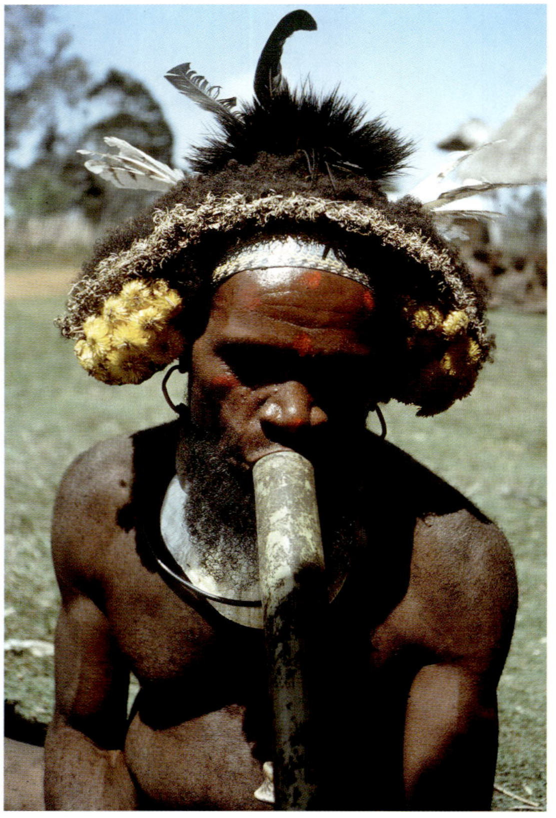

Huli Man, Tari, Southern Highlands, Papua New Guinea, 1965

Older Huli men wear wigs of human hair decorated with everlasting daisies and a crown of black cassowary and other feathers. At other times the wig may be decorated with bird of paradise feathers, snake skin or marsupial fur. These wigs are worn for daily activities but especially at the periodic pig-killing festivals and other occasions of heightened social activity and political display. This man is puffing on his bamboo tobacco pipe, a favourite pastime for older Huli men.

Photo: Mick Pendergrast, Auckland Museum CT 2143

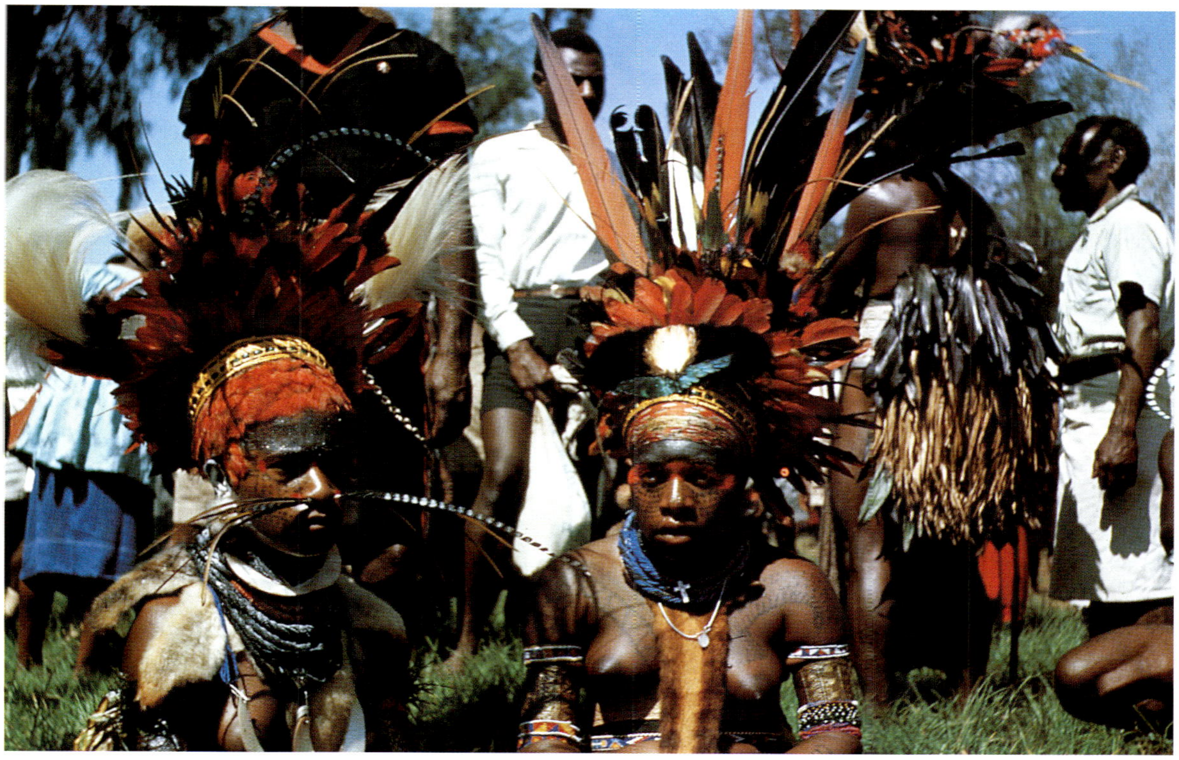

Young Women From Minj, Middle Wahgi Valley, Western Highlands, Papua New Guinea, 1963

For special occasions such as bridewealth payments, pig-killing festivals, warfare compensation payments, and festivals for religious cult ceremonies, Papua New Guinea highlands men and women decorate themselves with various flamboyant arrangements of feathers, furs, shells and body paint. These body adornments convey specific meanings depending on the occasion and the particular ornaments chosen. These women from Minj in the central Wahgi valley have head-dresses of bird of paradise and other feathers, with shell valuables, bead necklaces and marsupial fur around their necks.

Photo: Mrs A. Grace-Jones, Auckland Museum CT2272

MAKING JEWELLERY

MAKERS OF PACIFIC jewellery could be anybody from young children, to adults filling in spare time, to old people no longer able to carry out the heavy tasks of gardening and fishing. Or in some of the ranked hierarchical or stratified Pacific societies, there were specialist part-time craftsmen and women who employed their special skills, training and experience to create intricate or bold jewellery of special quality and distinction for the superior individuals to wear. Some materials required minimal preparation before they could be incorporated into jewellery, many others had to pass through complex and lengthy skilled processes before manufacture could even begin. An old generalisation is sometimes made that in pre-industrial societies, men work with hard materials such as stone, bone, shell and wood using a variety of special tools, while women work soft materials such as clay and fibres, usually with just the skill of their hands. This gender distinction holds to some degree in Pacific societies but with such a variety of cultures there are innumerable exceptions. For some of the more complicated jewellery, both men and women contributed their special skills and materials to create the final composition.

Before the advent of pliable metals and the ability to make clasping structures to hold valuable stones, Pacific jewellery was constructed mainly by stringing items together on fibre, stitching individual units to a fibre base or textile, plaiting them into cords, or setting them as inlay in a resin or gum. Most of these techniques, which required fine detailed and tedious repetition, were the preserve of women, while men concentrated on shaping and cutting the required stone, shell and bone materials to form the individual elements. But in the Solomon Islands, it was the men who also worked the *Parinarium* gum into a paste and designed the intricate patterns of *Nautilus* and *Conus* shell inlay on combs, bowls and canoes.

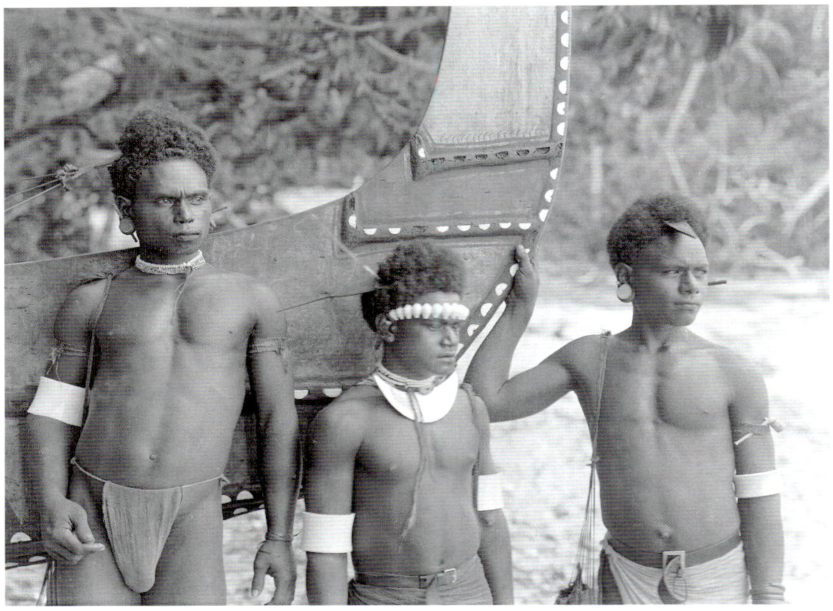

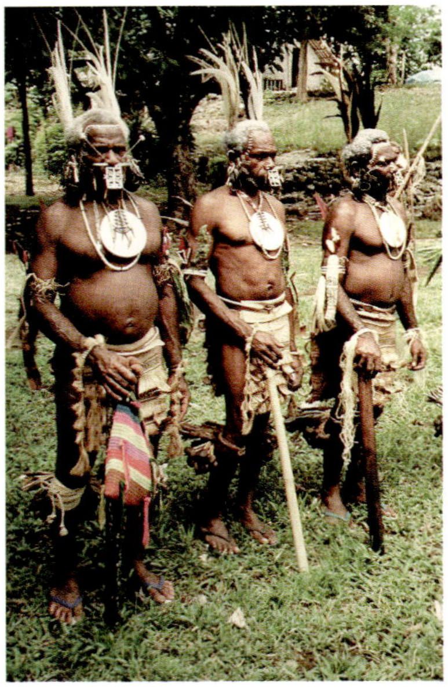

above: ***Nelo* Dancers In Full Costume, Graciosa Bay, Santa Cruz Islands, Solomon Islands, 1998**

Performed in a special dancing circle enclosed in a wall of coral blocks next to their custom house, the nelo *dance is named after the pearl shell* nelo*—nose ornaments worn by the men. To wear the* nelo*, the man inserts it through the septum of his nose, which has been pierced when he was younger. Their full* nelo *dance costume includes turtle shell ear rings,* Tridacna *shell* tema *chest pendants, necklaces of drilled shell-money discs, face paint, tapa cloth arm ornaments, leg rattles of* Pangium edule *nuts, and loom-woven breech cloths of banana fibre. The* nelo *dance is one of a range of different dances, each with their special costume and ornaments, relating to men's initiation.*

Photo: M. Pendergrast, Auckland Museum

left: **Young Men Wearing Shell Ornaments, Heuru, San Cristobal (Makira), Solomon Islands, 1906**

Standing in front of their shell-inlaid war canoe, these young men of San Cristobal Island in the south-east Solomon Islands wear decorative combs in their hair and a variety of shell ornaments. On their upper arms, all are wearing extremely valuable large polished arm rings cut from Tridacna *(giant clam) shell with much labour using flints and coral abrasors. In addition to his necklace of drilled shell disc currency, the man at centre wears a* dafe*—a crescent-shaped, pearl shell, breast ornament. Across his forehead is a band of cowrie shells on a fibre backing.*

Photo: John Watt Beattie, Auckland Museum 5889/6326

In another reversal of this broad generalisation, in many areas, the small shell disc units manufactured for traditional shell currency and for jewellery were cut, shaped and polished by women, who also drilled the suspension hole in every individual disc with the widespread Pacific type of cord-operated pump drill tipped with a piece of flint. This process is continued today by women of Auki village on the Langalanga Lagoon of Malaita in the Solomon Islands. In the Massim district of south-east New Guinea, the *Spondylus* shells, called here *kaloma*, for making red shell discs also called *kaloma*, can be gathered by diving at only two or three lagoon localities in the Trobriand Islands, accompanied by much magic ritual. The diving, the breaking of the shells into suitable pieces and the drilling are all done exclusively by men, but the final polishing of the discs is women's work.

In the past, this process must have been a major occupation for many women and men in villages of the Pacific from Micronesia to New Caledonia, wherever shell, coconut shell or small stone discs were prepared to be strung as currency or threaded into jewellery. However, everywhere in Melanesia, the manufacture of large *Tridacna* clam shell and *Conus* shell arm rings was definitely the province of men, as it required large-scale cutting and sawing, grinding and polishing to a range of prescribed shapes.

Among the most sculptural forms of Pacific jewellery are the stylised human figures of Maori nephrite *hei-tiki* breast ornaments. Special techniques of cutting and sawing nephrite with sandstone files and grindstones were developed by Maori, centuries after they had settled in New Zealand, to make nephrite adzes, which were much more efficient than other stone blades. These new techniques were then applied to making a variety of nephrite personal ornaments such as *hei-tiki*, *pekapeka*, *koropepe*, *poria kaka*, *hei-matau* and other straight and

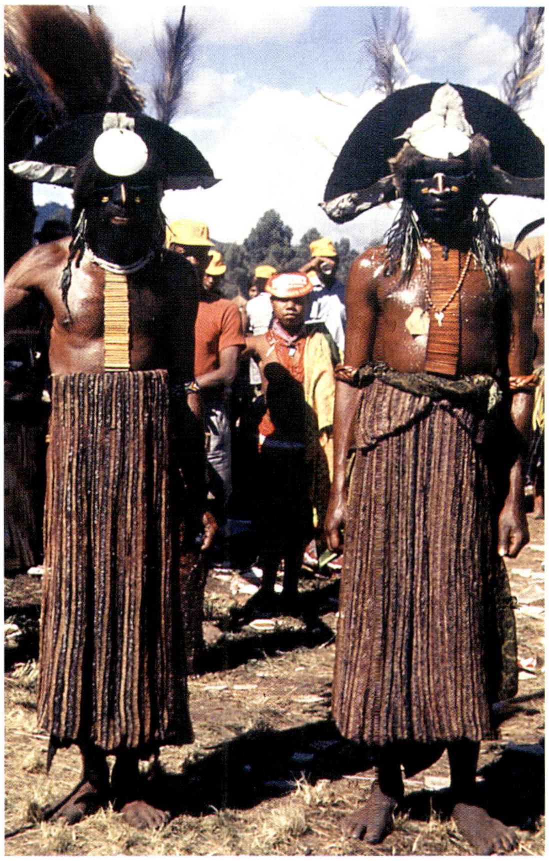

Men From Wabag, Western Highlands, Papua New Guinea, 1970s

Photographed at the Goroka Show, these men of the Enga people who live west of Mount Hagen wear heavy netted aprons and the Enga style of hair wig. Their bodies are oiled and their faces darkened with charcoal. The sets of bamboo tally sticks, called omaak, *hanging on their chest indicate the number of times they have given away sets of valuable pearl shells in* moka *ceremonial exchanges with other clans. Their total outfit tells onlookers that they are men of growing influence and importance in their clan.*

Photo: Karl Every, Auckland Museum CT4233

curved pendants. To some extent, *hei-tiki* figure styles followed the regional and tribal styles of woodcarving, which was very much a men's sacred or *tapu* art. Hence the working of nephrite jade for tools, weapons and ornaments was restricted to men, some of whom became famous as skilled specialists.

The *hei-matau* breast pendant of the Maori, a stylised fishhook, was just one example of the close connection between fishhooks and ornament throughout much of the Pacific. For Oceanic peoples whose whole history and present livelihood are so closely bound up with the sea and its products, this relationship is to be expected. Consequently, in many Oceanic cultures, fishhooks or parts of them or imitations of them were transformed into neck ornaments of deep cultural significance.

On Tobi in the westernmost Caroline Islands, an atoll society very reliant on the sea, fishhooks worn as ornaments served as key symbols of birth, rank, and connections with the ancestors. On Tikopia, women wear a necklace of turtle shell fishhook points, or a single point as a neck pendant, while older men may wear a pearl shell fishhook shank as a single pendant. On the atolls of Tokelau, the wedding ceremonies feature a presentation to the bride by her mother's brother of a *kahoa* pearl shell pendant that he places around her neck. But the *kahoa* is not just an ordinary pendant; indeed it is the shank of a pearl shell lure fishhook that has been unbound for the occasion. Later, it will be bound again as a complete fishhook with turtle shell point and attached line, to be used in fishing for skipjack by the groom and his male relatives. By transferring this supreme masculine valuable made out of treasured pearl shell across the marriage bond via the person of the female bride, the importance of the marriage and the promised creation of a new family have been marked for the whole community to see.

In much of the traditional Pacific, it was the custom for men to wear their hair long and often made up into complicated styles while women kept theirs short or even shaved away completely. For actually dressing the hair, needles of palm midrib or bone were preferred to combs; the latter serving more as decorative ornaments and personal adornment, therefore qualifying as jewellery. Consequently, men rather than women wore combs more frequently and used them to mark status and ritual seniority. As such, the combs themselves were delicately and often elaborately decorated in a huge variety of ways, requiring and exhibiting all the special skills of each cultural area. Pearl or *Nautilus* shell was inlaid and cemented with *Parinarium* (putty nut) paste, feathers or tassels were attached to long slender handles to sway elegantly with every step, coconut midribs were woven together with human hair and fine tendrils so that the bindings formed intricate patterning, abstracted icons and ancestral figures were incorporated into the structure, and the prized red feathers of Polynesia ornamented chiefly combs. The head and hair are *tapu* (sacred), especially in Polynesia where to pass anything over the head, to touch the head and even to stand so that one's head is above another's are grave insults. Therefore anything that came into contact with the head was handled with care and respect. Combs continue today as items of adornment and are decorated according to a more personal taste and style.

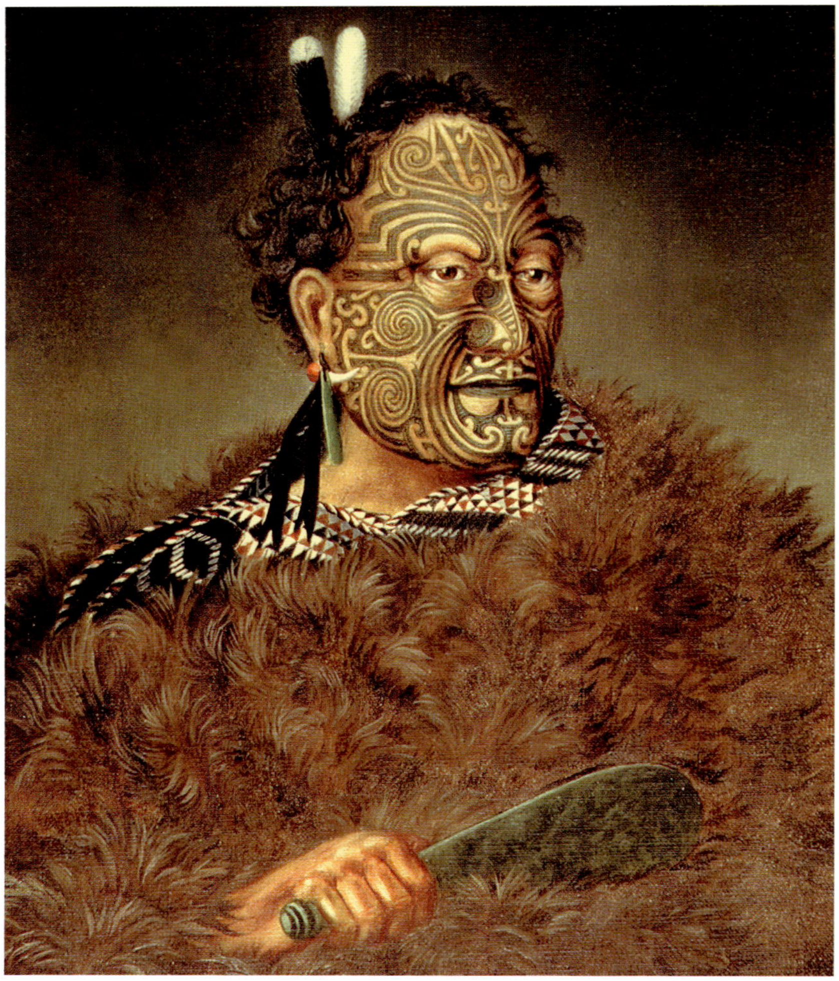

WEARING MESSAGES

FROM TIME IMMEMORIAL, people have had to make decisions about what jewellery to wear. What have always changed through time and across cultures are the reasons for wearing jewellery and the concepts on which people base their decisions to wear one piece rather than another. Modern Westerners and those Pacific Islanders who have embraced the global scene now make their decisions based mainly on aesthetic values, which are becoming increasingly universal. Nevertheless, these moderns also carry over some older attitudes towards jewellery, especially the wearing of family heirloom jewellery for sentimental reasons and the display of expensive and ostentatious jewellery to signal status and wealth.

But in the traditional Pacific, the reasons for wearing particular jewellery were much more varied and yet also more prescribed. The messages conveyed by a piece of jewellery were public knowledge and were usually quite specific, so that the wearer had to be more careful about what he or she had the right or reason to wear. Correspondingly, the viewers could read the traditional messages with more certainty. Since the messages of jewellery and body adornment were so widely understood and recognised within a particular culture, it was quite common for helpers to assist with the dressing where a complicated assembly of feathers and ornaments was worn, such as in the highlands of New Guinea. Without the need for too much consultation about the intended message, these helpers can attach the appropriate feathers, put on the right

TAMATI WAKA NENE, CHIEF OF NGAPUHI TRIBE, NORTH AUCKLAND, NEW ZEALAND, 1860S

Waka Nene was a prominent chief of the Ngapuhi in the Hokianga and Bay of Islands areas, the largest tribal group in the north of New Zealand. In his hair he wears a black and white-tipped huia tail feather, as a recognised sign of his chiefly rank. In his pierced earlobe he wears a mako shark tooth ornament, embellished with European-introduced red sealing wax and a black ribbon. Below this hangs an ear pendant of nephrite jade. Wearing a kiwi feather cloak, he holds a tribal heirloom jade weapon as an attribute of his warrior reputation.

Painting by S. Stuart, Auckland Museum

ornaments, and paint the wearer's face and body in the correct colours and patterns. A small hand mirror has also become a much-desired possession especially in the highlands of New Guinea so that the wearer can monitor the effect of his ensemble as it is constructed.

Some of the main themes informing the wearing of jewellery in the Pacific can be explored here. The most obvious is the connection between jewellery as currency and currency as jewellery, especially in those areas of Melanesia and Micronesia where a form of shell disc currency was in use. It has been said that Pacific ornaments of shell money may be regarded either as the most valuable of ornaments or the most decorative form of money. This crossover between shell money and ornament is paralleled by the relationship between Santa Cruz red feather money and the decorative head sticks of the same red feathers worn by dancers in Santa Cruz. Not only shell money but a wide range of items regarded as currency were also worn as ornaments, among them dog and porpoise teeth, boar tusks and New Caledonian fur and jade money.

Wearing jewellery as a message about wealth could be located along a wide continuum. At one extreme was the wearing of objects with purely a wealth or economic value, which were simply hung temporarily on the owner's body or his wife's body for display. This would include the wearing of *kina* pearl shells set in red ochre and resin plaques among the Melpa people of the Wahgi Valley in the Western Highlands of New Guinea, and the display of bride price on the body of the bride in the Admiralty Islands. Further along the continuum is the wearing of items of monetary value also for their aesthetic and communicative value. This would apply to much of the shell money jewellery in the Solomon Islands. This modality grades into jewellery made of valuables but where the aesthetic value is paramount and any commercial value is minimal or obsolete; this also applies to certain types of Solomons jewellery. Finally, at the other end of the continuum, are ornamental objects that are not valuable in themselves but which symbolise value and wealth. The prime examples of this are the *omaak* sticks of bamboo worn hanging down a Melpa man's chest in the Wahgi Valley of the New Guinea highlands, where each stick denotes the number of times he has participated in a ritual *moka* pig and pearl shell exchange ceremony to demonstrate his economic power.

Some jewellery attains its meaning and significance by virtue of its connections with the world of trade and commerce. The possession of *kula* ornaments and valuables, which is always temporary because of the nature of this trade system, demonstrates that the holder is a man of enterprise and influence recognised in the whole Massim district. As discussed above, many of the raw materials of jewellery can only be obtained by trade and therefore their possession indicates that their wearer is a participant in this commerce. Ornaments made of dog teeth from the Vitiaz Straits trade system, red feathers in Santa Cruz or Samoa, Maori ornaments of jade, and the combs and ear sticks covered with red and yellow plaiting made by the Kwaio in inland Malaita and traded down to coastal peoples are all instances of the incorporation of rare and valuable trade materials into jewellery, where their possession can be displayed publicly.

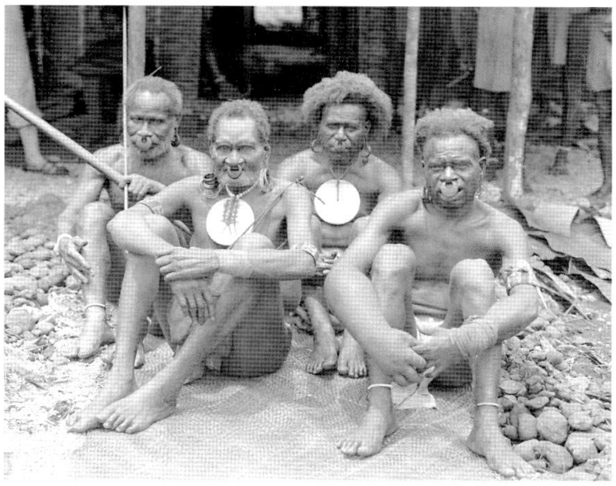

Elders in a Santa Cruz village, Solomon Islands, 1906

Photographed while they watched the activities of a visit by missionaries from the Melanesian Mission ship Southern Cross, *these pagan elders all wear their everyday ornaments of a turtle shell nose ring, ear rings of turtle shell, and armlets of bark string and shell beads. One carries his tobacco pipe through his extended ear lobe. Two of them wear heavy* tema *discs of clam shell on cords of shell money around their necks. For more formal ceremonial occasions or a dance, they would also wear eight to ten shell armlets. Young boys could not wear these ornaments until their twelfth or thirteenth year, after several pigs had been sacrificed.*

Photo: John Watt Beattie, Auckland Museum 6599

Another common motive for the wearing of jewellery in the Pacific is the connection between jewellery and protection. Apart from the obvious armour of cane basketry worn in the Star Mountains of New Guinea or the plaited sennit body suits of Kiribati and the Marshall Islands, some types of jewellery are said to have been worn simply for the physical protection that they offered from clubs and projectiles. These include the ivory and shell breastplates of Fiji and the breastplates covered in red *Abrus* seeds worn along the central north coast of mainland New Guinea. However, the reasons for wearing jewellery and the messages inherent in jewellery are never 'simple' in the Pacific and these two types of breastplates also carry powerful messages about moral protection and status. In those areas where powerful bows were used in warfare and hunting, a wrist band or lower arm cover protected the bowman from the force of his bowstring and these items were nearly always elaborated into patterned jewellery.

More pervasive than the physical protection provided by jewellery is the way that some Pacific jewellery acts with symbolic power to counter the physical aggression of others. When an Admiralty Islands man donned his feathered 'war charm' at the nape of his neck before entering dangerous territory or going to war, he placed himself under the symbolic protection of the famous mythical warrior depicted on the ornament or the protection of his ancestors represented by their bone incorporated into it. An executioner appointed by the elders in Malaita in the Solomon Islands wore the shell-inlaid *wari-hau* baton down his back to show that he acted with the approved authority of the community leaders. Other jewellery items were worn clasped in their teeth by warriors going into battle, to signify that they intended to fight seriously and with the approval of their community, such as the *gibigibi* of the Collingwood Bay people or the *musikaka* of the Koiari inland from Port Moresby or the *karahut* of the Abelam to the north of the mid-Sepik River. The English artefact collector James Edge-Partington noted that for Malaita, only warriors who had committed a homicide were entitled to wear their clam shell nose pins with flattened ends. A special head-dress of hornbill beaks from the Wanigela area also signalled that the warrior had already committed homicide previously and was therefore an opponent to be feared and respected.

While the jewellery described above acted with symbolic power to protect its wearer against actual physical force, other jewellery conferred symbolic protection from the dangerous forces of the supernatural world. When a person of the Tolai nation on the Gazelle Peninsula of New Britain wore certain flowers and herbs as ornament, he was not just making himself pretty with sweet smelling and colourful decorations. Here the message of specific flowers, leaves and herbs, besides conferring protection in battle or awakening the love of a desired woman, could also provide protection from sorcery. Many of the more elaborate headbands and nose ornaments worn by the Tolai had special protective powers invested in them by a sorcerer of the secret Ingiet society. Some of these powers were automatically transferred to the person when he donned the ornament. Others had to be renewed by an Ingiet expert each time the item was worn. Yet others, especially the headbands, served as an external sign that the wearer had been protected by taking powerful magic potions before putting on the ornament.

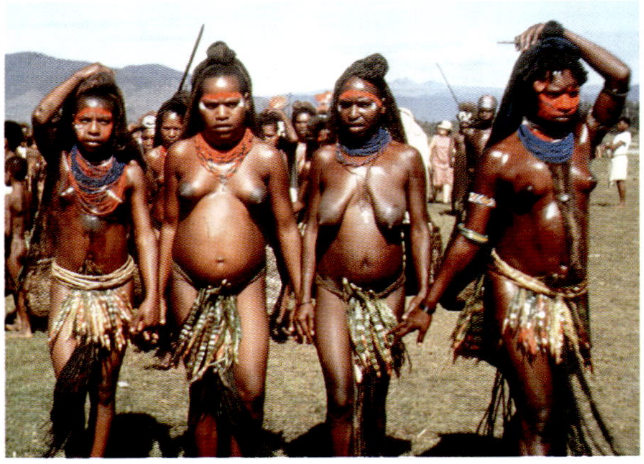

Young Women, Mount Hagen, Wahgi Valley, Western Highlands, Papua New Guinea, 1963

These young women are dressed to enjoy themselves as onlookers at an interclan festival near the highland town of Mount Hagen. Their costume consists of aprons of crimped cordyline leaves and large netted bilum *bags knotted on their heads and covering their backs. The* bilum *serves jointly as costume, clothing and carry-all; but it is often worn empty, especially when at social gatherings. Strings of glass tradebeads around their necks, face paint and fresh oil on their skin complete their outfits.*

Photo: Mrs A. Grace-Jones, Auckland Museum CT 2261

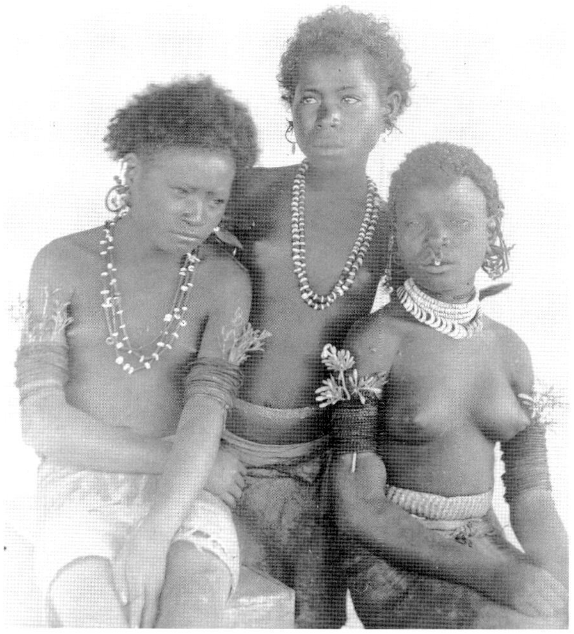

Young girls before their tattooing ceremony, Wanigela, Collingwood Bay, Oro Province, Papua New Guinea, between 1901 and 1911

These young Wanigela girls have not yet reached the age when their faces will be tattooed. They wear necklaces of shells and teeth; the one on the left consists of Nassa *shells separated by short sections of cassowary quills. Turtle shell rings and short strings of beads are attached through their pierced earlobes. Tucked into their fibre arm bands are sprigs of sweet-smelling herbs.*

Photo: Percy Money, Auckland Museum 97/53

Jewellery like this is part of the realm of charms, talismans and amulets, which operate to protect against evil or to achieve some desired aim. People in the Solomon Islands wore small shell constructions as charms to help them increase their wealth in shell money. Many young and not so young men and women in the Pacific wore charms to help them seduce the opposite sex, such as the little wooden image from the mouth of the Fly River in Papua, worn suspended on the chest by young men when singing and dancing to attract the girls. Another very important message conveyed by jewellery was membership of a particular group or category of person. One of the most obvious category distinctions is the gender one of male and female. However, in the traditional Pacific, as with much of the jewellery in this book, this gender distinction did not always follow the pattern that a person from Western cultures might expect. Occasionally, for very specific reasons, the wearing of gender specific jewellery was reversed, as by the widows of Onjob in Collingwood Bay who dance in their men's war regalia.

Social status was often marked by jewellery. Girls in the Torres Strait Islands wore small triangular *Conus* shell neck pendants to show that they were already betrothed to a man and therefore had to be treated with circumspection. In many Pacific societies, certain ornaments or body decorations could only be worn by men after they had passed through the rites of passage and initiation rituals that admitted them to full adulthood. Huli men in the Southern Highlands of Papua New Guinea who have passed through the initiation rituals as young bachelors are entitled to wear large crescent-shaped hair wigs as a sign of their adult status. Ornaments such as a head-dress of hornbill beaks or certain shapes of nose pins that announce a man's membership of the category of successful homicide have already been mentioned.

Throughout the Pacific, certain jewellery items functioned as symbols of rank and leadership. The *bakiha* or *tarkola*—a decorated clam-shell ring chest ornament of the western Solomon Islands worn only by chiefs—are a dramatic case in point. The *lei niho palaoa* whale tooth pendant of Hawai'i probably fulfilled a similar role. In Samoa, the young sons and daughters of chiefs carrying out the high ceremonial roles of *manaia* and *taupou* in preparing and serving the kava or performing the most important dance at the end of a ceremony are clearly marked for the occasion by wearing the elaborate *tuiga* head-dress. Circular boar tusks from valuable, ritually killed pigs in Vanuatu served as a mark of status in the *suque* graded society. But in Vanuatu and the Solomons, some old men who have reached the highest status in their society virtually stop wearing jewellery, limiting themselves to a single plain but prestigious piece.

In those societies of the Pacific organised by clans or other types of lineage groups, some particular jewellery items were intended to mark their wearer's clan membership. Among the Mekeo living along the south-east coast of the Gulf of Papua, each clan had its own distinctive body ornaments, called *kangakanga*, to identify membership of a clan. These *kangakanga* ornaments were usually named after a plant or a small animal. In a totemic type of relationship the specific *kangakanga* of a clan could not be eaten but parts of that animal or plant were incorporated into the clan body decoration. When Mekeo clans entered into their periodic singing contests they had to make sure that their *kangakanga* body decorations were perfect, otherwise they would face certain defeat.

In a manner directly comparable to Western jewellery, Pacific jewellery often became heirloom jewellery, treasured because of its close association with those ancestors who had worn it through the years. But the ancestral and kin associations of jewellery, using the word in its very widest sense, may extend to much further and less familiar lengths in the Pacific world. Parts of the body of the deceased relative may be worn for shorter or longer periods, including teeth, bones, fingers and skull. Suspension cords for neck ornaments might be woven out of their hair. In the Polynesian outlier of Tikopia in the Solomon Islands, mourning relatives wear teeth, hair or pieces of their deceased's clothing around their necks, including nowadays their cotton shorts or shirts until they become shapeless begrimed rags. Even a Tikopian deceased man's wooden headrest may be worn as a back ornament by his son or daughter. For Maori needing to mourn the death of a relative lost in battle whose body cannot be recovered, his *hei-tiki* could be used as a surrogate through the funeral ceremonies.

In many Pacific societies, as in much of the ancient world, a person's jewellery was buried with them to accompany them to the next world. That this practice is also an ancient one in the Pacific is evidenced by the jewellery buried with the dead at the thirteenth century archaic Maori site of Wairau Bar, in New Zealand's South Island, and the rich range of ornaments buried about 500 years ago with the legendary chief Roy Mata and his retainers on the sacred island of Retoka near Efate in Vanuatu.

Coix lachryma-jobi or Job's tears seeds have a close and curious association with mourning in the eastern New Guinea mainland. In many of these cultures, widows are expected to debase themselves by shaving their heads and covering their bodies with white clay for an extended period of mourning. At the end of this period, usually the only sort of body decoration and ornament that they are allowed to wear is composed of the white grey pearly seeds of Job's tears.

For New Zealand Maori, jade or *pounamu* maintains a very close association with the mythical homeland of Hawaiki, the place the ancestors came from in their migrations to New Zealand and where they return to after death. Ngahue, the first ancestor to reach New Zealand, took a treasured piece of *pounamu* back to Hawaiki, where he cut it up to make two famous adze blades and some ear pendants. The adzes were used to shape out the migratory ancestral canoe that his relatives sailed back to New Zealand. One of the ear pendants was called Kaukaumatua and was brought to New Zealand by Tamatekapua, the captain of Te Arawa migration canoe. This ear pendant, or at least its named successor, was passed down through the chiefly generations; it was lost and found again in various adventures, and finally lost in 1887 by a chief's daughter while swimming in Lake Taupo. Treasured heirlooms like Kaukaumatua are remembered by their personal names, and are referred to in songs and legends to honour and mourn those ancestors who have passed on, back to Hawaiki.

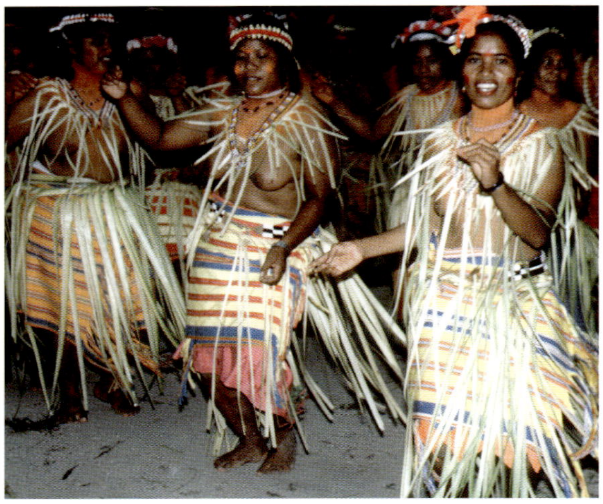

Women Dancing For Visitors, Pulap, State of Chuuk (Truk), Caroline Islands, 1987

For this dance, the women have anointed their bodies with red turmeric powder and coconut oil. The woman in front has a hibiscus flower in her hair while others wear headbands of plastic flowers. Most wear necklaces of fine glass trade-beads. Their colourful wrap-around skirts are woven with modern cottons on traditional back-strap looms. The two women at the front wear beaded belts of traditional geometric patterns that are probably family heirlooms.

Photo: K.Nero, Courtesy of Karen Nero

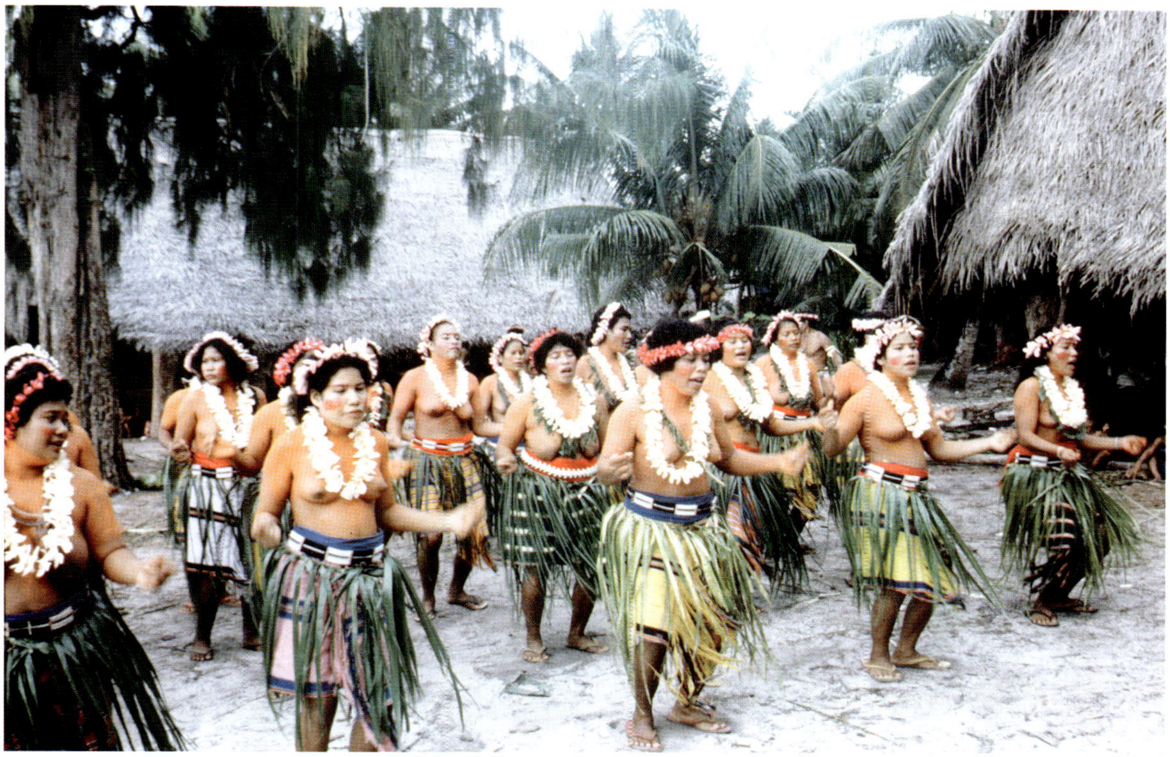

CHANGES IN PACIFIC JEWELLERY

PACIFIC JEWELLERY HAS always been changing and adapting to new materials, new situations and new cultural configurations over the many centuries of human colonisation of the Pacific Islands. Jewellery made of more permanent materials such as stone, bone and shell that has survived in archaeological sites constitutes some of the best evidence available for understanding the development and spread of ancient Pacific peoples and their cultures.

With the arrival of Europeans and Christianity in the Pacific, these changes in jewellery were accelerated and continue today at an ever-faster rate. Along with clothes, jewellery became one of the most powerful messages that people employed or were directed to use to show their allegiance either to a traditional pagan way of life and belief or to the new Christian way. Some new materials from the commercial world replaced the traditional, leading to a loss of ancient skills and sensitivities. Crass modernity and the sheer power of globalisation have not been kind to traditional Pacific jewellery. Some of the messages conveyed have changed drastically, often beyond the conscious control of the people who wear the jewellery.

Although Pacific Islanders very quickly appreciated the advantages of metal for utilitarian purposes, it rarely made its way into jewellery until modern times when contemporary Pacific jewellers have adopted Western ways of working metal for jewellery. Silver and copper inlays on turtle shell became popular in some places, such as Samoa. But nowadays, contemporary Pacific jewellers of indigenous descent working in the islands and around the Pacific rim in a new diaspora are looking back at the work of their ancestors for instruction and inspiration, while taking full advantage of modern techniques and materials, sometimes with a mischievous or ironic comment on our contemporary world.

Women Dancing For Visitors, Satawal, State of Yap, Caroline Islands, 1986

Performing a dance for visitors in front of the village canoe house, these women wear necklaces and decorations of white frangipani and red ginger flowers, with fresh green leaves around their waists. A few wear yellow plastic necklaces. Their wrap-around skirts have been woven on traditional back-strap looms using modern coloured cottons. Over their skirts, many are wearing heirloom belts of black and white beads strung in strict geometric patterns. Several have anointed their bodies with red turmeric powder and coconut oil.

Photo: K.Nero, Courtesy of Karen Nero

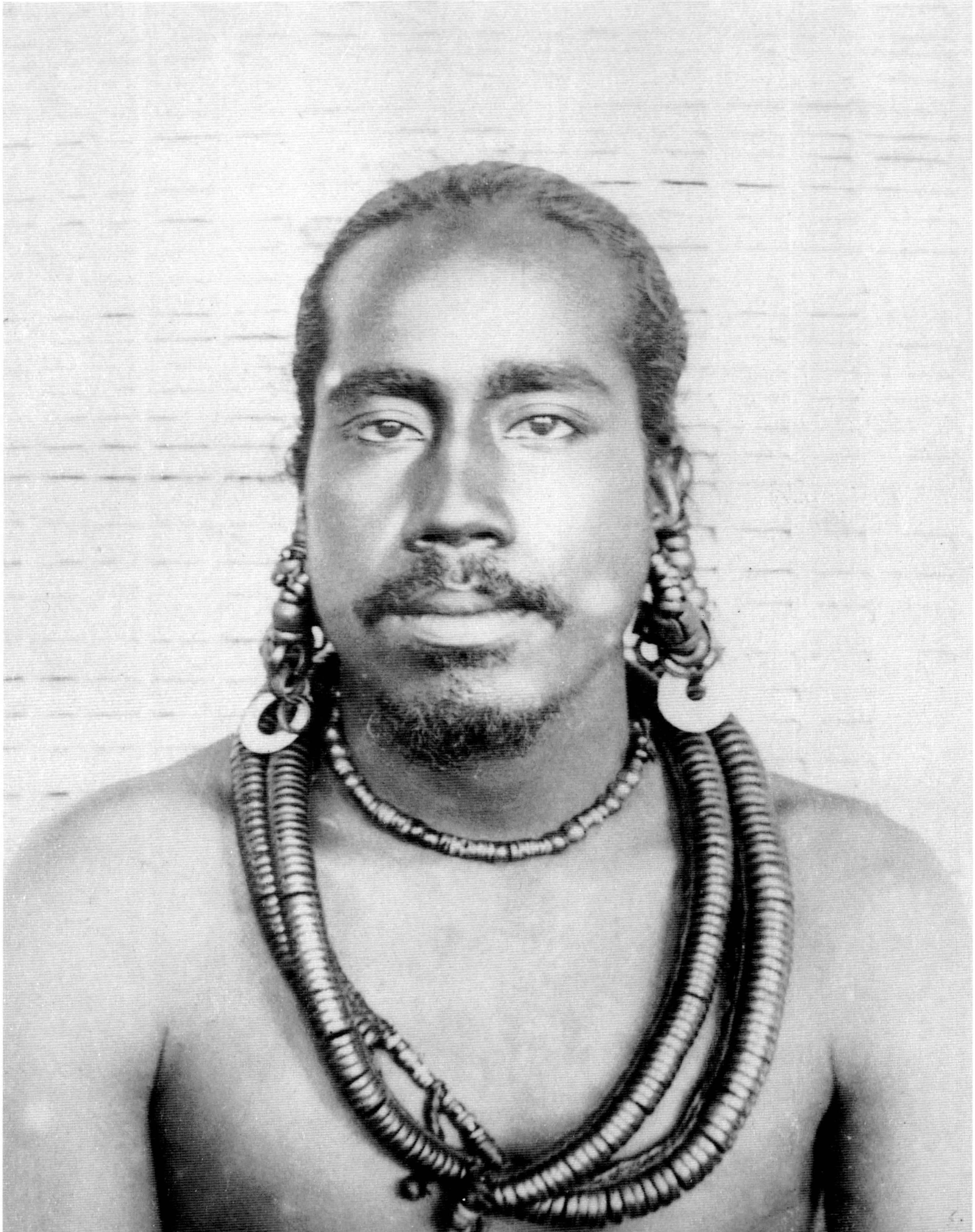

CHAPTER ONE

MICRONESIA

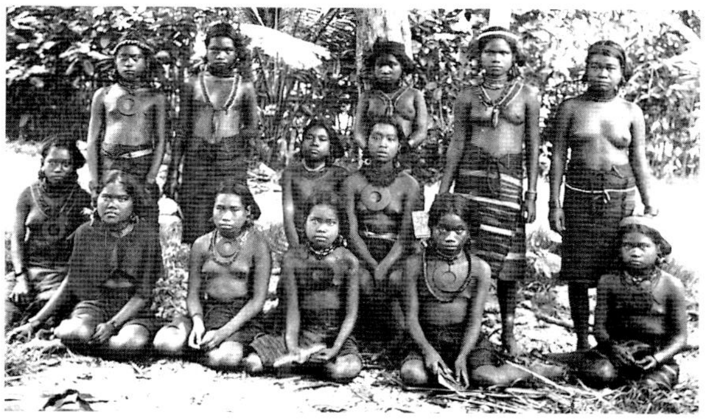

Girls of Satoan (Satawan) Island, Mortlock Group, State of Chuuk (Truk), Caroline Islands, 1887

Thomas Andrew may have photographed these girls at an American Mission school on Mwokil (Mokal) Island to the east of the Mortlock Islands group, but girls' dress on Mwokil and Satawan was very similar. Most of these girls wear a woven wrap-around skirt. This is topped with a belt of plaited strands and perhaps beads strung between wooden or turtle shell spacers. Their most frequent neck ornament is an open flat ring of turtle shell suspended on a string of black and white drilled shell discs. Others wear various shell disc, plaited fibre and coconut ring necklaces, and three of them also wear a wooden breast pendant.

Photo: Thomas Andrew, Stephenson Percy Smith Collection, Alexander Turnbull Library, Wellington, PA1-o-469-34.

left: **Man of Satoan (Satawan) Island, Mortlock Group, State of Chuuk (Truk), Caroline Islands, 1887**

This young man wears in his pierced and extended earlobes the typical Chuukese heavy collection of coconut shell and turtle shell rings from which is suspended a larger flat Conus *shell ring. Tight around his neck he has a necklace of small drilled coconut and shell discs. In a longer neck loop, he also wears a double string of larger coconut shell rings, each of which is lashed individually to a thicker fibre cord. For some men, this assemblage of ornaments in their earlobes was made with larger and more numerous rings, so that the* Conus *rings hung down onto their chests.*

Photo: Thomas Andrew, Stephenson Percy Smith Collection, Alexander Turnbull Library, Wellington, PA1-o-469-47-1

MICRONESIA IS A term introduced by Europeans to refer to the wide scatter of islands in the north-western Pacific that consists of the Caroline, Mariana and Marshall Islands, as well as Kiribati (Gilbert Islands), Nauru and Banaba (Ocean Island). This is now a politically diverse area. The Caroline Islands are divided into the states of Yap, Chuuk (Truk), Pohnpei (Ponape) and Kosrae (Kusaie), which make up the Federated States of Micronesia (FSM), all sovereign states in free association with the United States of America. Separate in the western Caroline Islands is the Republic of Belau (Palau). To the north of the Caroline Islands is the Commonwealth of the Northern Mariana Islands, commonly referred to as the Mariana Islands, and to the east of the Caroline Islands are the Marshall Islands. To the south of the Marshall Islands is Kiribati (formerly Gilbert Islands), to the west of which lie Nauru and Banaba. Geographically this is also a diverse area with several different types of land formation. The Marianas are volcanic, the Carolines have both volcanic and coral islands, the Marshalls and Kiribati are exclusively coral atolls, and Nauru is a raised coral island.

Micronesian art reflects a complex history of ancient cultural influences from Indonesia, Melanesia and Polynesia, tempered by more recent influences from a series of ruling colonial powers from Europe, Japan and America. This art is expressed through an extraordinarily limited range of materials, mainly plant fibre, wood, various sea shells, turtle shell and feathers. Limitations in materials focussed artistic expression on both embellished detail and simplicity of form, from the heavily ornamented sashes to the exquisitely minimal form of a fishhook lure or fishhook-point neck pendant.

Being so geographically isolated, inter-island contact was crucial for the cultures of this corner of the Pacific, particularly for the low-lying atoll groups. Long distance canoe voyaging became a speciality, and navigational skills were highly valued and carefully taught to selected young men. Complex systems of trade, tribute, and ceremonial and religious exchanges developed, within which personal items of adornment such as ear rings, necklaces, belts and skirts circulated as exchange valuables and tributes. Some of these valuables also functioned as forms of currency.

For the atolls of Kiribati, comparatively poor in raw materials, song and dance are two of the greatest art forms. In 1900 Robert Louis Stevenson wrote 'Of all dancing in the South Seas that which I saw at Butaritari (in the Kiribati group) stands easily the first, it leads on the mind; it thrills, rouses, subjugates; it is the essence of all art, an unexplored imminent significance.' Consequently much attention is given to dance costume and ornamentation, from head wreaths, to elegant necklaces and arm and finger ornaments, through to treasured sashes and belts of shell and human hair.

Much change and adaptation has occurred through the centuries, accelerating rapidly in the nineteenth century. Much knowledge and skill has been lost, yet the articulation of cultural values, hopes and dreams continues strongly in the arts of Micronesia, even in this era of satellite technology and rampant globalisation.

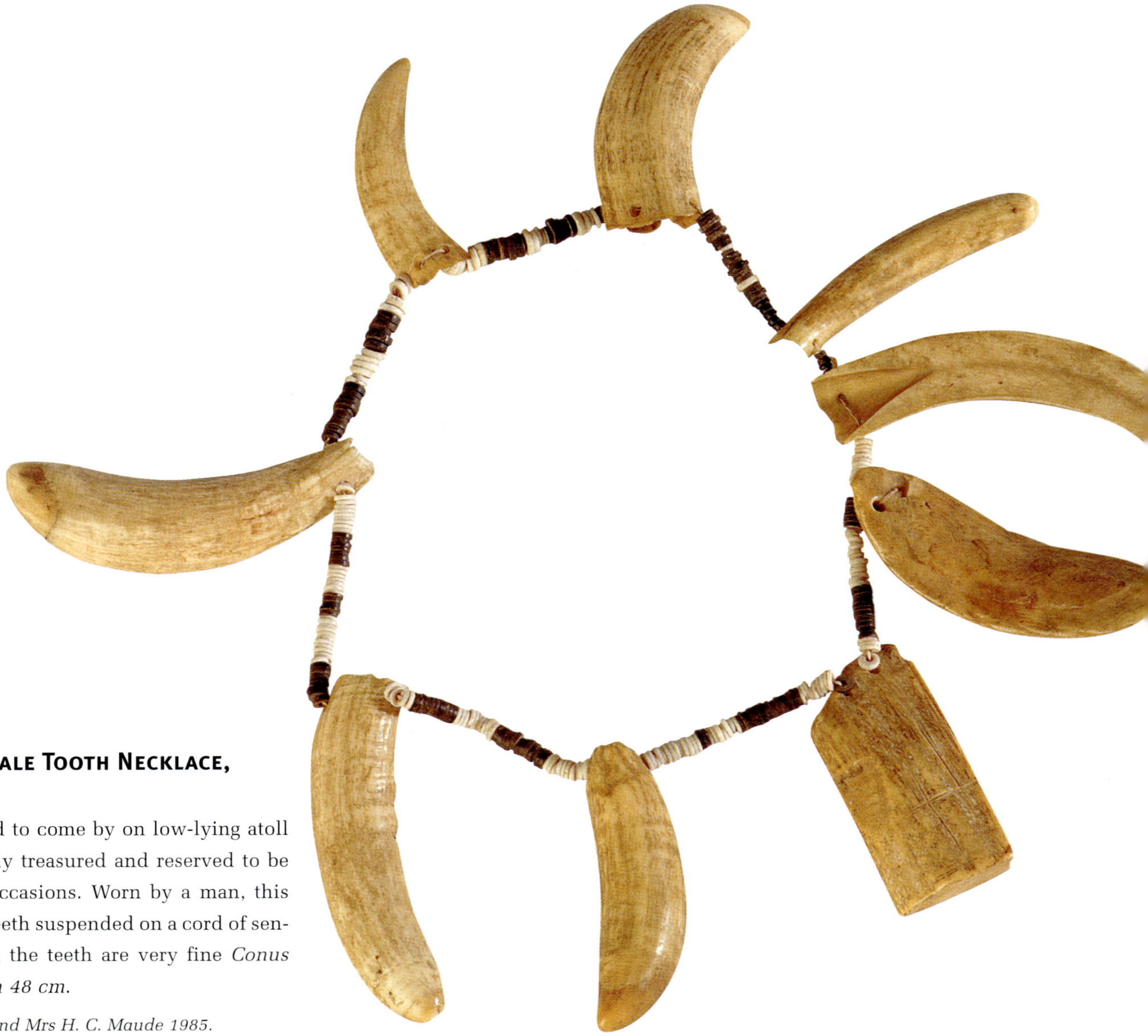

***Te Kauae Te Buangui*, Whale Tooth Necklace, Nonouti, Kiribati**

Whales' teeth are rare and hard to come by on low-lying atoll groups, and therefore are highly treasured and reserved to be worn only during important occasions. Worn by a man, this necklace has nine split whale teeth suspended on a cord of sennit fibre. Interspersed between the teeth are very fine *Conus* and coconut shell discs. *Length 48 cm.*

AM 25182. Presented by Mr H. E. and Mrs H. C. Maude 1985.

opposite: **Fishhook necklace, Tobi, Caroline Islands**

Situated close to Indonesia and south of Palau (Belau) in the westernmost Caroline Islands, Tobi has a very small population with a distinctive language of its own. As an atoll society with limited natural resources, fishing is very important for the maintenance of their culture. If a foetus or baby died at birth, a special fishhook was buried with the body at the birthing house. Elders wore a fine quality fishhook like this turtle shell one on a delicately plaited pandanus cord as a sign of rank and as a protection for their ultimate journey into the afterlife. In many Oceanic cultures, fishhooks were transformed into neck ornaments of deep cultural significance. *Length 45 cm.*

AM 14550. James Edge-Partington Collection. Presented by Dr Thomson Wilson Leys Memorial 1924.

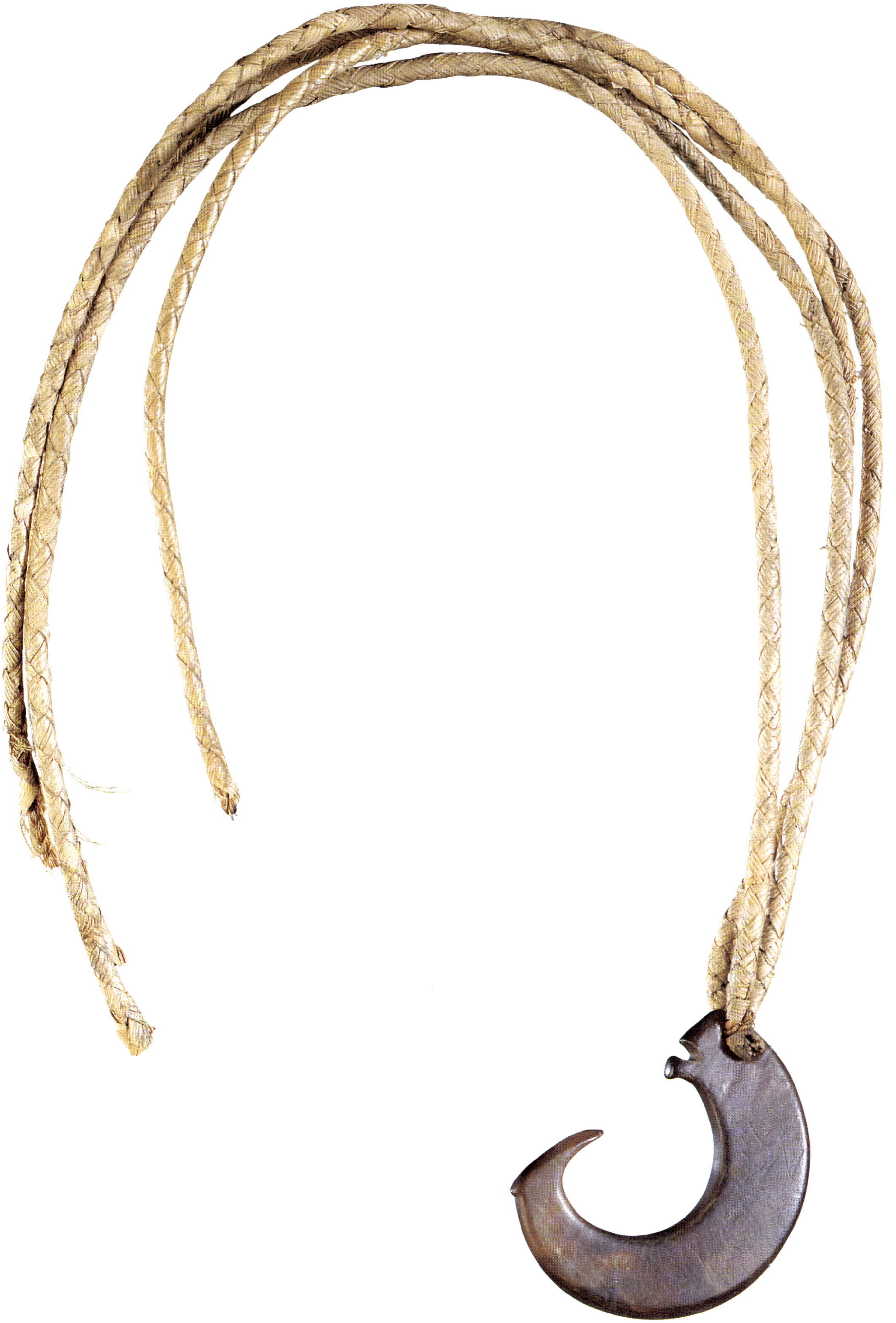

Pearl-shell Breast Pendant, Yap

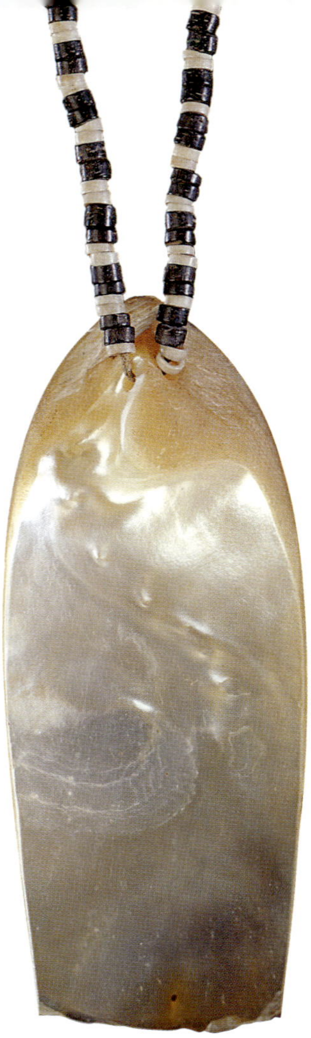

Cut to a spade form, which is a shape with a long Pacific heritage, this piece of pearl shell has been highly polished to emphasize the natural beauty of the material. Its maker has cleverly preserved the thick hinge portion of the shell to provide a strong perforation for the neck cord. Whole pearl shells and pieces cut like this served as a special currency in Yap where they arrived as tribute from the eastern Caroline Islands of the Yapese Empire. This is a more refined ornamental version of this pearl shell currency. Its value here has been enhanced by the addition of alternating black and white shell currency discs on the neck cord. Patterns composed of alternating black and white shell discs are very popular in Micronesian jewellery. *Length 16.5 cm, width 6 cm.*

AM 17481.2. Presented by Mrs G. J. Clark 1932.

Katau, Belt, Nonouti, Kiribati

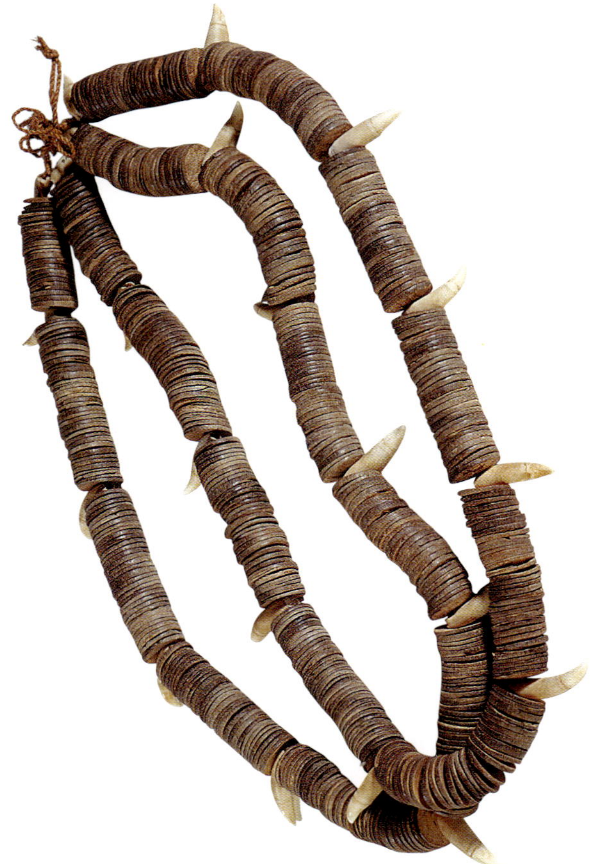

Ornamental belts are a very important part of dance attire in Kiribati. *Katau* are kept by the senior women within families, and are worn at major festivals or in performance of the ceremonial *ruoia* dance. Men make the belts from coconut shell. After initial cleaning and shaping into discs, a central hole is drilled through each disc with a pump drill. Interspersed between the coconut shell discs here are porpoise teeth through which suspension holes have also been drilled. Porpoise teeth are regarded as highly valuable. *Length 80 cm.*

AM 25116. Presented by Mr H. E. and Mrs H. C. Maude 1985.

opposite: **Breast Ornament, Caroline Islands**

There is some uncertainty about the Caroline Islands origin of this beautiful whalebone breastplate but this locality was recorded by the nineteenth century British collector and author James Edge-Partington whose scrupulous attention to such details must be taken seriously. Breastplate forms in whalebone and ivory are much more characteristic of Fiji, while the notched edges and overall form are reminiscent of archaic stone and bone breast pendant ornaments of the New Zealand Maori. *Length 16 cm, width 18 cm.*

AM 15873. James Edge-Partington Collection. Presented by Dr Thomson Wilson Leys Memorial 1924.

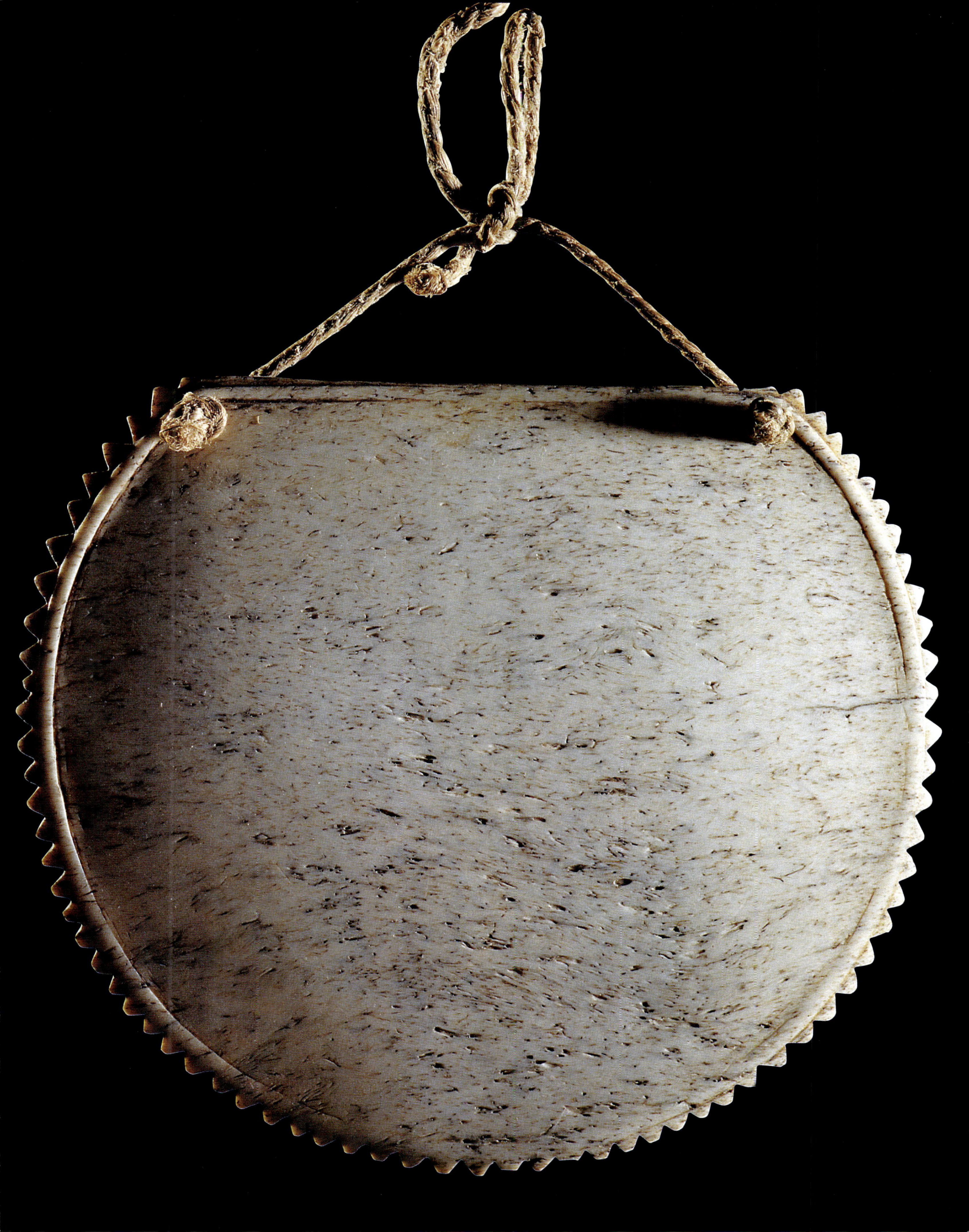

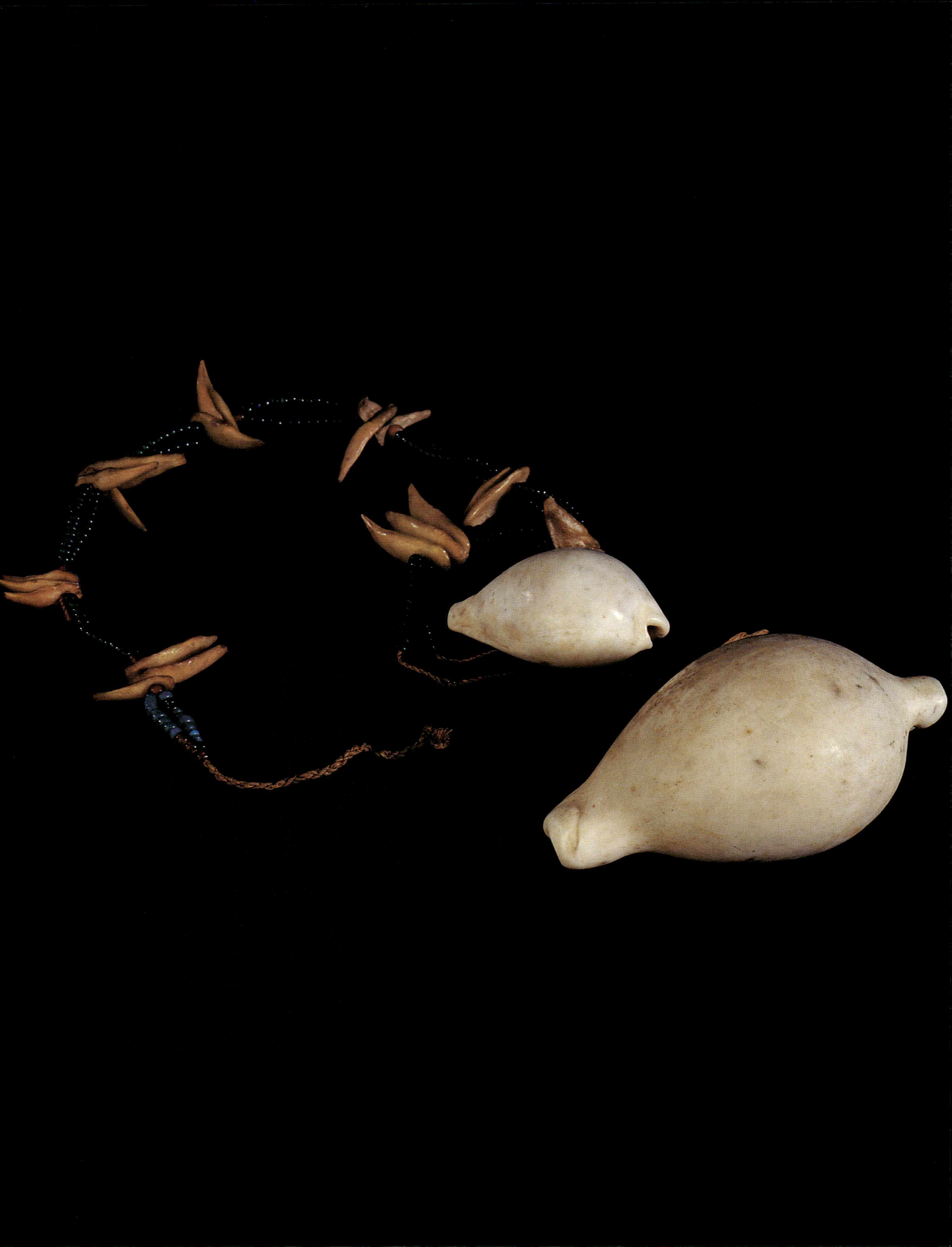

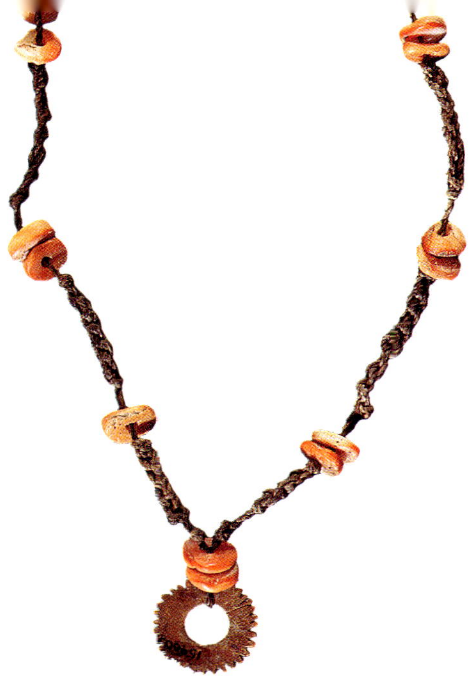

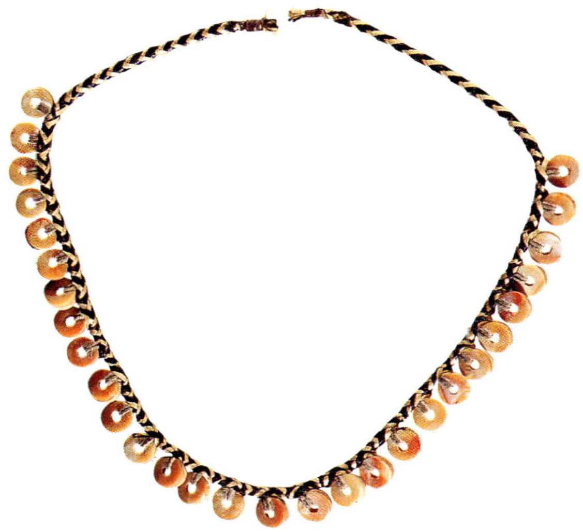

Necklaces, Marshall Islands

One of the most characteristic types of jewellery in the Marshall Islands of Micronesia are various forms of necklaces with a constant component being small drilled discs shaped out of red *Spondylus* shell. These discs may be strung through their central hole, either continuously or grouped between beads of other materials, or suspended on their edge from a plaited neck cord. Sometimes a pendant of shell or turtle shell might be suspended from the necklace. Strings of these red shell discs also served as currency in the Marshall Islands. *Lengths from 32.5 to 48 cm.*

AM 15900.1–3. James Edge-Partington Collection. Presented by Dr Thomson Wilson Leys Memorial 1924.

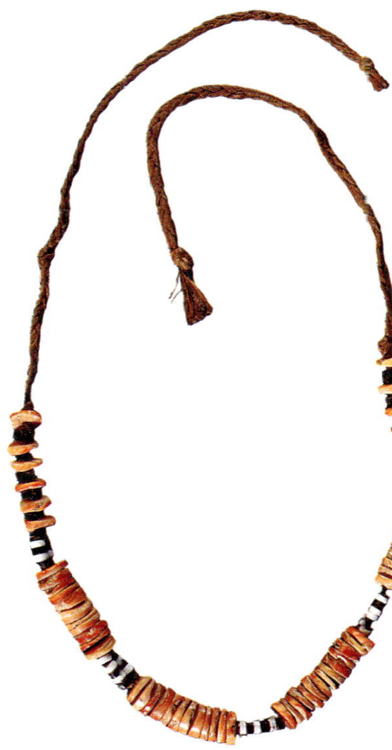

opposite: ***Te Mae Ae Kingkingaki***, Necklace, Beru, Kiribati

Bure, cowrie shells, are rare and therefore highly valued. Two cowrie shells are here strung on fine sennit cord, and coloured beads and fish bones are also incorporated to produce this fine and attractive necklace. *Bure* shells may also be worn individually around the upper arm as part of the dance costume when performing *ruoia* dances. The *ruoia* is a traditional dance form with several distinct types. Children are taught to dance even as they learn to walk and may become skilful dancers before their teenage years. *Length 30 cm.*

AM 22945. Presented by Mr H. E. and Mrs H. C. Maude 1985.

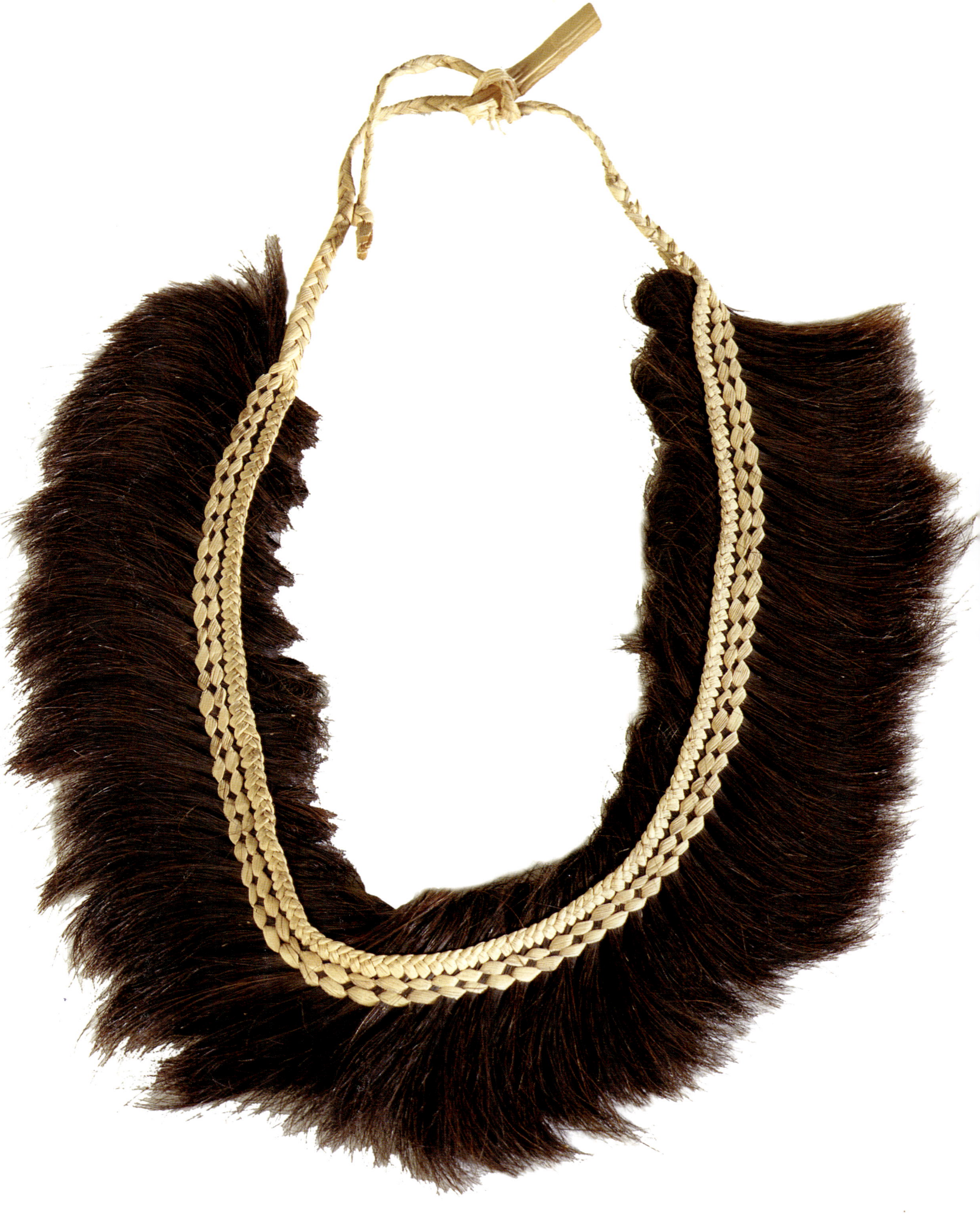

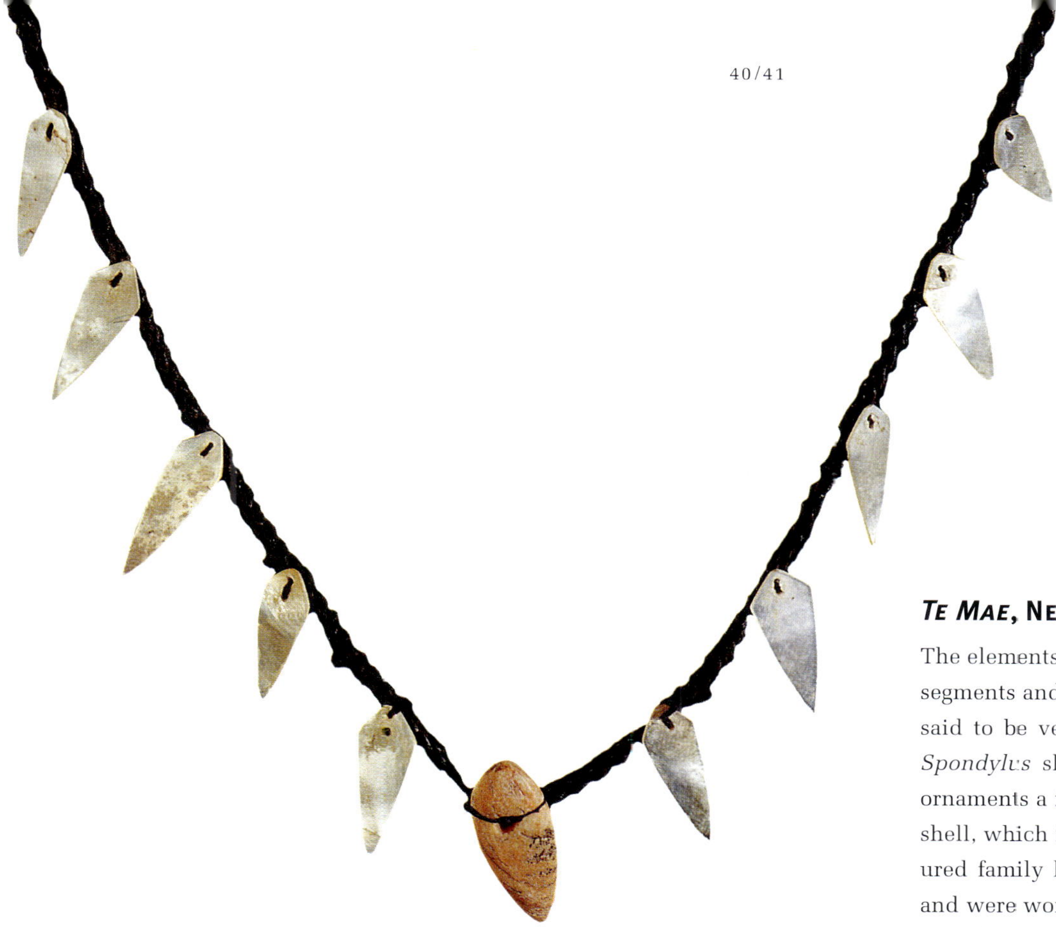

Te Mae, Necklace, Beru, Kiribati

The elements of this necklace consist of ten *baeao* pearl shell segments and one central *Spondylus* shell segment, which is said to be very rare in Kiribati. A pendant made from red *Spondylus* shell was considered one of the most valuable ornaments a family possessed. In combination with the pearl shell, which is also rare, this article would have been a treasured family heirloom. These necklaces were made by men, and were worn in the performance of *ruoia* dances.
Length 53 cm.

AM 24017. Presented by Mr H. E. and Mrs H. C. Maude 1985.

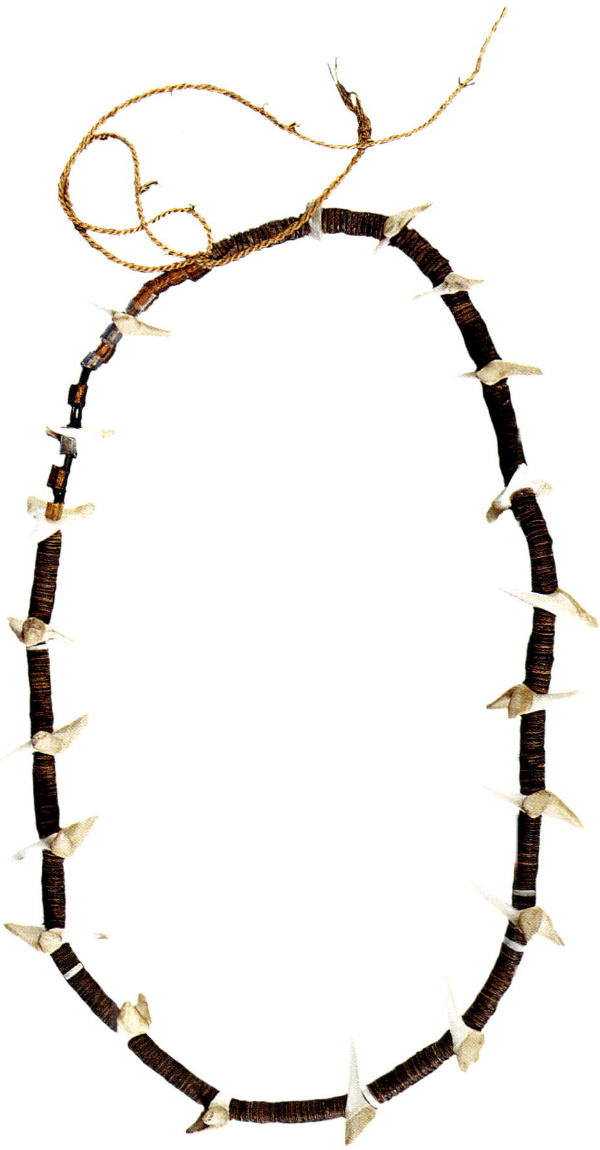

Necklace, Marshall Islands

Drilled coconut shell discs have been strung with interspersed shark teeth and a few trade beads to produce a necklace that was probably intended for sale to visitors as an art piece, as it would be most uncomfortable to wear. However, the prominence of shark teeth in this composition reflects an ancient preference for their use in ornament and weapons among the people of the Marshall Islands and Kiribati.
Length 89 cm.

AM 30059. Presented by Mrs Sidney Aris 1948.

opposite: *Te Mai Te Iranatu Ae Rarangaki*, Human Hair Necklace, Tabiteuea, Kiribati

Ornaments of human hair are of extreme significance due to the sacred properties hair is believed to possess. As treasured objects, they are carefully guarded and passed down within families. Human hair is incorporated into a wide range of objects from personal ornaments and clothing to fishing lines and cord bindings. Small bundles of hair of roughly equal length have been folded in half and banded together with finely plaited pandanus leaves, to form this neck ornament.
Length 40 cm.

AM 22937.1. Presented by Mr H. E. and Mrs H. C. Maude 1985.

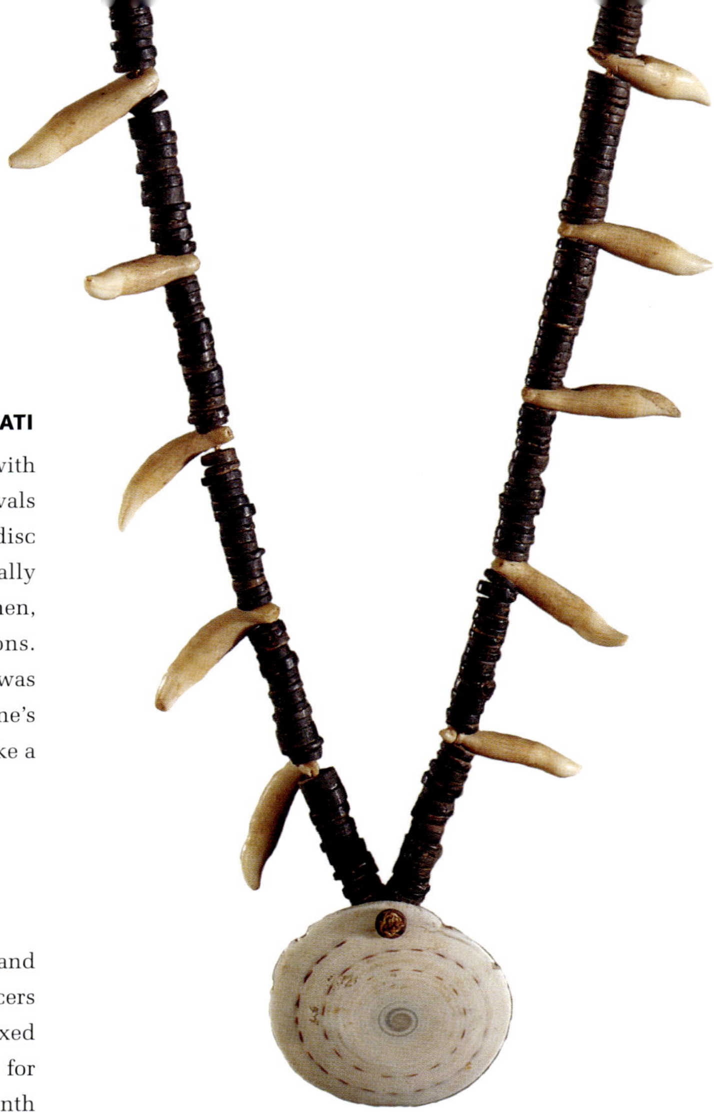

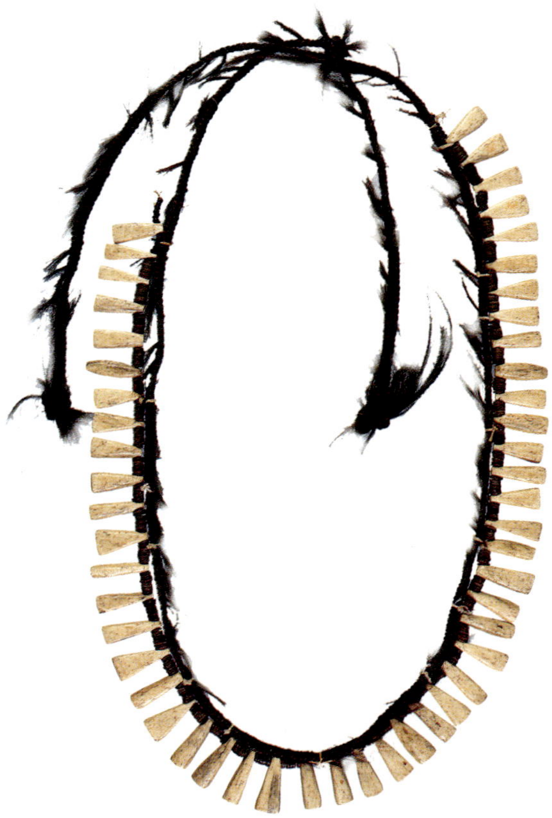

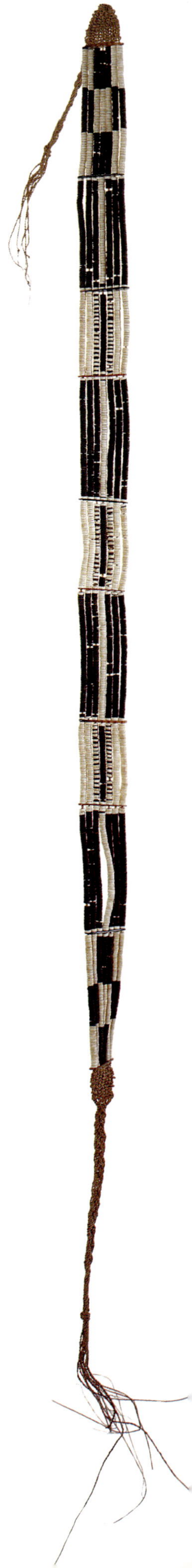

clockwise from right:

Te Nikabono, Conus **Shell Necklace, Beru, Kiribati**

A treasured and now rare item, this necklace is strung with finely worked coconut shell discs interspersed at intervals with ten porpoise teeth, and with an attached *Conus* shell disc pendant called a *nikabono*. Necklaces of this type are usually worn by women and girls, and only very occasionally by men, during dance performances or other festive occasions. Porpoises were of special significance to the chief, as it was believed that one's chiefly status should be reflected in one's physical size, so a chief should be 'round in the middle, like a porpoise'. *Length 39 cm.*

AM 23014. Presented by Mr H. E. and Mrs H. C. Maude 1985.

Dance Belt, Yap

In this woman's dance belt, strings of white mussel shell and black coconut shell drilled discs are held in place by spacers of turtle shell. The maker has created the numerically-fixed pattern of black and white strings that has been standard for this item of body adornment from at least the mid-nineteenth century to the present. When worn over a woven loincloth, this pattern resonated with the geometric designs of the weaving. Belts of this pattern were made in the Yap Outer Islands of the western Caroline Islands from where they passed as tribute to Yap, eventually becoming chiefly heirlooms. Decorative belts and necklaces were the major components of personal adornment for both men and women in most of Micronesia. *Length 122 cm, width 3.5 cm.*

AM 32634. Presented by Lady Ellis 1951.

Necklace, Nonouti, Kiribati

The foundation of this necklace is a cord of plaited human hair forms. An ornament like this was probably a family heirloom with the human hair emphasising an ancestral connection. Attached to this at intervals is a string of drilled coconut shell discs separated into groups of about eight each by a perforated spade-shaped piece of bone perhaps carved to represent teeth. Necklaces like this were worn by women and girls in the festive *ruoia* dances held in the large *maneaba*, or meeting houses. Coconut shell discs strung alternately with white *Conus* shell discs were also a major component of the shell currency called *tekaroro*, formerly used widely in Kiribati and the Marshall Islands. *Length (decorated area only) 69 cm.*

AM 25183. Presented by Mr H. E. and Mrs H. C. Maude 1940.

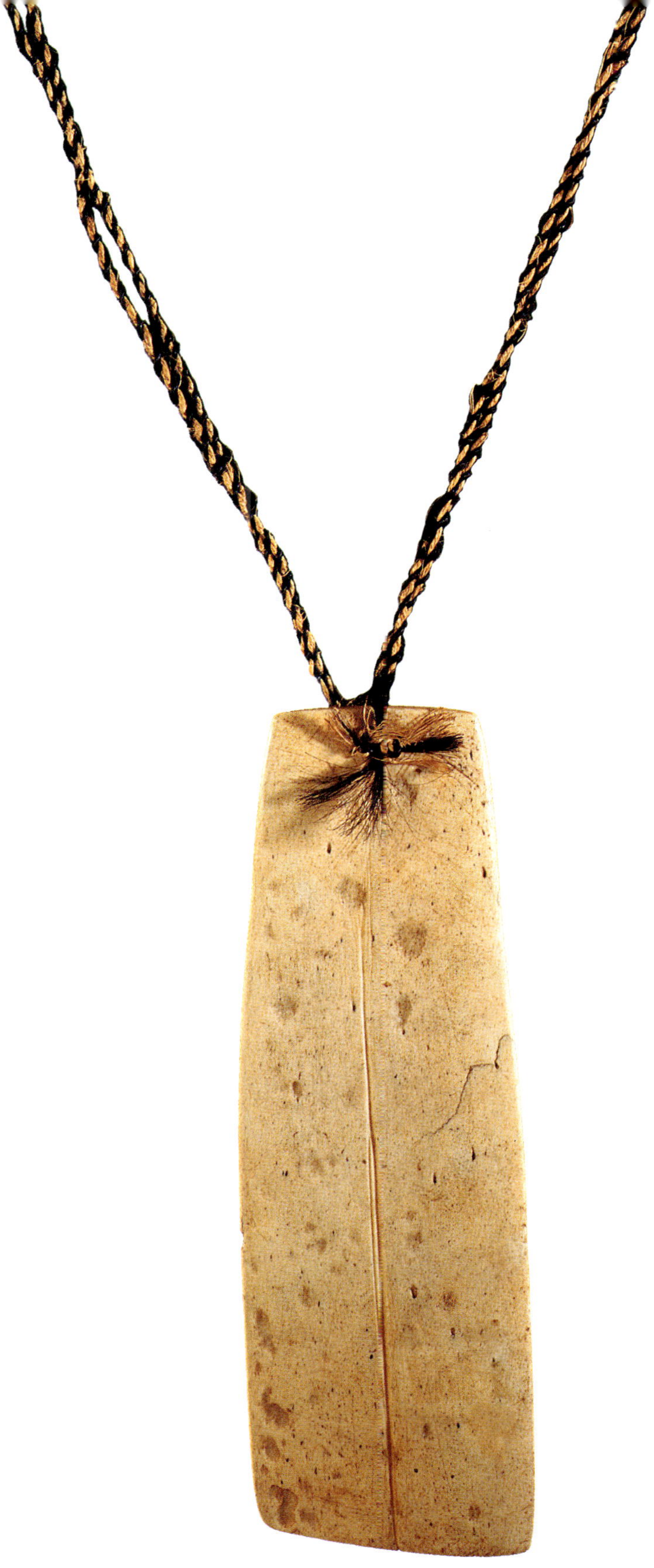

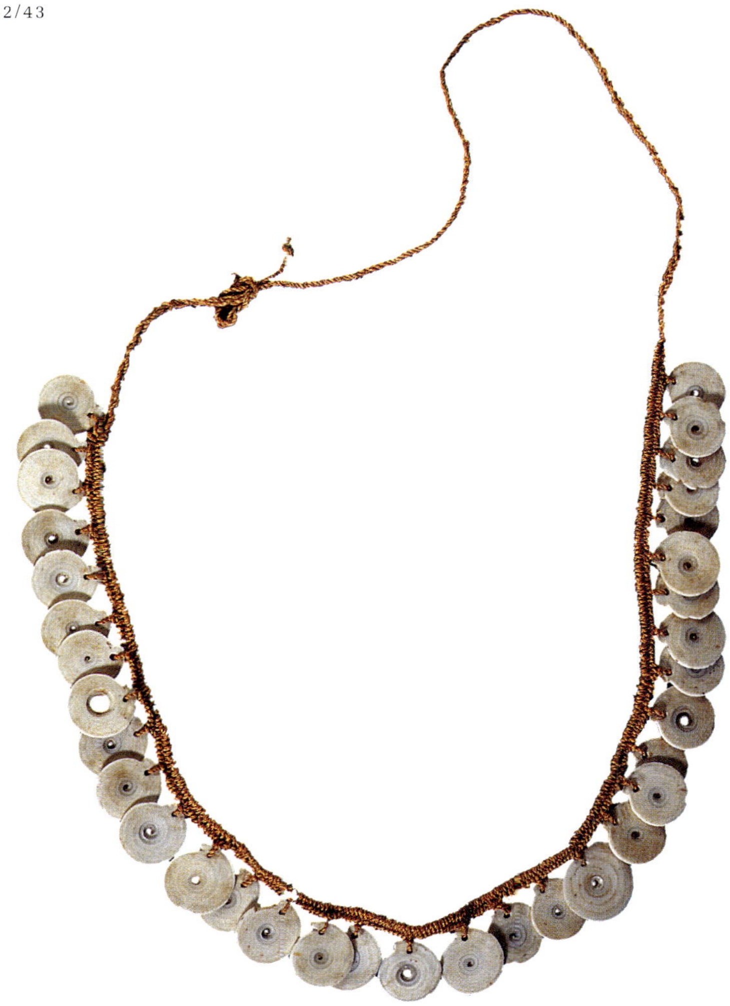

above: ***TAONA N RIRI*, DANCE BELT, TABITEUEA, KIRIBATI**

This ornamental belt was made specifically for a young girl. *Nikabono* discs formed from *Conus* shell, have been attached to a foundation of finely plaited sennit fibre cord, called *kora*. Extremely finely processed *kora*, as in this example, is used in the manufacture of clothing, belts and personal ornaments. The raw material for *kora* is the husk of the coconut shell. Coconut shell husk is also processed to produce sturdier rope, *ro*, which is used in the construction of canoes and houses, as well as in the manufacture of suits of armour. *Length 45 cm.*

AM 24105.1. Presented by Mr H. E. and Mrs H. C. Maude 1985.

left: ***TE BUANGUI*, CEREMONIAL NECK PENDANT, TABITEUEA, KIRIBATI**

Whale-derived raw material is very rare and therefore highly prized in Kiribati culture. Consequently, objects and items of adornment fashioned from whale bone and ivory are greatly valued and become treasured family heirlooms. *Te buangui*, a sign of wealth and status fashioned from the jawbone of a whale, are worn only during ceremonial occasions in the *maneaba*, the large traditional meeting house. *Te buangui* are of such significance that even land could be exchanged for this article. *Length 24.5 cm, width 8 cm.*

AM 24051 Presented by Mr H. E. and Mrs H. C. Maude 1985.

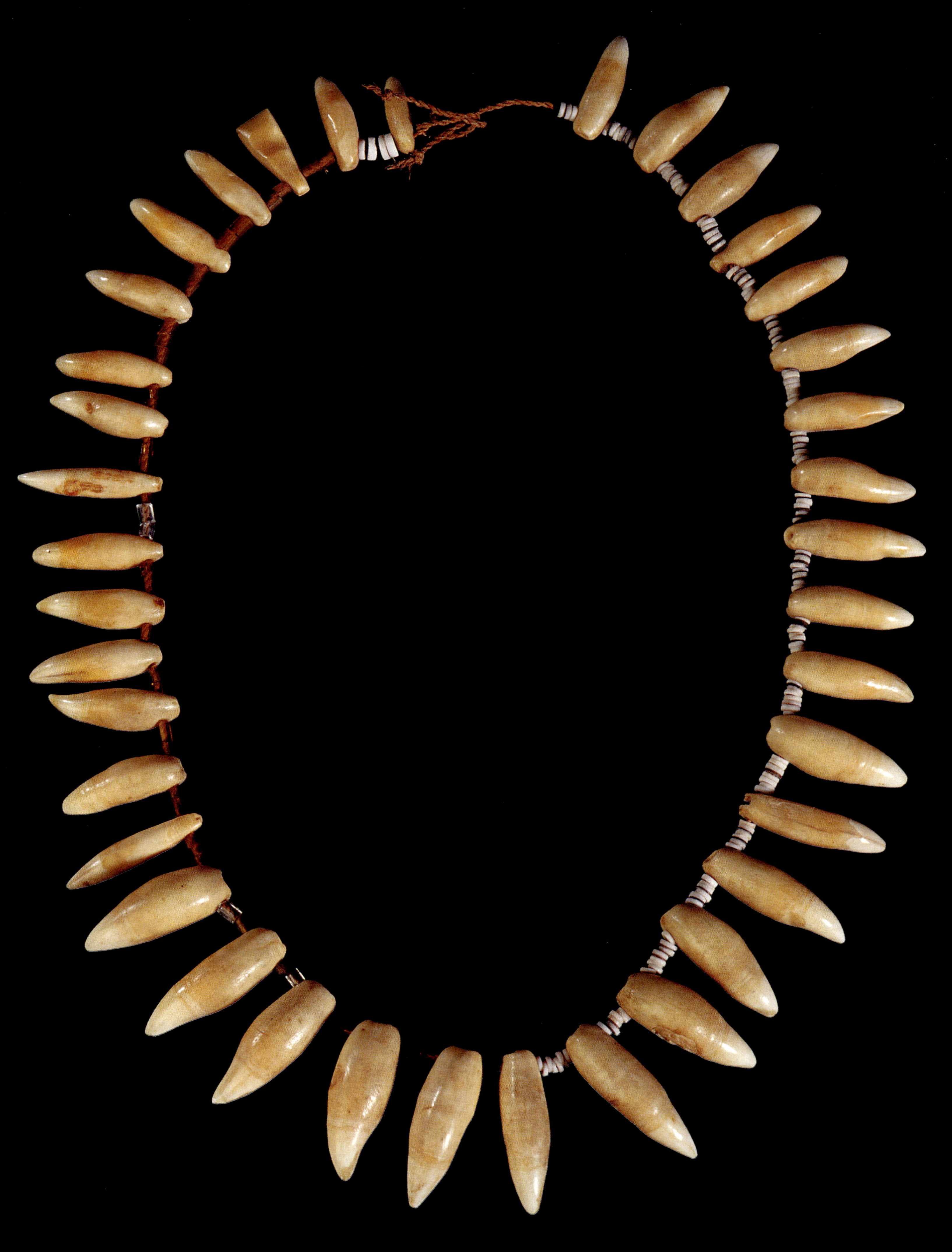

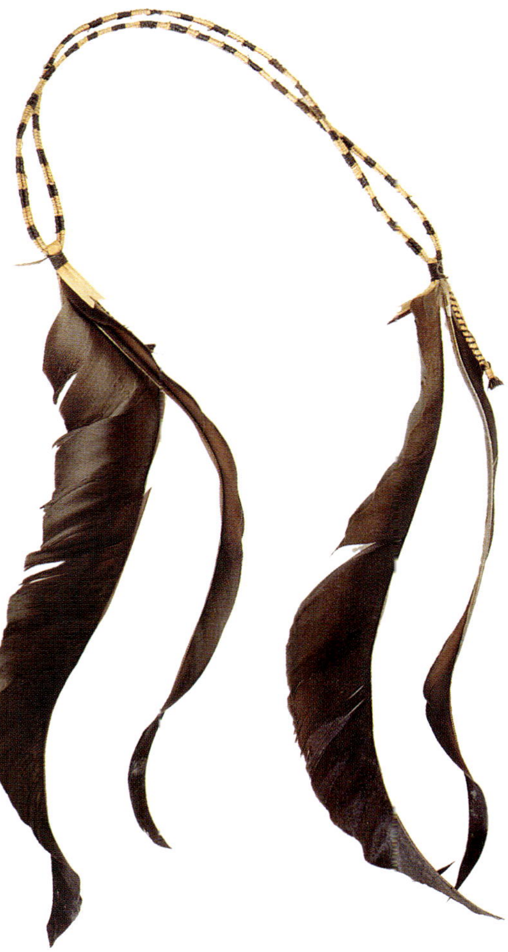

Damoon Or *Emar*, Head Ornament, Nauru

A cord of tightly wrapped and plaited pandanus and hibiscus bast is decorated with long curling feathers of the frigate bird. As well as body ornaments, many of the baskets, belts and mats made by the craftswomen of Nauru were decorated with these black curling frigate bird feathers, reflecting the great regard for this bird in Nauruan culture and serving almost as a badge of Nauru handicraft. *Length of cord 60 cm.*

AM 19956. Presented by British Phosphate Commission 1934.

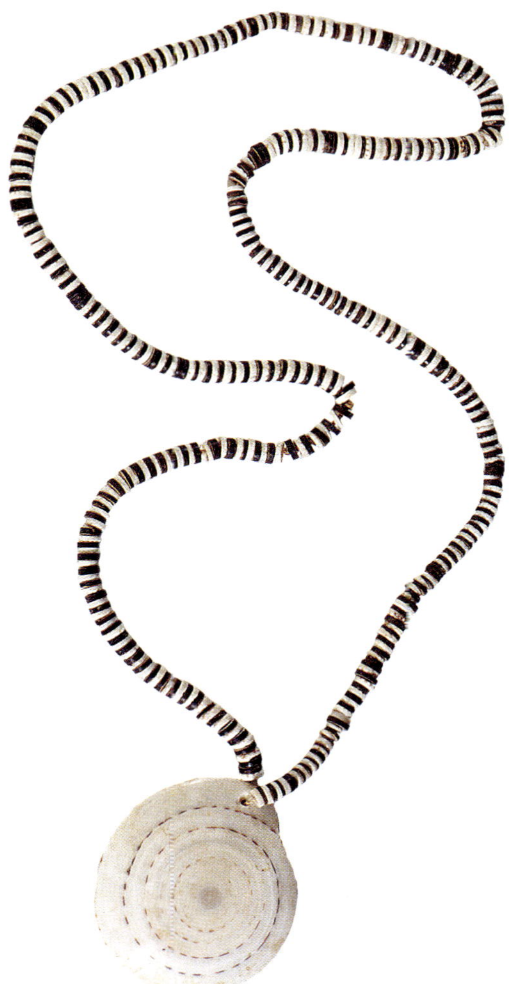

Te Nikabono, *Conus* shell necklace, Nonouti, Kiribati

The name *nikabono* strictly refers to the ground *Conus* shell disc pendant but is often applied to the whole necklace. Usually worn by women and girls for festive dancing, the *Conus* shell pendant is treasured both for its beauty and for its rarity value. Individually drilled coconut shell discs and *Conus* shell discs have been strung in an alternating pattern on the neckcord, another illustration of the Micronesian preference for alternating black and white geometric patterns. *Length 54 cm.*

AM 25185.1. Presented by Mr H. E. and Mrs H. C. Maude 1985.

opposite: Porpoise Teeth Necklace, Kiribati

Thirty-eight porpoise teeth are strung on a fine sennit fibre cord. Strung between the teeth are *Conus* shell discs and introduced coloured glass and plastic beads. Though of little worth, the coloured beads added colour and some interesting texture. The porpoise teeth on the other hand are held in particular esteem and are greatly valued. It was widely believed that members of certain Kiribati clans possessed the ability to call porpoises onto the shore, as witnessed by Arthur Grimble, the British Resident Commissioner between 1914 and 1933. *Length 60 cm.*

AM 32556. Presented by Lady Ellis 1951.

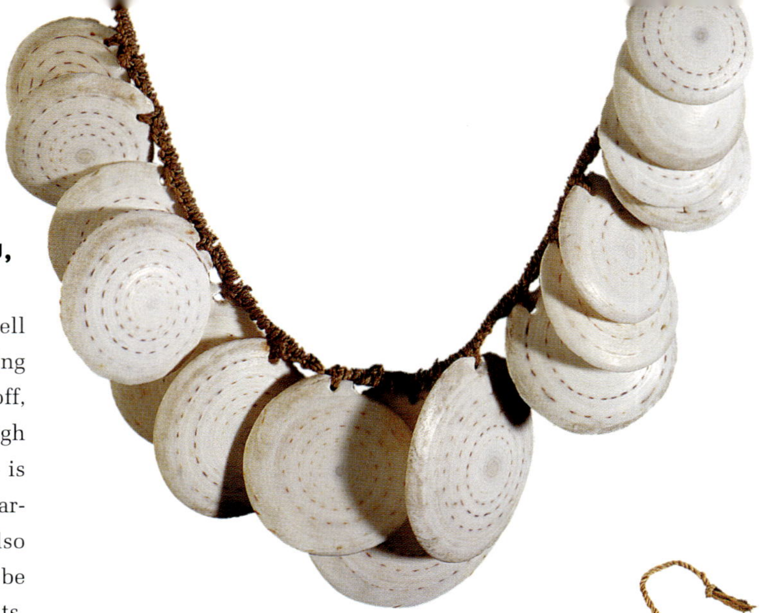

Te Itua Nikabono, Conus Shell Necklace, Beru, Kiribati

Both men and women may wear this type of *Conus* shell necklace. The manufacture of these is a time consuming process in which the flat end of the *Conus* shell is sawn off, the edges smoothed and a suspension hole is pierced through the outer whorl. Through this suspension hole the disc is attached to the plaited sennit band. The sennit bindings, particularly the fine material such as in this example, are also achieved through a lengthy process, particularly if it is to be included in the manufacture of belts and personal ornaments. *Length 58 cm.*

AM 24112. Presented by Mr H. E. and Mrs H. C. Maude 1985.

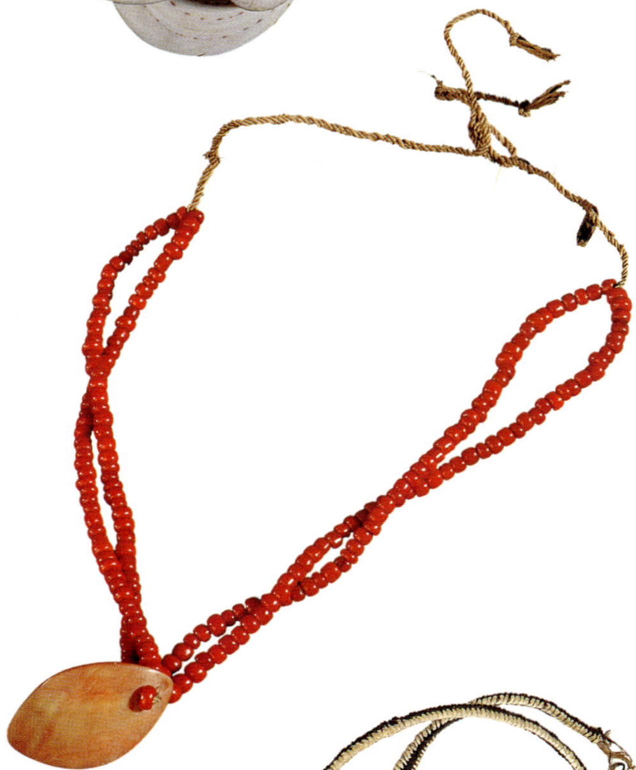

Te Nta, Spondylus Shell Necklace, Kiribati

Red commercial beads have been strung on fine cord with a shaped elliptical reddish *Spondylus* shell pendant. The shell is rare and is found with difficulty below the water line on the reefs of the outer lagoon. For the I-Kiribati people, mystery surrounds the origin of the *Spondylus* shell, hinted at by the intriguing name they have given to the shellfish—*koikoi-n-anti*, 'small shell of the spirits'—but unfortunately no further information was recorded. Edmund John Finny acquired this article while serving in the Western Pacific High Commission during the 1940s. *Length 29.5 cm.*

AM 54924. Presented by Lieutenant-Colonel E. J. Finny 1995.

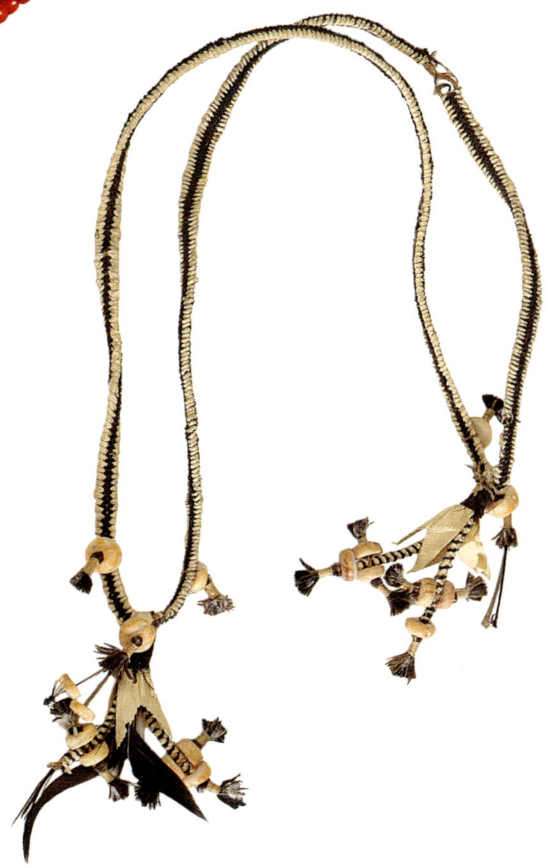

Necklace, Nauru

The cord of this necklace consists of tightly plaited and wrapped hibiscus bast, human hair and pandanus fibres. This cord is decorated with tassels of drilled red shell or coral discs, feathers and pandanus leaf pieces, which form a very characteristic feature of Nauruan personal ornament. Similar pieces were also worn as head ornaments. *Length of cord 56 cm.*

AM 30060.2. Presented by Mrs Sidney Aris 1948.

opposite: *Te Uba*, Pearl Shell Pendant, Nonouti, Kiribati

This beautifully polished pearl shell has been attached to a necklace of coconut and *Conus* shell discs and ten univalve shells. The shell discs have been painstakingly shaped, polished and drilled, then threaded on to a beautiful fine sennit fibre cord. These necklaces are usually reserved to be worn during dance performances. Another important use for pearl shell is as shanks for bonito trolling lures to which are lashed turtle shell points. *Length 42 cm.*

AM 25186. Presented by Mr H. E. and Mrs H. C. Maude 1985.

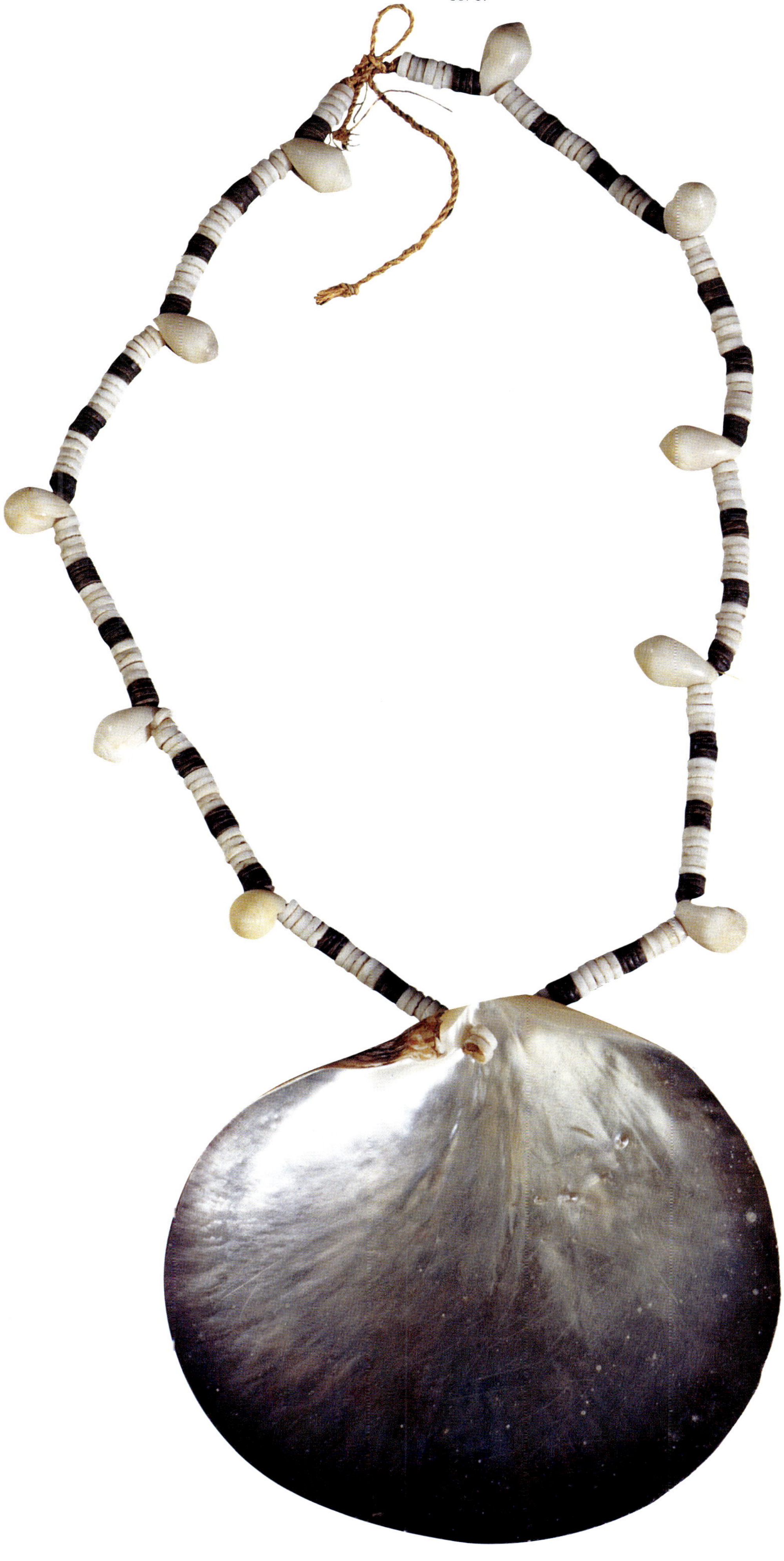

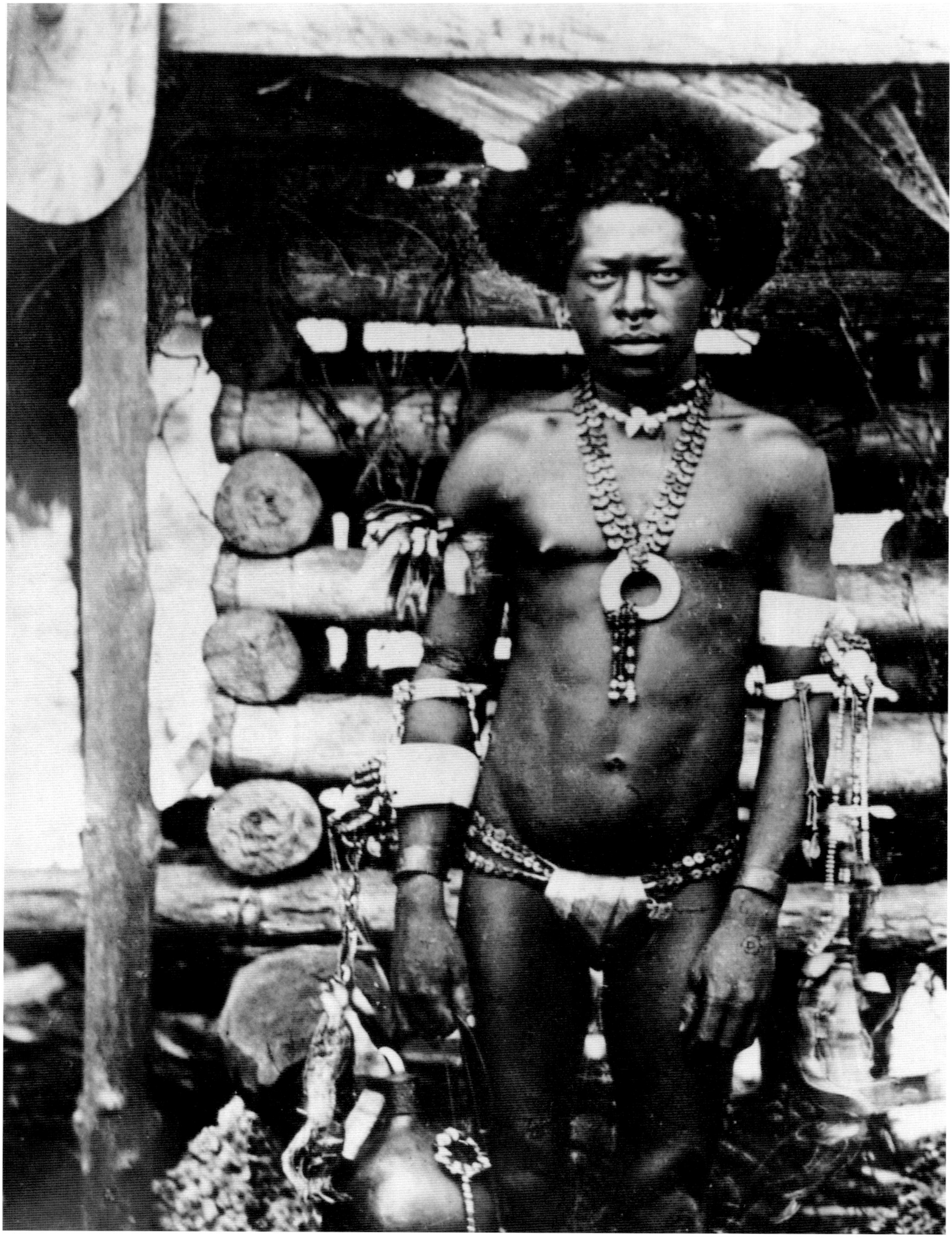

CHAPTER TWO

MAINLAND NEW GUINEA

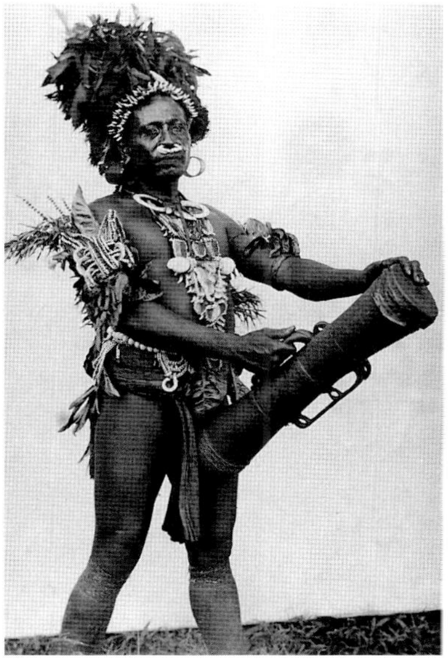

WARRIOR WITH DANCE DRUM, NORTH-EASTERN PAPUA NEW GUINEA, ABOUT 1900

Dressed in his best personal ornaments of feathers, boar tusks, dog teeth, and Nassa *and* Ovula *shells, this dancer from the Astrolabe Bay area presents himself as the epitome of strong prosperous aggressive manhood, according to the ideals of his culture.*

Photo: Carter Album, Auckland Museum C41090.

opposite: **MAN WEARING *KULA* VALUABLES, TROBRIAND ISLANDS, PAPUA NEW GUINEA, ABOUT 1911**

Standing in front of a yam storage house, this young man wears Conus *shell arm bands called* mwali *and a rare* doga *necklace of red* Spondylus *shell discs called* sapisapi, *all valuables associated with the* kula *trading cycle linking the islands of the Massim district. The two main items traded ceremonially between trading partners in the* kula *are shell necklaces called* soulava *or* bagi, *and* mwali, *but very rarely are either of these items actually worn. This young man must be wearing the* mwali *and* doga *for a special occasion.*

Photo: Vosper-Warren Album, Auckland Museum C28444.

NEW GUINEA IS the second largest island in the world, after Greenland. Close to the mainland are many smaller islands, especially around the Vogelkop at the western end and the D'Entrecasteaux Islands and the Louisiade Archipelago at the eastern extremity. The mainland is very mountainous in the interior but with large, high-altitude, intermontane valleys now mostly covered in open grasslands. From these highlands, many tributaries form large rivers such as the Digul, Fly, Kikori, Ramu, Sepik and Mamberamo, which meander across the surrounding forested lowlands and flow into huge estuaries and swampy areas, especially along the southern coasts.

This diverse geography has nurtured many different modes of livelihood among the people, including coastal sea-fishers, riverine hunters and bush gatherers, swamp-dwelling sago processors, shifting agriculturists in the bush-covered hills, and elaborate agricultural systems in the highlands. Some of the coastal and off-shore islanders supplemented their agriculture and fishing by long-distance trading in large sailing canoes.

As a result of its complex colonial and political history the island is now divided into the independent state of Papua New Guinea in the eastern half and West Irian (Irian Jaya, formerly Dutch New Guinea) as a province of Indonesia in the west. This modern political division, and the older one between British/Australian Papua in the south-east and German New Guinea in the north-east, was imposed upon native cultures that were continuous across these borders.

This large island is also the most diverse cultural area of the world, with several hundred distinct languages and many different cultures, albeit with an underlying unity and common approach to the necessities of life. The total population now numbers about one million Melanesians in West Irian and about four million in Papua New Guinea. Highlands societies are generally large in scale, with some very dense populations, while groups in the lowlands tend to be smaller and more diverse. Societies around the forested fringes of the highlands are often very small and mobile through a large territory. In social organisation, these societies range from egalitarian to those with 'big-men' who have achieved their leadership status by economic and political success, those with some hierarchy, and a few with chiefly institutions.

Extensive trade moved materials between coastal and inland groups, including materials used in jewellery and adornment. Very broadly, this involved shells travelling to inland areas and bird feathers going out to coastal societies.

MAP OF NEW GUINEA

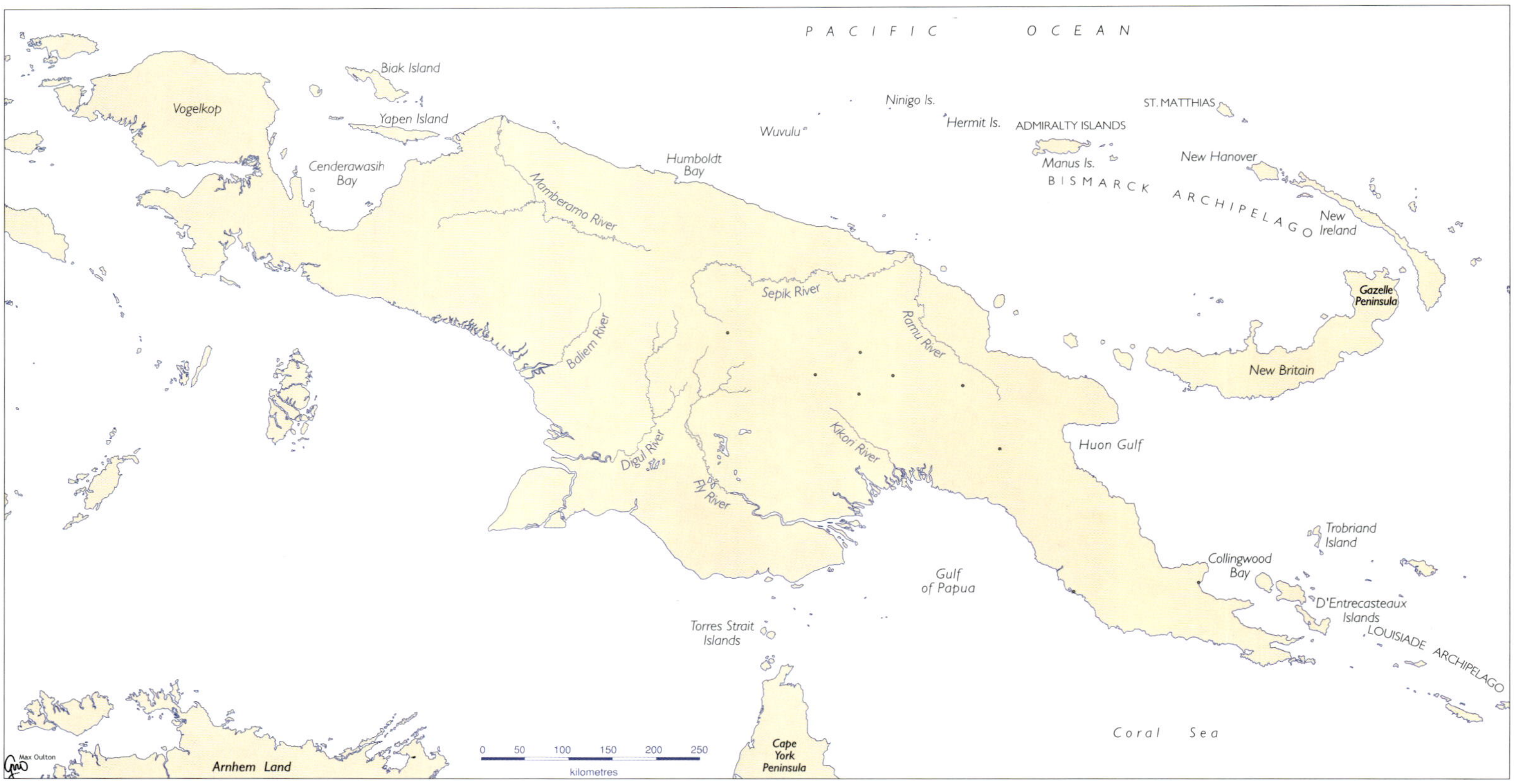

Around the coasts there were several complex trading systems such as the *hiri* between the Motu of Port Moresby and the Elema and Namau of the Gulf of Papua, the *kula* around the islands of the Massim district, and the Vitiaz Straits trading system linking islands off the coast and areas of the mainland around Huon Peninsula with western New Britain. Finished jewellery items and trade valuables that might be worn also travelled along these trade routes. Being very portable, jewellery and body adornment items, or at least the ideas and patterns behind them, moved very easily over long distances across cultural divisions. Therefore, while major distinctions are often drawn between the highlanders' concentration on ephemeral body art as opposed to the lowlanders' concern with sculptural and architectural painting arts, these differences are not so prominent when considering jewellery and body adornment.

Men From A Mountain District Of The Fly River, Papua New Guinea, 1890s

Men from the mountain headwaters of the Fly River wear an assortment of jewellery consisting of shell and pig tusk pendants, bands of animal teeth and shells, and cassowary quills. In order to wear all these different ornaments, these men have had their nasal septa and the sides of the nose pierced and their earlobes extended. Their small fragmentary shell ornaments are usual for people living in areas a long distance from the sea, where even small pieces that have survived the trade routes have a significant value.

Photo: Alexander Turnbull Library, Wellington 144857-1/2.

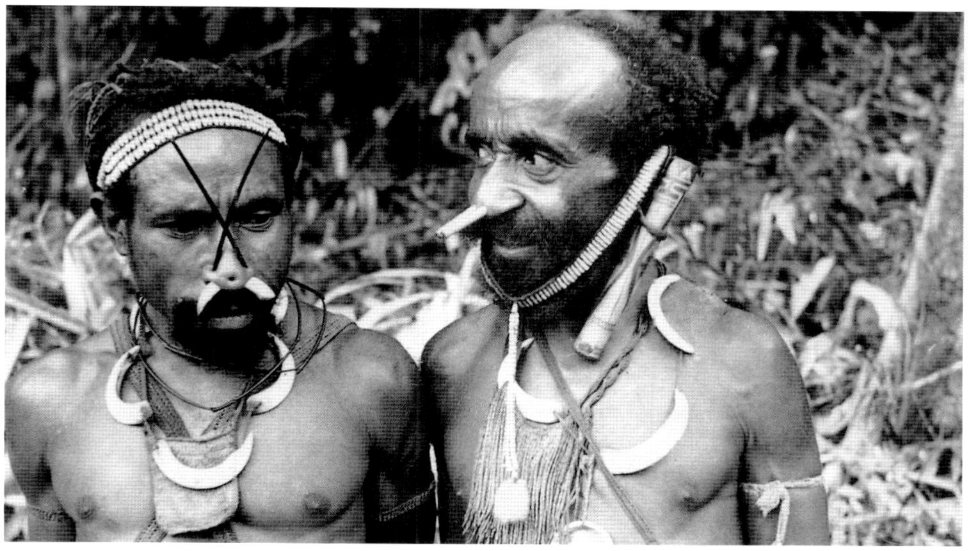

Men Dressed For Dancing, Wanigela, Collingwood Bay, Oro Province, Papua New Guinea, Between 1901 and 1911

Wearing new barkcloth loincloths with patterns specific to their clan membership, these men also display their fighting ornaments. Two have their boar-tusk face ornaments, gibigibi*, hanging on their chests, but during dance and fighting these were held in the teeth to frame their face. Others wear the head-dress of hornbill beaks, originally reserved for warriors who had killed an enemy. This photograph clearly shows how a clan group correlated the messages conveyed by their self-decoration, even though they are wearing three different types of head-dresses.*

Photo: Percy Money, Auckland Museum B11016.

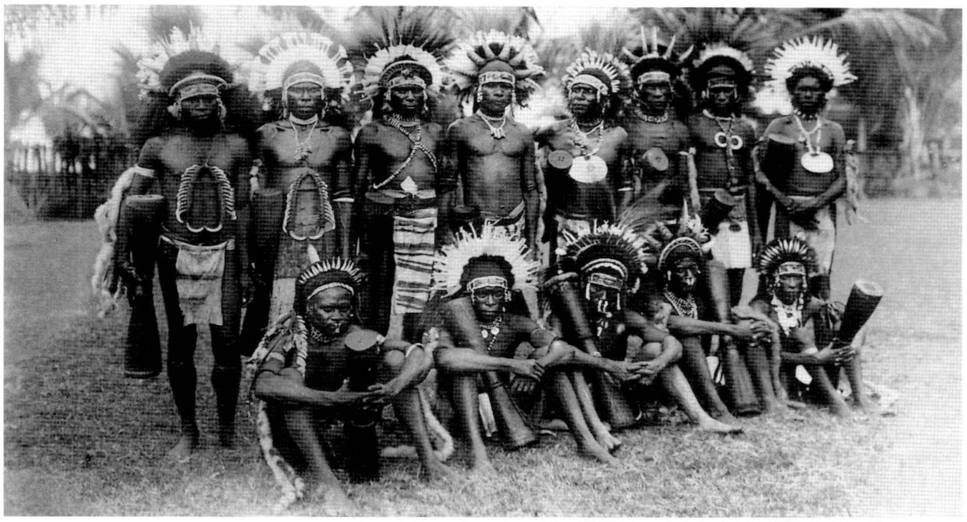

Presentation of Valuables, Trobriand Islands, Massim District, Papua New Guinea, About 1911

Men of the Trobriand Islands, dressed in their finery of white cockatoo feather head-dresses and necklaces, line up for a formal presentation of valuables. Trobriand men and women dress up frequently like this for dancing, especially for the two months of nightly dancing to celebrate the yam harvest. Adults dress in their traditional costumes and feather head-dresses, apply face paint and use other magical herbs and preparations to increase their beauty and to make themselves feel young again like the teenagers, who welcome these dances as an opportunity for sexual freedom.

Photo: Vosper-Warren Album, Auckland Museum C28446.

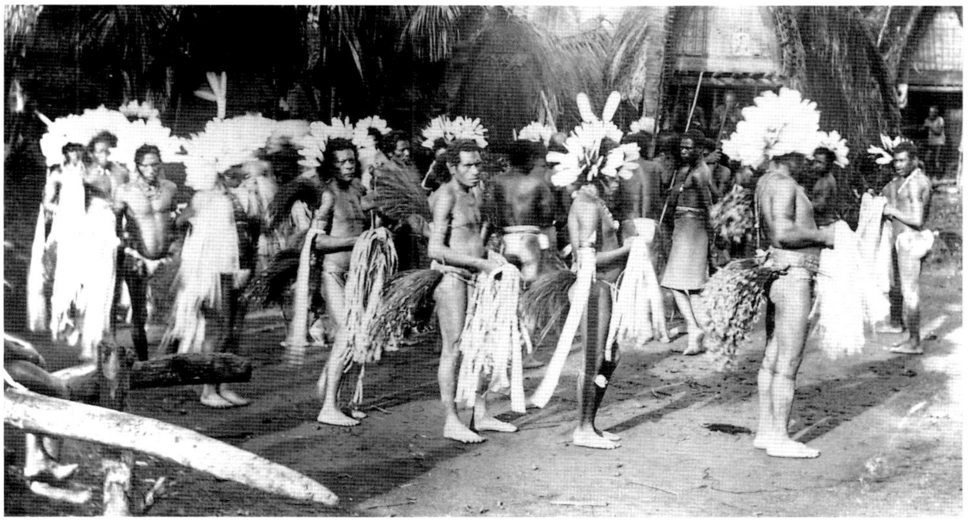

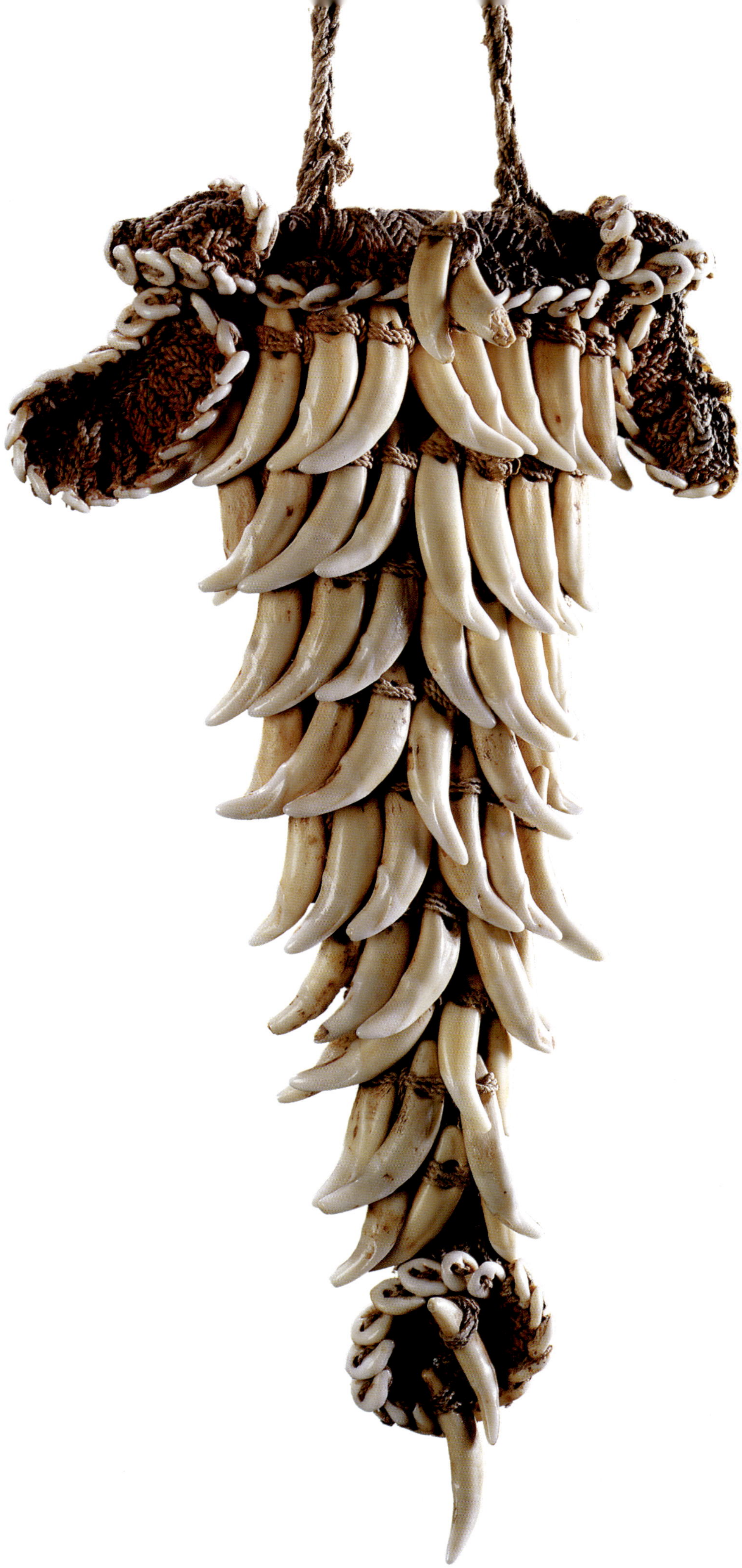

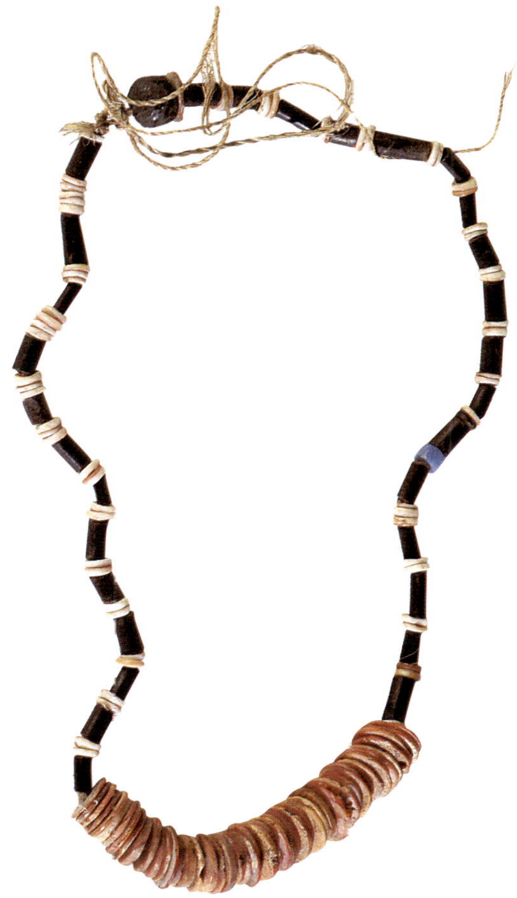

Necklace, Massim District, Milne Bay Province, Papua New Guinea

Red *Spondylus* shell discs drilled so that they can be strung onto cords are virtually the trademark of Massim district trade valuables and body ornament. They are found strung as components of necklaces either alone or with other bead elements and attached on short cords to numerous other forms of jewellery. In this necklace, the *Spondylus* discs are grouped at the centre of a cord that is strung on each end with alternating white shell beads and cassowary feather quills. *Length 23 cm.*

AM 48032.2. Presented by Mr Tucker 1977.

***Siripya/Fofona*, Chest and Back Ornament, Benabena and Kamano, Eastern Highlands, Papua New Guinea**

Women plait the fibre backing of a *fofona*, which is then decorated with small *Nassa* shells and pigment by men, who also attach the valuable *Ovula* shells that have been brought into the Highlands from the coast. *Fofona* are badges of male initiation, worn by young men in warfare and at festivals as a sign that they have been through the painful initiation rituals. Modern examples like this are still being made and also serve as bride price and compensation payments. *Length 34 cm, width 30 cm.*

AM 55925. Purchased 2002.

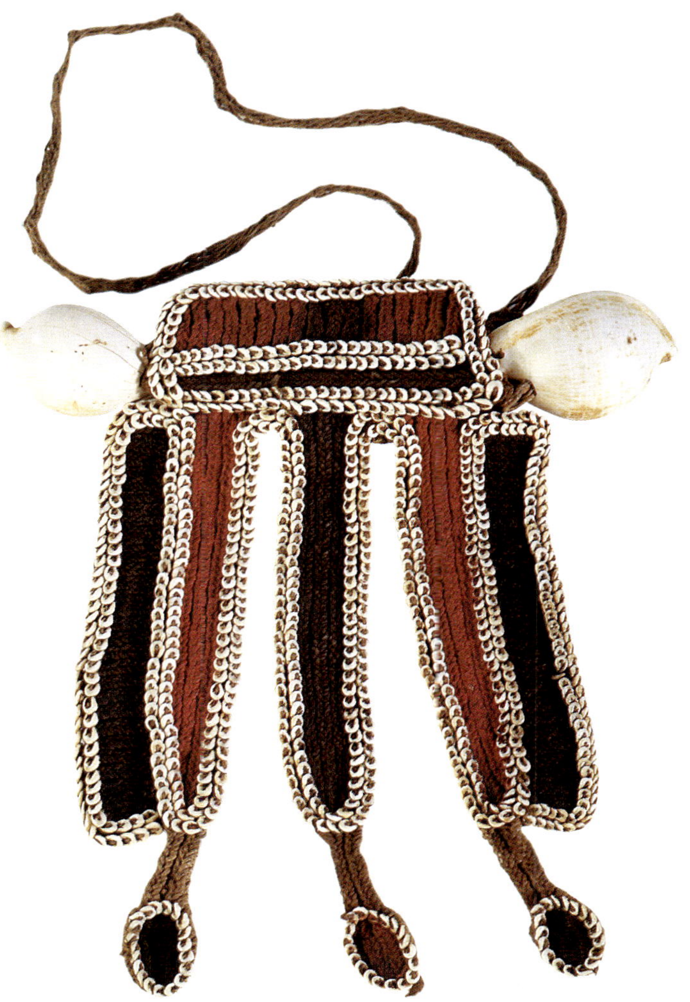

opposite: **Breast Ornament, Astrolabe Bay, Madang Province, Papua New Guinea**

Large dog teeth and *Nassa* shells on a fibre base have been combined into this breast ornament, which a man would wear as a sign of his wealth. However this was quite a common ornament, worn by many men in this area. Dog teeth were a major form of currency in much of New Guinea. *Length 40 cm, width 13 cm.*

AM 11424. Presented by Mr R. Recknagel 1892.

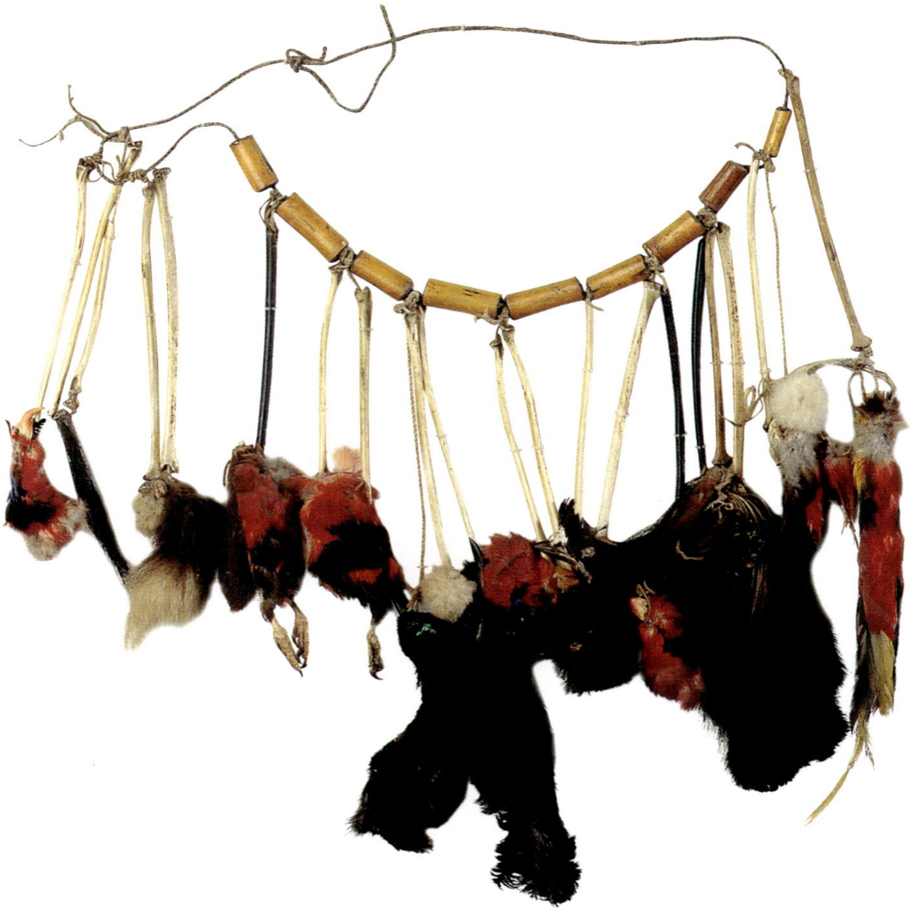

Necklace, Anga People, Morobe Province, Papua New Guinea

This necklace is designed to be worn so that all the attachments will hang down over the chest of the man wearing it. Threaded on the cord are sections of reed serving as spacers to separate the attachments. Bird bones and three cassowary quills support the attachments, which consist of cuscus tails, bird heads, pig hair and feathered bird skins—some still with their feet attached. An elaborate necklace like this was probably only worn on special occasions. *Length 72 cm.*

AM 54838. Purchased from Karl Every 1994.

***Nanemo*, Forehead Ornament, Collingwood Bay, Oro province, Papua New Guinea**

Worn only by warriors across the forehead as part of a much larger ensemble of feather head-dress and shell necklaces, this ornament has been constructed of cut sections of orange *Spondylus* shell, outlined with white *Nassa* shells, all mounted on a fibre base. This form of ornament is especially characteristic of the Orokaiva people living around Mount Lamington. *Length 30 cm, width 6 cm.*

AM 9991. Presented by Miss Anne Tomlinson 1926.

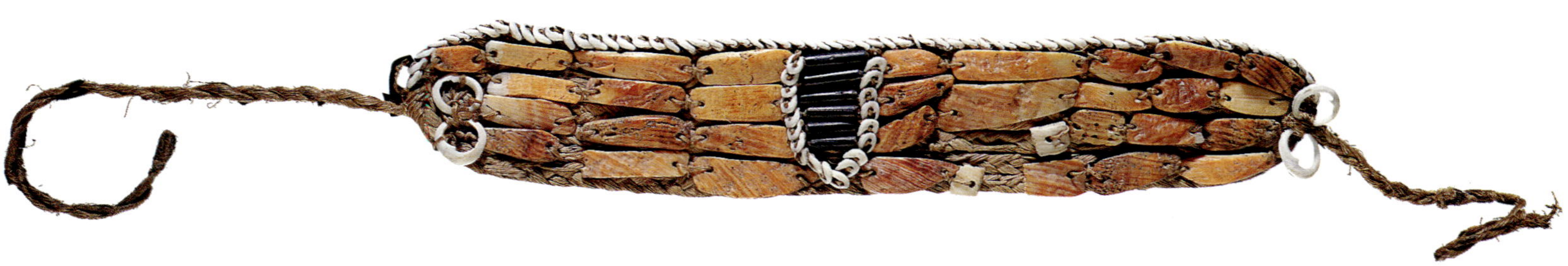

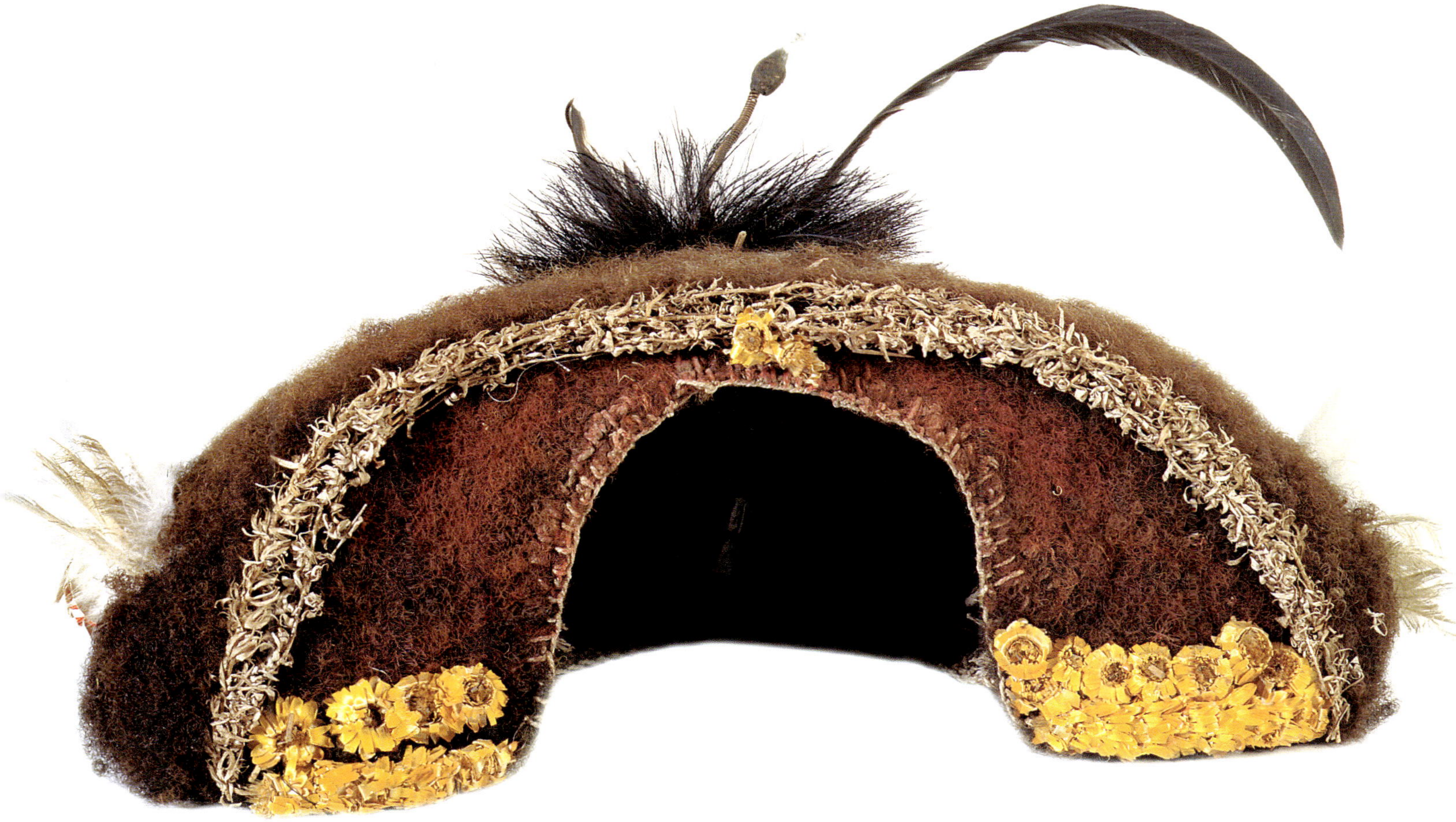

Human Hair Wig, Huli People, Tari Valley, Southern Highlands Province, Papua New Guinea

Huli men who have passed through the initiation rituals as young bachelors are entitled to wear large crescent-shaped hair wigs as a sign of their adult status. Wigs are worn especially at the periodic festivals and other occasions of heightened social activity and political display. Older men wear this sort of wig made of human hair on a twine network, decorated with everlasting daisies, cassowary and other bird feathers, and with red dye dabbed on the front. At other times the wig may be decorated with bird of paradise feathers, snake skin or marsupial fur. *Width 47 cm.*

AM 55464.

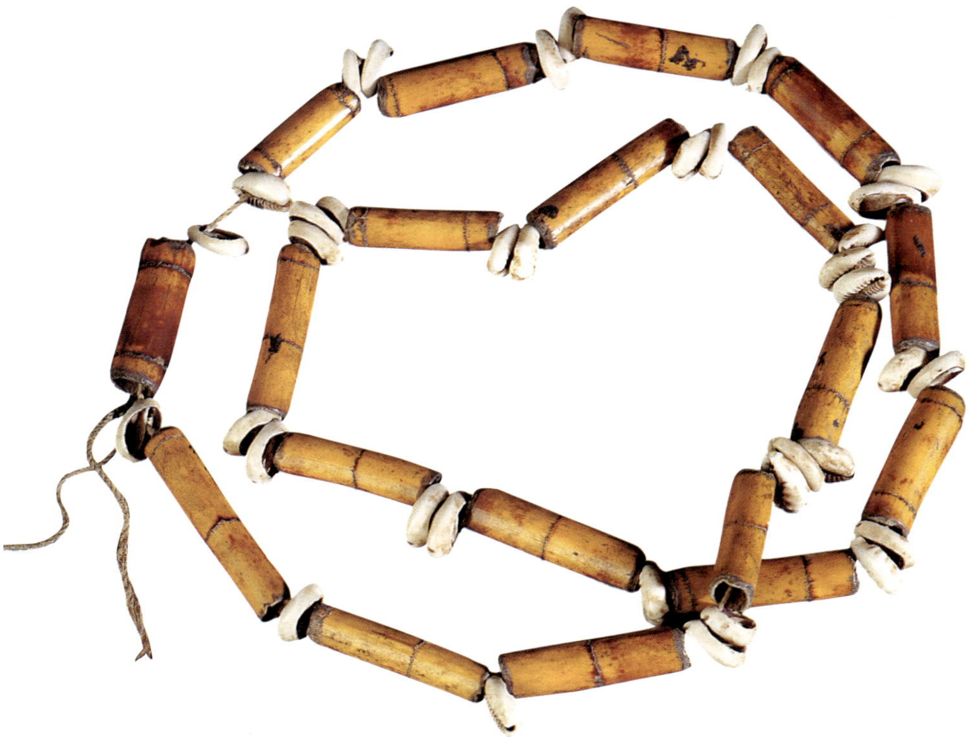

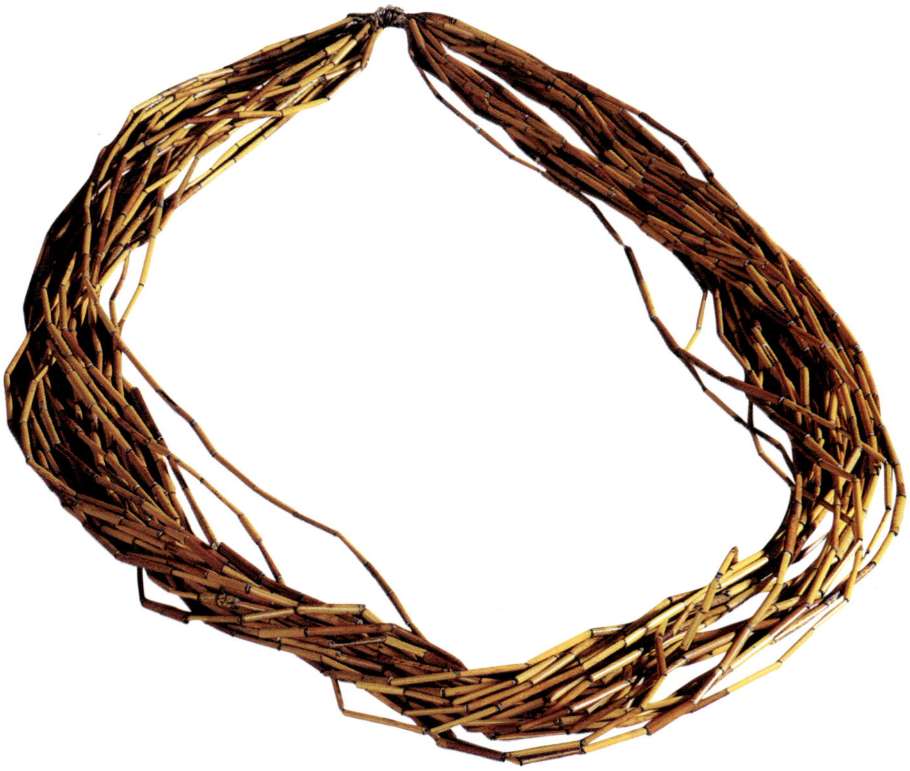

Necklace, Betiana, Oksapmin People, West Sepik Province, Papua New Guinea

Unlike their Mountain Ok relatives to the west in the Star Mountains of central Papua New Guinea, the Oksapmin live not in villages but in scattered homesteads. These homesteads are located at the very centre of the huge island of New Guinea, and the *Nassa* shells of this necklace have been traded in from the coast through many hands over many miles, gaining value as they travel. Here they have been strung by local women between sections of reeds, to be worn as a highly valued ornament that complements their minimal costume of a layered reed skirt. *Length 40 cm.*

AM 44656. Presented by Lynne Owen 1971.

Reed Necklace, Dani Tribe, Baliem Valley, Central Highlands, West Irian

This simple necklace of sections of yellow reed strung on native fibre string is one of the few ornaments worn by Dani women, and then only rarely. Usually Dani women are too busy gardening and cooking to be concerned with self-decoration. *Length 53 cm.*

AM 55418. Purchased from Mr Russell Bond 1992.

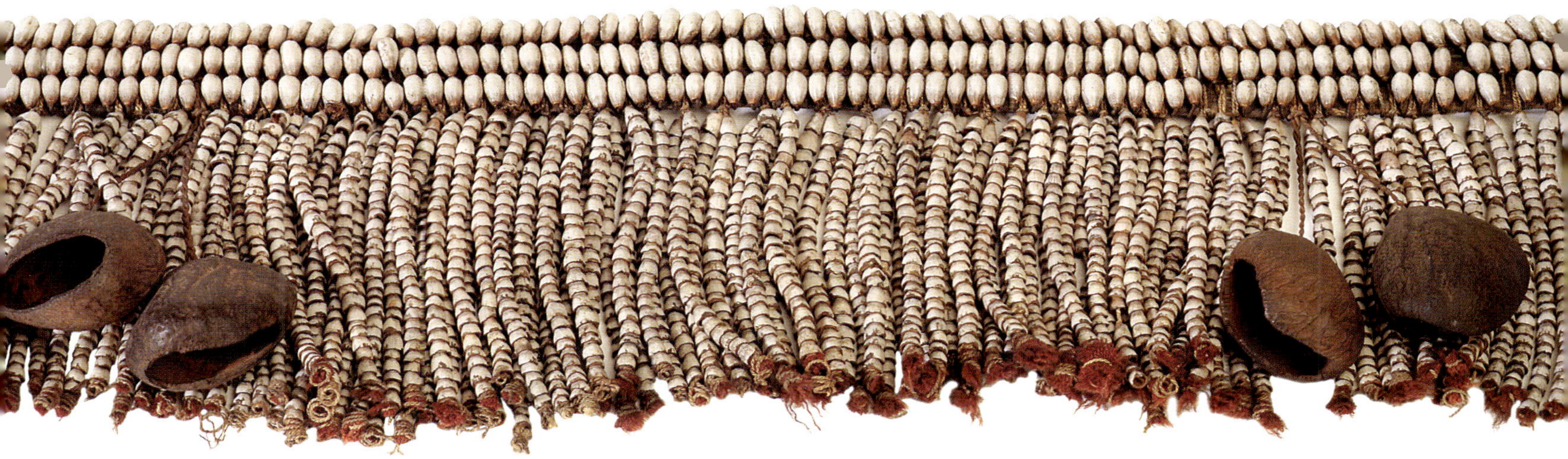

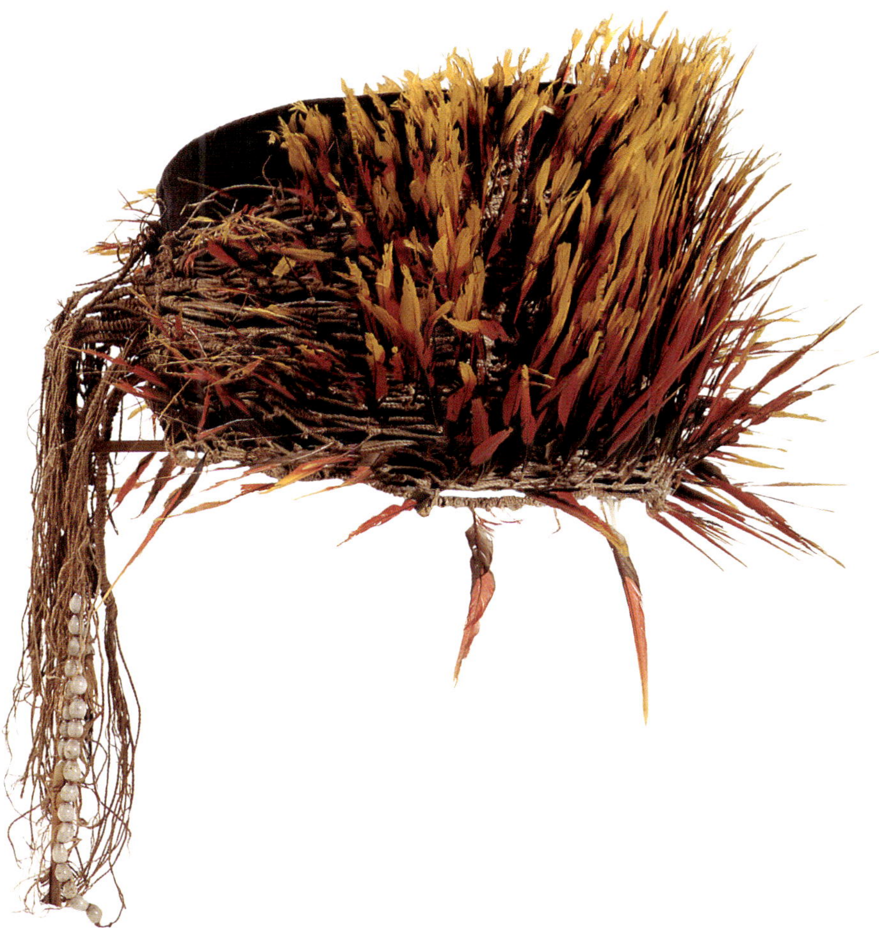

Ornamental Belt, South-East Papua New Guinea

Like so many museum artefacts, the exact locality where this belt was obtained is now unknown. The belt has been constructed on a foundation of three strips of cane forming the waistband, then these have been covered with whole *Coix* seeds, and cut-off *Coix* seeds have been strung on red wool to form a thick fringe. Finally, two pairs of *Pangium* nuts have been attached and these would provide a rhythmic sound as the belt swayed during dancing. *Coix lachryma-jobi* or Job's tears seeds have a strong association with mourning in this area of Papua New Guinea, perhaps suggesting that a woman wore this belt during funeral rites. *Length 65 cm, width 12 cm.*

AM 45711.

Head Ornament of Feathers, Motu People, Port Moresby area, Papua New Guinea

Motu and Koita men and women living in the off-shore villages raised on stilts along the coast east and west of Port Moresby decorated themselves with very elaborate feather head-dresses and shell valuables. These were worn at the large dance and feast festivals sponsored by important men to mark special occasions such as the annual departure of the *hiri* trading fleet for the Gulf of Papua. Such festivals also gave the sponsors an opportunity to demonstrate their wealth and community commitment. *Length 58 cm, width 20 cm.*

AM 13265. Presented by Miss Isaacs 1921.

opposite: ***Doga/Dona/Doana*, Chest Ornaments, Massim District, Milne Bay Province, Papua New Guinea**

A true *doga* or *dogadoga* chest ornament featured a boar tusk that had grown into a full circle. *Doga* formerly accompanied the *mwali* arm ring in *kula* trading and were extremely valuable. These became very rare and were often replaced by *doga* with an imitation boar tusk made out of *Conus* shell or *Tridacna* clam shell, as in the examples here. These *doga* retain the traditional red *Spondylus* shell discs in the necklace, with the addition of red, blue and white glass tradebeads. This ornament was known as *dona* among the Motu people around Port Moresby, where it was an important valuable featuring in first-child ceremonies and bride price. from left: *Length 46 cm; length 45 cm.*

left: *AM 15341. James Edge-Partington Collection. Presented by Dr Thomson Wilson Leys Memorial 1924.*
right: *AM 30815. Purchased from Mr W. E. Browne 1949.*

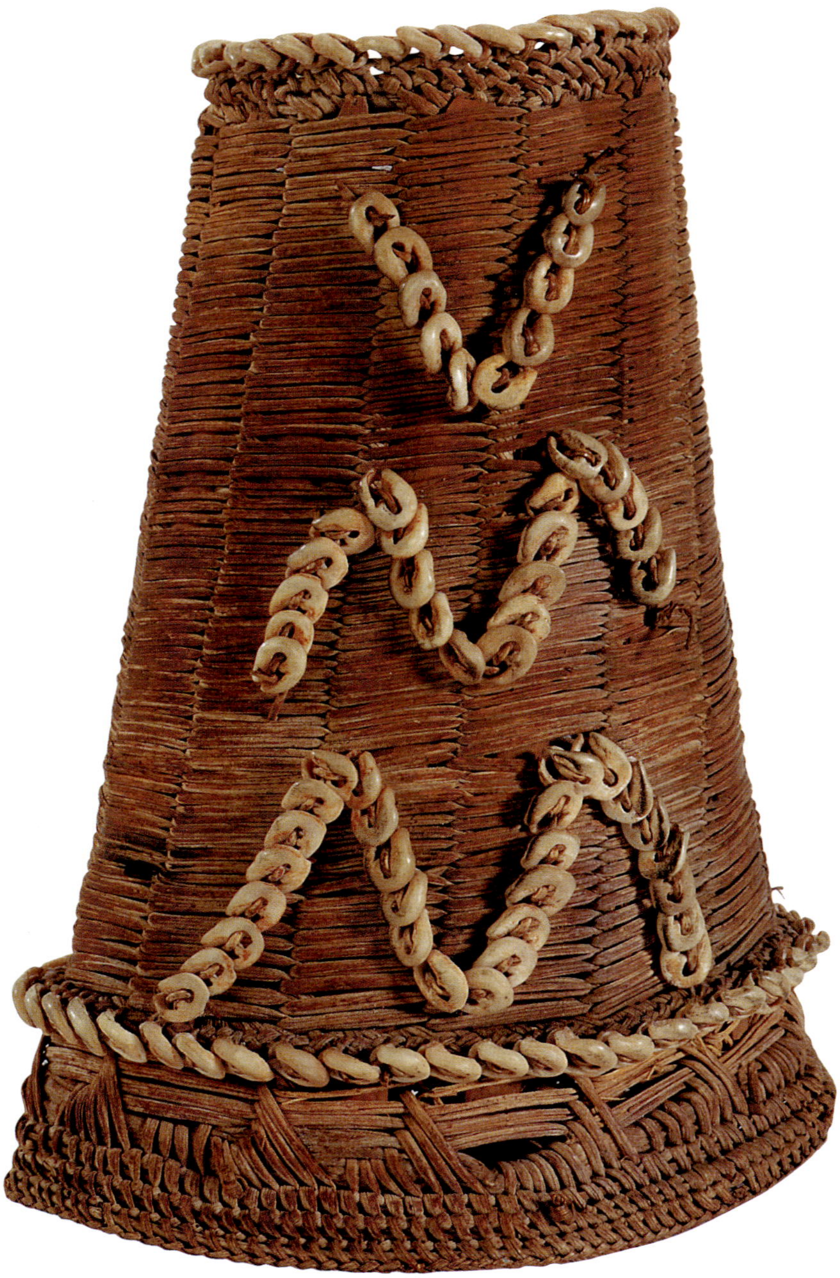

Hair Cylinder, North Coast, East Sepik/ Madang Provinces, Papua New Guinea

Plaited with fine cane, this hair cylinder has been decorated with patterns of *Nassa* shells, which have been stitched on and the whole ornament coated over with red ochre. Men wore their hair cut short except for a long clump at the back of the head. This hair was pushed through the cylinder, forming a bunch at the narrow top that might be further decorated with a comb or a pendant string of beads. Hair cylinders were worn by young men along much of the north coast between Madang and Wewak. *Length 17 cm.*

AM 13296. Presented by Mr R. A. Meek 1924.

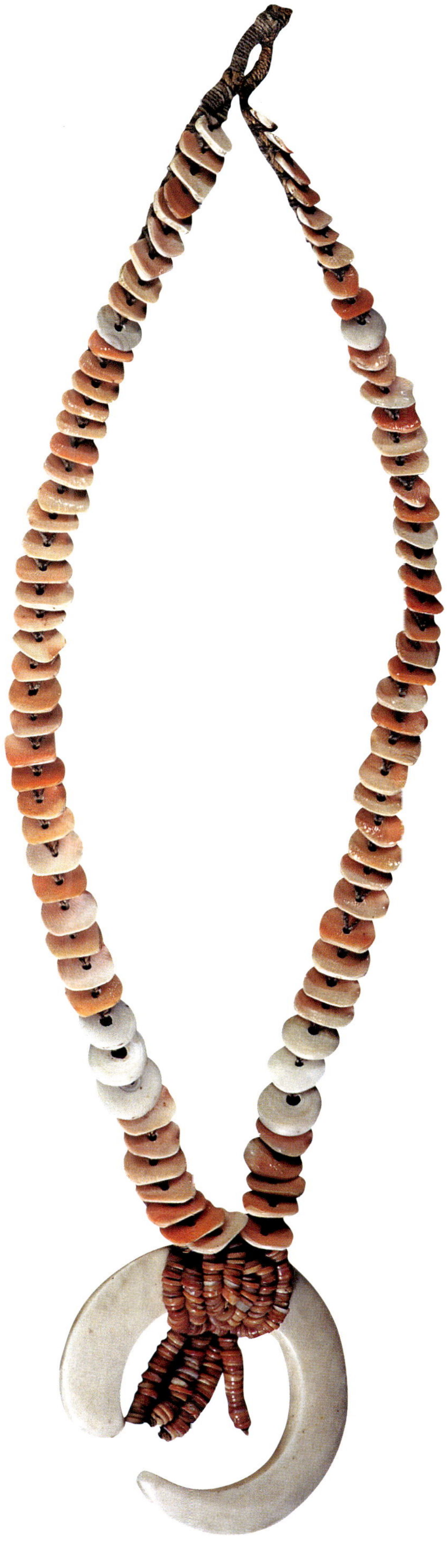

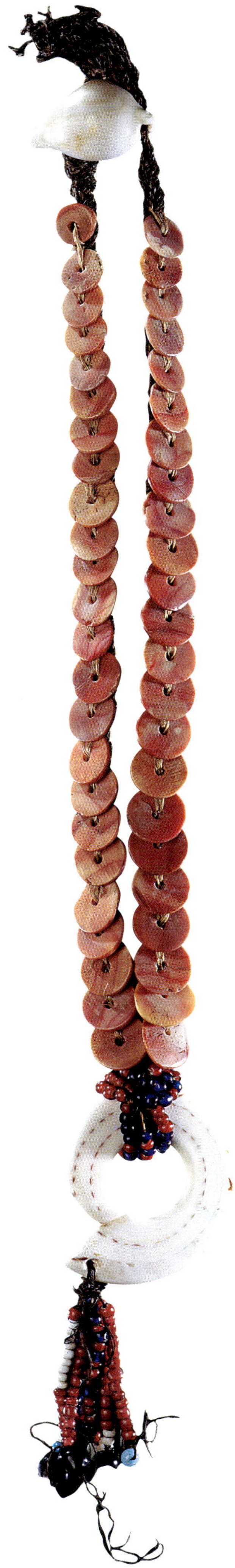

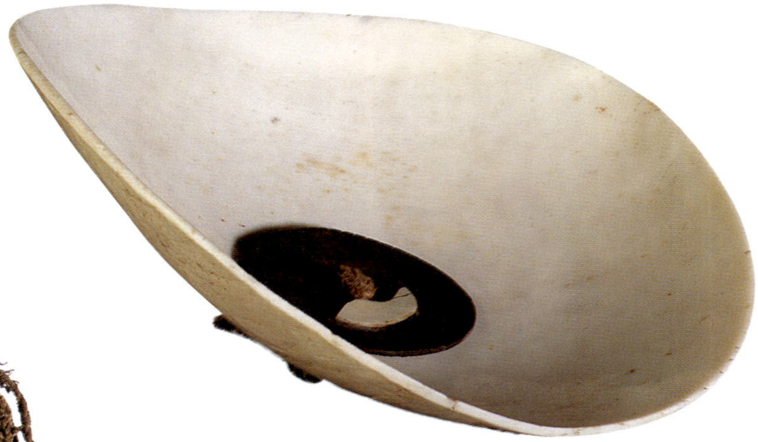

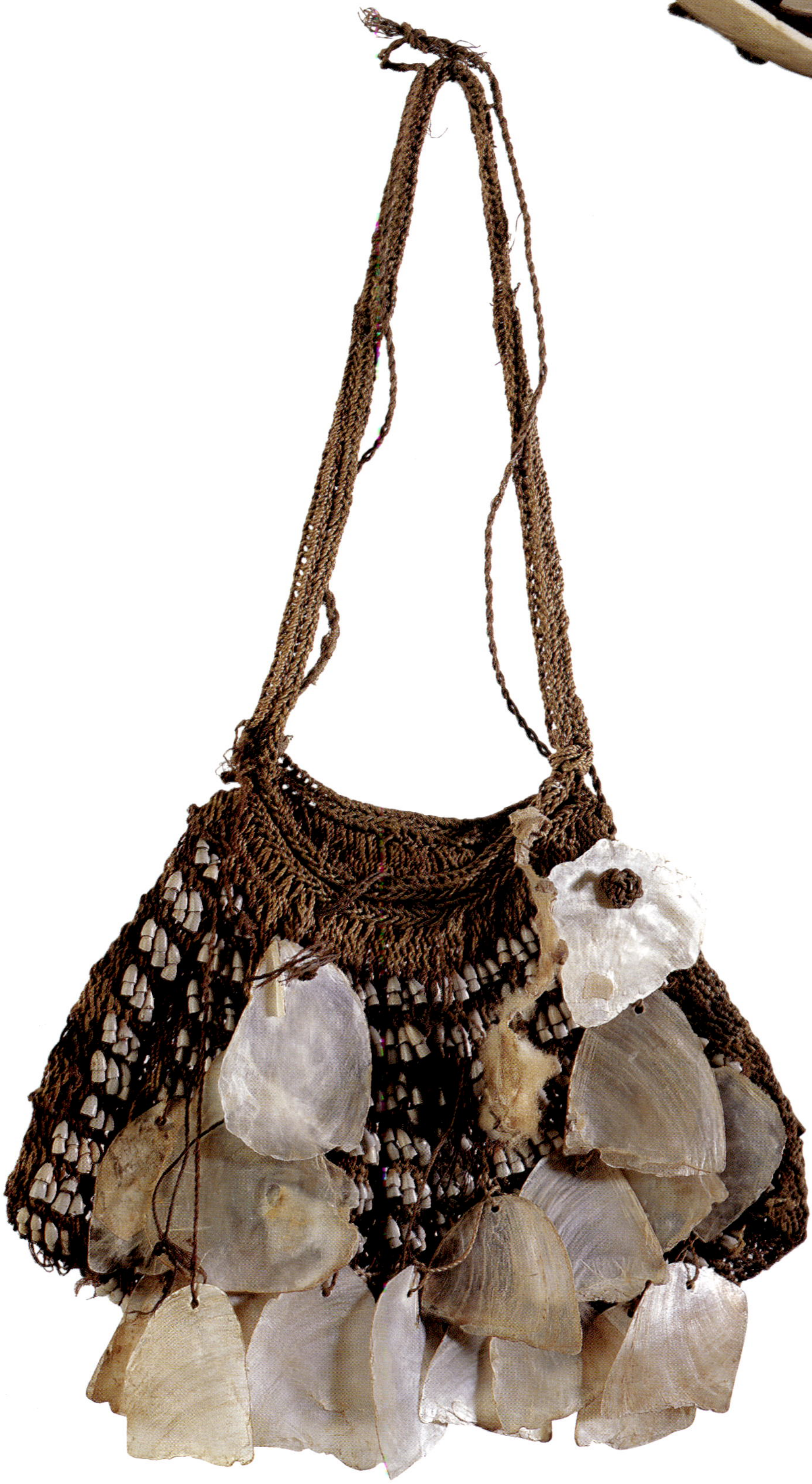

Shell Ornament, Brumer Island, Near Samarai, South-east Papua New Guinea

Cut from a portion of a *Melo* 'bailer' shell, this ornament is said to have been worn either on the head or on the hip of a man, depending whether the wearer was at peace or at war. Its design follows a composition of large curved shell with a central decoration held in by the suspension cord, a structure quite common to this area of south-east Papua New Guinea. *Length 14.5 cm, width 12.5 cm.*

AM 15353. James Edge-Partington Collection. Presented by Dr Thomson Wilson Leys Memorial 1924.

***Bilum* String Bag, Guap (Juo) Island, Wewak Coast, Papua New Guinea**

Oyster shells and Job's tears seeds (*Coix lachryma-jobi*) with one end cut off for stringing decorate this small bag, which a man wore over his upper arm. In it he probably carried some of his betel-chewing equipment and some charms. *Length 42 cm, width 25 cm.*

AM 15609. James Edge-Partington Collection. Presented by Dr Thomson Wilson Leys Memorial 1924.

opposite: ***Bilum* String Bag, West Sepik Coast, Papua New Guinea**

Small *bilum* string bags made by women and decorated with arrangements of shells and seeds can be regarded as jewellery for men and women in New Guinea, fulfilling both functional and aesthetic purposes. This bag has been decorated with Job's tears seeds (*Coix lachryma-jobi*) with one end cut off for stringing. *Length 42 cm, width 33 cm.*

AM 12902. Purchased from Messrs Rinaldo and Eder 1914.

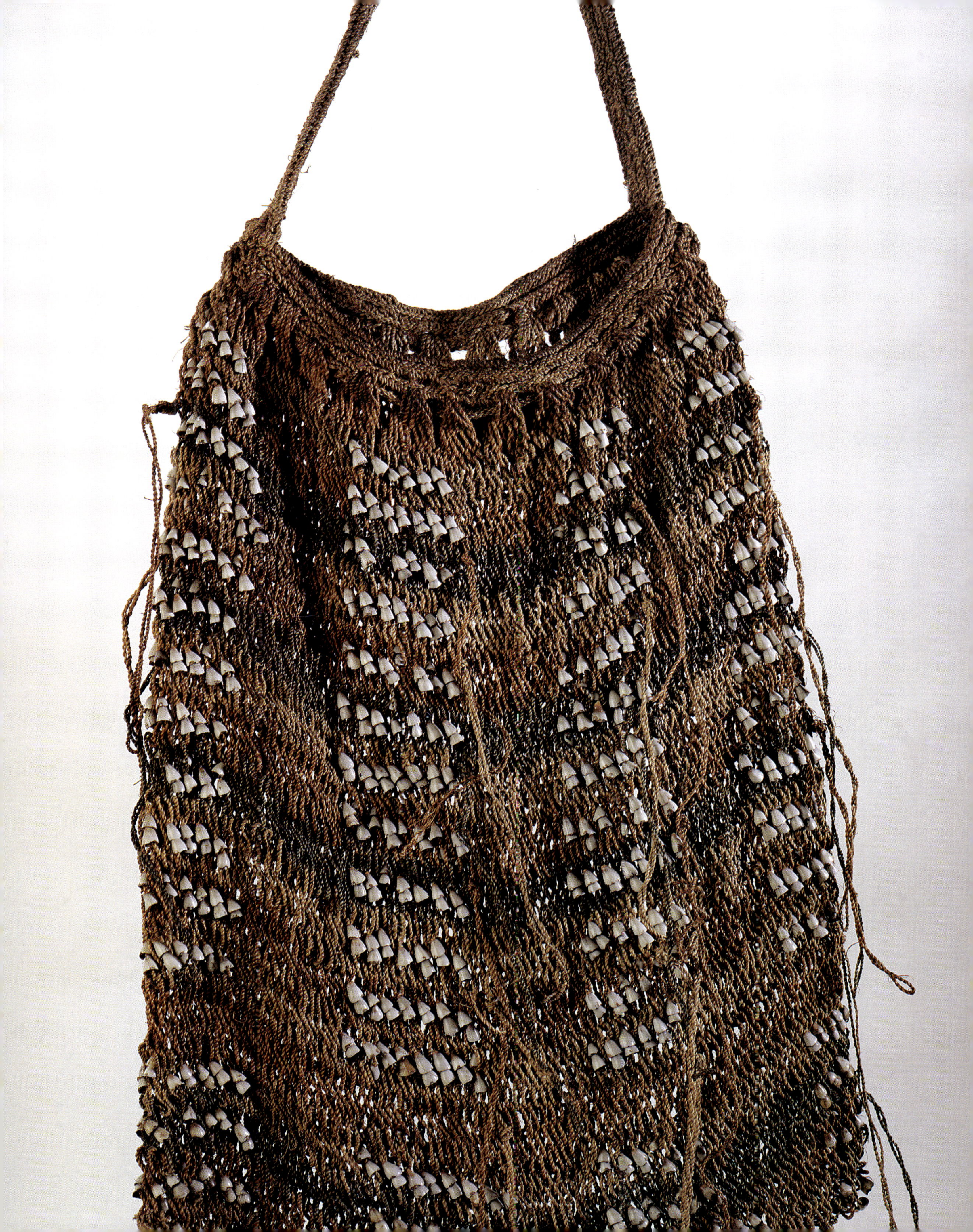

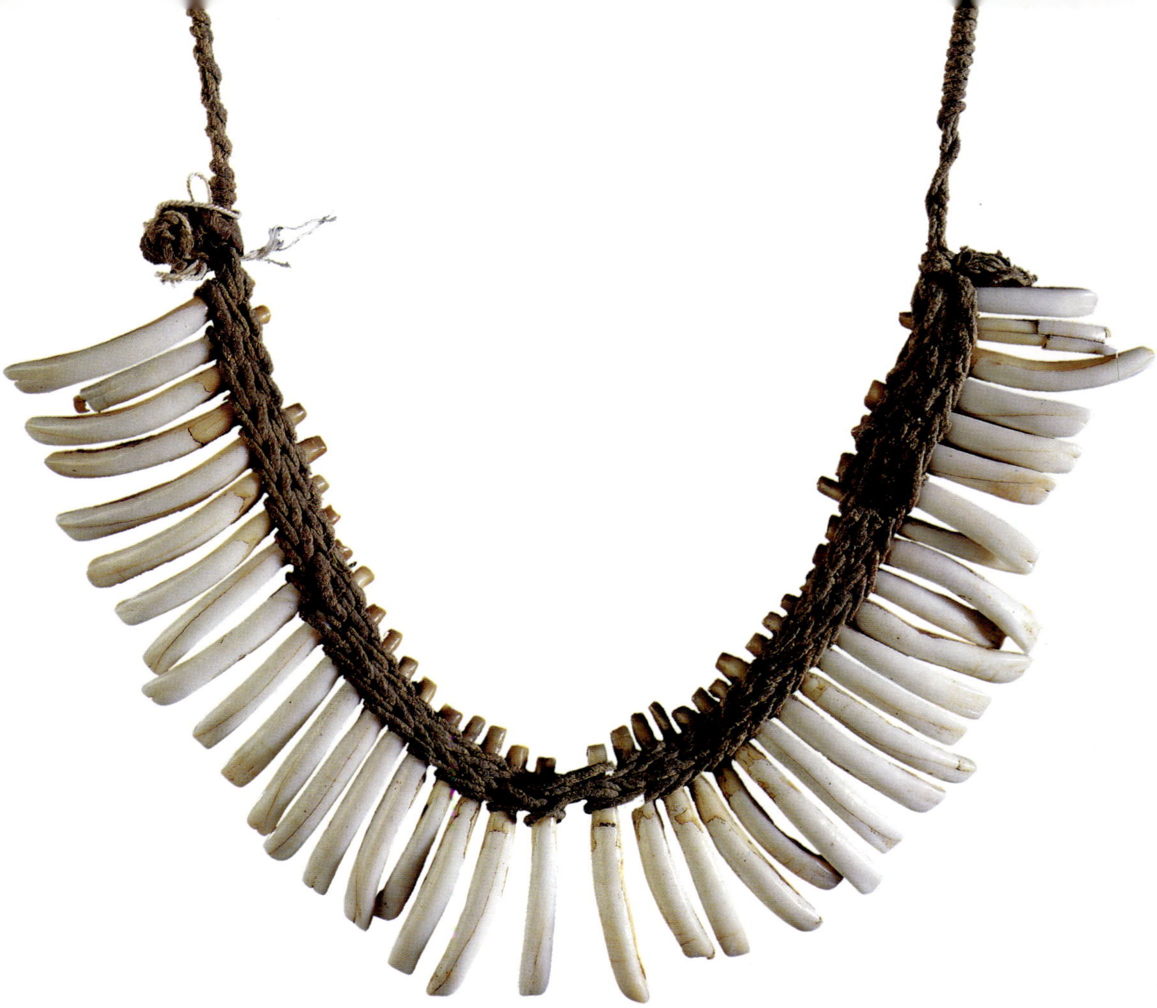

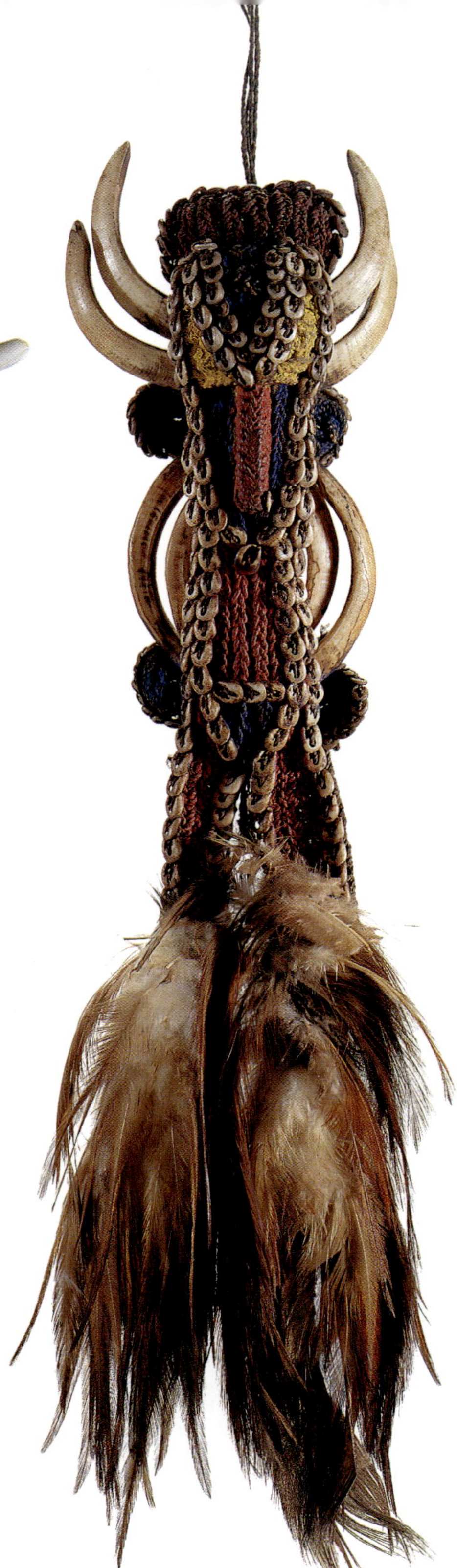

NECKLACE OF PIGS' TEETH, SISIMIN PEOPLE, OM RIVER, WEST SEPIK PROVINCE, PAPUA NEW GUINEA

The people of the Om River valley at the headwaters of the Strickland River are closely related in culture to their Mountain Ok neighbours to the west, although the Om live in a lower altitude valley. The Sisimin had very little contact with Europeans at the time this necklace was made. Pigs continue to be the main source of wealth and status among these people. Some claim that each tooth represents a pig that has been killed by the wearer. *Length 30 cm.*

AM 44658. Presented by Miss Lynne Owen 1971.

***KARAHUT/ANDAKARA* MOUTH ORNAMENT, ABELAM PEOPLE, EAST SEPIK PROVINCE, PAPUA NEW GUINEA**

For everyday use and at festivals, an Abelam warrior who has passed his initiation into manhood wore his *karahut* ornament hanging on his back. Made of boar tusks and *Nassa* shells on a netted human shape, this ornament refers to the bravery and aggression of the wild boar. When attacking an enemy village the warrior held the *karahut* in his teeth, thereby taking on the qualities of the fierce boar for himself. *Length 44 cm, width 10 cm.*

AM 55193. Purchased 1996.

opposite: **BREAST ORNAMENT, NORTH COAST OF NEW GUINEA**

Curved pig tusks were often a sign both of wealth and aggression in much of New Guinea. This ornament was usually worn on the chest, but in warfare it was also carried in the mouth. Beaten and coloured barkcloth has been attached to cover the bindings. *Length 30 cm, width 23 cm.*

AM 15763. James Edge-Partington Collection. Presented by Dr Thomson Wilson Leys Memorial 1924.

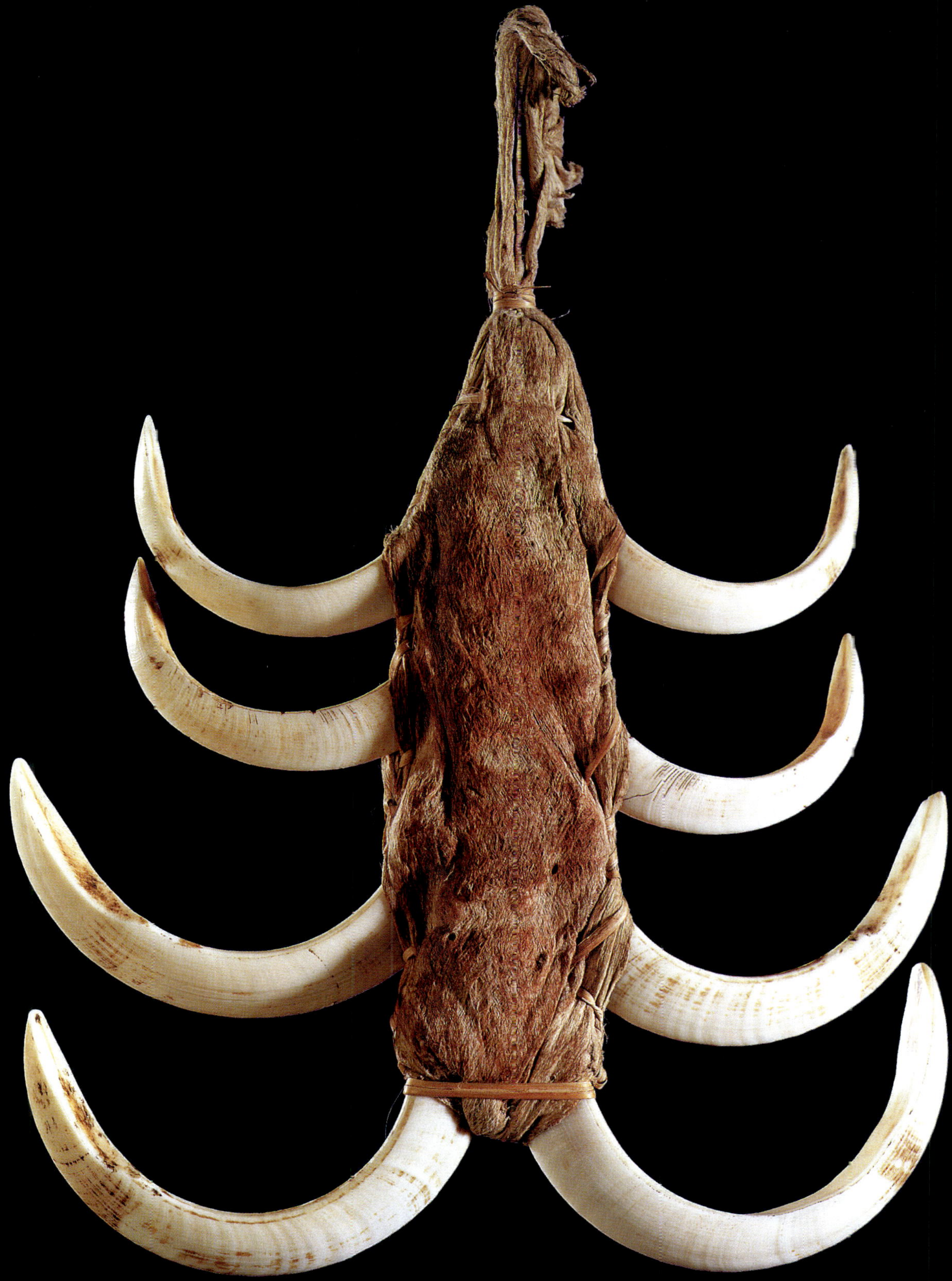

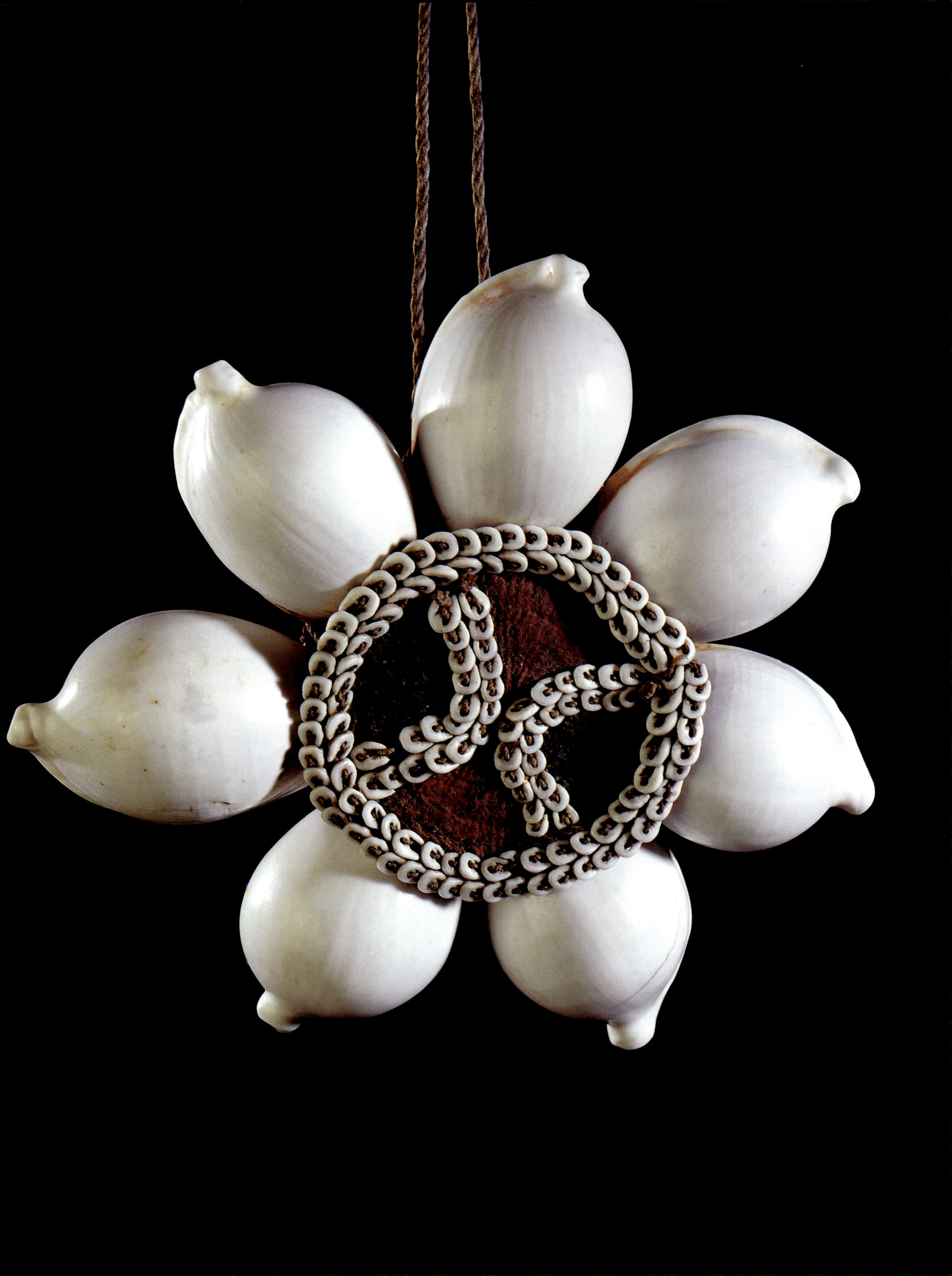

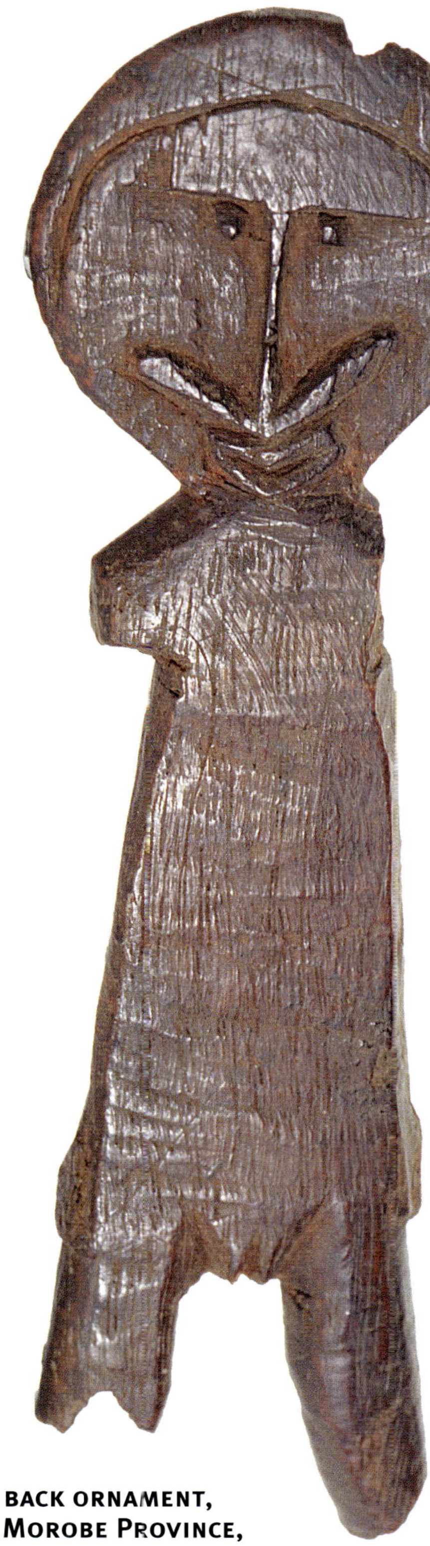

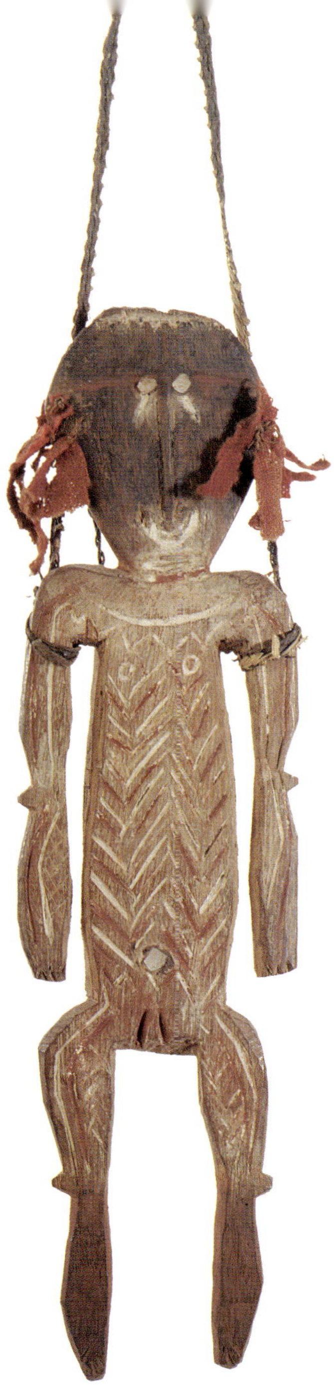

opposite: **Breast or back ornament, Huon Peninsula, Morobe Province, Papua New Guinea**

This large ornament of cowrie shells mounted on a base decorated with *Nassa* shells was worn around the neck, either on the back or the breast, by men of importance. For special ceremonies it was worn on the back. Similar ornaments were worn along much of the north-east coast of New Guinea. *Diameter 20 cm.*

AM 15734. James Edge-Partington Collection. Presented by Dr Thomson Wilson Leys Memorial 1924.

***Mimia*, Charm Figures, Kiwai People, Mouth of the Fly River, Western Province, Papua New Guinea**

These little wooden charms in the form of a female figure were worn suspended from the neck, hanging on the chests of initiated Kiwai men or on the backs of young uninitiated Kiwai boys, when singing and dancing to attract the attention of women and young girls. Larger wooden *mimia* figures were suspended along the aisle of the *darimo* longhouse and carried in the prows of war canoes to weaken the spirits of their enemies. from left: *length 30 cm, width 8 cm; length 17 cm, width 4 cm.*

above left: *AM 15481. James Edge-Partington Collection. Presented by Dr Thomson Wilson Leys Memorial 1924.*
above right: *AM 15480. James Edge-Partington Collection. Presented by Dr Thomson Wilson Leys Memorial 1924.*

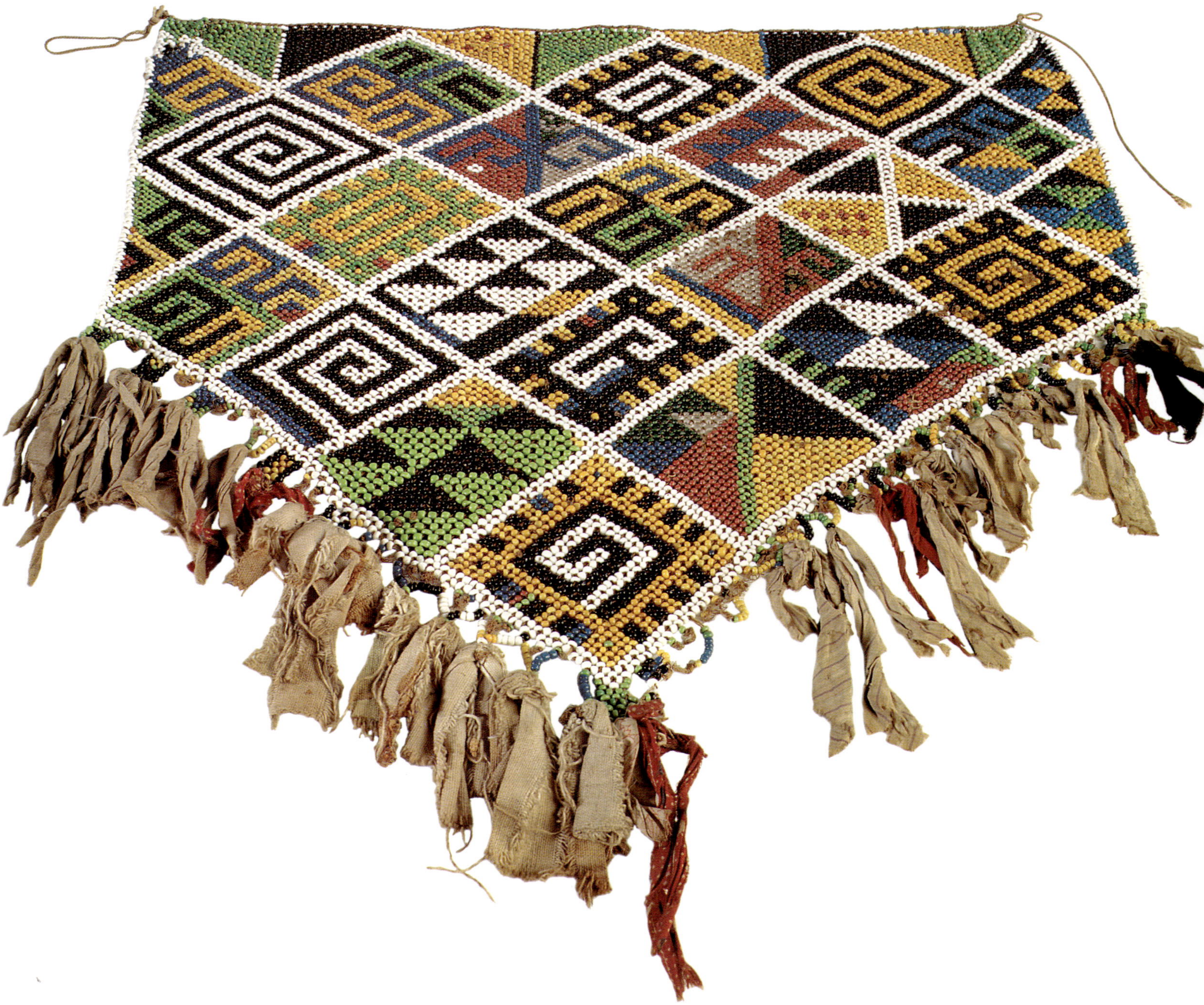

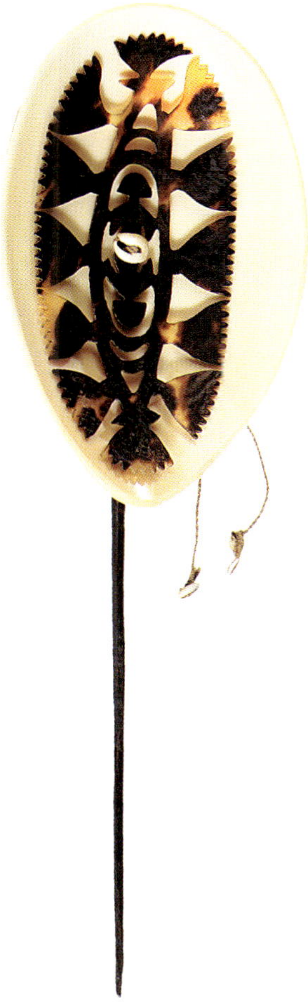

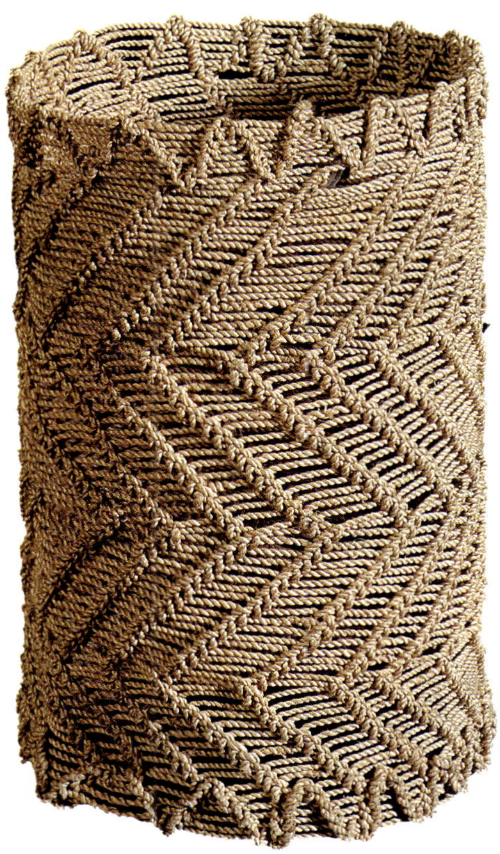

HAIRPIN IN *KAPKAP* FORM, COASTAL SEPIK AREA, PAPUA NEW GUINEA

Unlike most *kapkaps* that are mounted on a fibre headband to be worn as a forehead ornament, this Sepik area variation of the *kapkap* form is mounted on a pointed stick that can be thrust through a man's hair. The oval shape of its shell backing and turtle shell overlay also differs from the circular *kapkaps* of most other regions. *Kapkaps* are an ancient and widespread form of Pacific ornament, most common in Melanesia but extending into Micronesia and out to the Marquesas Islands of Eastern Polynesia, where some have been found that can be archaeologically dated to over two thousand years ago. *Length 23.5 cm, width 7.5 cm.*

AM 55210 Purchased 1997.

TAE, NETWORK ARM BAND, MOTU PEOPLE, PORT MORESBY, PAPUA NEW GUINEA

This arm band is distinguished from most of the common arm bands plaited from leaf materials by the fine delicacy and precision of its plaited patterns. These patterns have been realised in native string that is made by women rolling fine bark strips on their thighs. Showing no signs of wear, it may have been made for sale. *Length 10 cm.*

AM 15417.2. James Edge-Partington Collection.
Presented by Dr Thomson Wilson Leys Memorial 1924.

opposite: *SIREWU*, CEREMONIAL APRON, CENDERAWASIH (GEELVINK) BAY, WEST IRIAN

Glass trade-beads of many different colours have been threaded by skilled women to form complicated patterns in this ceremonial apron, worn by both men and women. Originally, these aprons were probably made using local drilled shell beads, but since very early contact with Indonesian traders, who were seeking bird of paradise plumes and sandalwood, glass trade-beads have been available in this area. These geometric designs may also owe some of their inspiration to Asian designs imported on cloth. *Length 63 cm, width 57 cm.*

AM 54686. Purchased from Mr A. Pendergrast 1993.

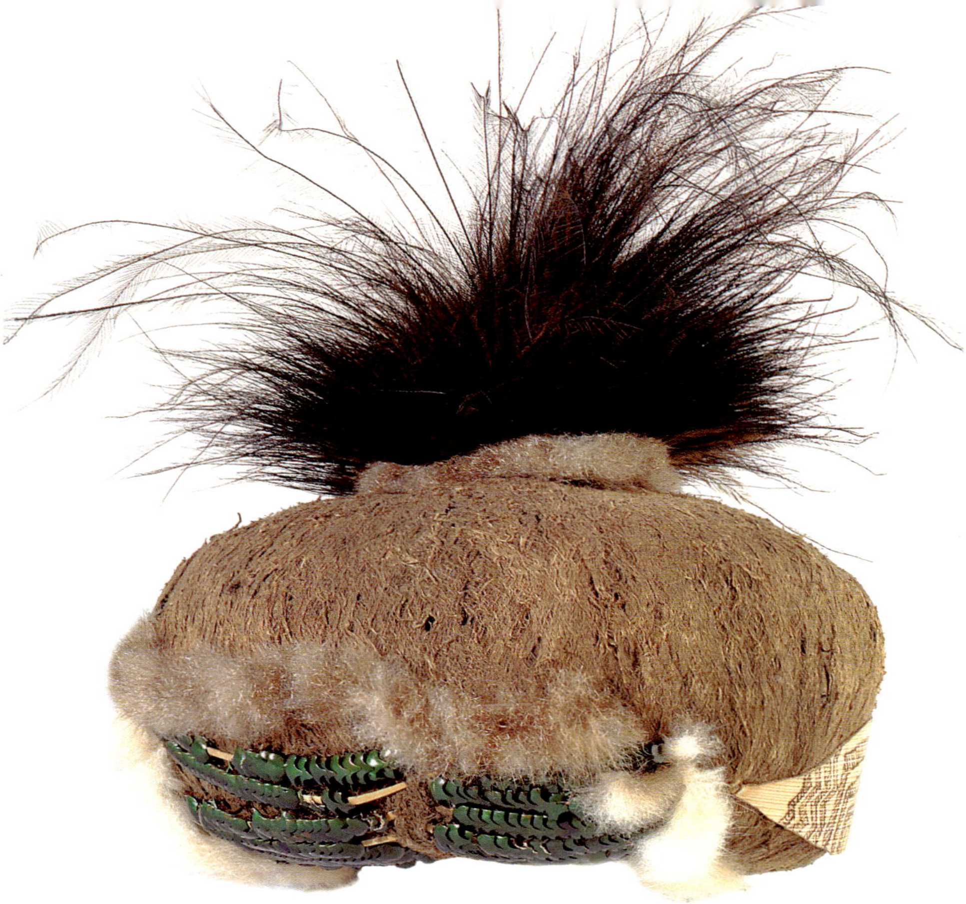

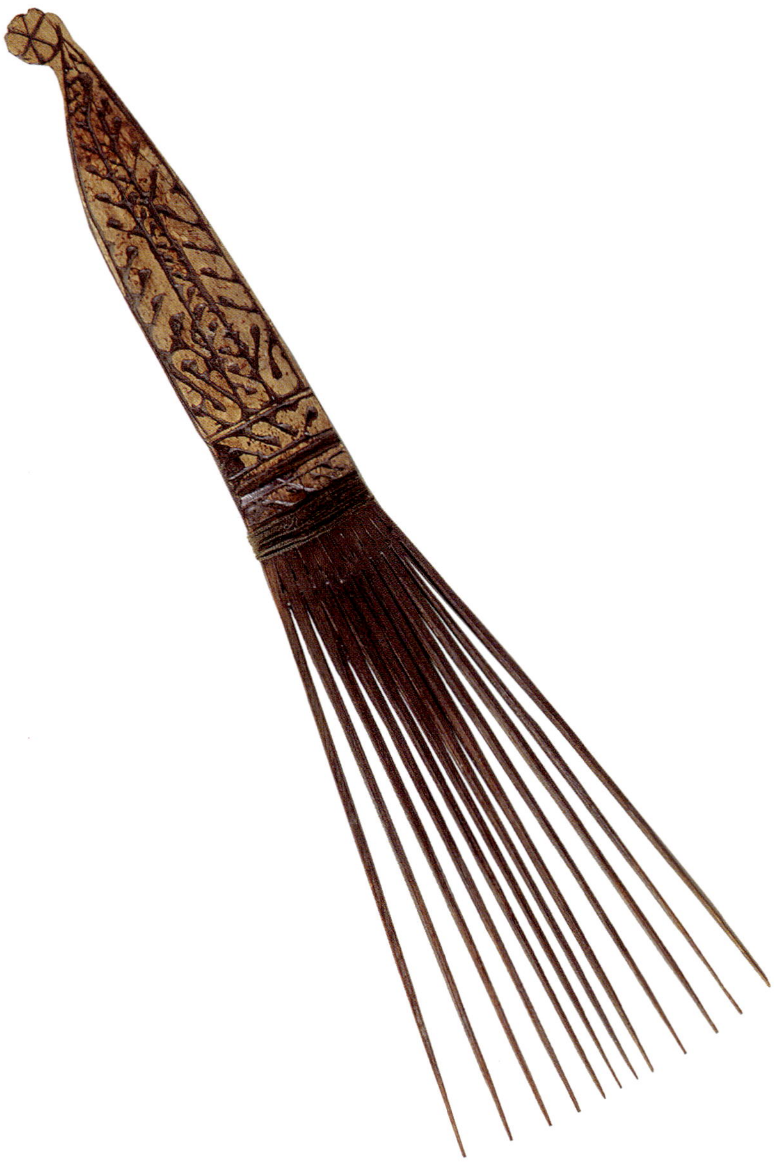

Foij, Wig, Kalam People, Kaironk Valley, Schrader Ranges, Western Highlands Province, Papua New Guinea

The bulk of this head-dress is a wig of human hair set on a basketwork frame and covered by a bark-cloth sheet. It is decorated with cuscus fur and a bunch of cassowary plumes. A bamboo leaf ornament with incised geometric designs is attached to the lower back, and green beetle carapaces are strung on cane strips at the front. Kalam men wore these wigs at *smy* dance festivals, where their visitors were feasted on pork and taro, their sons had their nasal septa pierced for wearing ornaments, and their wives' relatives were compensated for all the hard work that the women had invested in the gardens and pig-raising. *Length 35 cm, width 29 cm.*

AM 37045. Presented by Dr and Mrs Ralph Bulmer and Dr Bruce Biggs 1963.

Bamboo Comb, Probably Cenderawasih (Geelvink) Bay, West Irian

To make this comb, the lower portion of a single piece of bamboo has been separated into twelve teeth, which were then held apart by small blocks of wood. A floral-derived pattern has been carved into the upper unsplit portion, leaving the design to stand out in the original yellow surface of the bamboo. These scroll patterns are common in this area of West Irian and have an Indonesian appearance, perhaps indicating that they were introduced during the nineteenth century through contact with other cultures from islands to the west. *Length 26 cm, width 8 cm.*

AM 54681. Purchased from A. Pendergrast 1993.

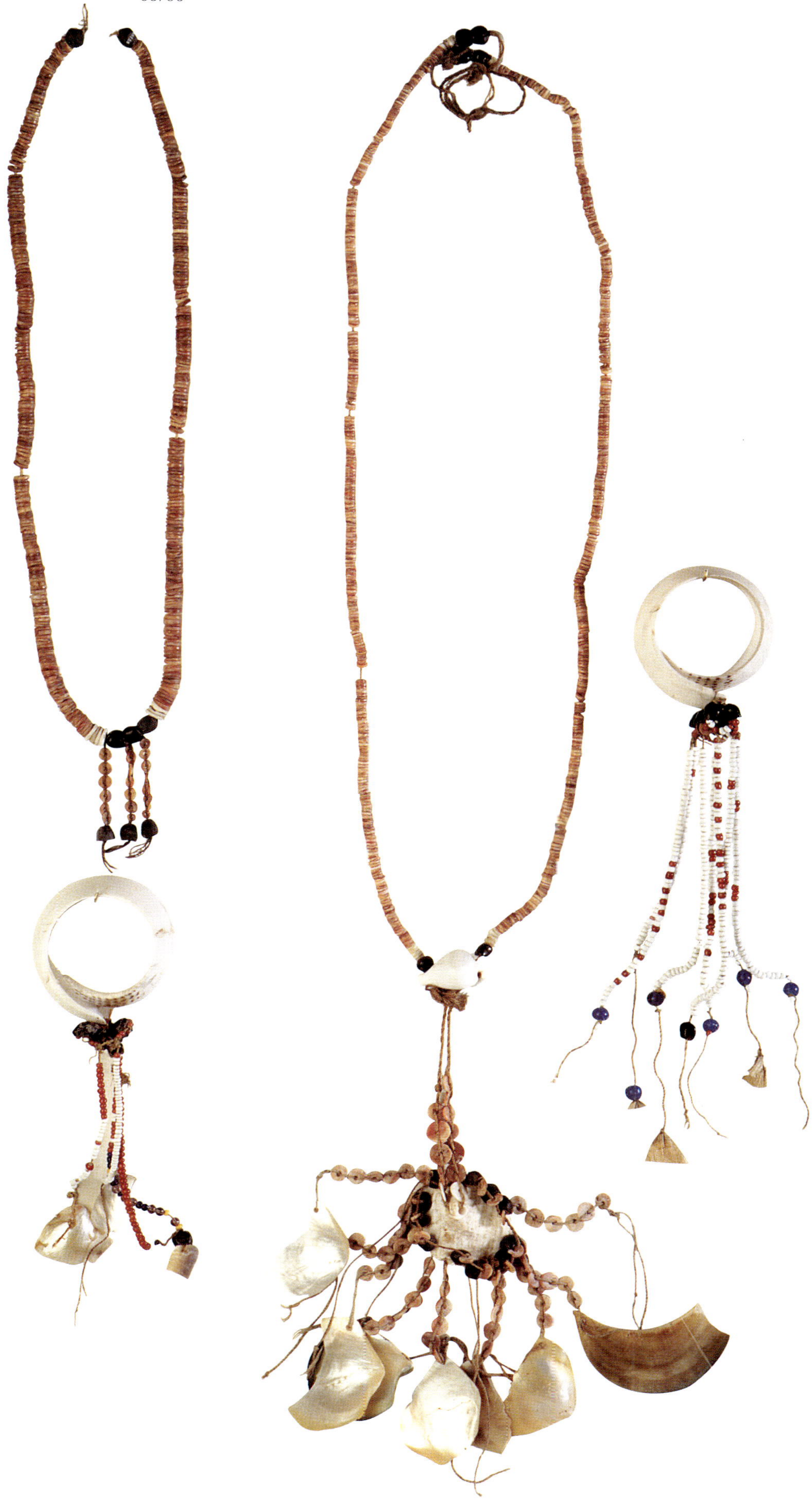

KULA VALUABLES, MASSIM DISTRICT, MILNE BAY PROVINCE, PAPUA NEW GUINEA

Partners in the *kula* exchange and trading cycle around the islands of the Massim district ritually exchange *soulava* necklaces (middle) for *mwali* arm rings of *Conus* shell travelling in the opposite direction. Much preparation and magic is needed to ensure safety on the long, open sea voyages when *kula* valuables and trade goods are carried in their outrigger canoes. The importance of these valuables is directly related to their ceremonial role as exchange valuables in the *kula* and they have no other function. *Mwali* are worn only rarely, on very special occasions, by men prominent in the *kula* trade. The *katudababile* or *samakupa* necklace on the left with its black banana seeds and red *Spondylus* shell discs is a subsidiary *kula* item, often leaving the system. Other useful items such as cooking pots, stone adze blades, and food were also traded at the same time. clockwise from top left: *Length 51 cm; length 61.5 cm; length 24 cm; length 22 cm.*

clockwise from top left: *AM 55388.*
AM 48011. Presented by Mr Tucker 1977.
AM 23330.2. Presented by Mrs Ballantyne 1937.
AM 47995.4. Presented by Mr Tucker 1977.

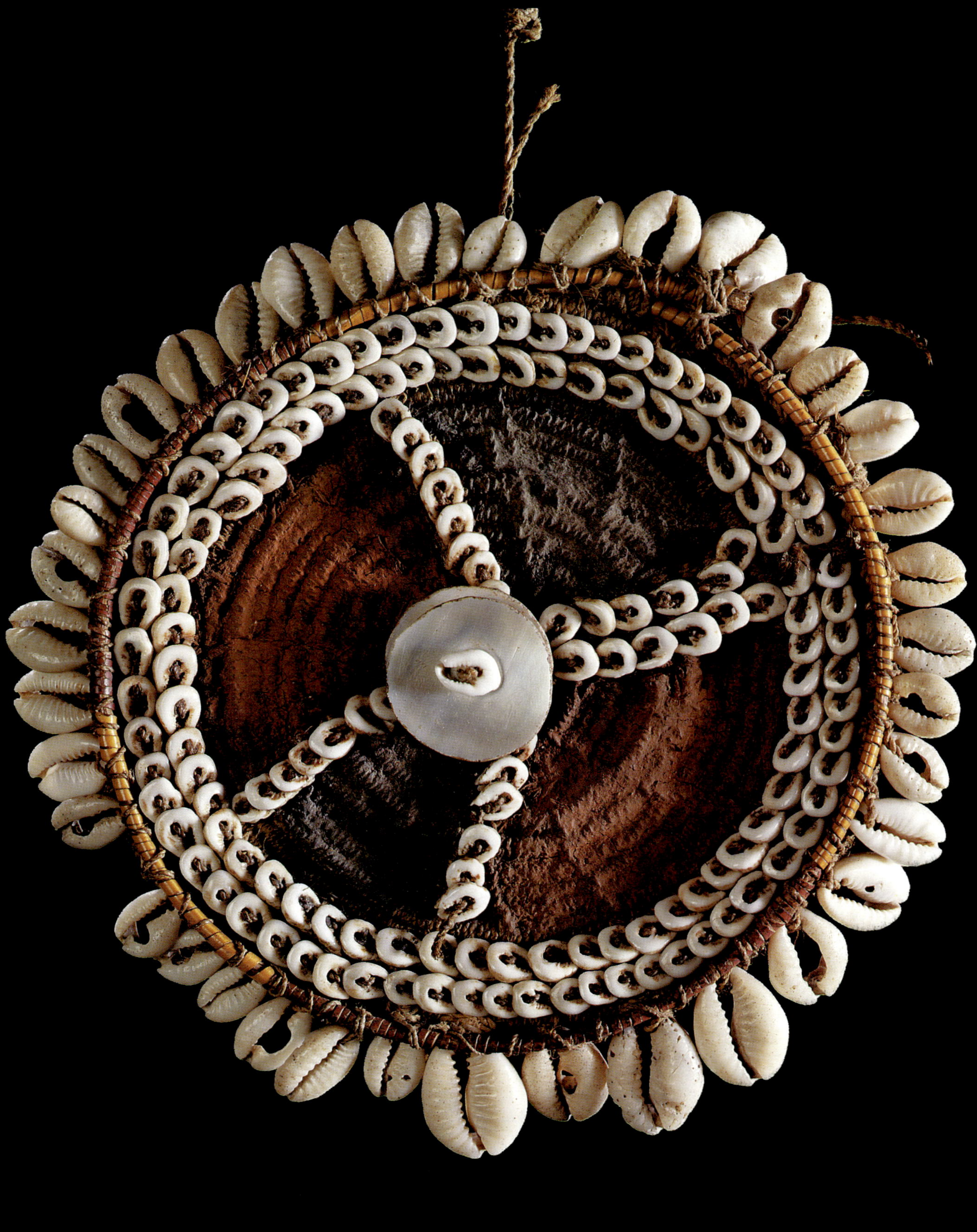

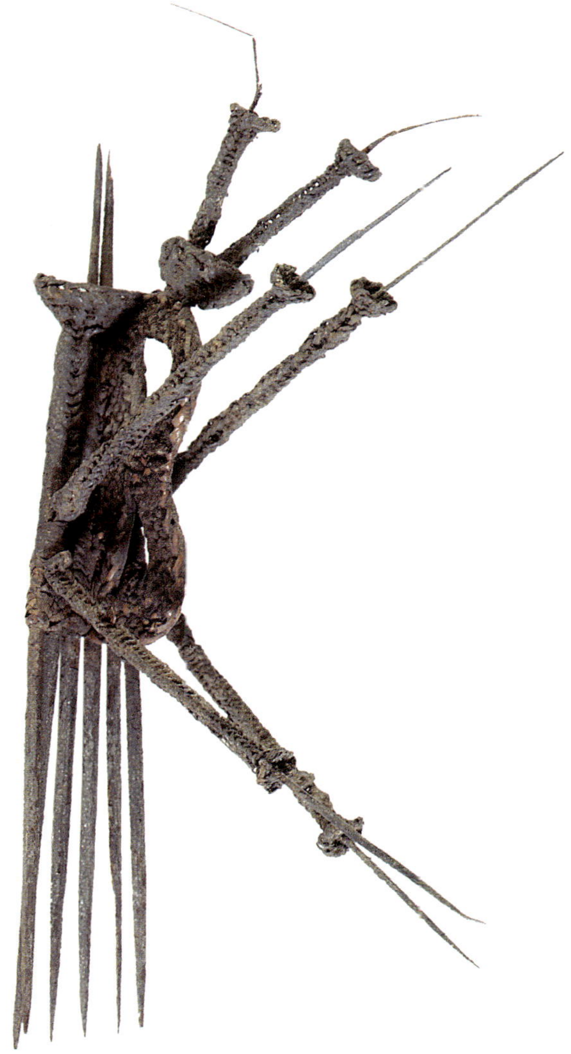

Comb, north-west of Maprik, East Sepik Province, Papua New Guinea

The Abelam people of this area are renowned for the great towering *korumbo* houses dominating each village, with rows of ancestral spirits painted in bright colours on the facade. These houses, called *haus tambaran* in local pidgin, provide a venue for the boys' initiation ceremonies into the secrets of the long-yam cult and the *tambaran*, clan spirit cult. The long yams are decorated with fibre basketry masks and basketry figures are hung on the lower facade of the *korumbo*. This complicated comb has been made with the same skilled fibre techniques and has spikes for fresh flowers and herbs to be attached when worn in the context of the *tambaran* ceremonies. *Length 21 cm, width 4.5 cm.*

AM 50957. Presented by Mr Brian Watts 1984.

Chest Ornament, South Coast, Papua New Guinea

Two curved boar-tusks on a plaited hair cord are the main element in this ornament. They are decorated with a solitary red trade bead and strings of Job's tears *Coix* seeds ending with parrot feathers. A note recorded by the collector says that this ornament was held in the warrior's teeth when he went into battle, a common practice in much of coastal south-east Papua New Guinea. This type of ornament was called a *hono* by the Orokaiva and Binandere peoples of Oro Bay, where it signified that the wearer had killed an enemy. *Length 10 cm, width 12.8 cm (pendant only).*

AM 15435. James Edge-Partington Collection. Presented by Dr Thomson Wilson Leys Memorial 1924.

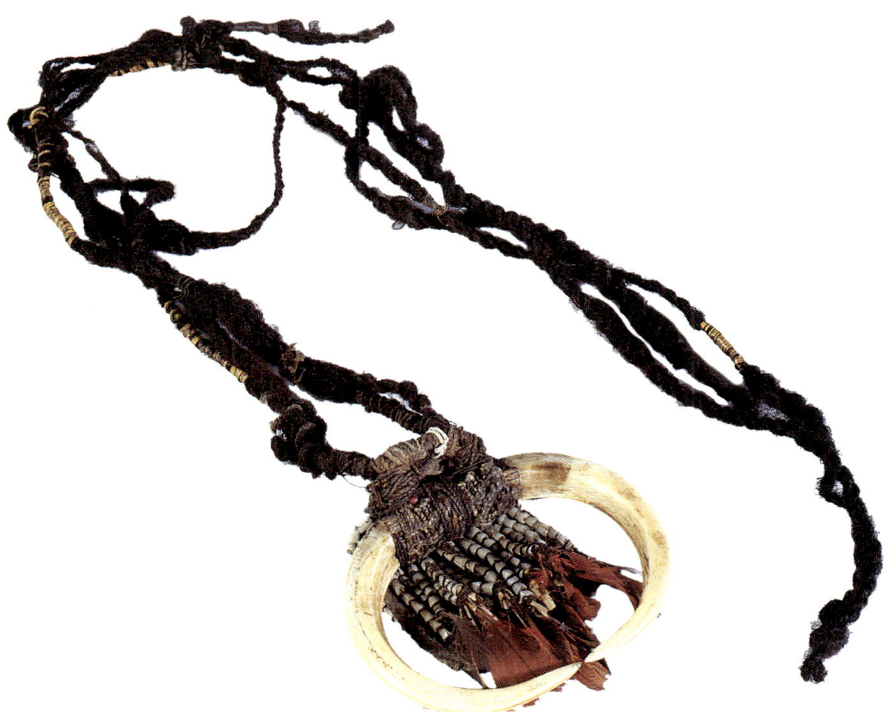

opposite: Breast Ornament, Huon Gulf, Morobe Province, Papua New Guinea

A woven fibre circlet coloured with red and grey pigment is decorated with *Nassa* and small cowrie shells. This would have been worn on the chest suspended by a woven fibre neck-cord. This form of ornament is found along the north coast of New Guinea from the Huon Gulf to the Ramu River estuary. *Diameter 13 cm.*

AM 11425. Presented by Mr R. Recknagel 1892.

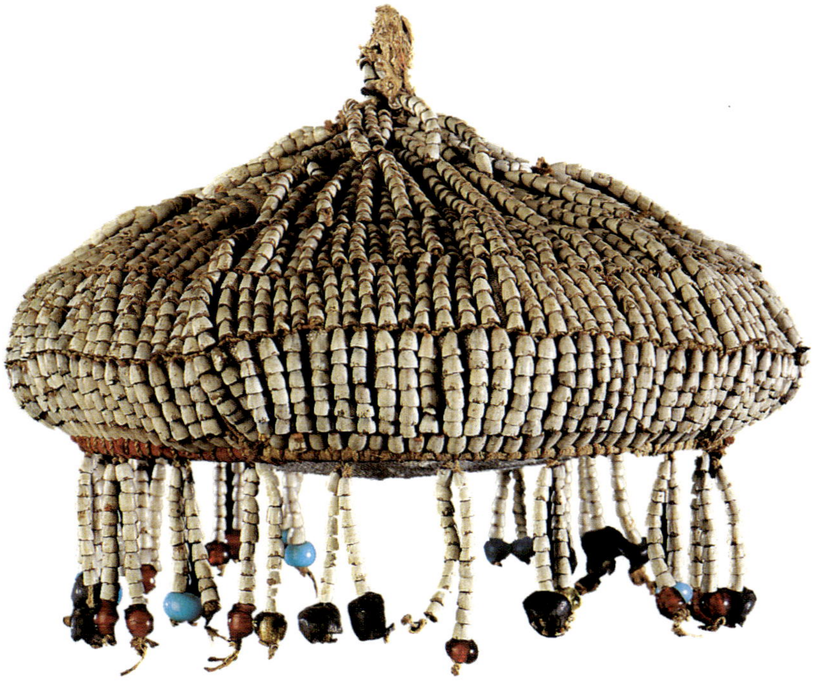

Widow's Wig, Collingwood Bay, Oro Province, Papua New Guinea

Widows in this area went into seclusion for at least a year, during which time they made a mourning dress of a wig, armlets and openwork bodice all decorated with *Coix lachryma-jobi* or Job's tears seeds. They wore this outfit after emerging from seclusion. This widow's wig of *Coix* seeds has been decorated with extra coloured glass trade-beads. *Diameter 22 cm.*

AM 45709.

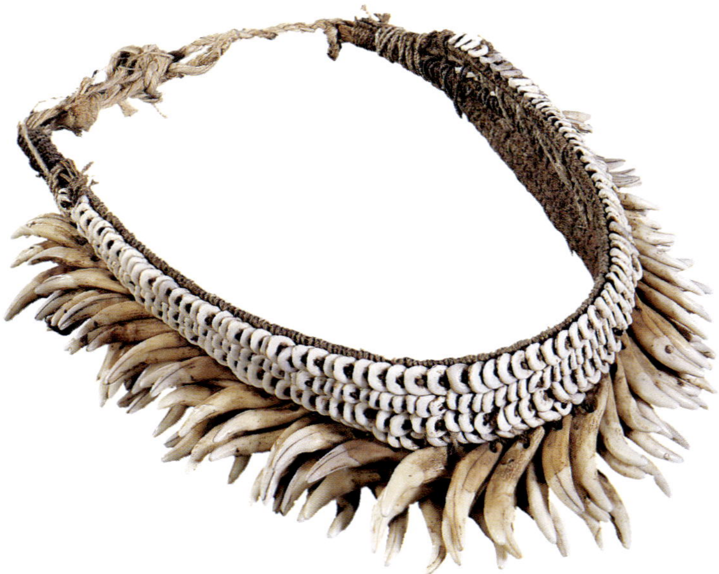

Head Band Ornaments, Wain People, Gairen Village, Huon Gulf, Papua New Guinea

These head ornaments of *Nassa* shells and dog teeth are some of the valuables that circulated in the regional trading system of the Vitiaz Strait and Huon Gulf, linking the north-east coast of mainland New Guinea with the western end of New Britain and the islands in between. Canoe traders from the small islands of Bilibili, Tami and Siassi carried specialised products around the trade system, including ornaments of boar tusks and dog teeth that later became valuables used in bridewealth payments. from top: *Length 62 cm; length 31 cm.*

from top: *AM 53146. Purchased from Graham Jackson 1989.*
AM 53147. Purchased from Graham Jackson 1989.

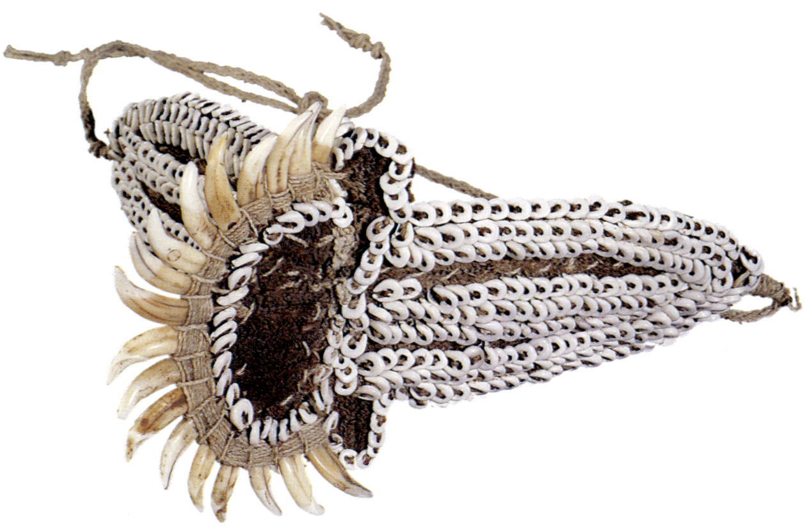

opposite: ***Houe*, Shell Arm Rings, Selepet, Huon Peninsula, Papua New Guinea**

Six *Trochus* shell arm rings have been attached together with native fibre string to form a composite arm ornament. Some of the rings have geometric patterns incised and carved into them. *Height 4.5 cm.*

AM 20217. Rev. A. H. Voyce Collection. Presented by Sir William Goodfellow 1934.

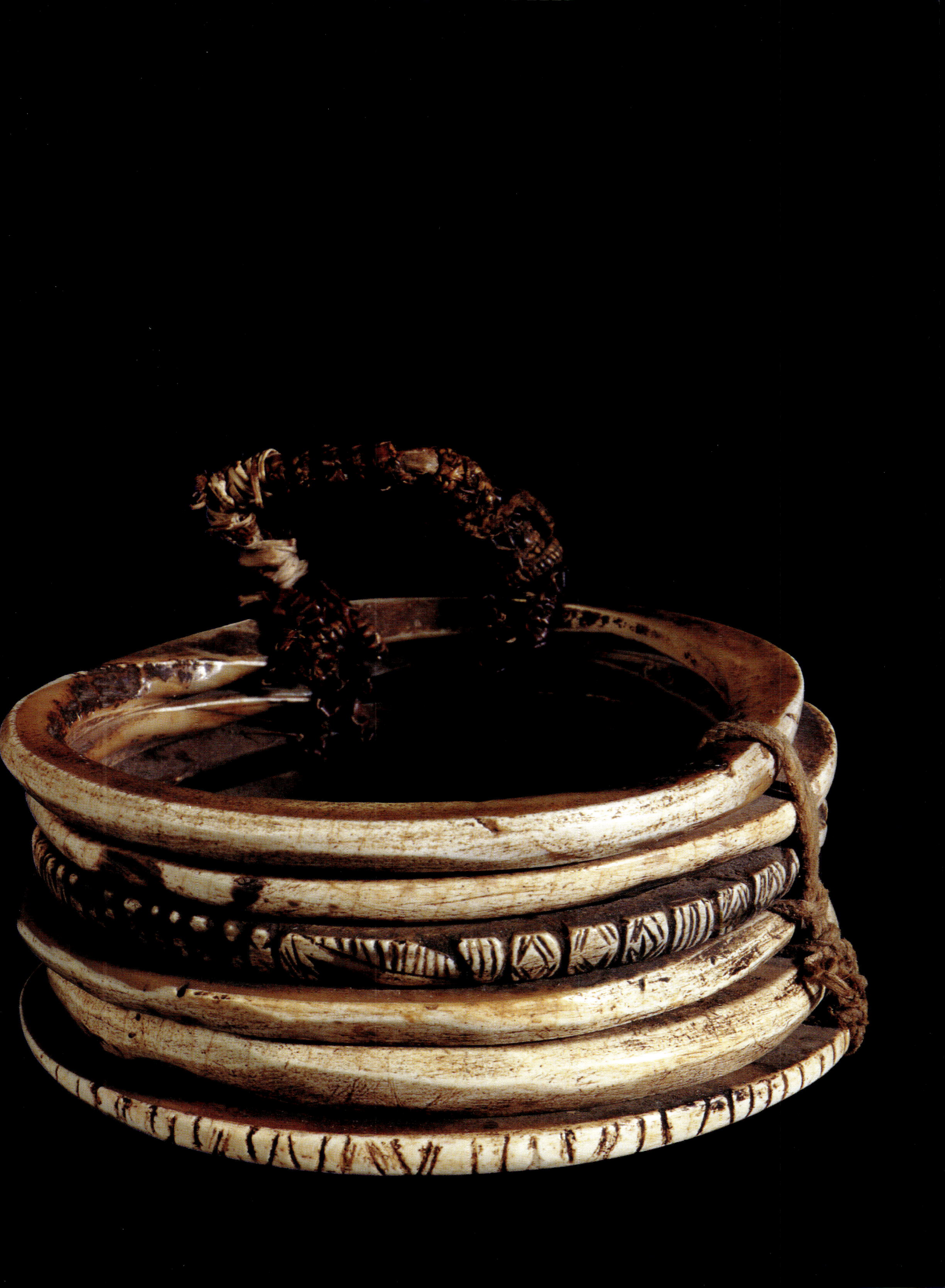

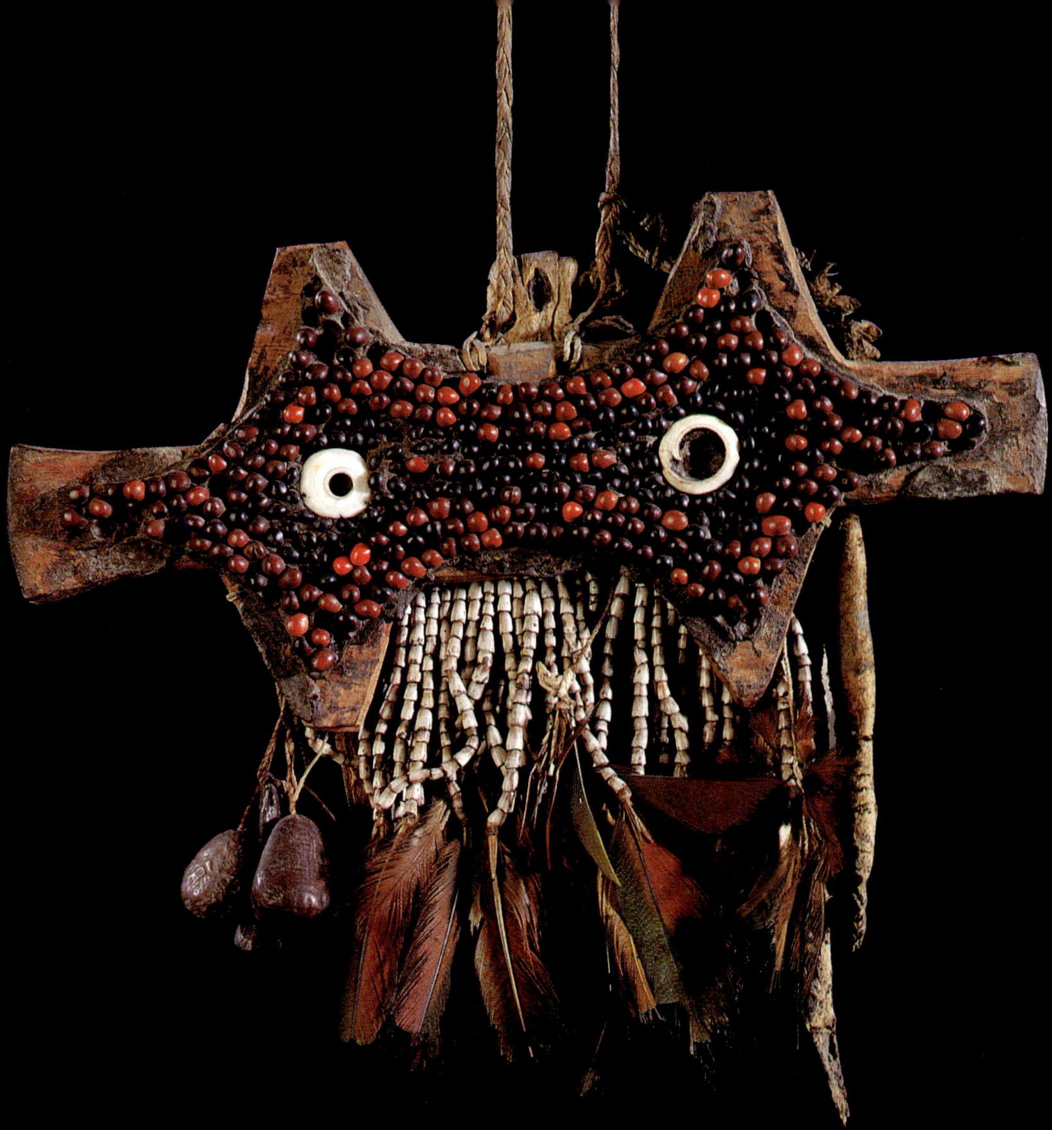

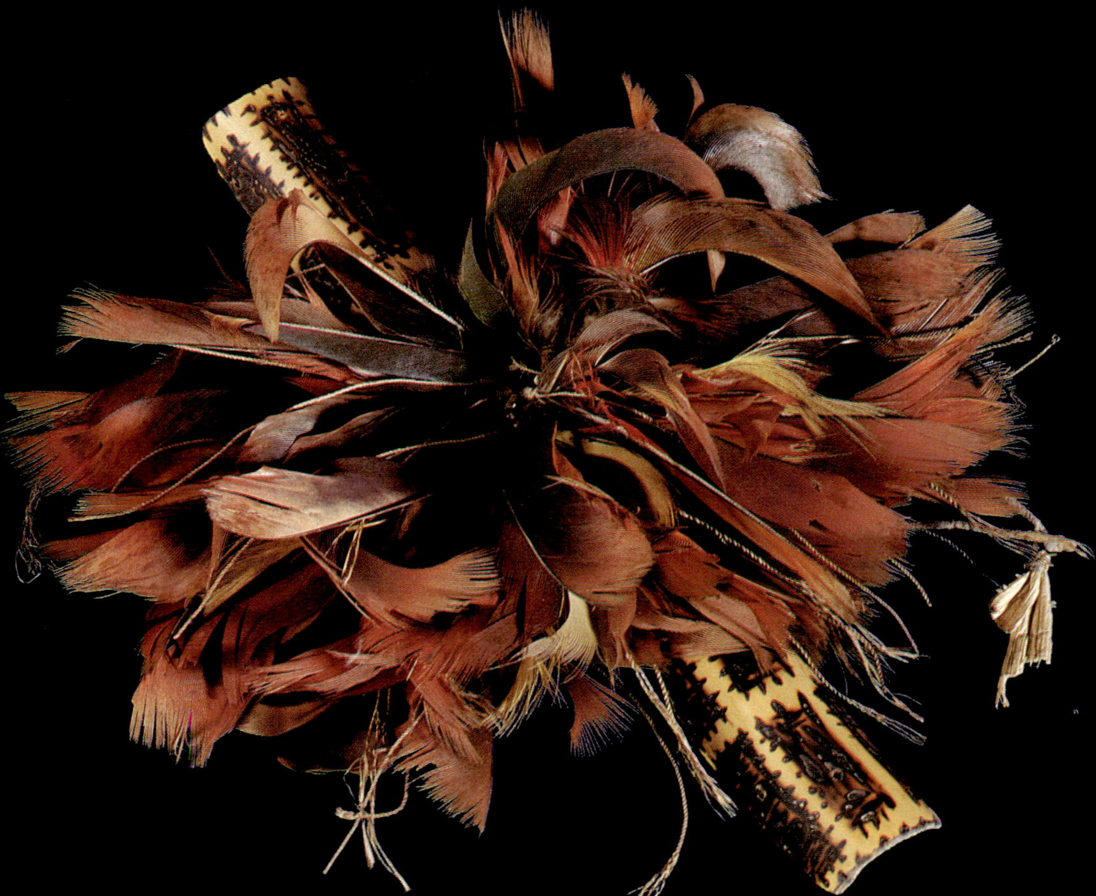

opposite top: ***Musikaka*, Breast and Mouth Ornament, Koiari People, Central Province, Papua New Guinea**

Normally worn hanging from the neck onto the chest, a warrior of the Koiari people living inland from the Port Moresby area, would clench this ornament in his teeth when going into battle. It consists of a wooden plaque decorated with red *Abrus* seeds supporting strings of white *Coix lachryma-jobi* seeds and feathers. The *Pangium* nuts would add a rattle to the overall threatening effect. *Width 25 cm.*

AM 16644. Presented by Mrs M. W. Millar 1931.

opposite bottom: ***Musikaka* or *Kotsiva*, Breast and Mouth Ornament, Motu People, Hula Village, Central Province, Papua New Guinea**

A different form of *musikaka* to that usually seen, this one has been constructed of a short half-section of bamboo with pokerwork designs burnt into it and a cluster of parrot feathers attached. It was collected in the late nineteenth century from the large coastal Motu village of Hula, which was built out on piles over the sea. The gardens were on nearby coastal land and the villagers traded with people further inland, which is how they obtained the parrot plumes. *Width 22 cm.*

AM 15342. James Edge-Partington Collection. Presented by Dr Thomson Wilson Leys Memorial 1924.

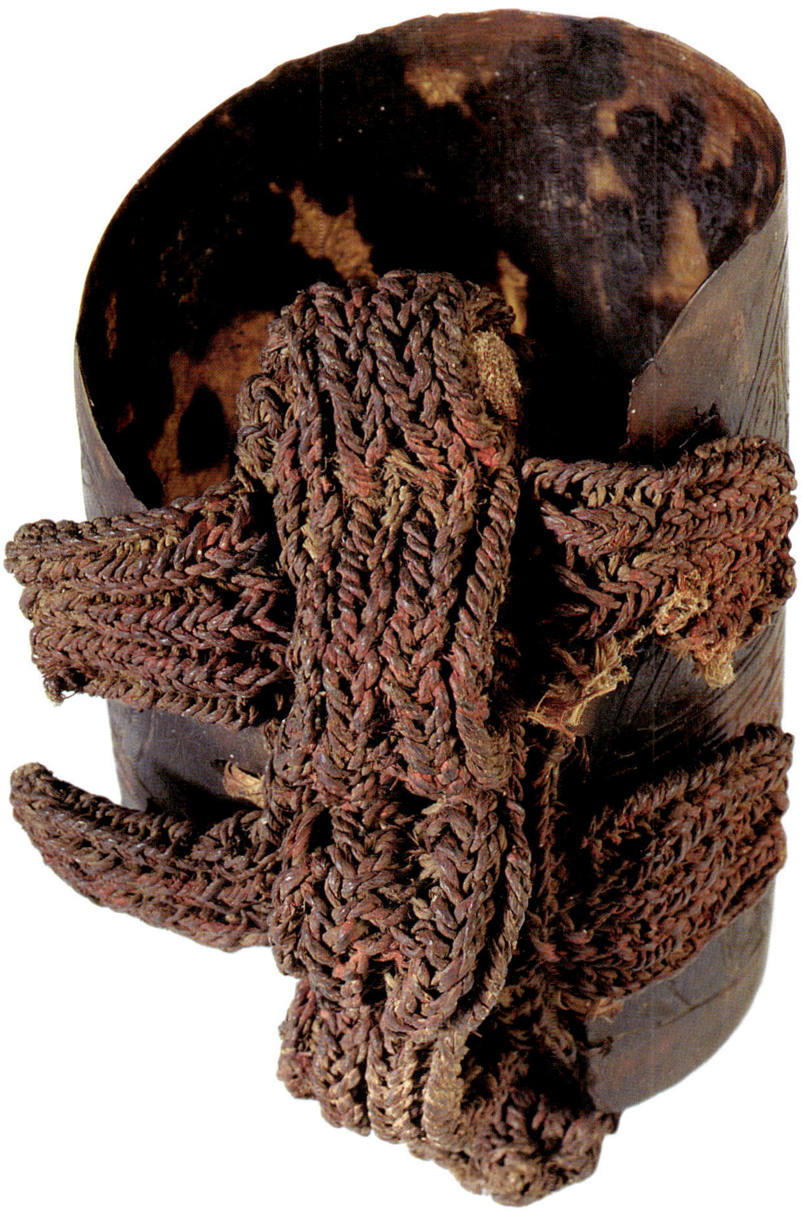

Arm Ornament, North Coast of Sepik District, Papua New Guinea

Made on the north coast of mainland New Guinea, this type of arm ornament was traded far into the interior, where such ornaments are highly valued and used in marriage transactions and other ceremonial payments. The ring has been cut from turtle shell, probably from the *Caretta imbricata* turtle and decorated with incised geometric patterns. A large, native fibre construction coloured with red ochre has been attached over the join. *Height 14 cm.*

AM 35227. Purchased from E. E. Vaile Trust Fund 1958.

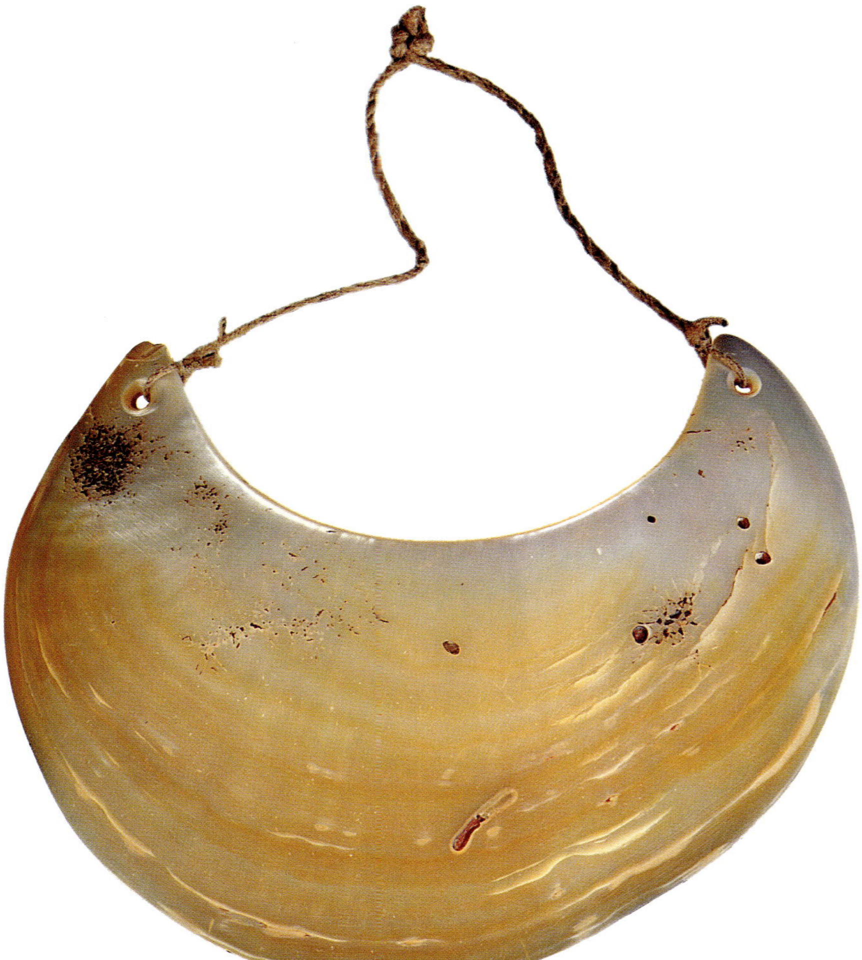

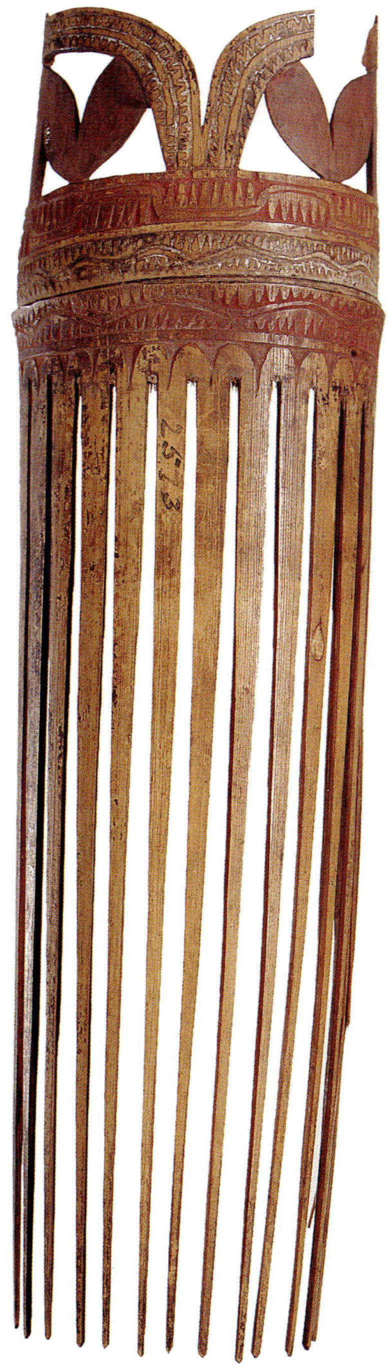

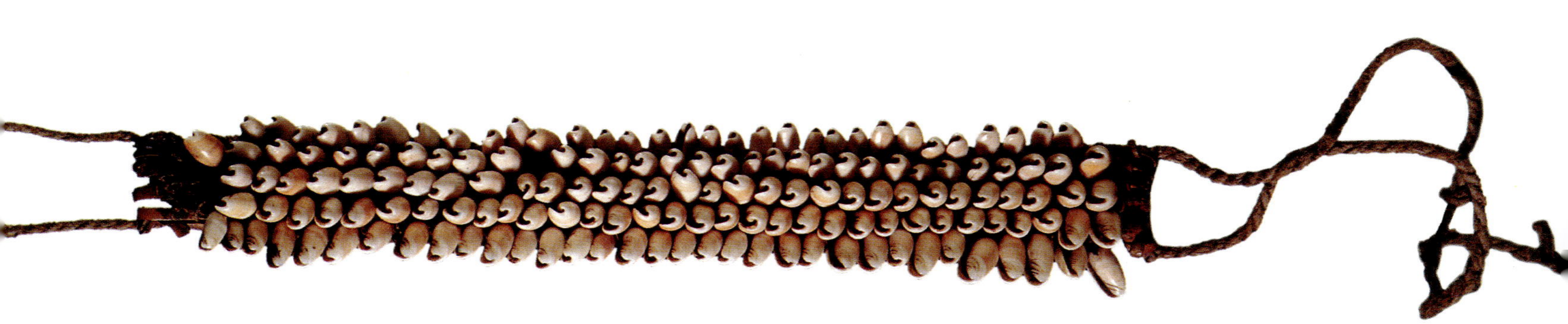

opposite (clockwise from top left):

KINA, GOLD LIP PEARL SHELL BREAST ORNAMENT, ENGA PEOPLE, KANDEP VALLEY, WESTERN HIGHLANDS

A missionary of the Apostolic Church obtained this ornament in the Kandep Valley in 1965 from an Enga man named Yendard. Traditionally, *kina* pearl shells traded up from the coast served as a specialised currency in the Western Highlands but their value was soon degraded by huge numbers of shells flown in by Europeans in the 1930s. In 1965, this missionary reported that this ornament was said to be worth three months' wages, and 20 such shells amounted to a reasonable bride price. *Length 19 cm.*

AM 45755. Presented by Mr L. H. McGrath 1972.

BAMBOO COMB, HUON PENINSULA, PAPUA NEW GUINEA

Melanesian men are more likely than women to wear hair combs, as part of their ceremonial dress. This form of comb cut from a large bamboo stem is characteristic of the Kate language group who live on the extreme eastern coast of the Huon peninsula. They would probably identify this design as representing the legs of frogs. *Length 25.5 cm, width 7 cm.*

AM 2573. Purchased from Mr Ives 1928

FOREHEAD ORNAMENT, PORT MORESBY AREA, PAPUA NEW GUINEA

Worn across the forehead below a feather head-dress, this ornament has been made of small pink shells attached to a rattan and fibre base. Such ornaments were only worn for ceremonial occasions. *Length 27 cm, width 5 cm.*

AM 15436.2. James Edge-Partington Collection. Presented by Dr Thomson Wilson Leys Memorial 1924.

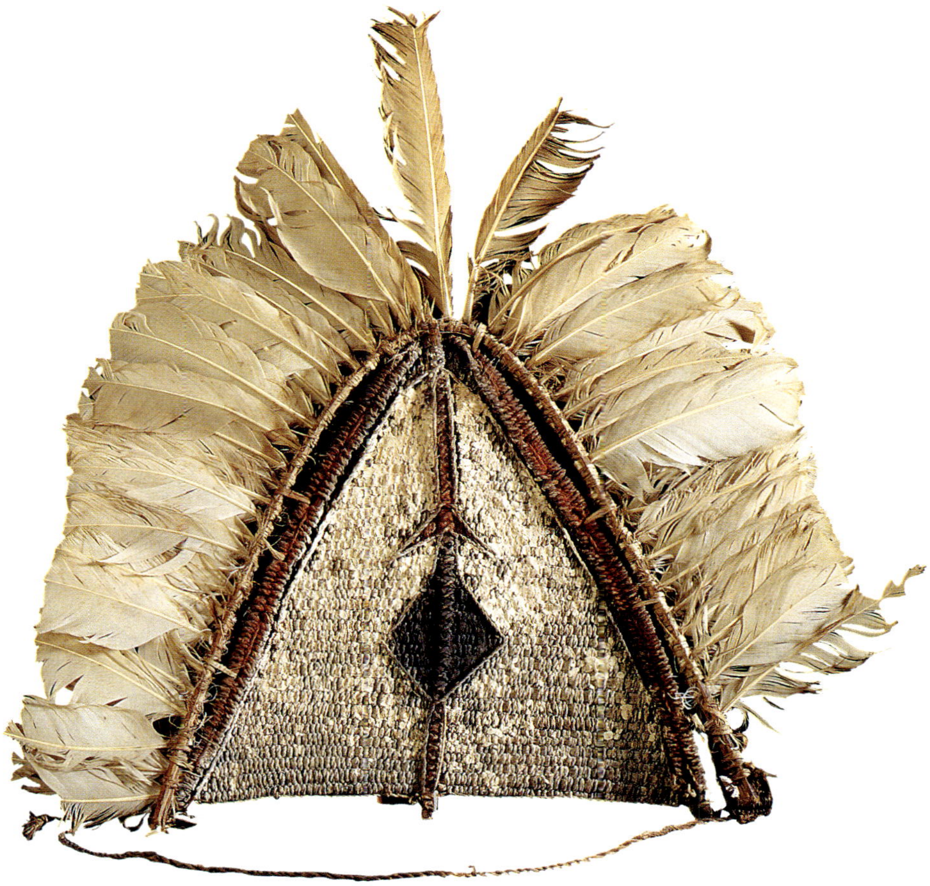

BURURU, FEATHER HEAD-DRESS, KIWAI PEOPLE, WABUDA ISLAND, MOUTH OF THE FLY RIVER, WESTERN PROVINCE, PAPUA NEW GUINEA

Worn when going into a fight or for dancing, this head-dress is constructed of fibre-work on a cane frame with white seabird feathers attached. The fibrework has been coated over with white lime and black and red pigment to produce the pattern. *Length 41 cm, width 40 cm.*

AM 15512. James Edge-Partington Collection. Presented by Dr Thomson Wilson Leys Memorial 1924.

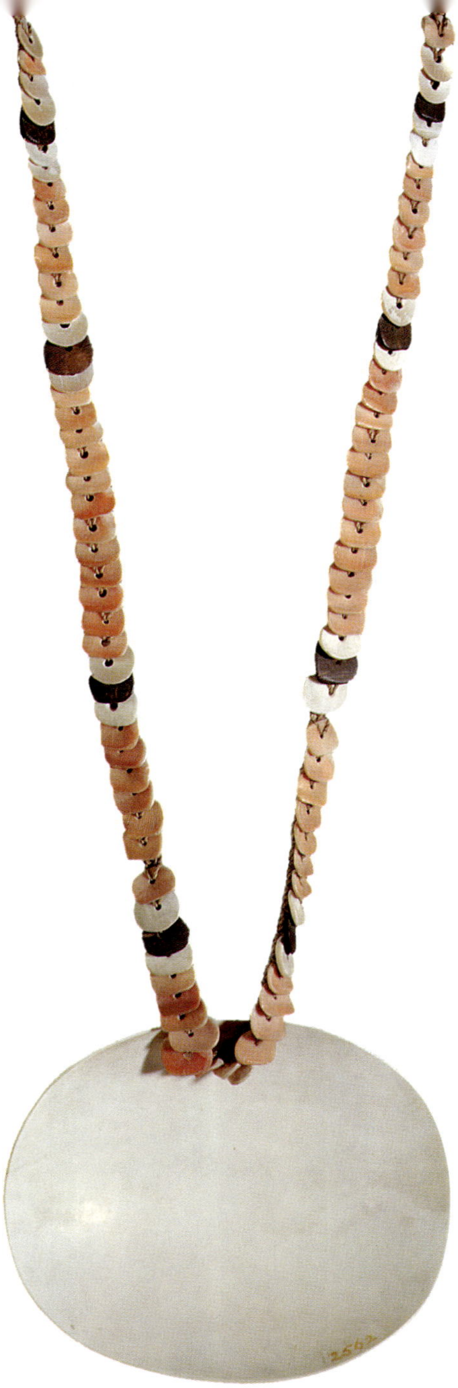

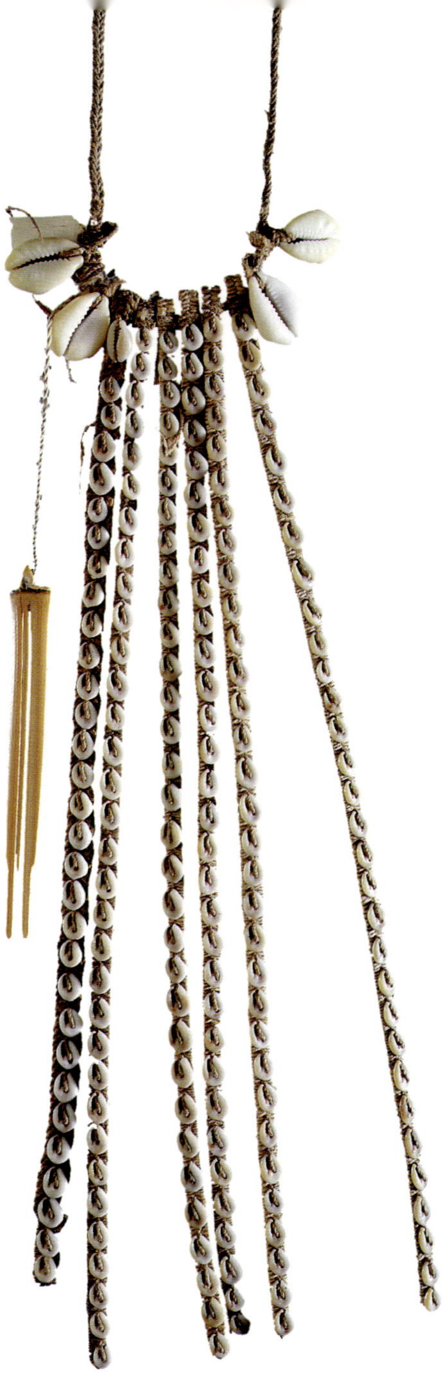

BREAST ORNAMENT, EASTERN GULF OF PAPUA, PAPUA NEW GUINEA

A concave dish cut out of a large white 'bailer' shell suspended on a string of red *Spondylus*, coconut shell and pearl shell discs have been combined to produce a type of breast ornament very widespread around the coasts of the eastern Gulf of Papua. Some are fitted with a shell, bead or turtle shell decoration at the centre of the dish. *Length 50 cm.*

AM 2562. Presented by M. C. Cleland 1928

NECKLACE, DANI TRIBE, BALIEM VALLEY, CENTRAL HIGHLANDS, WEST IRIAN

In the high mountain valleys of New Guinea, certain shells traded in from the coast, especially the cowrie and *Nassa* shells as on this necklace, attained a monetary value in addition to their ornamental role. The owner of this necklace has also found it a convenient place to carry his bamboo jew's harp. Young Dani men especially favour these *Nassa* shell necklaces, perhaps as a reminder of the closely woven *Nassa* shell *wopok* chest covers formerly worn in warfare. *Length 16 cm, width 6 cm.*

AM 36844. Purchased from Mr Russell Bond 1992.

opposite: ***GIBIGIBI* FACE ORNAMENT, GOMEDU, WARIA RIVER, ORO PROVINCE, PAPUA NEW GUINEA**

When a warrior from Gomedu village entered a fight, he clasped his *gibigibi* face ornament between his teeth so that his face was framed and disguised. Composed of boar tusks, dog teeth, trade beads and bright red *Abrus* seeds, his *gibigibi* conferred supernatural protection on the warrior and warned his enemies that he was protected from their attack. At other times the ornament was worn hanging on his chest from its neck cord. *Length 28 cm, width 24 cm.*

AM 32549. Presented by Lady Ellis 1957.

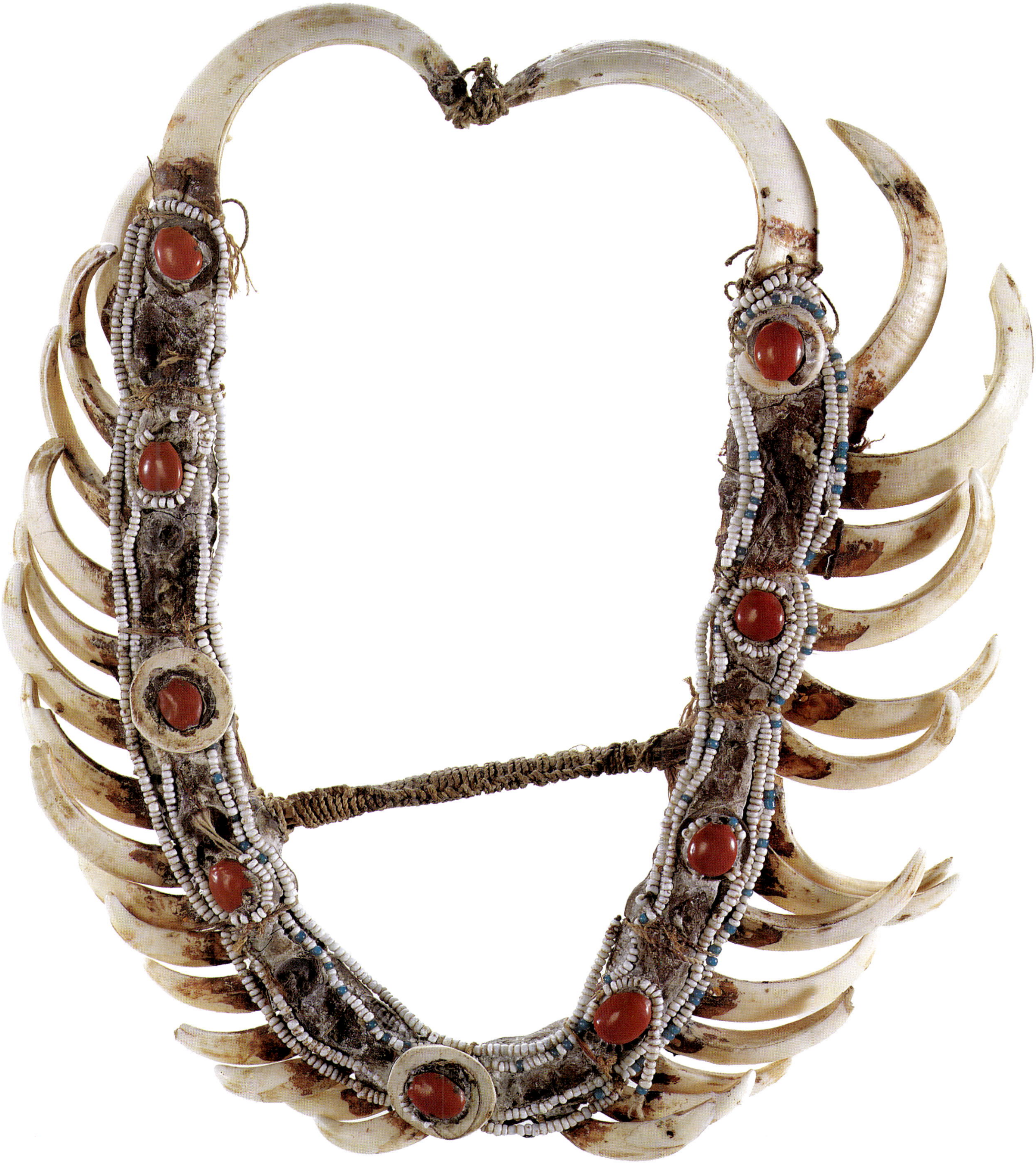

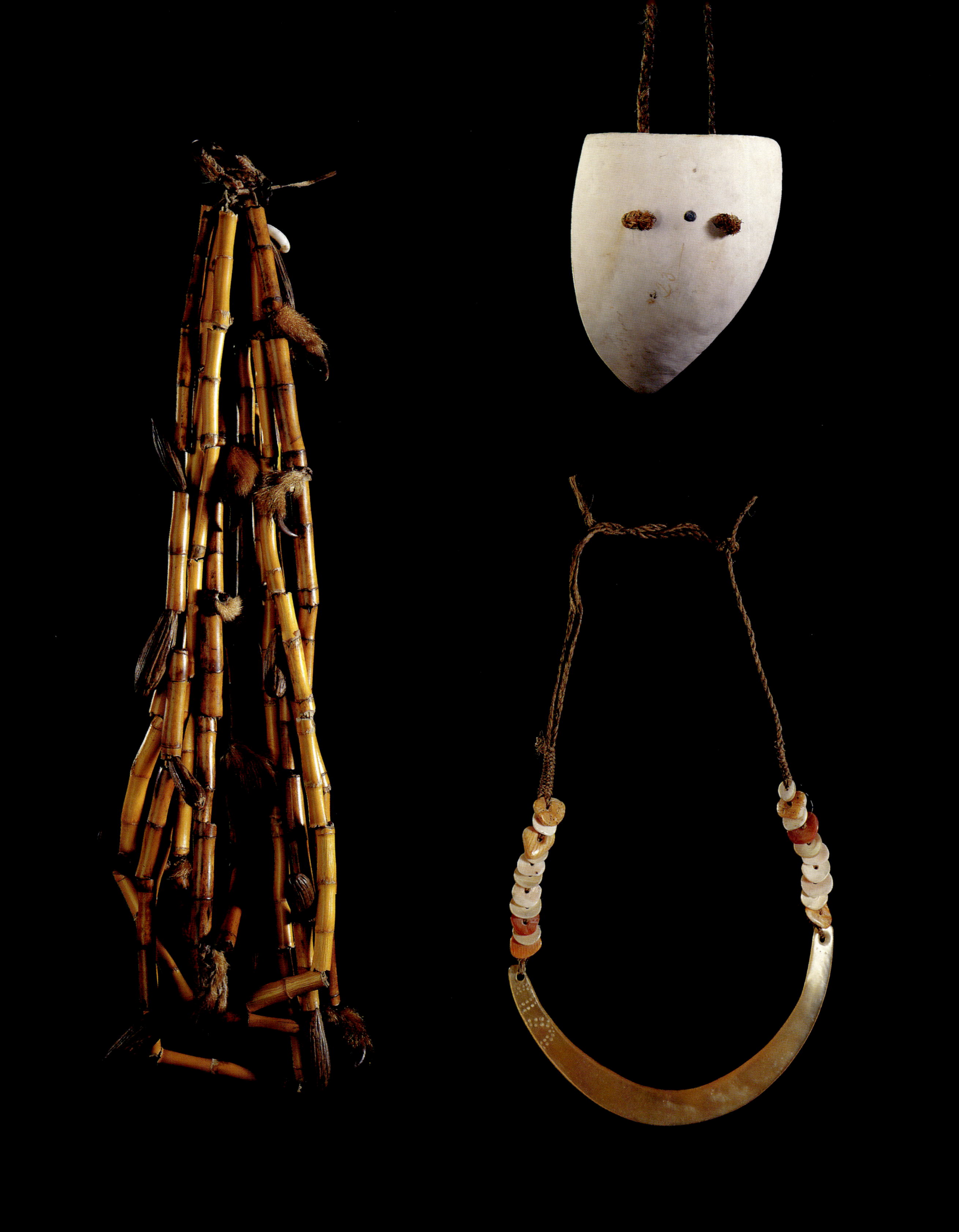

opposite (clockwise from top left):

Necklace, Aseki, near Menyamya, Anga (Kukukuku) People, Morobe Province, Papua New Guinea

This necklace consists of four strings of short lengths of yellow orchid stems, interspersed with brown seeds and cuscus claws, still with attached fur. Anga men usually wore a thick fibre skirt, a necklace of shell or other materials and a cassowary feather head-dress. *Length 210 cm.*

AM 55018 Purchased from Mr A. Peterson 1995.

Yadere-ere, Pubic Shield, Kiwai People, Mouth of the Fly River, Western Province, Papua New Guinea

Men of the tribes living around the muddy estuarine western shores of the Gulf of Papua from Goaribari Island to the mouth of the Fly River and further into the islands of Torres Strait wore a pubic shield cut from the large curve of a *Melo* 'bailer' shell. This was worn in fighting and raiding, and also when dancing on ceremonial occasions. This *yadere-ere* was collected during the 1890s by Reverend James Chalmers when the London Missionary Society was extending its work into the area around the mouth of the Fly River. *Length 22 cm, width 15 cm.*

AM 15506. James Edge-Partington Collection.
Presented by Dr Thomson Wilson Leys Memorial 1924.

Mairi, Neck Ornament, South-east Coast, Papua New Guinea

Crescent-shaped neck ornaments of pearl shell are one of the most widespread forms of Pacific jewellery, seen from the New Guinea highlands to the Solomon Islands and further east into Polynesia. This example is distinguished by the delicacy of the highly-polished, gold-lip pearl shell crescent, while the red *Spondylus* shell discs on the suspension cord indicate that it is from the south-east Papuan coast. Known by their Motu name as *mairi*, these crescents were traded among the Namau, Elema, Mekec, Roro and Motu peoples along the eastern Gulf of Papua coast and south-east towards the Louisiade Archipelago. *Length 36 cm.*

AM 32559. Presented by Lady Ellis 1951.

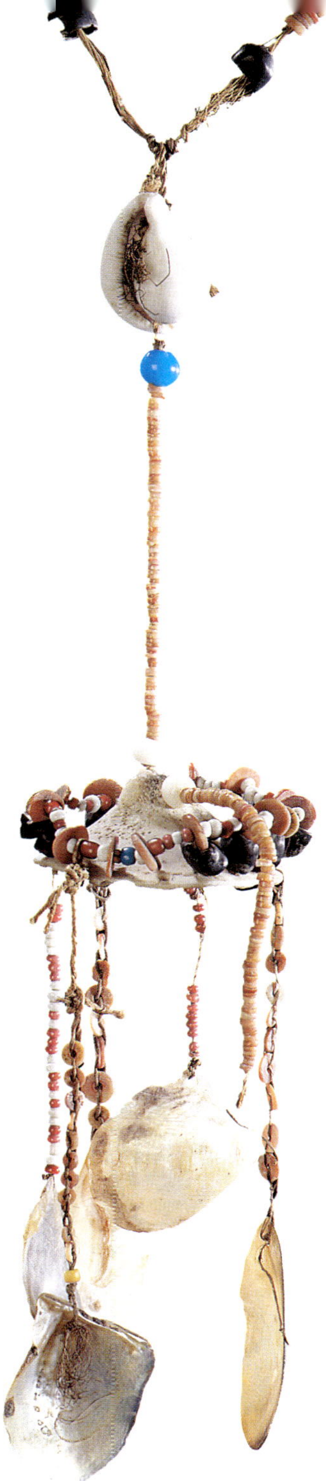

Soulava or *Bagi*, D'Entrecasteaux Islands, Milne Bay Province, Papua New Guinea

Kula is an exchange and trading cycle linking many of the islands in the Massim district of south-east Papua New Guinea. *Soulava* necklaces and *mwali* arm rings are ritually exchanged by *kula* partners from different islands. On very special occasions, such as yam harvest festivals, a *soulava* might be worn by a woman, hanging down on her back. The *soulava* consists of red *Spondylus* shell discs strung *sapisapi* style on native cord joining with a cowrie shell, then a *Cassis* shell pendant from which golden oyster shells and imported glass beads are suspended. *Length 94 cm.*

AM 23911. Purchased from Mrs Ballantyne 1937.

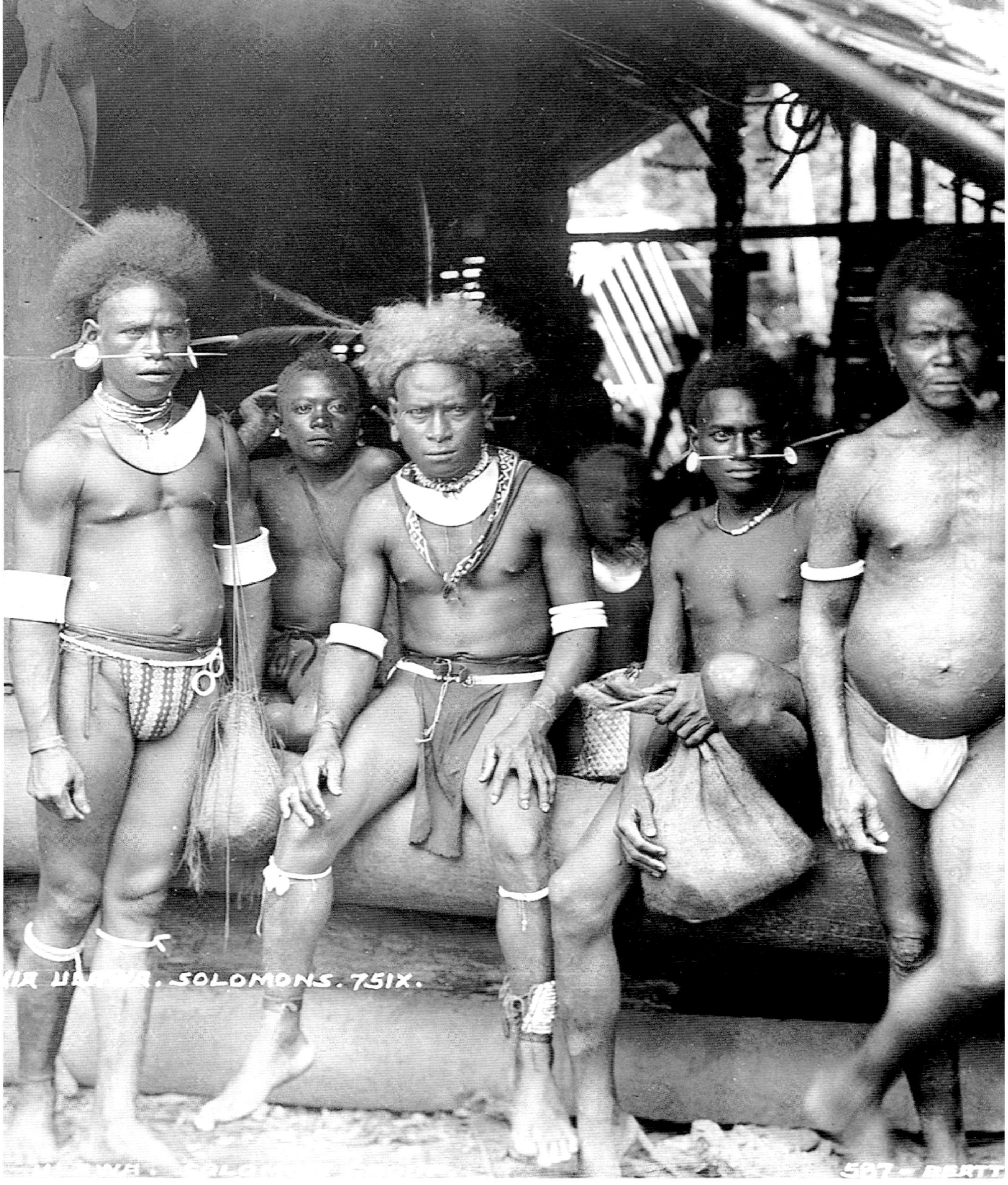
SOLOMONS. 751X.

CHAPTER THREE

ISLAND MELANESIA

BISMARCK ARCHIPELAGO, TORRES STRAIT ISLANDS, SOLOMON ISLANDS INCLUDING BOUGAINVILLE, SANTA CRUZ ISLANDS, VANUATU, NEW CALEDONIA

opposite: **Non-Christian Men of Ahia Village, Ulawa Island, Solomon Islands, 1906**

Posing in front of their men's custom house, where they spent much of their time, these young men who have been initiated into the bonito cult wear a wide variety of personal ornaments. Most obvious are their pearl-shell neck crescents and large Tridacna *clam shell arm rings representing wealth. Visitors to Ulawa at this time remarked that the young unmarried men were more conspicuous than their elders with their elaborate body ornaments and self decoration of arm bands, shell money belts, necklaces, nose and ear ornaments and arm and leg bands. This contrasted with the high-ranking men, who tended to discard their elaborate body ornament in favour of one or two large clam shell ornaments that simply marked their status.*

Photo: John Watt Beattie. Auckland Museum 5827/6381

ISLAND MELANESIA AS a general convenience term encompasses several major island groups as listed above, stretching south-eastwards from the New Guinea mainland to New Caledonia in the south. Some of these islands are extremely large, especially New Caledonia, Bougainville, New Britain and New Ireland. All of the larger islands are very mountainous and thickly forested, providing a wide range of stone, shell, animal and plant materials suitable for making jewellery. Smaller islands, and especially the low coral atolls, provide only limited food resources and raw materials.

These island groups have had a diverse political history and this is reflected in their present political status. The widespread Bismarck Archipelago is part of the independent state of Papua New Guinea, as is the large island of Bougainville. However, while politically included in Papua New Guinea, Bougainville and neighbouring Buka are culturally part of the northern Solomon Islands. Despite their Melanesian heritage, the Torres Strait Islands are part of Australia. The Solomon Islands, which include the Santa Cruz group, are an independent state, as is Vanuatu, formerly the New Hebrides. New Caledonia is a territory of France.

Any generalisation about the diverse cultures and arts of Island Melanesia is very difficult and fraught with exceptions. To the far west, the peoples of the small north-western islands such as Wuvulu, Sae, Kaniet, Ninigo and the Hermits have Micronesian affinities. People of the Admiralty Islands speak about twenty different Austronesian languages but form three main cultural groups; the Ussiai living in the interior of Manus Island, the Matankol of the surrounding islands, and the Manus on the south-east coast of the big island. Admiralty Islanders are famous for their woodcarvings of ancestors, bowls and spears, often coloured red and black with intricate coloured bindings. New Britain and New Ireland are famous for their diverse forms of wooden, plaited fibre and barkcloth masks and their sculptural carvings.

The Solomon Islands with their eighty or more distinct languages are the home of many forms of shell currency and ornaments, and intricate shell inlay on their canoes and carvings. Vanuatu is an extremely complex region culturally.

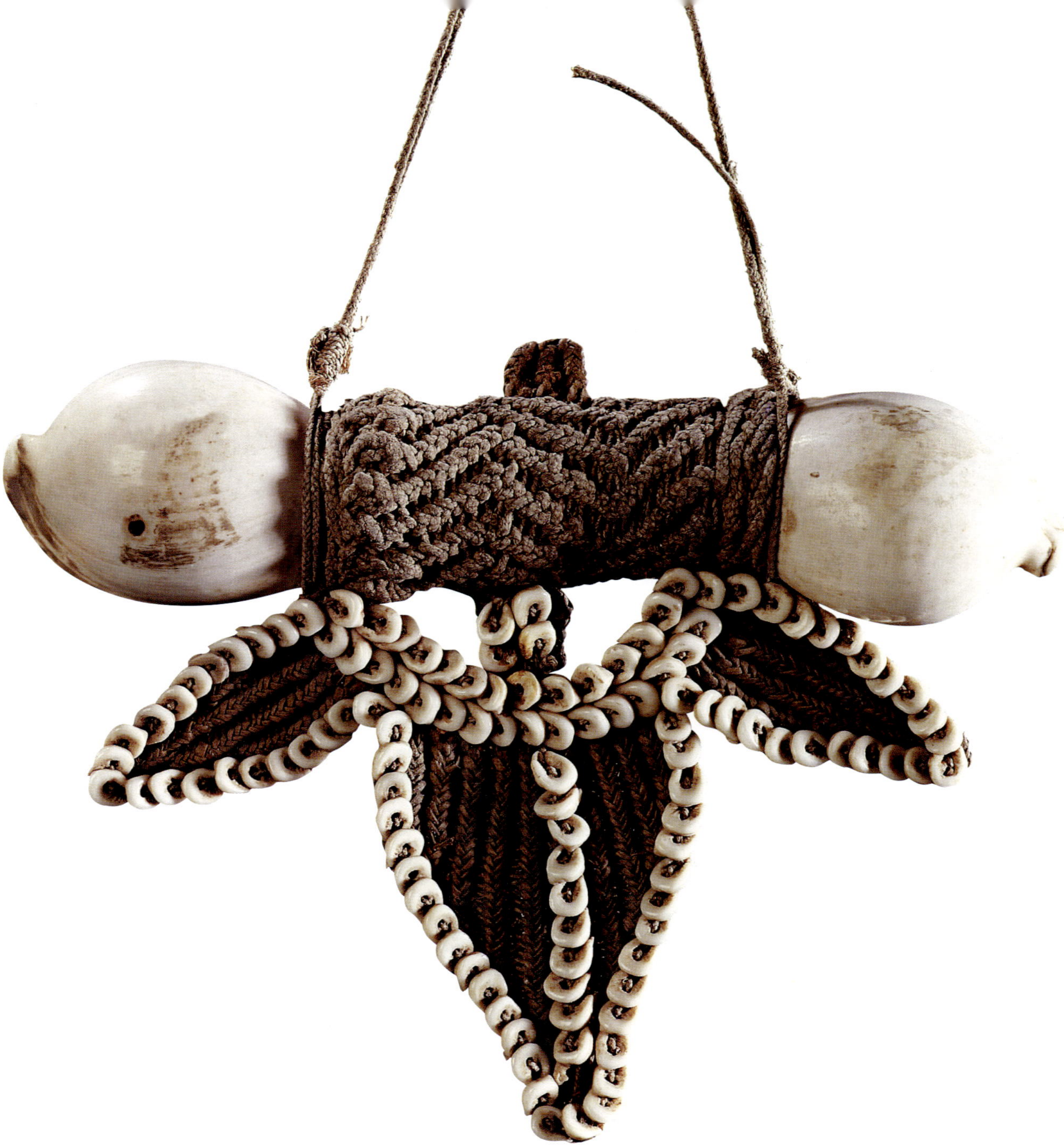

The population of about 170,000 people speak 113 different indigenous languages and their cultures overlap in many aspects. In the northern islands of Vanuatu, men advance to positions of power by taking steps up a hierarchy of grades by economic competition involving pig sacrifice. In the southern islands, a system of chiefly titles operates partly on heredity and partly on a pyramidal power structure. Both specific grades and titles have their own ritual paraphernalia and personal ornaments. New Caledonia has developed its own distinctive version of Melanesian artistic culture, characterised by large house carvings, wooden masks, and ritual objects of serpentine and flying-fox fur.

Jewellery and body adornment throughout this huge region is as diverse as would be expected from this cultural mix. However, some basic commonalities can be discerned, such as the widespread use of dog teeth, pig tusks, other mammal teeth and clam shell. Another frequent jewellery element are the large flat and concave white shell discs worn as forehead and breast pendants, often with the addition of a turtle shell fretwork or beads at the centre, as in the popular *kapkap* forms and their derivatives. Traditional small shell discs drilled for stringing are found very widely, whether as pure jewellery or as currency to be worn.

Breast Ornament, Witu (Garove) Islands, Papua New Guinea

Two large *Ovula* cowrie shells are linked by finely plaited fibre from which hangs three plaited-fibre lobes edged with *Nassa* shells. Worn for parade and warfare, this is a form of ornament characteristic of the Witu Islands, but like most ornaments here it shows close affinities with mainland New Guinea. *Length (including cord) 40 cm, width 20 cm.*

AM 11475. Purchased from Mr G. Stuart 1888.

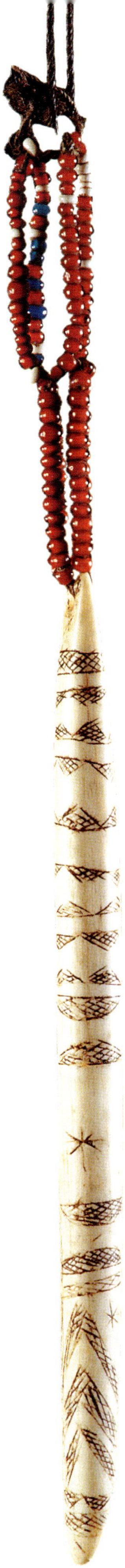

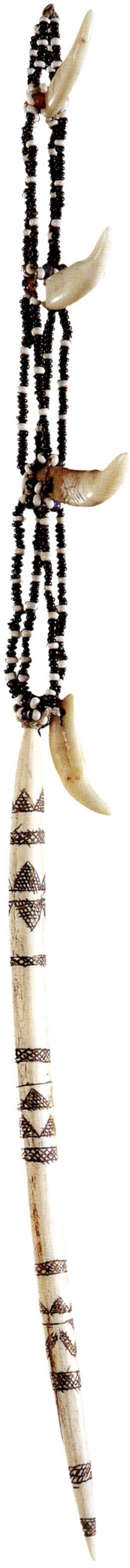

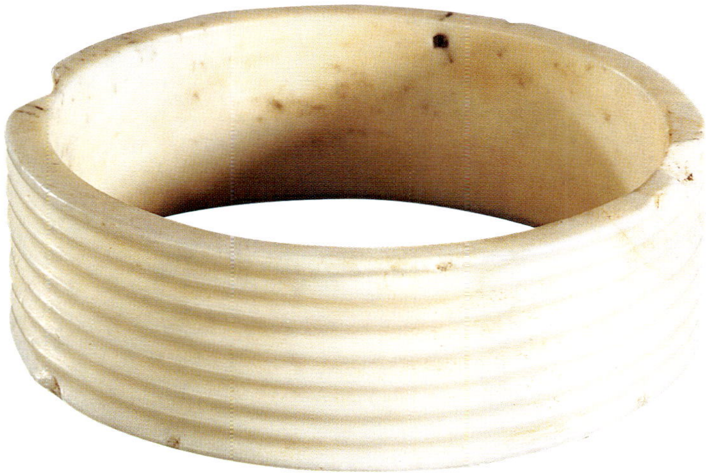

Anoa Ranguk, Arm Ring, Tanga Island, New Ireland, Papua New Guinea

Tanga has always been prominent as a manufacturing centre for *Tridacna* shell arm rings used in trading to the large island of New Ireland. They are produced not by drilling but by breaking a hole through with a sharp stone and smoothing it out with wood and pumice dust. Most famous and most highly valued are the distinctive Tanga shell rings ground very thin and decorated with several fine parallel grooves around the outside. In 1935 a good example of *anoa ranguk* could purchase 500 pounds of sago in New Britain. *Diameter 7.5 cm, width 2.5 cm.*

AM 25577. Presented by Mr A. Montgomery 1940.

Nose Ornaments, Admiralty Islands, Papua New Guinea

Both men and women in most of the Manus societies wear a variety of nose stick ornaments made from shell, wood, cane, tusk or coconut shell. At right is one of the most elaborate types, shaped by men from a giant clam shell and decorated with incised designs, trade beads and dog teeth. Sometimes an ornament like this was worn hanging from the pierced septum of the nose or from a stick passed through the septum. from left: *Length 20 cm; length 18 cm.*

from left: *AM 11481. Purchased from Mr G. Stuart 1888.*
AM 11482. Purchased from Mr G. Stuart 1888.

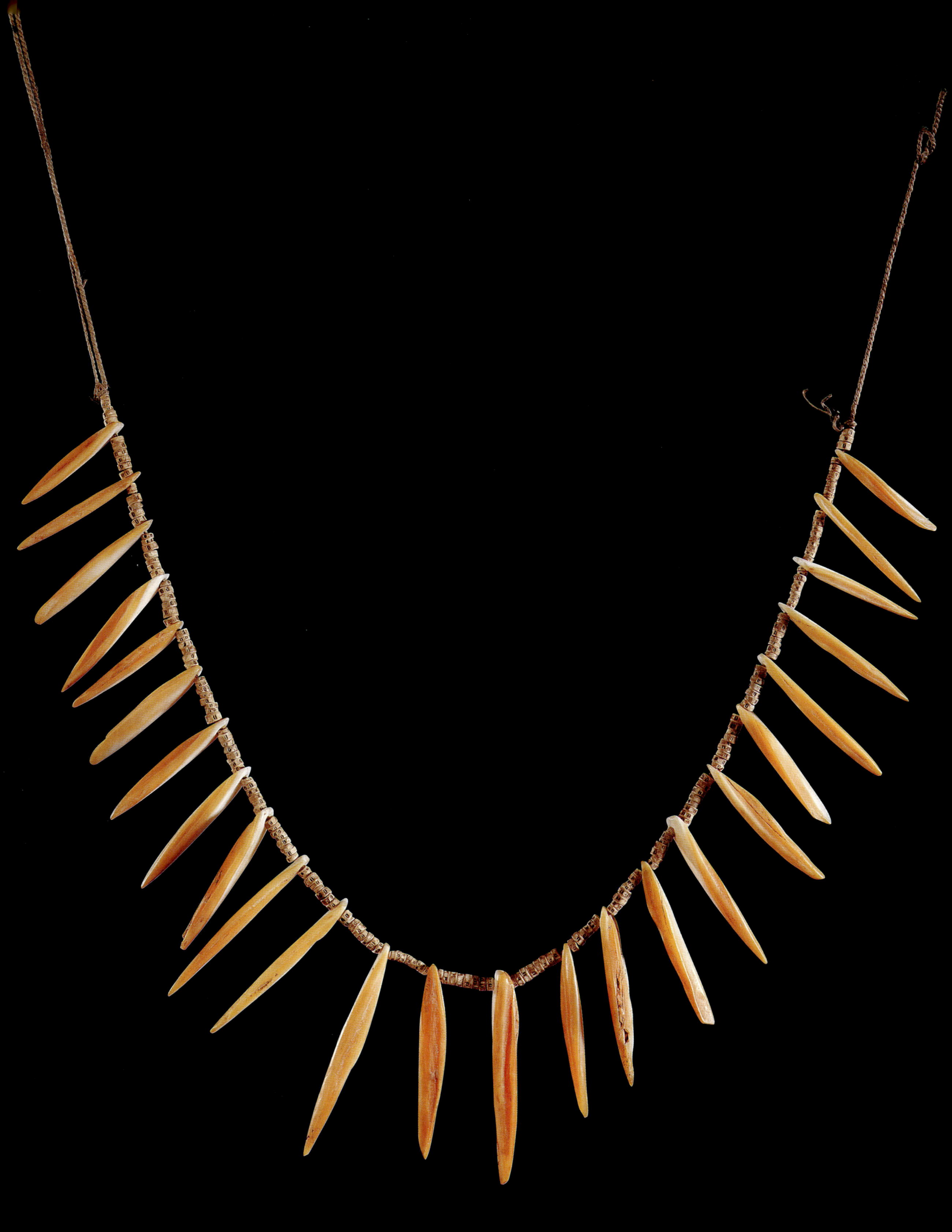

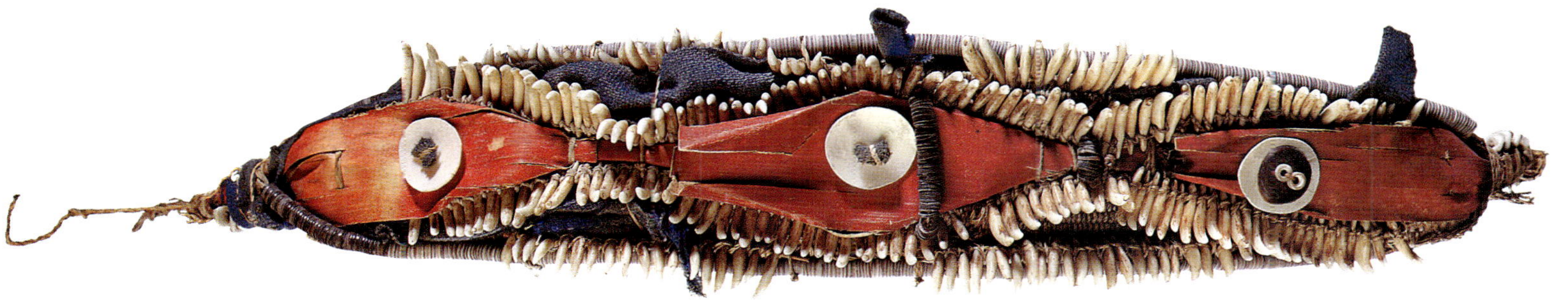

Rara, Head Band, Tolai people, Gazelle Peninsula, New Britain

Warriors among the Tolai people wore decorative head bands of various forms to provide supernatural protection from sorcery and danger in battle, making the wearer strong and courageous. This one incorporates cuscus teeth, imported blue cloth, leaves, and strings of drilled shell 'money' discs. Its supernatural power was instilled in it by rituals of the men's secret *Ingiet* society. *Length 32.5 cm, width 7 cm.*

AM 55345.

Neck Ornament, Admiralty Islands, Papua New Guinea

Described by early visitors as war charms, these neck ornaments were worn by men of all the population groups in the Admiralty Islands. It was attached to a tight neck cord so that it projected horizontally to the rear from the back of the man's neck. The carved head with its pendulous earlobes is said to represent a famous mythical warrior who had killed many enemies and could therefore provide protection for the wearer in dangerous situations, including visits to potentially hostile neighbours. Sometimes instead of the carved head there was a protective ancestor's bone. Frigate bird feathers clipped into a serrated edge complete the ornament. They are still worn today by dance groups. *Length 47 cm.*

AM 2138. Presented by Mr James Adams Wilkes 1928.

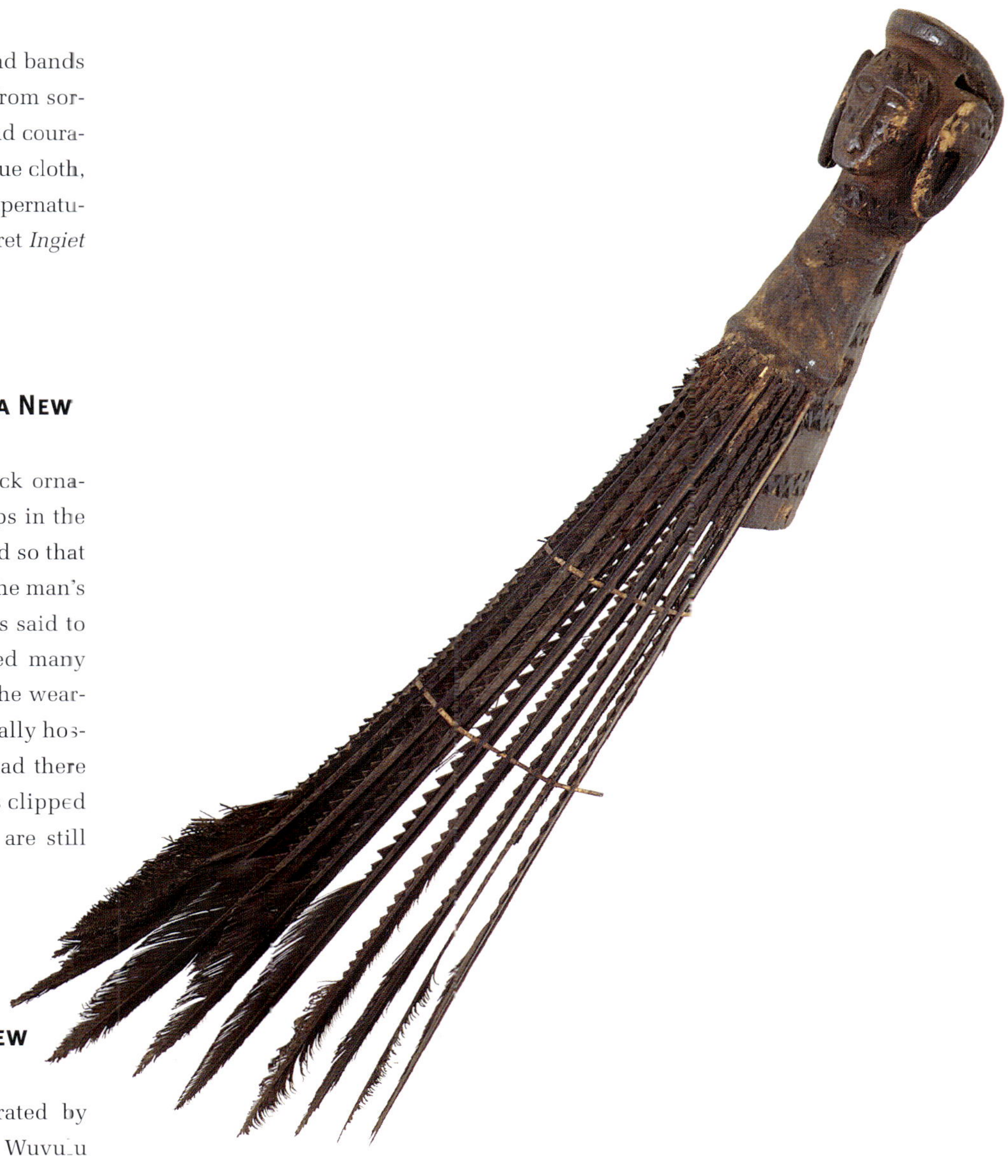

opposite: Necklace, Wuvulu (Maty) Island, Western Bismarck Archipelago, Papua New Guinea

Shaped pieces of *Cassis cornuta* shells are separated by strings of fish vertebrae in this necklace from remote Wuvulu Island, where Micronesian influences have reached Melanesia. Wuvulu people wore very little jewellery apart from necklaces of various shells, and women had turtle shell discs attached around their pierced and pendulous earlobes. *Length 82 cm.*

AM 15299.1. James Edge-Partington Collection. Presented by Dr Thomson Wilson Leys Memorial 1924.

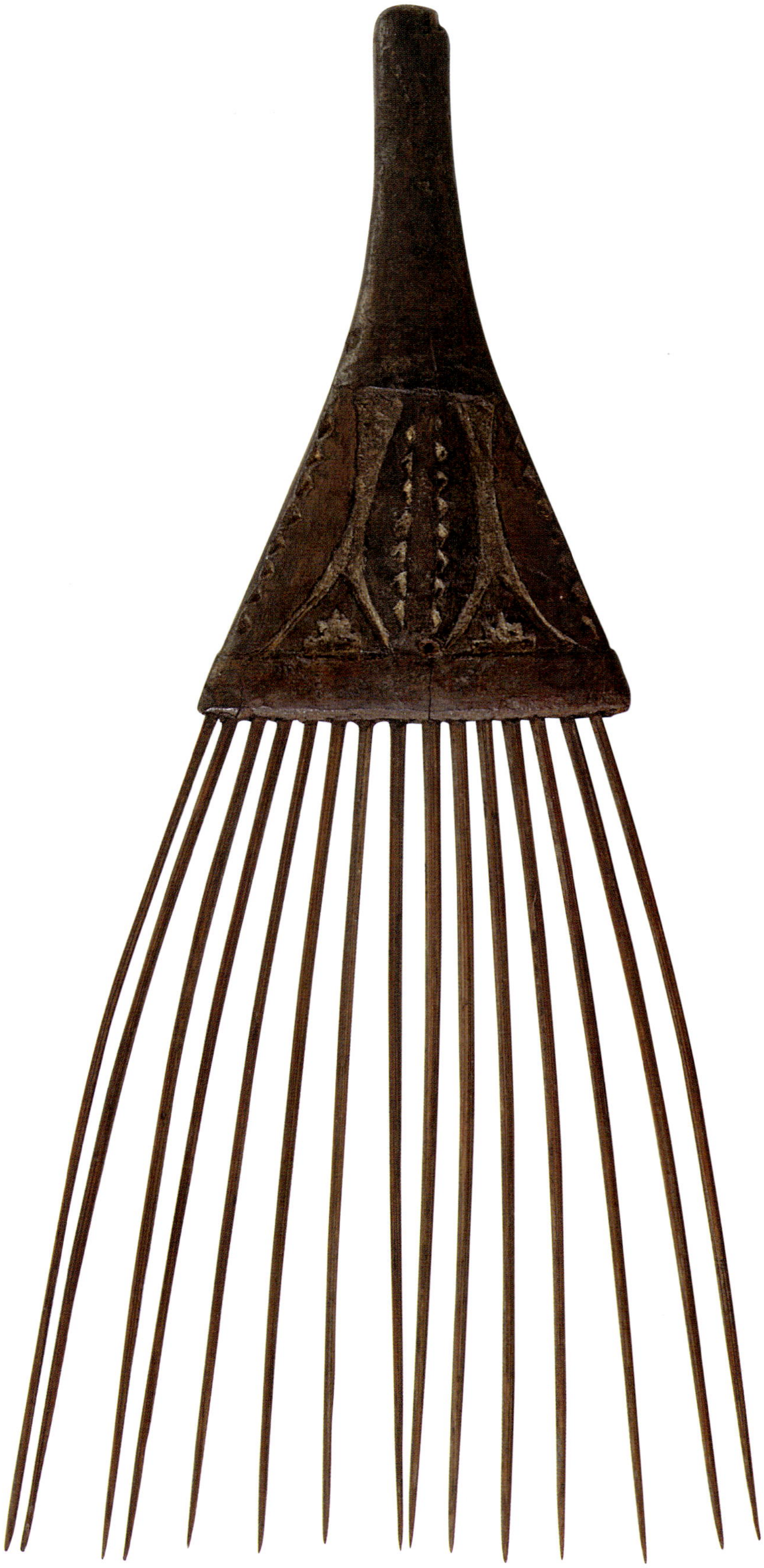

COMB, ADMIRALTY ISLANDS, PAPUA NEW GUINEA

Decorative combs in the Admiralty Islands were worn among all population groups by men rather than women, who usually kept their hair short or shaved completely. Only on special occasions such as a wedding would a bride wear a comb, but then mainly to display it for a short time as a part of the bride price. The teeth of this comb have been cut from wood, then bound together and the upper portion covered with paste made from *Parinarium* nuts. This paste has been coloured red with paint extracted from certain seeds, then carved with notched patterns and inlaid with white lime. *Length 30 cm, width 14 cm.*

AM 15325.2. James Edge-Partington Collection. Presented by Dr Thomson Wilson Leys Memorial 1924.

opposite: ***BAK*, BEADED APRON, PAK ISLAND, ADMIRALTY ISLANDS, PAPUA NEW GUINEA**

Part of an early collection from then German New Guinea, this apron has been made as an open network of traditional drilled shell-money discs hanging from a plaited fibre waistband decorated with parrot feathers and *Coix* seeds. Reports from this time state that these were the dance ornaments of men, especially chiefs who could afford the cost of shell money. By the 1930s, they were also worn by women at dances and festivals and in some areas were part of a bride's wedding dress. *Length 55 cm, width 34 cm.*

AM 11552. Purchased from Mr G. Stuart 1888.

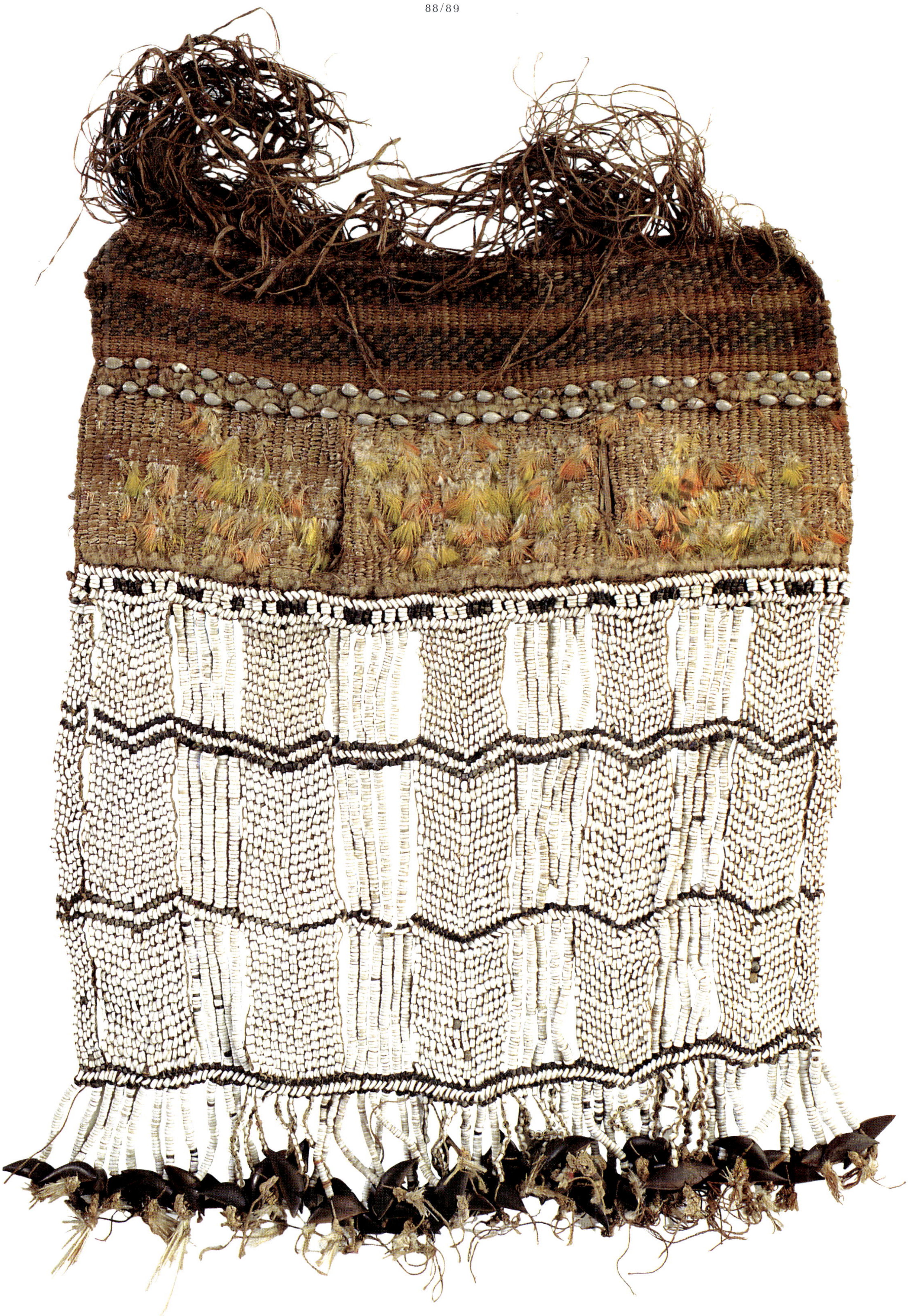

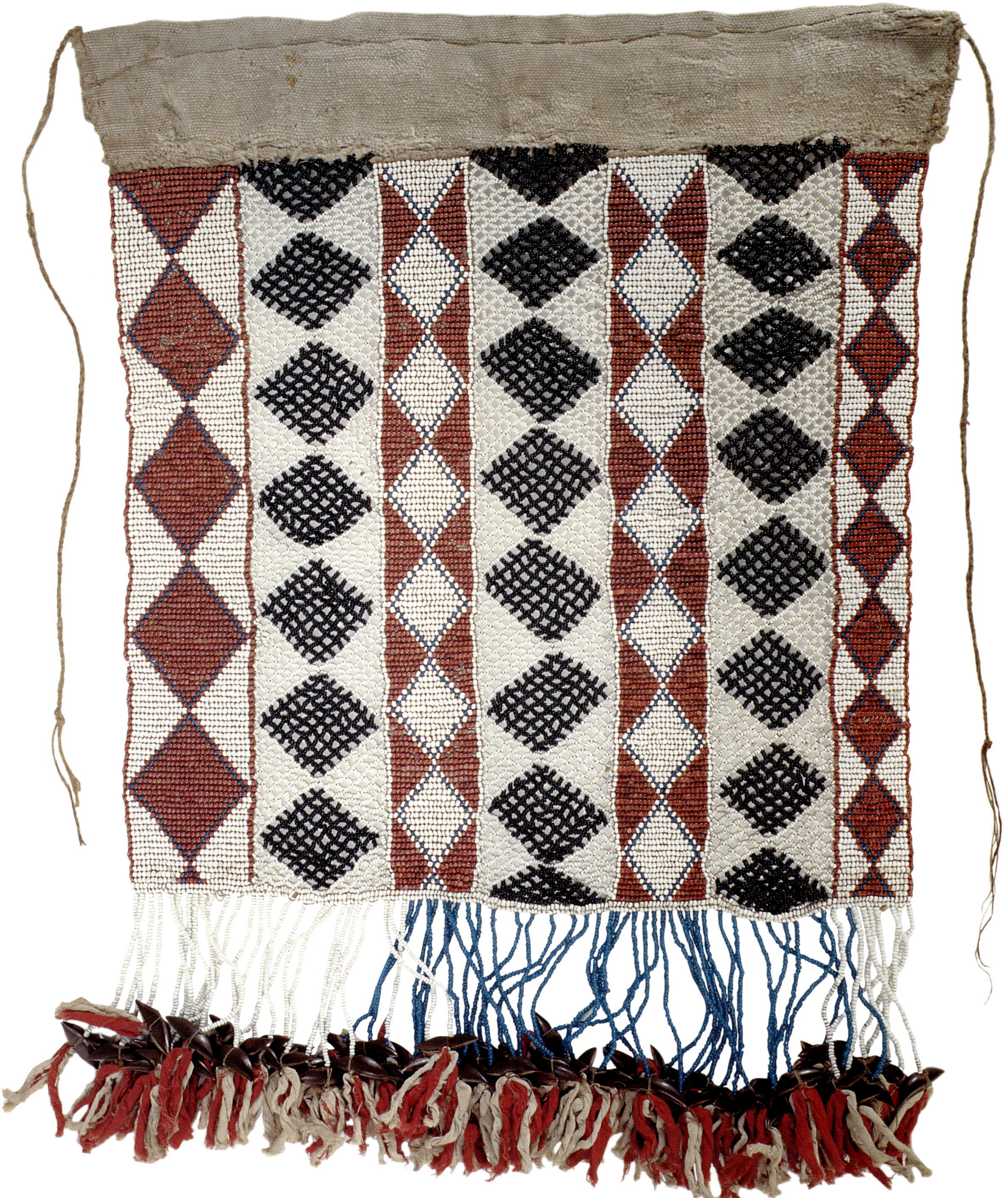

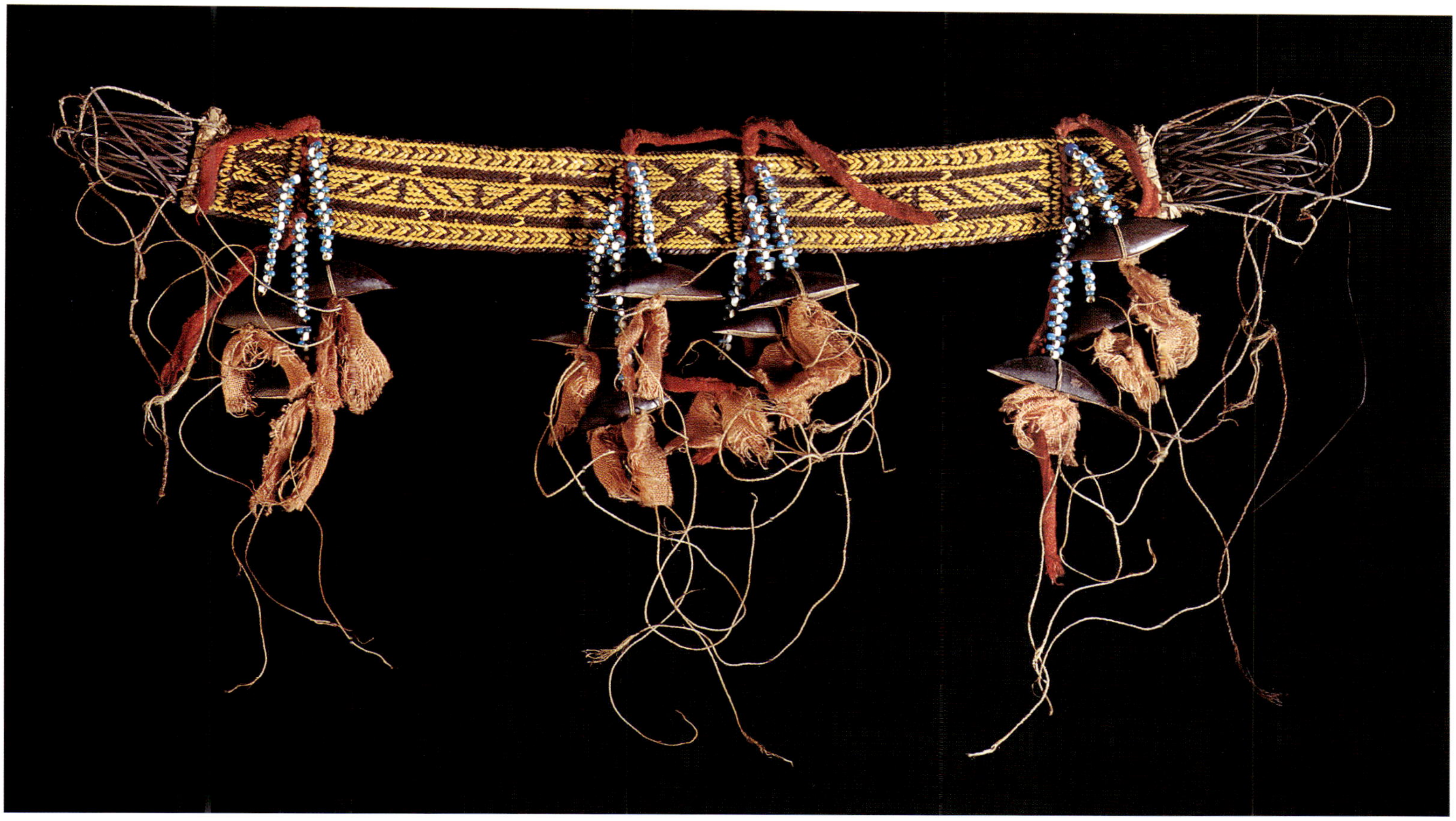

Leg Band, Admiralty Islands, Papua New Guinea

Designed to be tied around the leg just below the knee, this is a man's dance ornament. Probably made by women of the inland Ussiai people, the plaited band of yellow orchid fibre has attachments of shell beads, nuts and red trade cloth. *Length 27 cm, width 12 cm.*

AM 2392.7. Presented by Mr James Adams Wilkes 1928.

opposite: Beaded Apron, Manus, Admiralty Islands, Papua New Guinea

Traditionally, these beaded aprons made by the Matankol people of the south coast of Manus and off-lying islands consisted of traditional shell-money discs. But by the late nineteenth century, glass trade-beads with their wide range of bright colours had mostly replaced the old shell beads. Since the 1930s these modern versions have been worn by women at dances and festivals, including marriage and a special feast held by a rich man 15 to 20 years after his marriage. *Length 67 cm, width 47 cm.*

AM 2168. Presented by Mr James Adams Wilkes 1928.

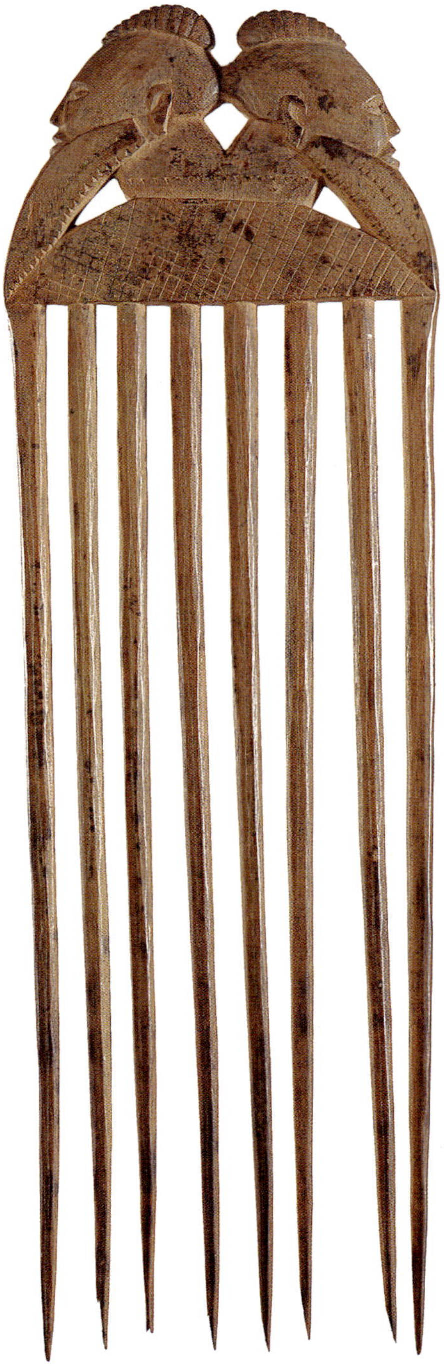

Kalakala, Comb, Kaniet (Anchorite) Islands, Western Bismarck Archipelago, Papua New Guinea

In the remote Kaniet Island group, influences from Micronesia mixed with Melanesian culture. Combs with bearded male heads, as on this one, were reserved for men, while women's combs had abstract geometric motifs. Men wore their *kalakala* above the forehead and fixed diagonally in their hair. As part of their initiation into manhood, Kaniet boys let their hair grow long during their seclusion and afterwards wore it in a complicated chignon that was *tapu* to a woman's touch. *Length 21 cm, width 6.5 cm.*

AM 15313. James Edge-Partington Collection. Presented by Dr Thomson Wilson Leys Memorial 1924.

Lal, *Trochus* Shell Arm Rings, Admiralty Islands, Papua New Guinea

Probably made mostly by the Matankol people of the off-shore islands around the big island of Manus, these arm rings have been shaped by knocking off the upper whorls of a *Trochus* shell, and polishing the resulting thin ring. This process is followed by many Melanesian craftsmen in different regions to make *Trochus* arm rings, but these are marked as distinctive to the Admiralty Islands by the particular geometric designs incised on them. These rings were then traded by their makers to all the other population groups of the Admiralty Islands and were worn by both men and women. from left: *Diameter 10.5 cm; diameter 10.5 cm; diameter 9.6 cm.*

from left: *AM 2277.4. Presented by Mr James Adams Wilkes 1928. AM 2277.1. Presented by Mr James Adams Wilkes 1928. AM 35335. Presented by Mrs S. Payne 1958.*

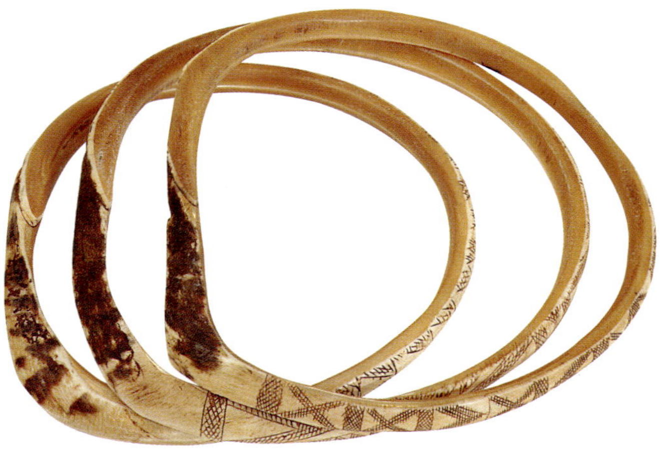

opposite: Widow's Head Ornament, Admiralty Islands, Papua New Guinea

Fine rattan strips have been tied into a lattice structure that supports patterned bands of glass beads. A plaited fibre cord was tied at the back of the head, holding the ornament across the forehead. This ornament was apparently worn by women of the Manus people on the south coast of big Manus and off-lying islands as part of a widow's attire. *Length 24 cm, width 25.5 cm.*

AM 52301.1.

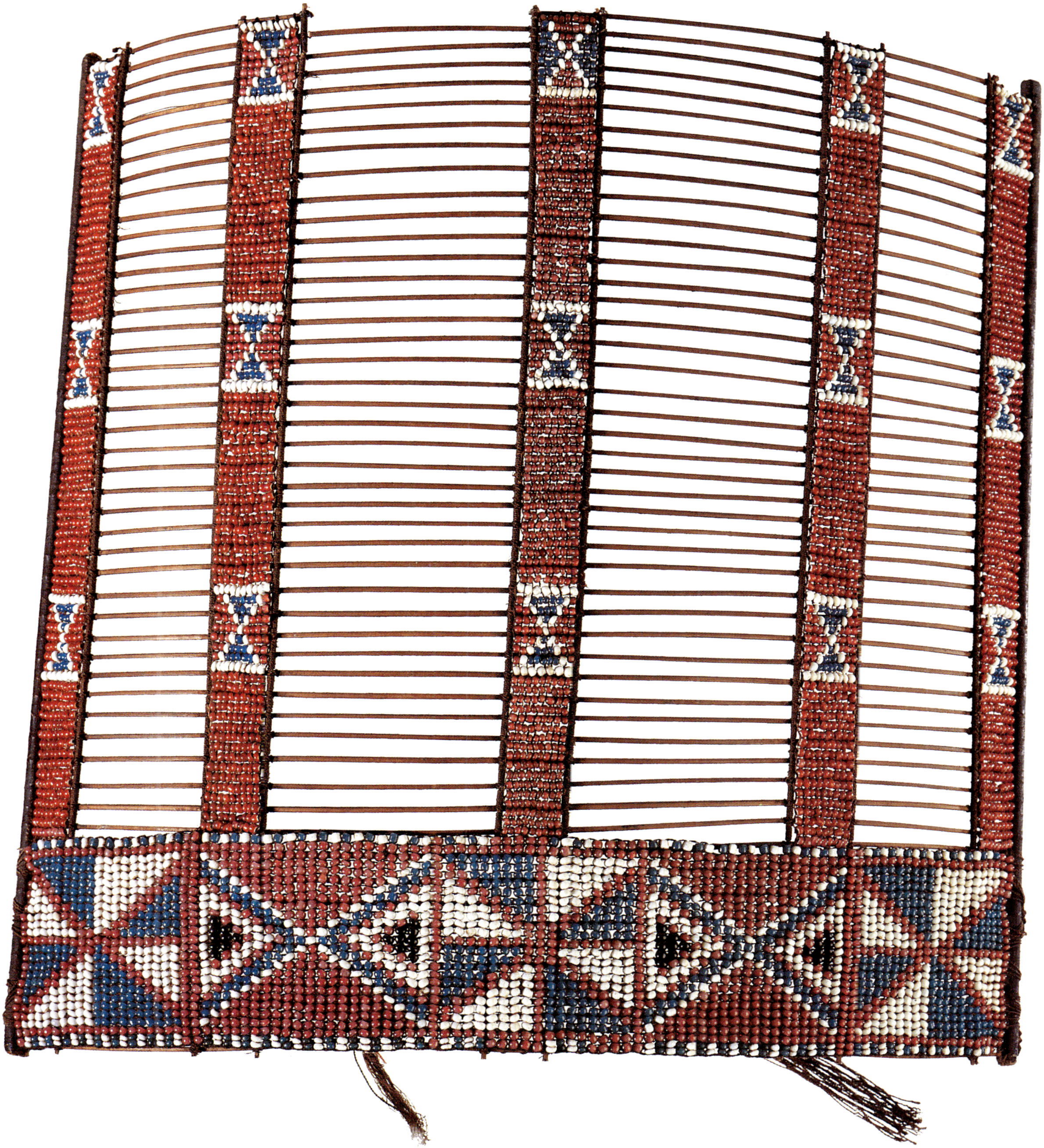

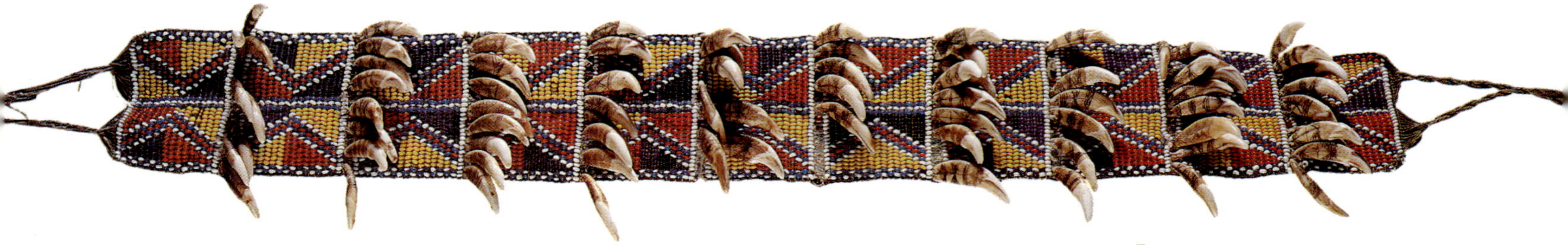

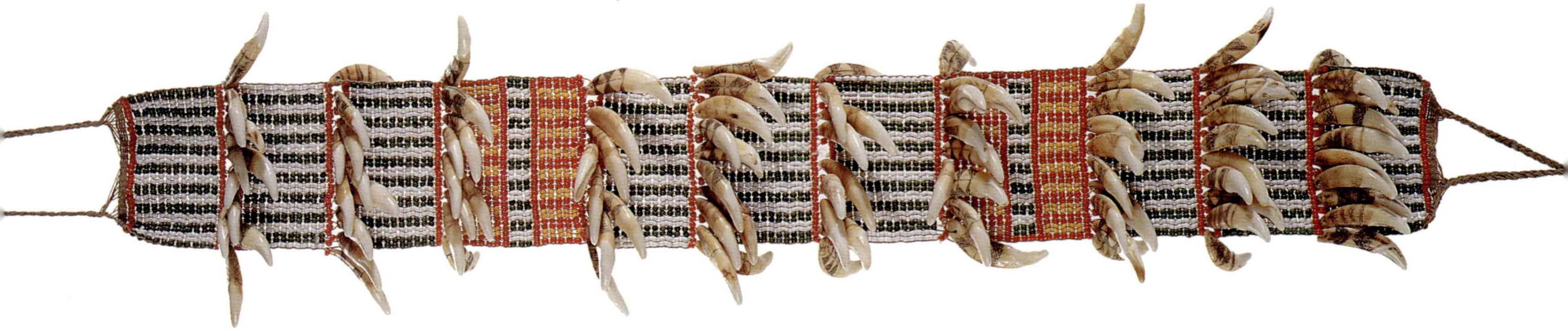

Beaded Belts, Admiralty Islands, Papua New Guinea

In this mid-twentieth century version of an old form, glass trade-beads have been strung in regular patterns to create a definite unit of monetary value, based on the traditional value of incised dog teeth, usually arranged in ten rows of ten teeth each. Men incise the patterns on the teeth and women plait them into the belt. Worn mostly as a belt or occasionally as a head band, these belts also figure as part of the bride price. from top: *Length 57 cm, width 9.5 cm; length 47 cm, width 10 cm.*

from top: *AM 55037. Purchased from Mr N. Devine 1995.*
AM 47815. Purchased from Rev. N. Basket 1976.

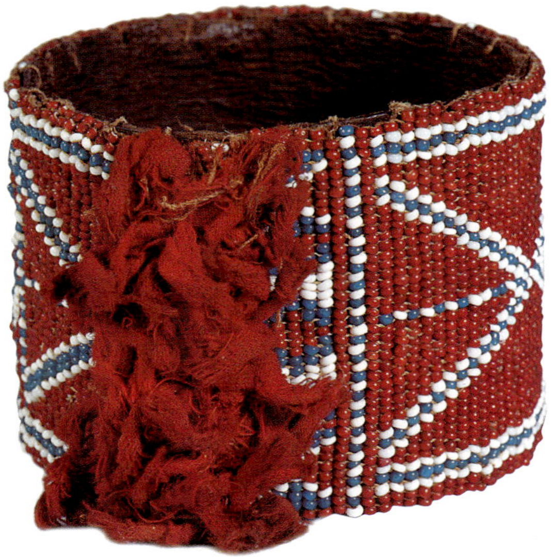

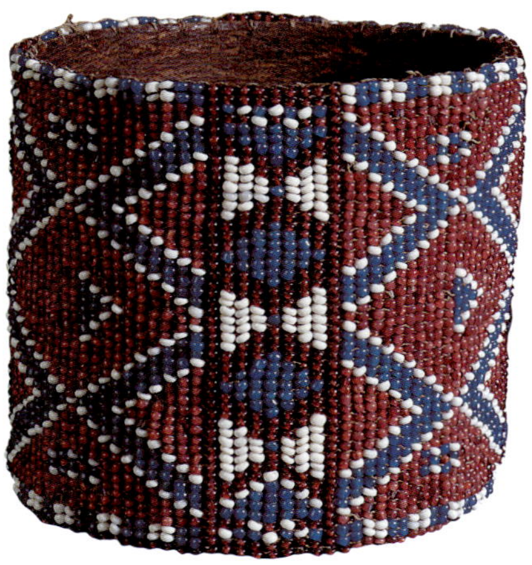

Arm Bands, Manus, Admiralty Islands, Papua New Guinea

Narrow arm bands were usually worn on the upper arm and wider bands like these were worn on the wrist as a cuff, by both men and women, especially among the Matankol and Manus peoples around the coasts and off-shore islands. They do not seem to have been present among the Ussiai groups of the interior. Women have made these arm bands by sewing small introduced glass beads on to a bark foundation. Beaded arm bands are worn as everyday ornament and more so on special occasions. They also serve as part of the bride price. from top: *Height 6.5 cm; height 8 cm.*

from top:*AM 2160. Presented by Mr James Adams Wilkes 1928.*
AM 55353.

opposite: Necklace, Admiralty Islands, Papua New Guinea

This is a woman's necklace of glass trade-beads supporting pendants of dog teeth attached together in pairs. Dog teeth featured prominently on many Admiralty Islands ornaments, and were often embellished with incised geometric designs. *Length 36 cm.*

AM 35337. Presented by Mrs S. Payne 1959.

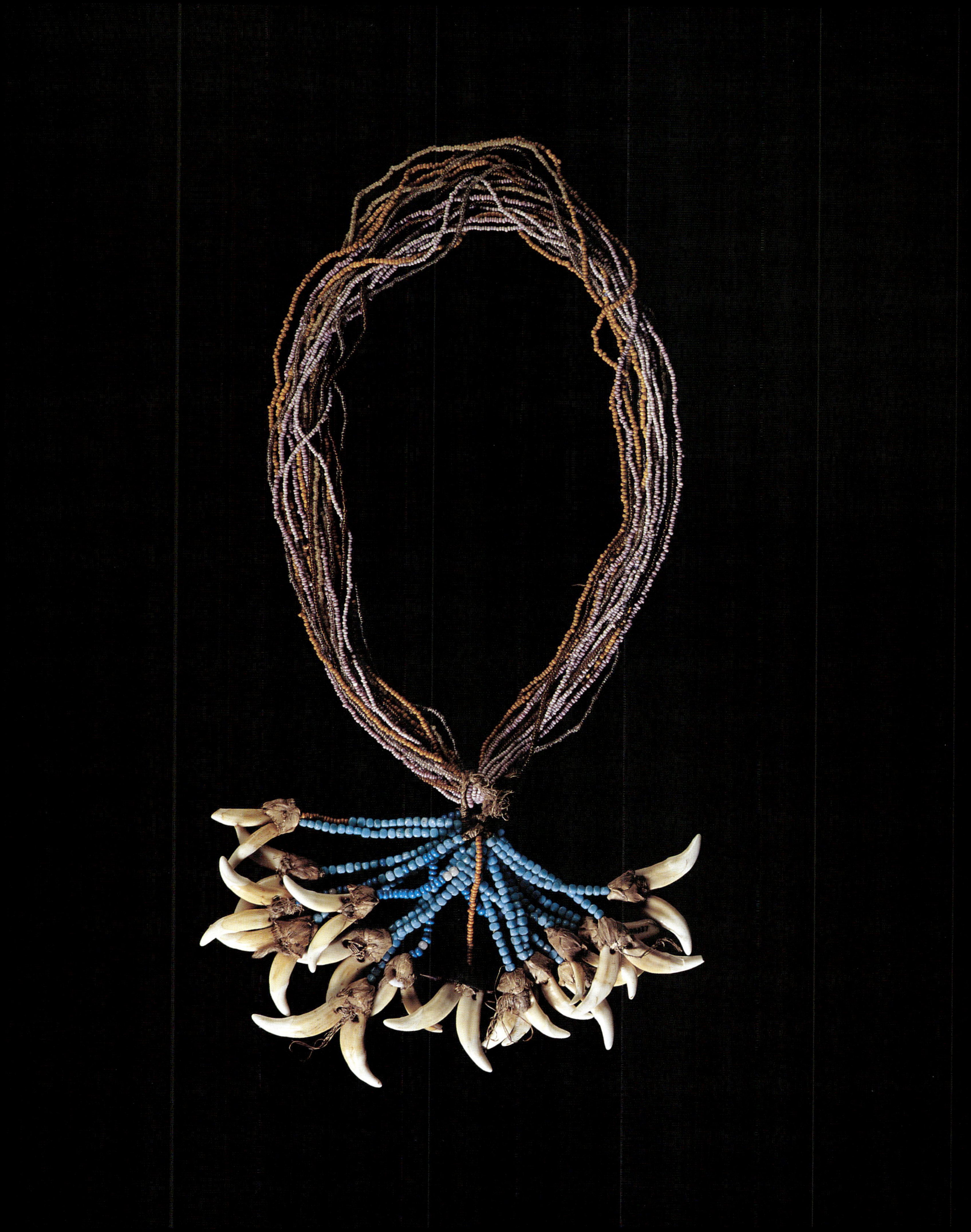

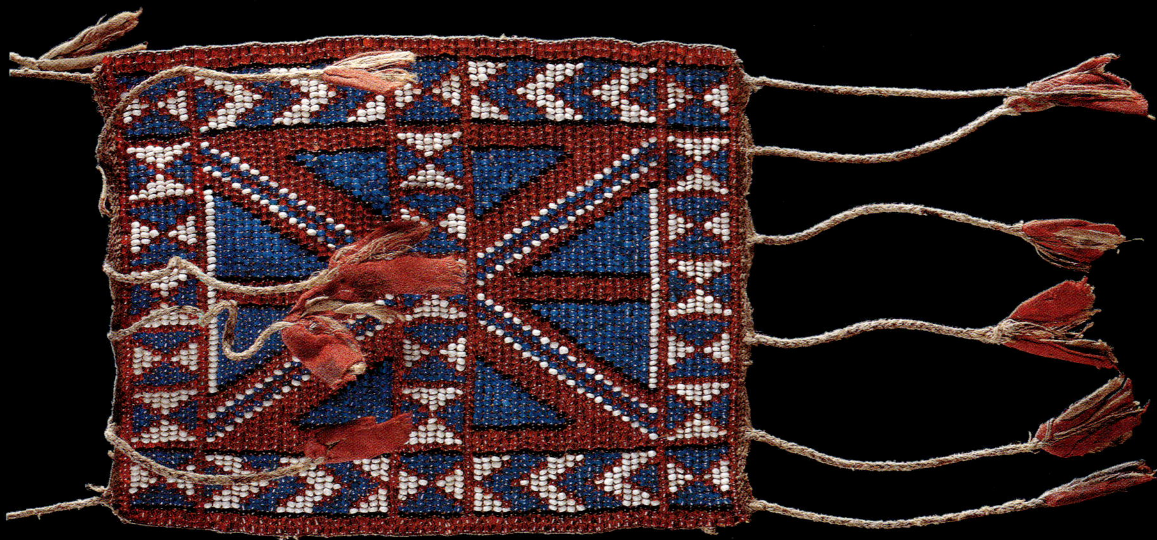

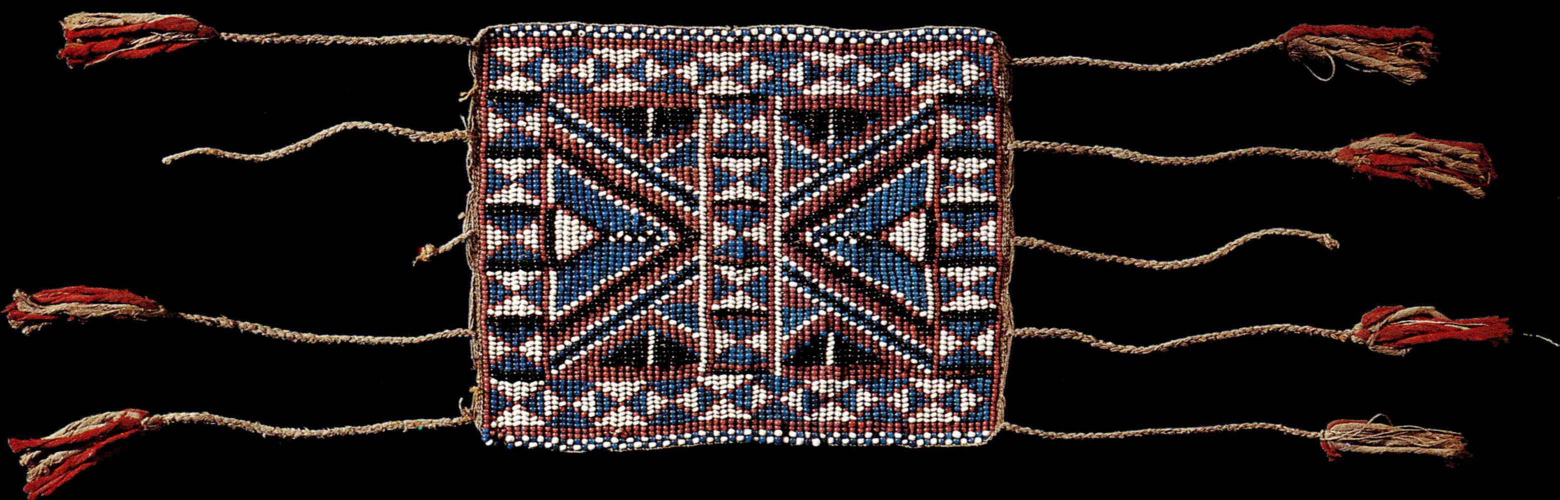

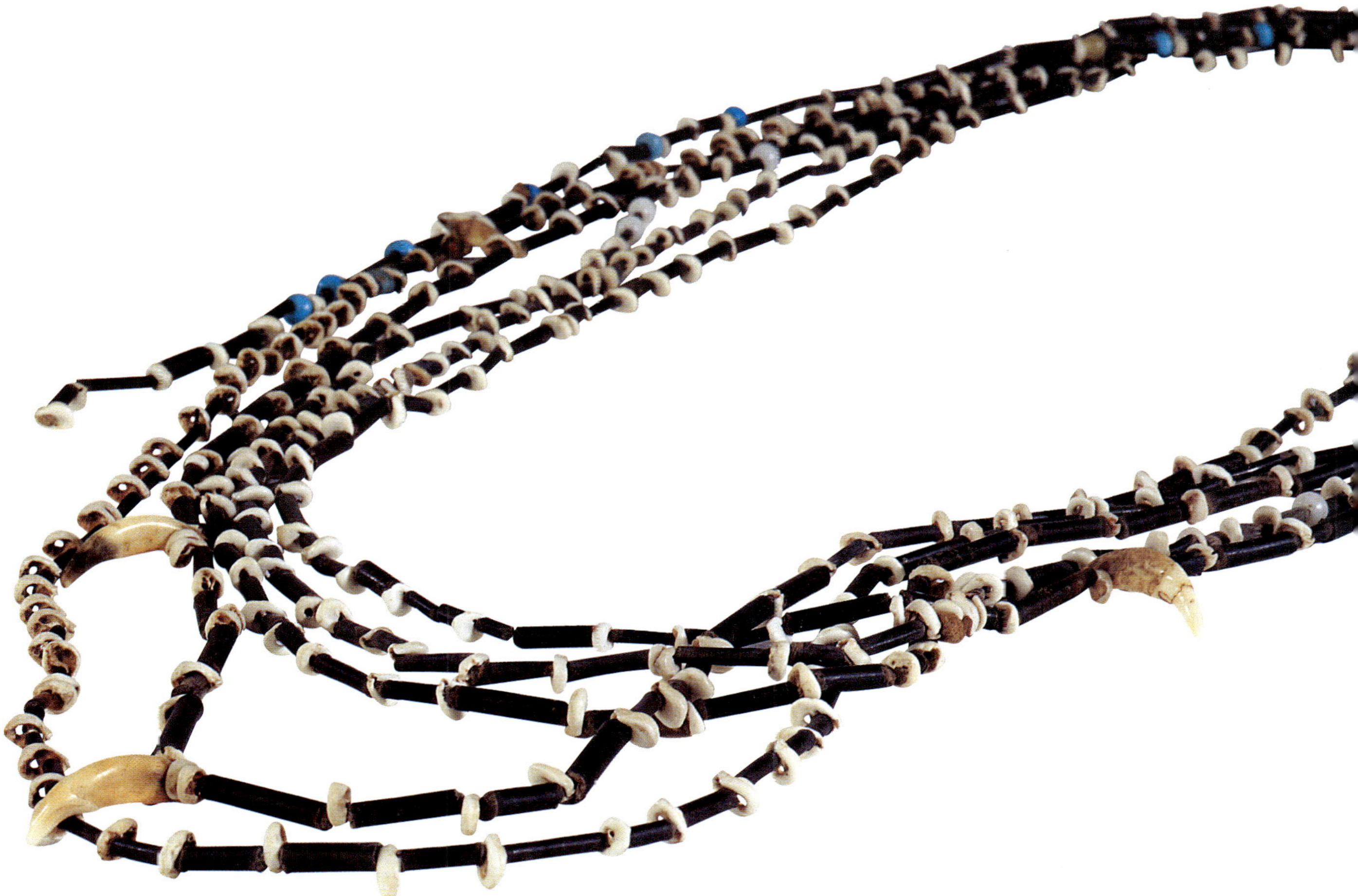

NASSA SHELL NECKLACE, NEW BRITAIN

In western New Britain on both the north and south coasts, strings of alternating *Nassa* shells and cassowary feather quills were worn as necklaces, usually consisting of a very long loop wound several times around the neck. They also served as currency and were stored in large quantities packed into baskets and kept in private houses. This string has been given extra monetary and ornamental aesthetic value by the addition of dog teeth and glass trade-beads. *Length 414 cm.*

AM 21063. Presented by Mr R. Holmes 1934.

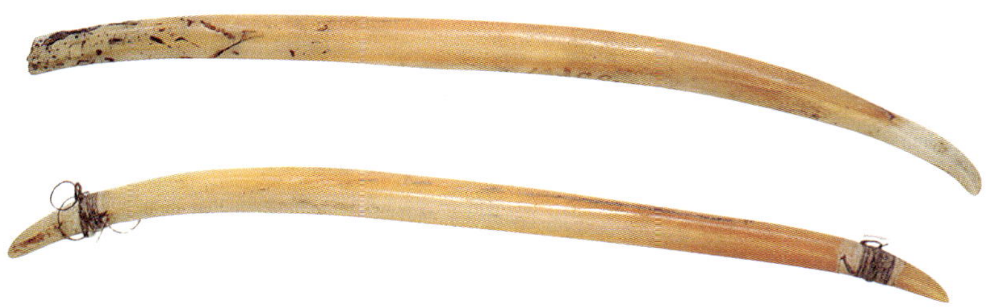

NOSE PINS, ADMIRALTY ISLANDS, PAPUA NEW GUINEA

Cut, ground and polished from sub-fossil *Tridacna* clam shell with its characteristic orange tinge, these nose pins were worn horizontally through the pierced nasal septum with the curved ends pointing downwards. In the Admiralty Islands, both men and women wore nose pins, with women favouring short downcurved models. Most people had their nasal septum pierced while quite young and wore various plugs and ornaments to keep it open, but this practice was discontinued in the later twentieth century. from top: *Length 14.8 cm; length 14.7 cm.*

from top: *AM 11480. Purchased from Mr G. Stuart 1888.*
AM 10309. Presented by Mr H. E. Vaile 1926.

opposite: LEG ORNAMENTS, ADMIRALTY ISLANDS, PAPUA NEW GUINEA

Admiralty Islands women use a complicated warp-plaiting technique to make patterned, glass beadwork leg cuffs. These are worn above the ankle with the tie cords towards the front. In the past it seems that both men and women wore these but today they are an important part of a bride's wedding outfit. from top: *Length (without ties) 17 cm, width 13.3 cm; length (without ties) 20 cm, width 16.5 cm.*

from top: *AM 13639. Rev. A. H. Voyce Collection. Presented by Sir William Goodfellow 1934.*
AM 4964. Rev. A. H. Voyce Collection. Presented by Sir William Goodfellow 1934.

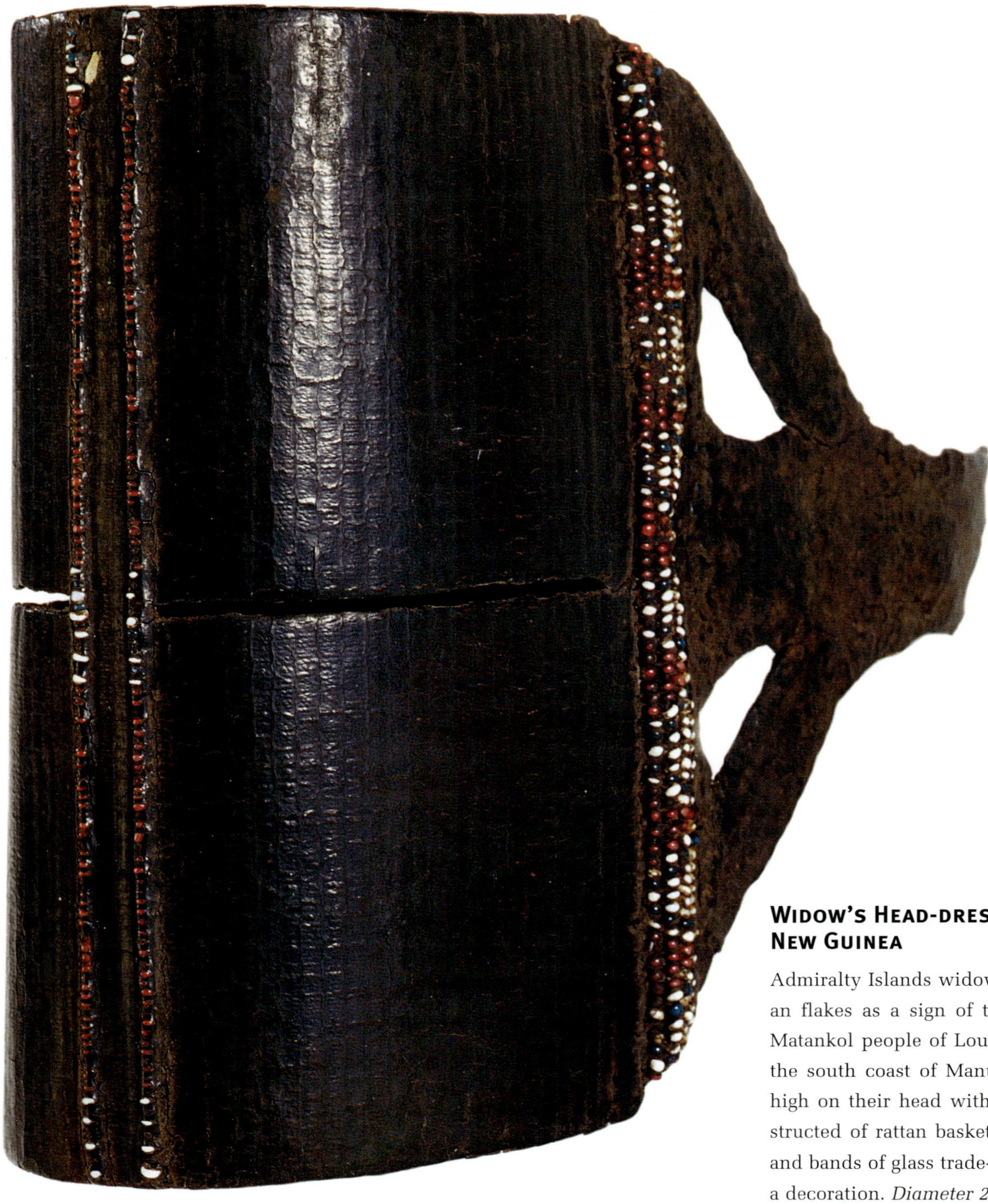

WIDOW'S HEAD-DRESS, ADMIRALTY ISLANDS, PAPUA NEW GUINEA

Admiralty Islands widows shaved their hair off with obsidian flakes as a sign of their mourning. Widows among the Matankol people of Lou and Pak Islands and the Manus on the south coast of Manus Island also wore this head-dress high on their head with the opening to the back. It is constructed of rattan basketwork coated with *Parinarium* gum, and bands of glass trade-beads have been set into the gum as a decoration. *Diameter 20 cm, height 17.5 cm.*

AM 2196.1. Presented by Mr James Adams Wilkes 1928.

opposite: ***MIDDI*, ORNAMENTAL COLLAR, TOLAI PEOPLE, GAZELLE PENINSULA, NEW BRITAIN**

To make this ornament, numerous *Nassa* shells have been perforated and sewn to a cane foundation. *Nassa* shells to be used as *tambu* shell currency were prepared differently, so that the *middi* did not have monetary value. Instead, because of their magical powers, *middi* were formerly worn by Tolai warriors seeking protection in battle. This one was collected by The Reverend George Brown, one of the first missionaries in the Gazelle Peninsula. *Length 68 cm.*

AM 11515. Presented by Rev. George Brown 1878.

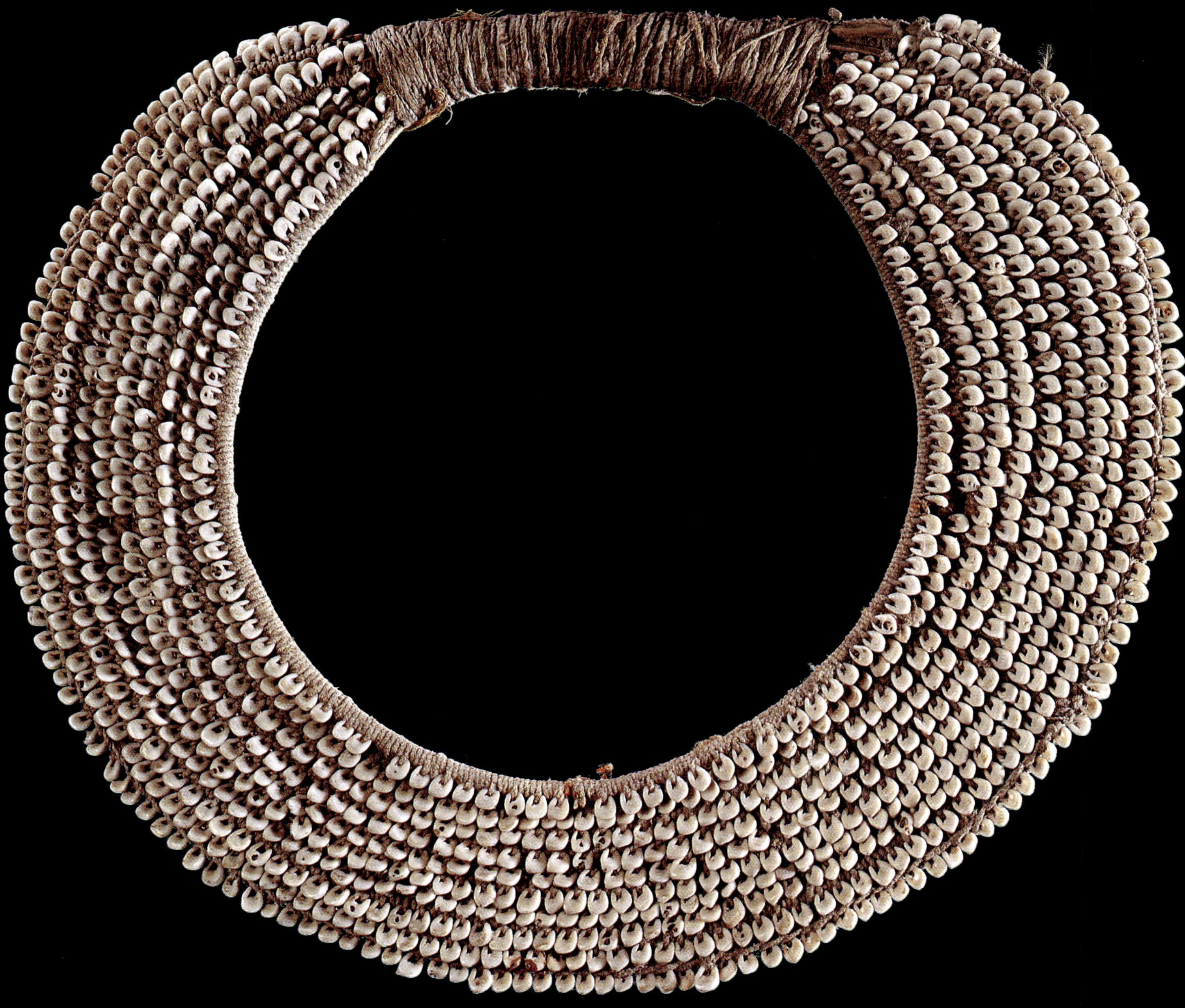

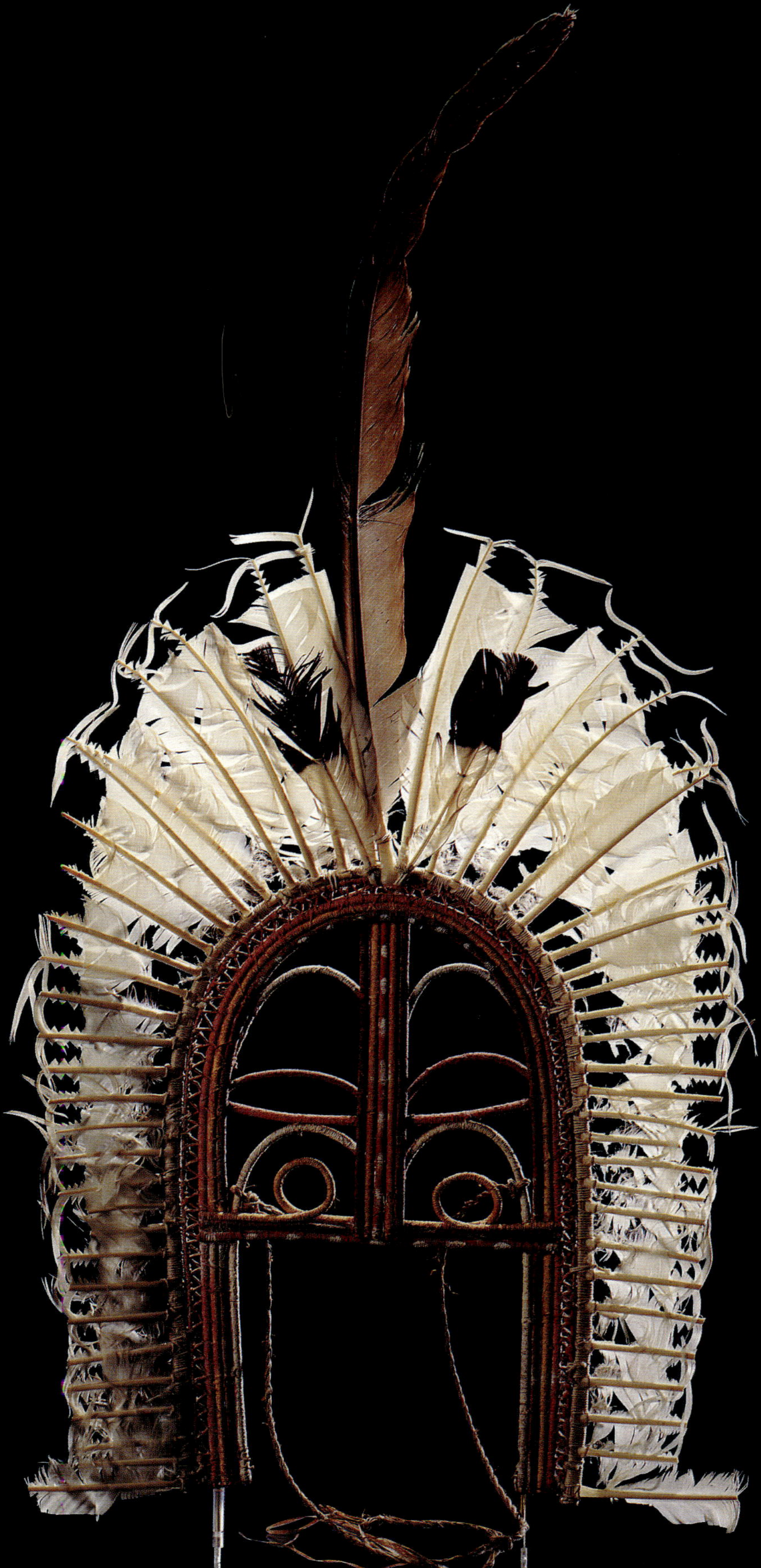

O, Betrothal Ornament, Torres Strait Islands

Usually cut from the side of a *Conus* shell, this triangular shell pendant was worn with various other ornaments down the back of a betrothed girl for about two months before her wedding. This alerted other men that she was spoken for and was therefore to be treated with respect. This example has been cut from a piece of introduced white ceramic ware which has been chosen because of its resemblance to the traditional shell. *Length 7.5 cm, width 6.5 cm.*

AM 15816. James Edge-Partington Collection. Presented by Dr Thomson Wilson Leys Memorial 1924.

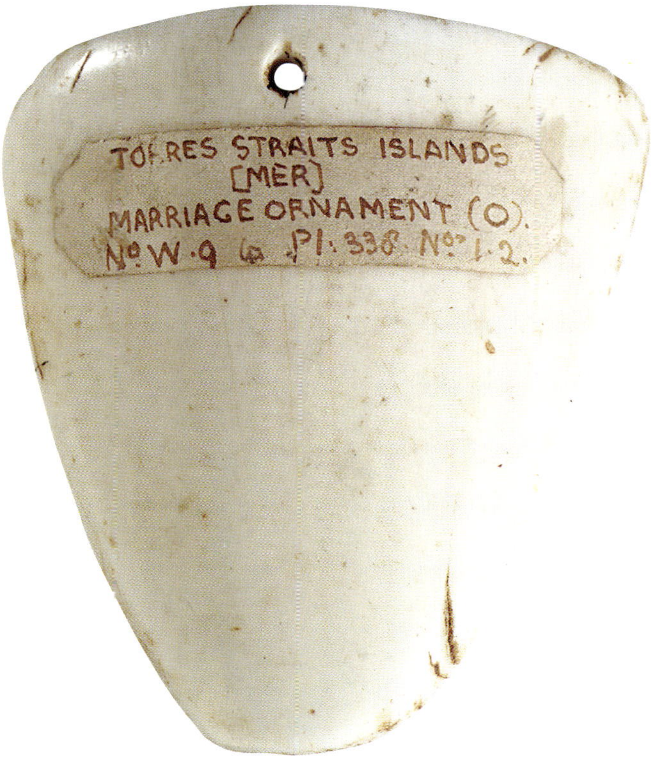

Musur, Arm Band, Torres Strait

This arm band is plaited from fine rattan and decorated with ribbons of introduced red cloth stripped from old garments. Some red and blue glass trade-beads have also been incorporated into the decorations. Worn constantly on the upper arm, especially by men, these arm bands are also accoutrements for dance costume, and often have sprigs of scented herbs tucked into them. When A. C. Haddon, the famous ethnographer of Torres Strait culture, collected this arm band, probably in 1888, he recorded that it was worn at the *Koppa-Koppa* (nowadays known as *kap-kap*), which is a general creole-pidgin term adopted by the islanders to cover all their secular dances performed on important social occasions. *Height 7.5 cm.*

AM 15820.3. James Edge-Partington Collection. Presented by Dr Thomson Wilson Leys Memorial 1924.

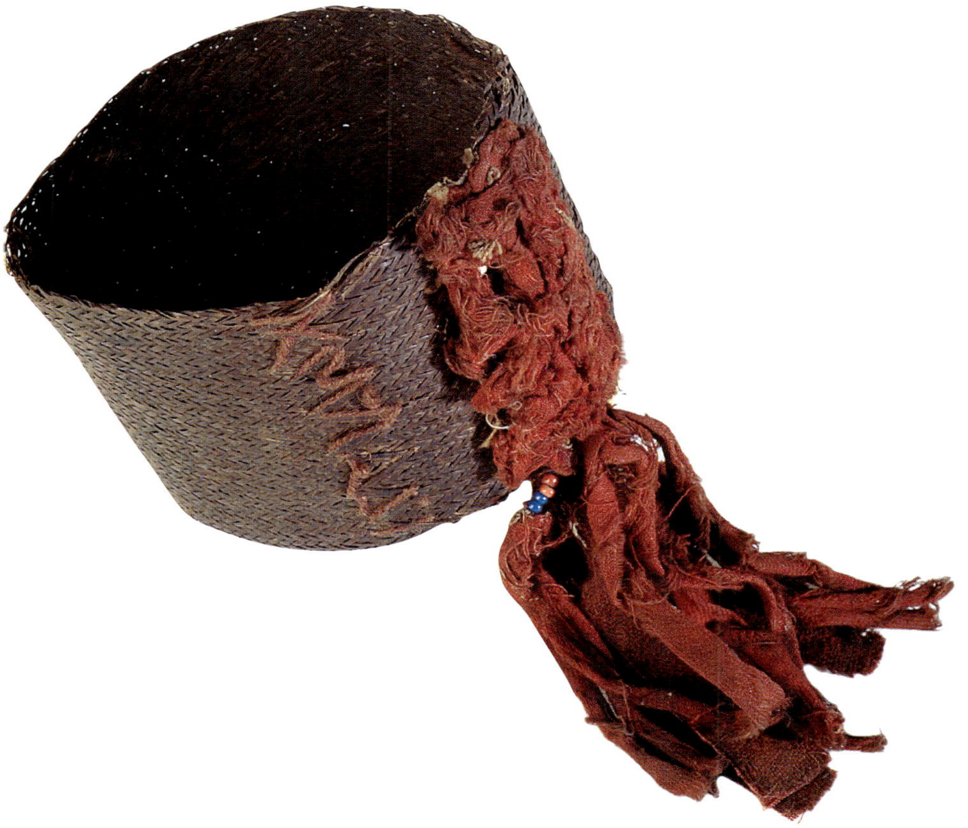

opposite: ***Dari* Head-dress, Mer (Murray) Island, Torres Strait**

Collected in 1964 and probably made not long before that, this modern *dari* retains all the traditional features of this head-dress, which has become a modern icon of Torres Strait culture and is featured on their flag. A cane frame wrapped in coloured wools supports specially trimmed and shaped seabird feathers. *Dari* were worn by men in warfare and ceremonial dance, and are still prominent in modern costume. *Height 64 cm, width 30 cm.*

AM 55223. Purchased at auction, 1997.

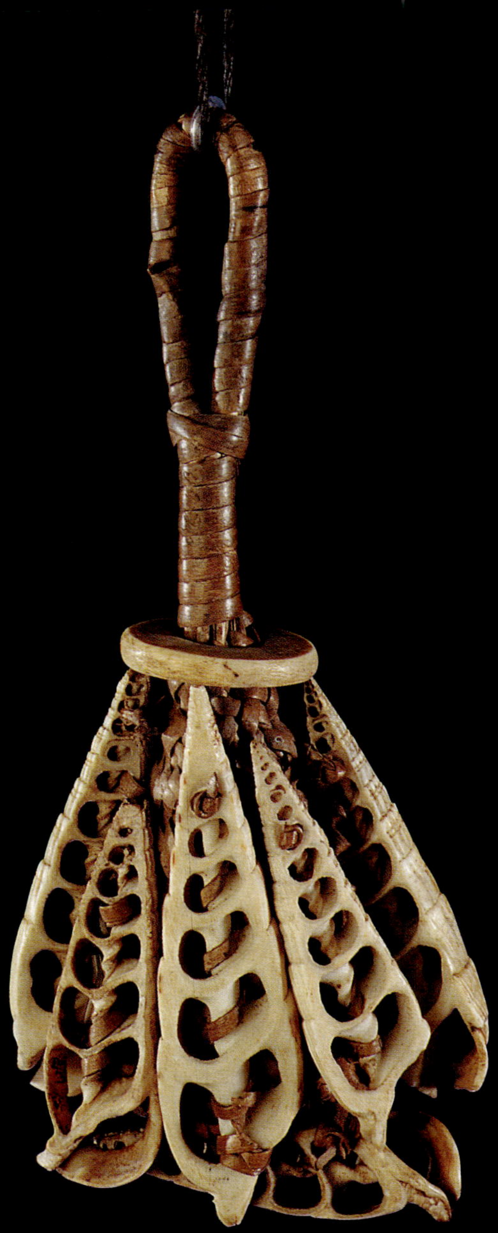

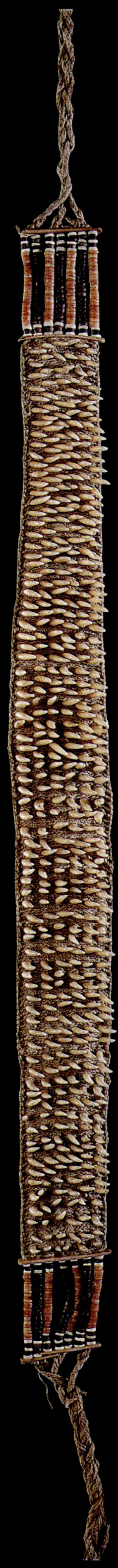

Hope, Charm, Marovo Lagoon, New Georgia, Solomon Islands

Charms in the Solomon Islands may be worn about the person or hung on canoes or houses. They are intended to convey or control the powers of the supernatural world and therefore may be used in magic to increase personal wealth, to ensure success in hunting, to protect the wearer from illness and sorcery, or to make the wearer attractive to the opposite sex. This charm, which was usually tied to the back of a warrior's shield, consists of a plaited cane case containing a human tooth and covered with cut sections of shells. *Length 14.5 cm, width 6.5 cm.*

AM 15241. James Edge-Partington Collection. Presented by Dr Thomson Wilson Leys Memorial 1924.

Belt, San Cristobal, Solomon Islands

Set in a fibre backing, this belt has porpoise teeth and the ends are decorated with red and black shell money discs. This would be worn as part of an elaborate outfit with a range of body ornaments. Porpoise teeth figure in many items of currency and body ornament, thereby combining these two values to enhance the status of the wearer. *Length 70 cm, width 4.3 cm.*

AM 11555. Purchased from Mr G. Stuart 1888.

opposite: Carved Bust, Vella Lavella, Solomon Islands

Naturalistic sculptures of men and women were produced in the New Georgia and Vella Lavella areas in the later nineteenth century, probably made for sale to European traders and possibly representing particular persons. Many have the same sorts of ornaments worn by living people at that time, such as the shell money necklaces, extended earlobes with plugs, and *Nautilus* shell inlay matching the patterns of contemporary fashionable face painting. *Height 25 cm, width 17.5 cm.*

AM 47645. Purchased from Mr A. M. Bensley 1976.

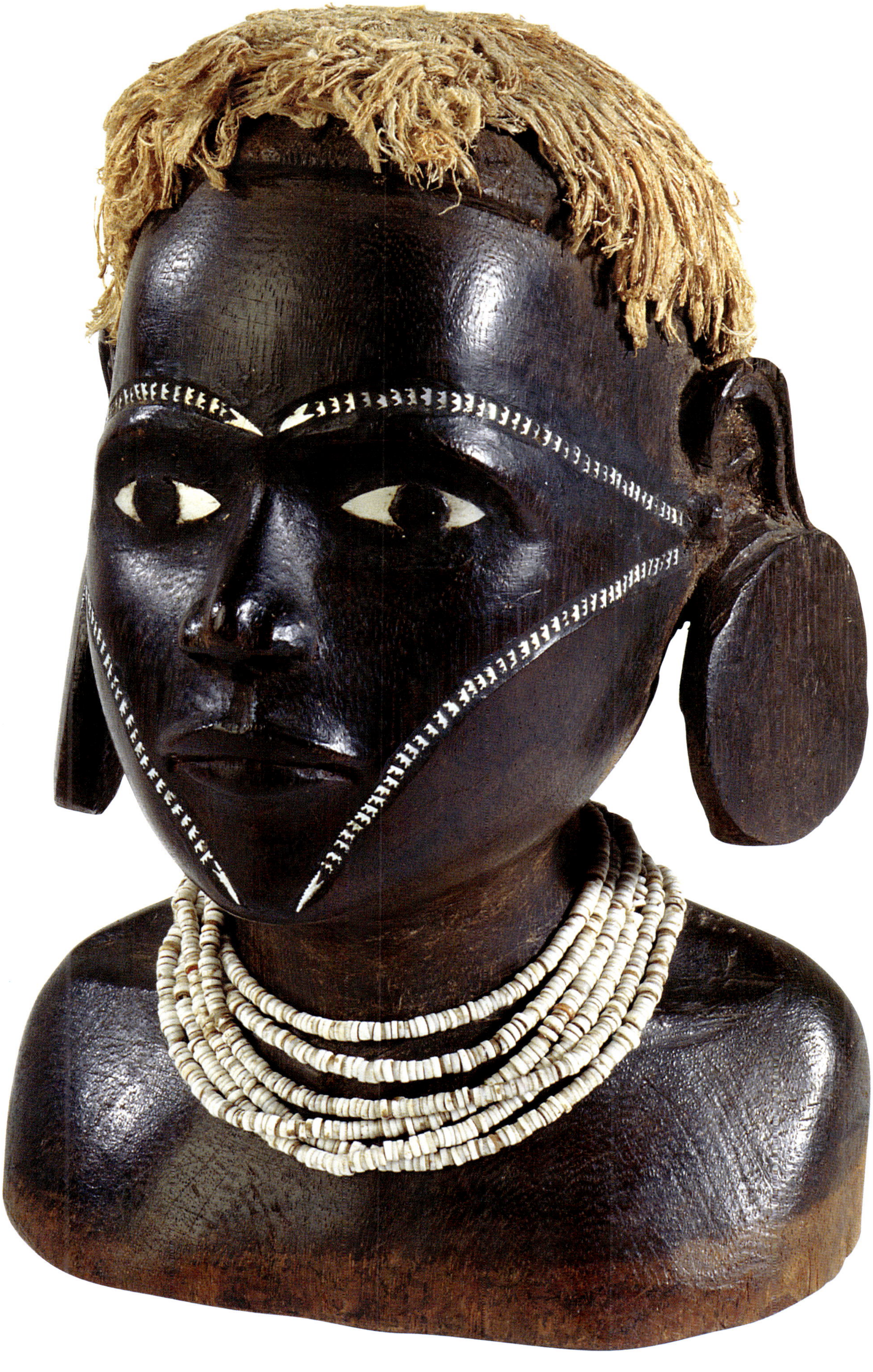

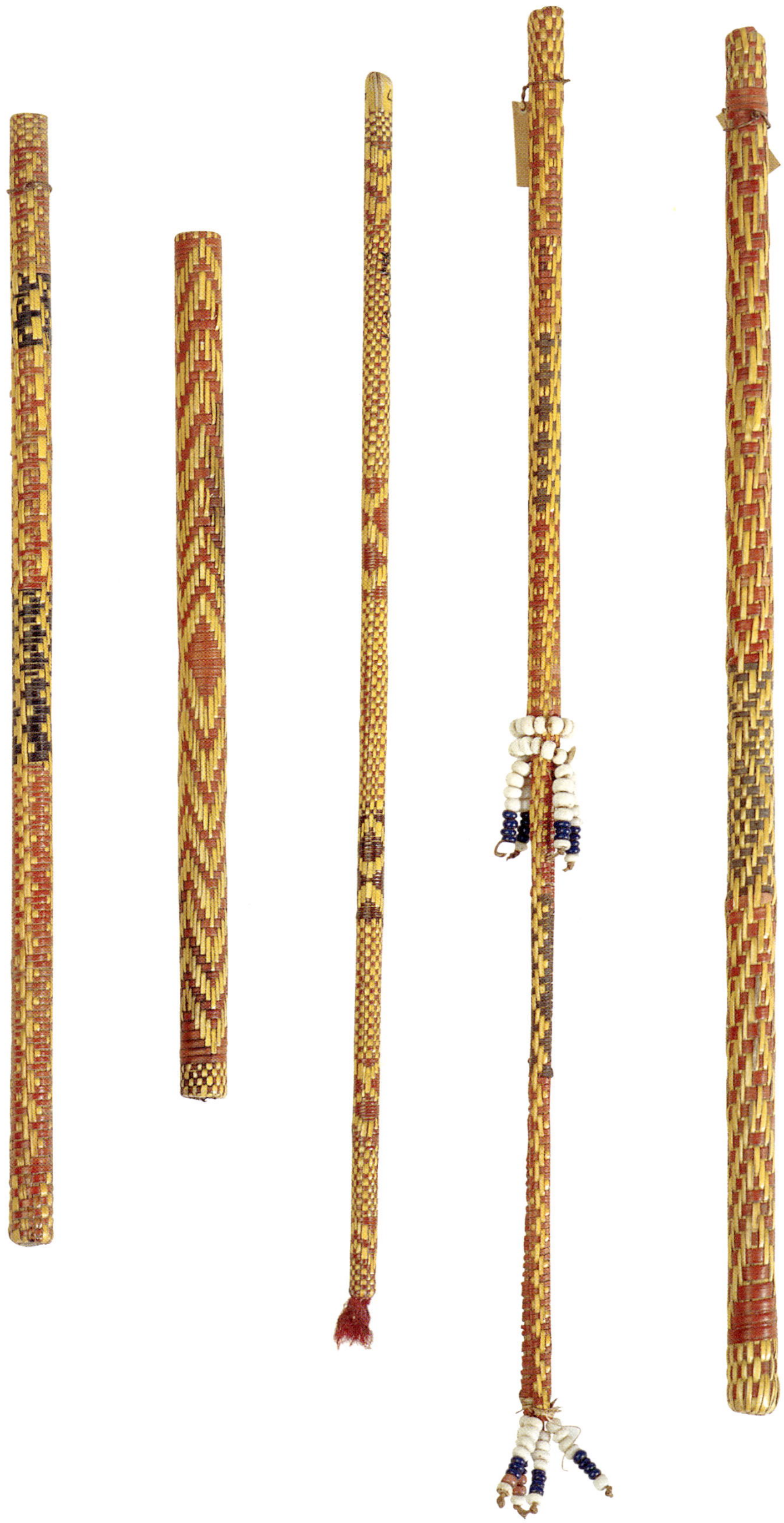

Ear Sticks, Malaita, Solomon Islands

Women of the East Kwaio hill people of Malaita construct these finely detailed ear ornaments by plaiting very narrow strips of coloured plant materials over a base of a cane or bamboo stick. The yellow is vascular tissue of orchid vine and the red is waxy tissue of coconut palm dyed red with an extract of *Morinda* root. Some sticks are also ornamented with glass trade-beads and red wool. These reached the coastal people of Malaita as trade items from the inland hill dwellers and were worn by men through their perforated earlobes. from left: *Length 18.7 cm; length 14.4 cm; length 21.1 cm; length 24.8 cm; length 22.7 cm.*

from left: *AM 8897.1. Purchased from Miss Poule 1920.*
AM 8897.2. Purchased from Miss Poule 1920.
AM 41767. Presented by Mrs F. Clarke 1969.
AM 8901. Purchased from Miss Poule 1920.
AM 8897.3. Purchased from Miss Poule 1920.

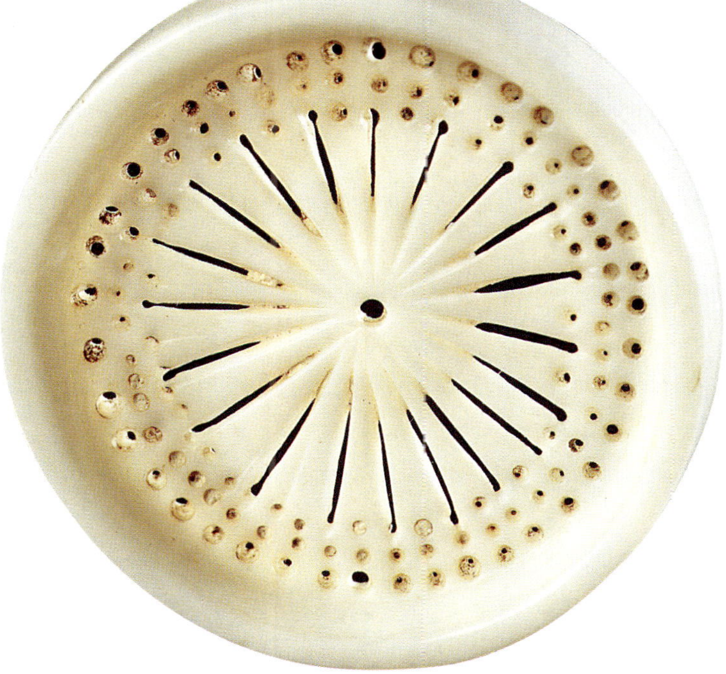

Shell Earlobe Ornament, Solomon Islands

Shaped from the shell of the giant *Tridacna* clam, these ornaments are worn in the pierced extended earlobe of men and women. Many carved figures from the Solomon Islands also show extended earlobes. As well as ornaments such as plugs and sticks, the open loop of the earlobe also became a handy place to carry small utensils such as a tobacco pipe. *Diameter 5 cm.*

AM 32291. Presented by Rev. C. Palmer 1951.

Kia, Chest Ornament, Shortland Islands, Solomon Islands

Made entirely from glass trade-beads with shell pendants at the bottom, this very rare form of ornament is said to have been worn by women, although it was probably owned by their husbands. Traditional forms of this ornament were made from individually and laboriously drilled shell discs; but in this one, the craftswoman has taken full advantage of the wide range of multicoloured imported glass beads becoming available in the later nineteenth century. *Length 69 cm.*

AM 15242. James Edge-Partington Collection. Presented by Dr Thomson Wilson Leys Memorial 1924.

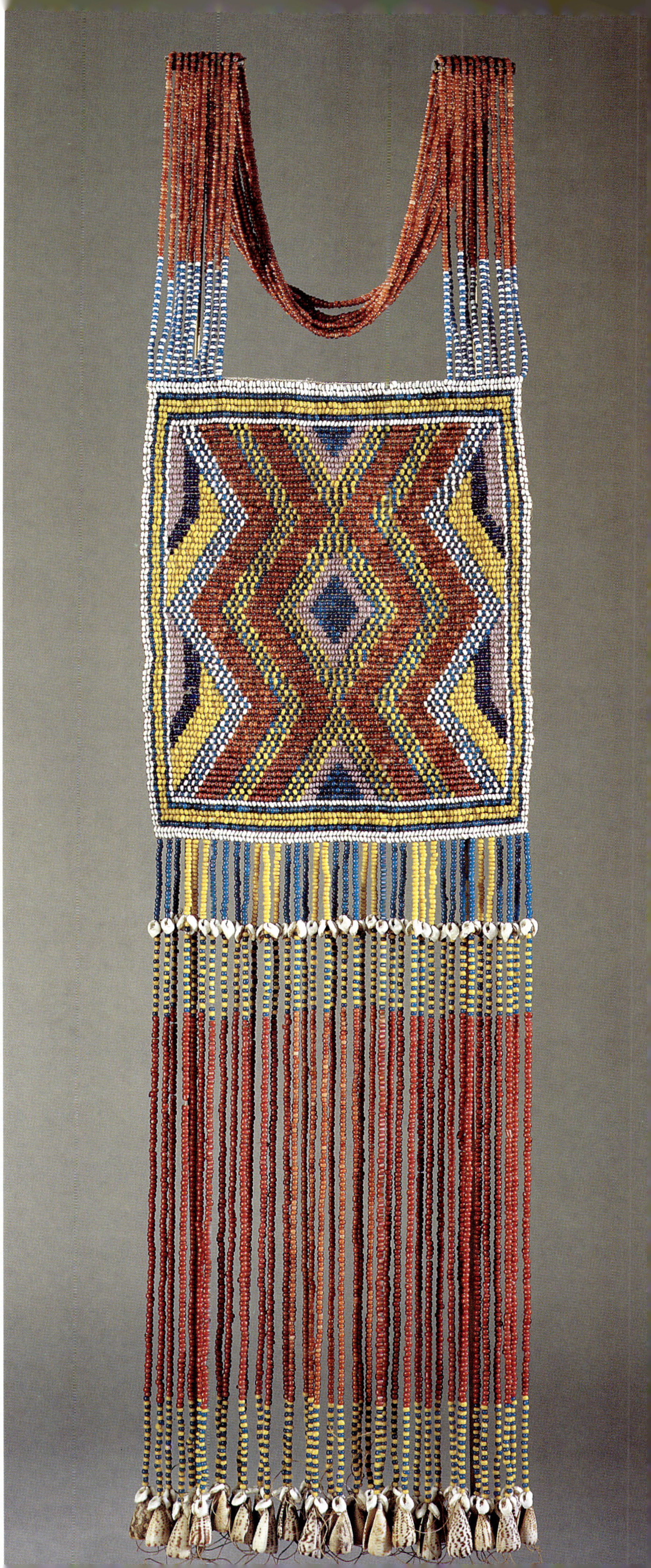

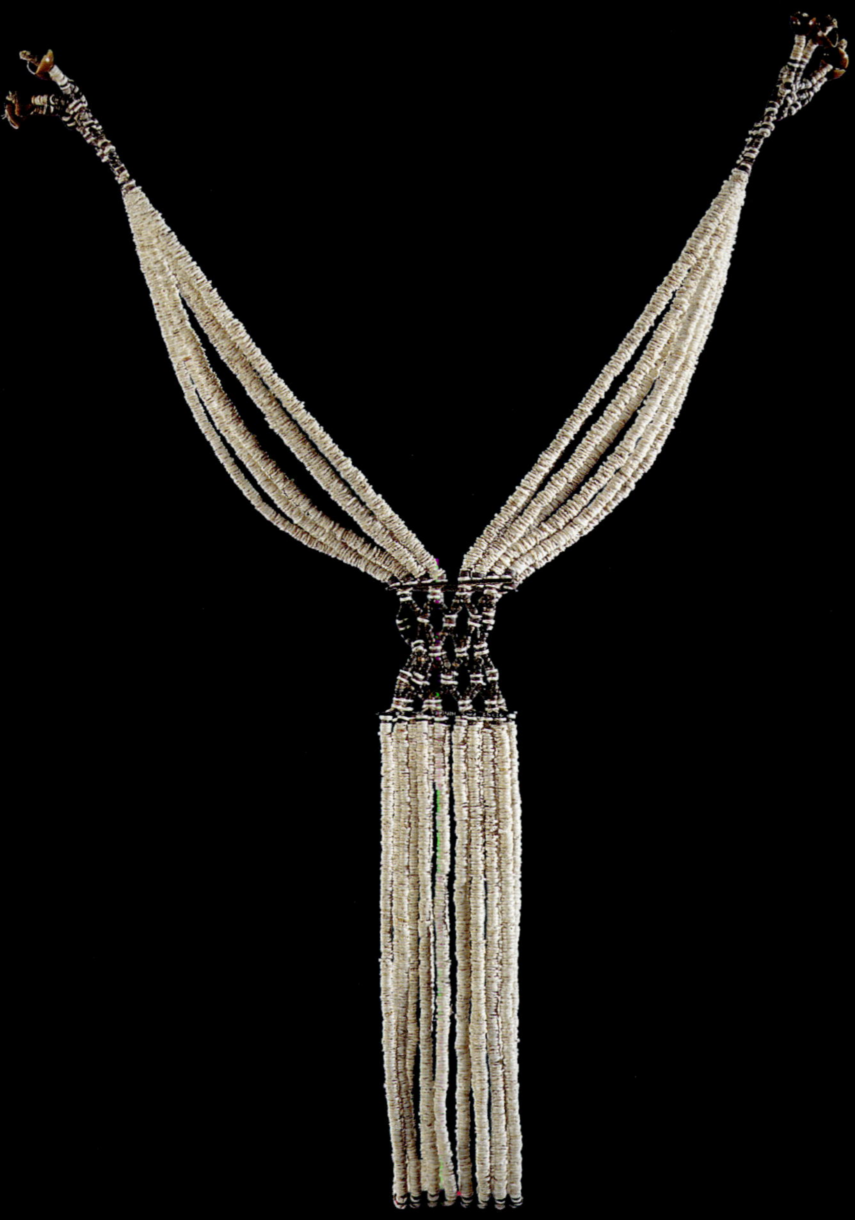

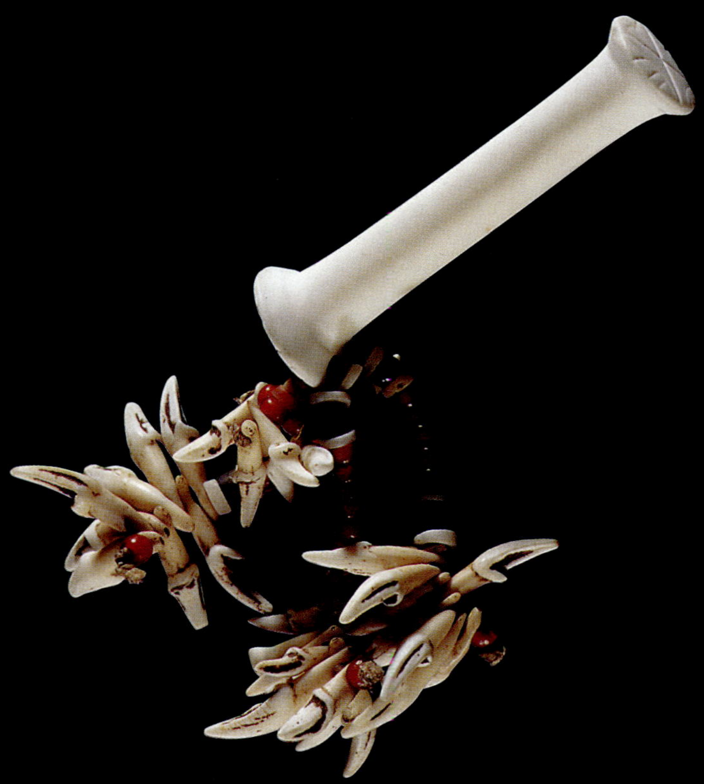

Chest Ornament, Malaita, Solomon Islands

This ornament consists of strings of fine, drilled, white shell discs held apart by spacers of turtle shell, and with seeds at the ends. A war leader or *ramo* of Malaita wore it as part of his ceremonial dress, around the neck and crossing over the chest with the criss-cross arrangement of brown and white shells at the centre of his chest. Shell discs like this also represent wealth, indicating the leader's status as a big-man who has achieved his position by sound economic management. *Length 64.5 cm.*

AM 47397. Presented by Miss Street 1976.

Ear Ornament, Solomon Islands

Glass trade-beads, shell money discs, and flying-fox teeth have been combined to form decorative tassels on the end of this delicate shell earplug. This is as much an expression of value as of aesthetics, but the red glass beads were probably considered more as a fashion statement. *Length (of ear plug) 4 cm.*

AM 32373.5. Presented by Rev. C. Palmer 1951.

opposite: Necklace, Ulawa, Solomon Islands

Highly polished *Conus* shell rings attached to a plaited fibre neck cord make a heavy necklace, worn by a man as part of his warrior's outfit. *Conus* shells were used to make two other main forms of ornament, either as open rings to be worn as arm bands or as discs ground flat that could be worn singly as a chest pendant or strung into a necklace. *Length 57 cm.*

AM 13164. Purchased from Mrs Porter 1919.

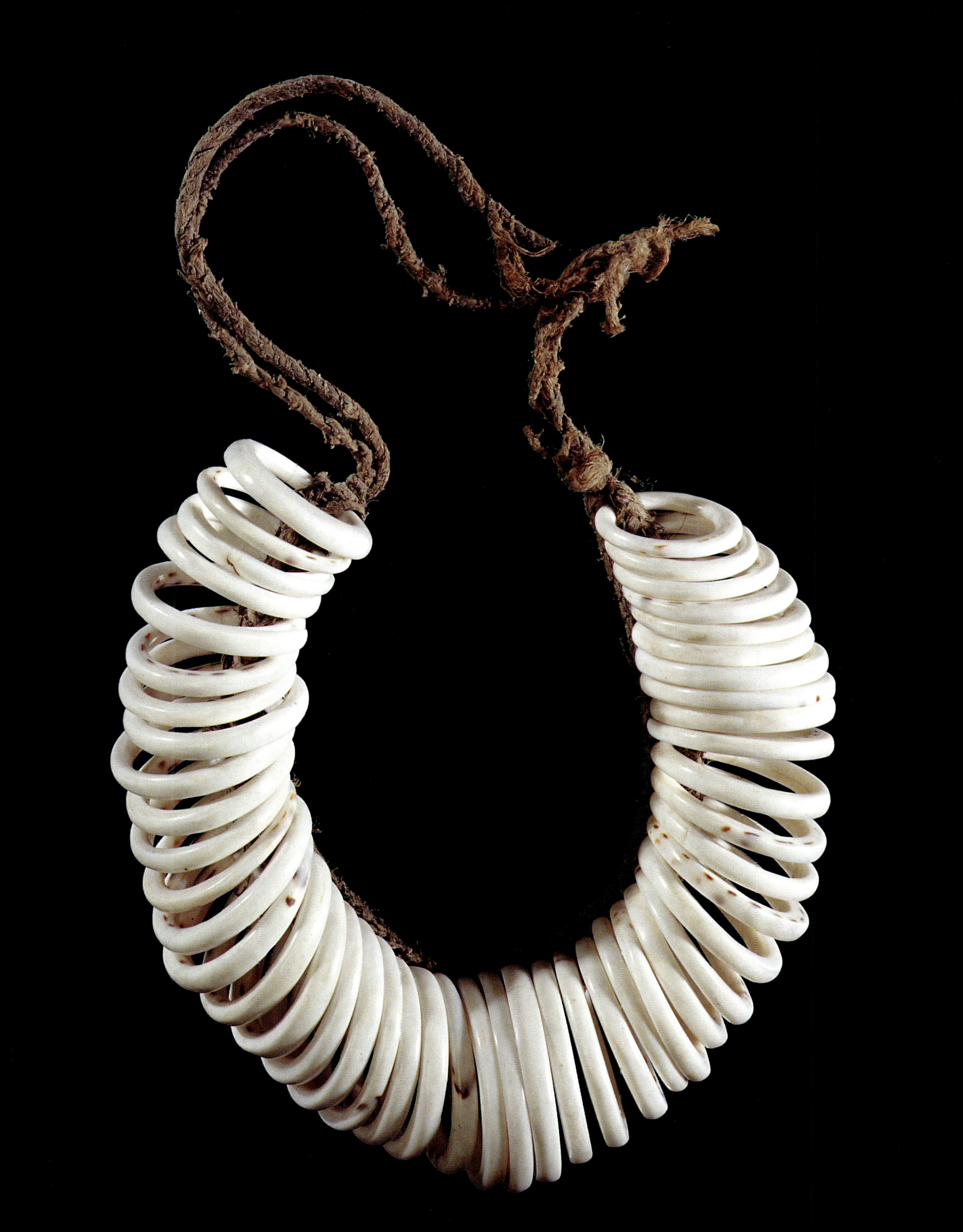

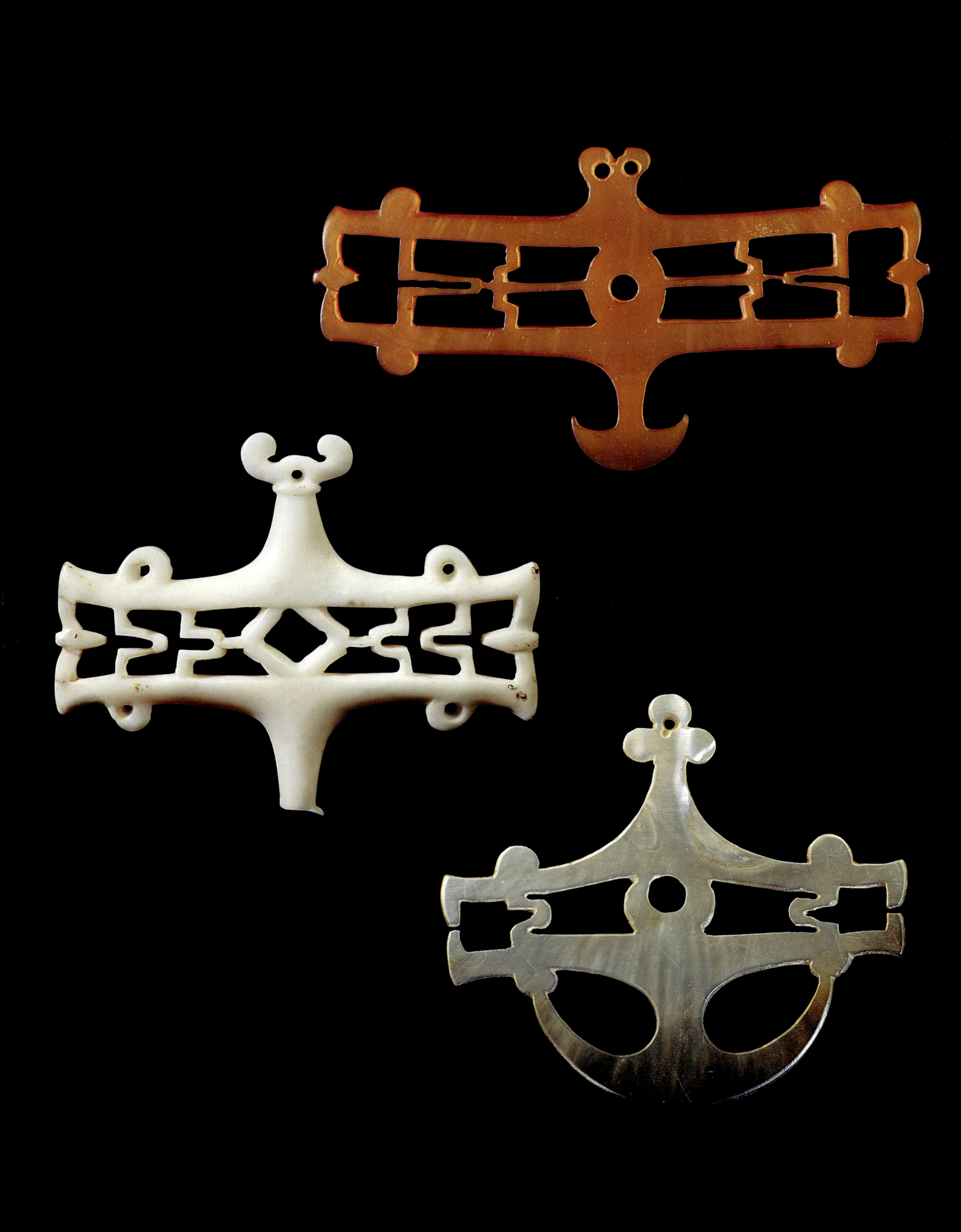

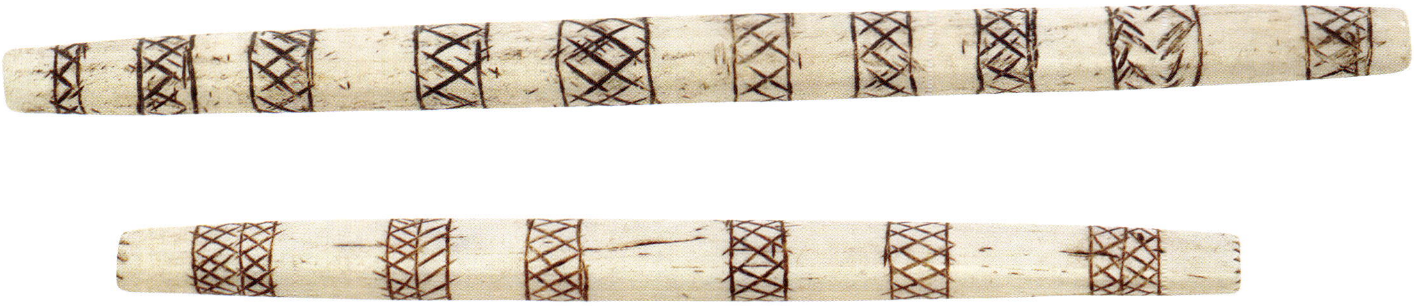

Nose Pins, Malaita, Solomon Islands

In their full ensemble of ornaments, coastal Malaitan men were weighed down with heavy shell head-dresses, combs, forehead bands, ear ornaments, necklaces, breast pendants, armlets, belts and nose pins. The British artefact collector James Edge-Partington noted that only warriors who had committed a homicide were entitled to wear their nose pins with flattened ends. These nose pins have been shaped out of *Tridacna*, giant clam shell, and are very heavy. Various shapes of nose pins made from shell, wood and bone were a widespread Pacific body ornament, worn usually by men but occasionally by women in full dress. from top: *Length 18.5 cm; length 14.7 cm.*

from top: *AM 32365. Presented by Rev. C. Palmer 1951.*
AM 55926.

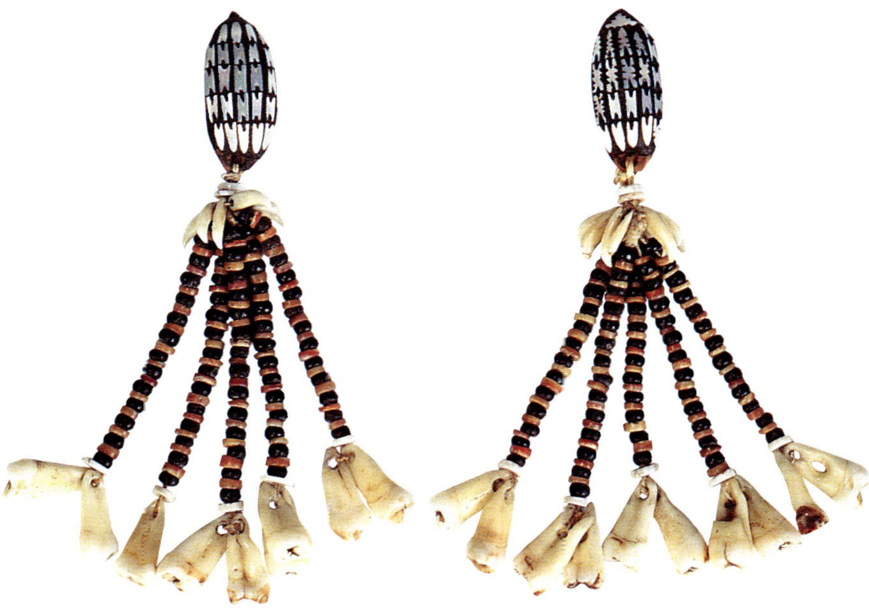

opposite: **Breast pendants, Solomon Islands**

Solomon Islanders make and wear a huge variety of breast pendants, usually cut out of pearl shell and sometimes from clam shell. A typical form worn by men for both everyday and special occasions is composed mainly of frigate bird motifs, which relate to the initiated men's *bonito* cult. from top: *Width 12 cm; width 9 cm; width 7.6 cm.*

from top: *AM 29462.1. Purchased from Rev. A. H. Voyce 1947.*
AM 29464.2. (From Roviana.) Purchased from Rev. A. H. Voyce 1947.
AM 31668. Presented by Mr W. J. Rutherford 1950.

Ear Ornaments, San Cristobal, Solomon Islands

Very fine detailed workmanship has been applied to this elaborate pair of ear ornaments. Delicate inlays of *Nautilus* shell have been inset on a *Canarium* nut which acts as the support for a set of tassels consisting of small porpoise teeth, shell money discs and seeds. Each string ends in a pair of human teeth, which have been drilled for attachment. *Length 14 cm.*

AM 15077. James Edge-Partington Collection. Presented by Dr Thomson Wilson Leys Memorial 1924.

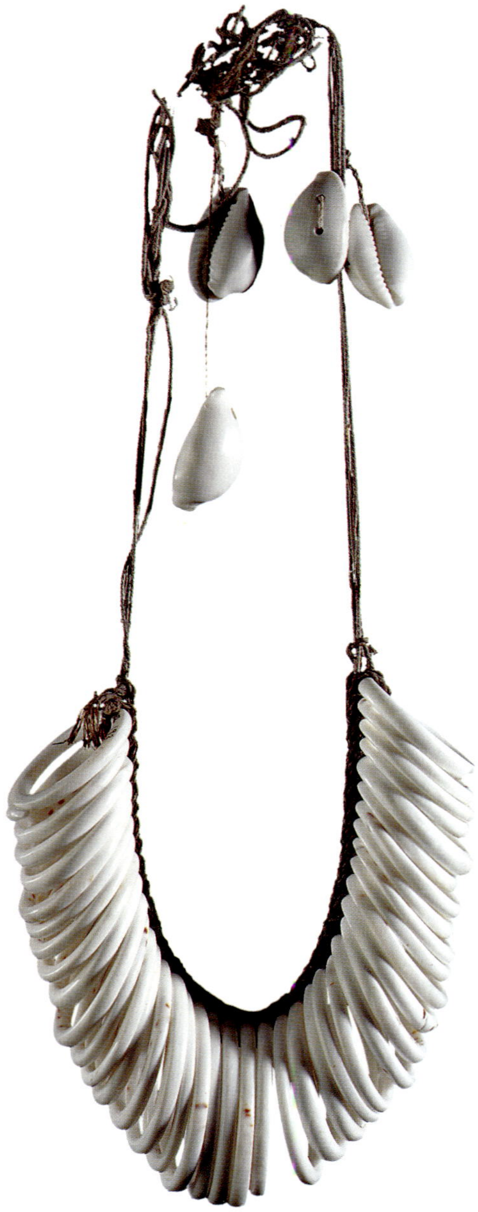

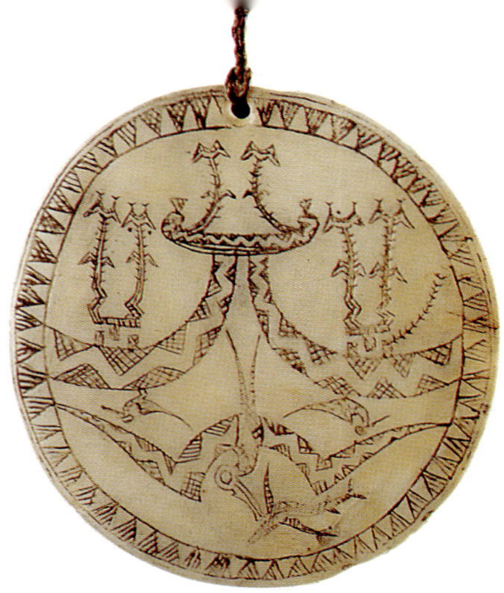

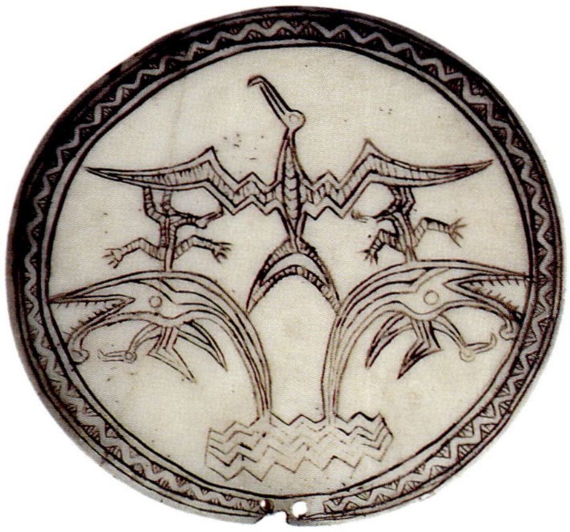

***Ulute*, Clam Shell Neck Pendant, Malaita, Solomon Islands**

Worn mostly by men of Malaita, Maramasike and Ulawa, the incised designs on *ulute* neck pendants usually depict frigate birds, often with fish in their beaks, and sometimes other fish and abstract patterns. On some, the main frigate bird figure stands upon abstracted wave patterns or an upturned canoe motif associated with sea spirits. These same pendants may also be strung together into a necklace. from top: *Diameter 8.8 cm; diameter 10 cm.*

from top: *AM 14421. Purchased from Mrs Goldsboro 1925.*
AM 33519. Purchased from Mrs C.V. Palmer 1953.

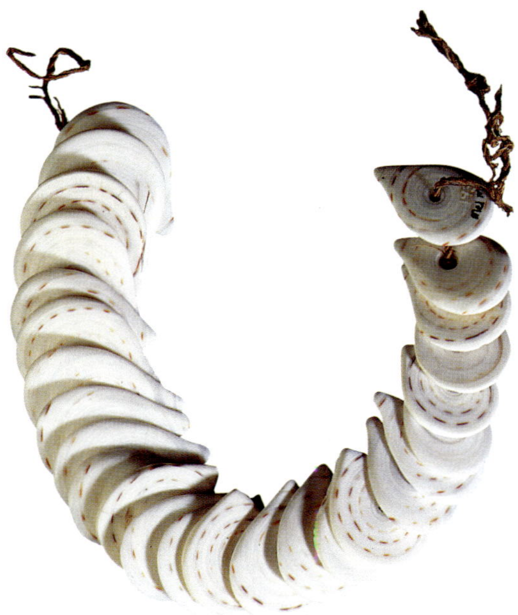

Shell Necklaces, Solomon Islands

Highly polished *Conus* shell rings were made into a wide variety of necklaces in the Solomon Islands. These two illustrate different ways that the *Conus* shells could be cut and ground to produce open rings or flat platelets, in this example with an unusual pointed feature that has been very deliberately worked in to each element of the necklace. These are part of the early collection assembled by the Anglican Melanesian Mission, whose ship *Southern Cross* was based at Auckland in New Zealand. Unfortunately, very few records were kept of where in Melanesia their artefacts were collected. from top: *Length 38 cm; length 29 cm.*

from top: *Nos. 192, 193. Melanesian Mission Collection.*

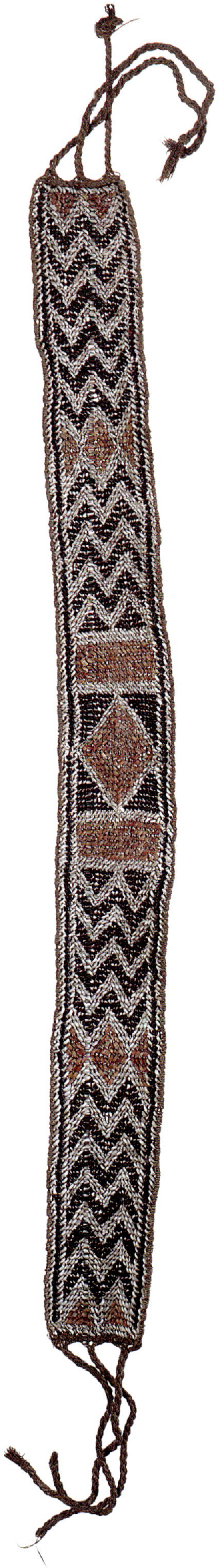

Waist Belt, Solomon Islands

Very fine red and white shell money discs have been plaited into black fibre to form this belt intended for both men and women to wear. The chevron motifs are probably derived from stylised frigate-bird patterns. Work as fine as this required patience and very close attention to planning and executing the pattern. Belts like this also constituted a currency in their own right. *Length 60 cm, width 6 cm.*

AM 12908. Purchased from Mrs Porter 1916.

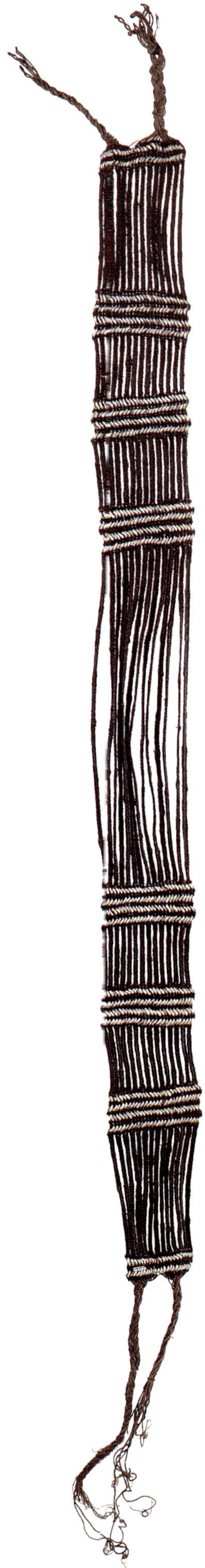

Waist Belt, Solomon Islands

This narrow belt follows the composition of belts made entirely of shell money discs, but most of this belt consists of very finely plaited black fibre interspersed with vertical bands of white shell money discs. This combination may indicate that the belt was intended as an item of lesser value or it may simply be a craftswoman's aesthetic choice. *Length 100 cm, width 6.5 cm.*

AM 14444. Purchased from Mrs Goldsboro 1925.

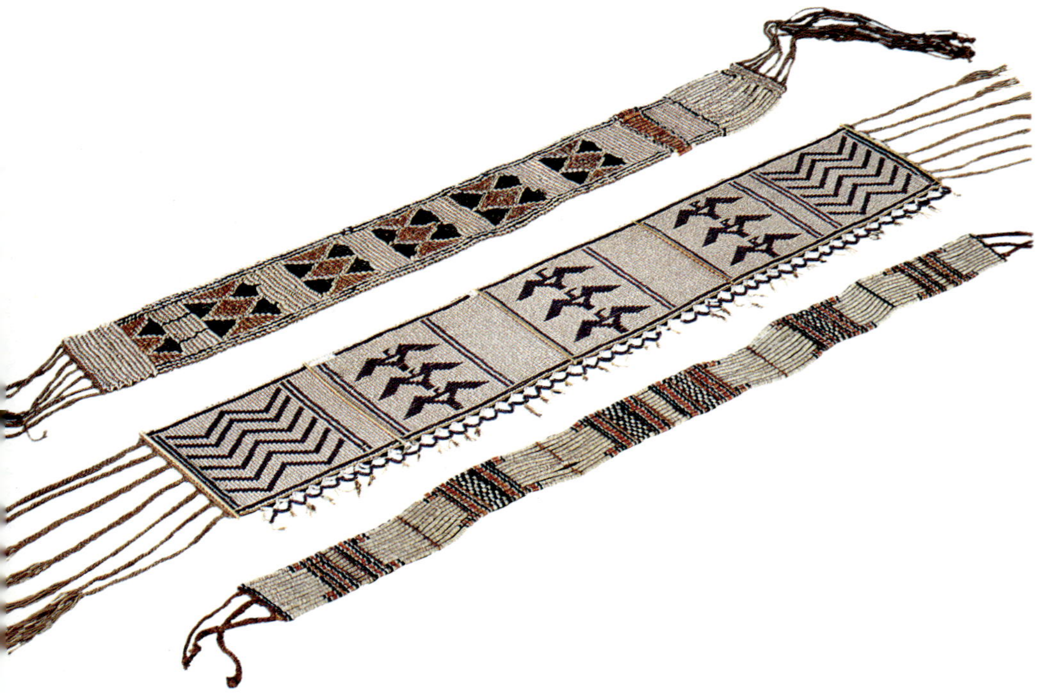

WAIST BELTS OF SHELL MONEY DISCS, MALAITA, SOLOMON ISLANDS

In the Solomon Islands, much of the shell disc money was made by women in the coastal villages of Langalanga, Auki and Alite along the Langalanga Lagoon on the west coast of Malaita. Some of this production was diverted into closely-worked patterned belts—either as strings held apart by turtle shell or wooden spacers, or forming a fabric on a fibre base. These wide belts were worn by warriors as part of their full regalia, the frigate bird motifs probably referring to their status as initiated members of the bonito cult, and other designs showing clan membership. from top: *Length 115 cm, width 9 cm; length 110 cm, width 14.5 cm; length 71 cm, width 6.5 cm.*

from top: *AM 32323. Presented by Rev. C. Palmer 1951.*
AM 15243. Langalanga Lagoon, Malaita. James Edge-Partington Collection. Presented by Dr Thomson Wilson Leys Memorial 1924.
AM 35924. Presented by Mrs F. Fraser 1960.

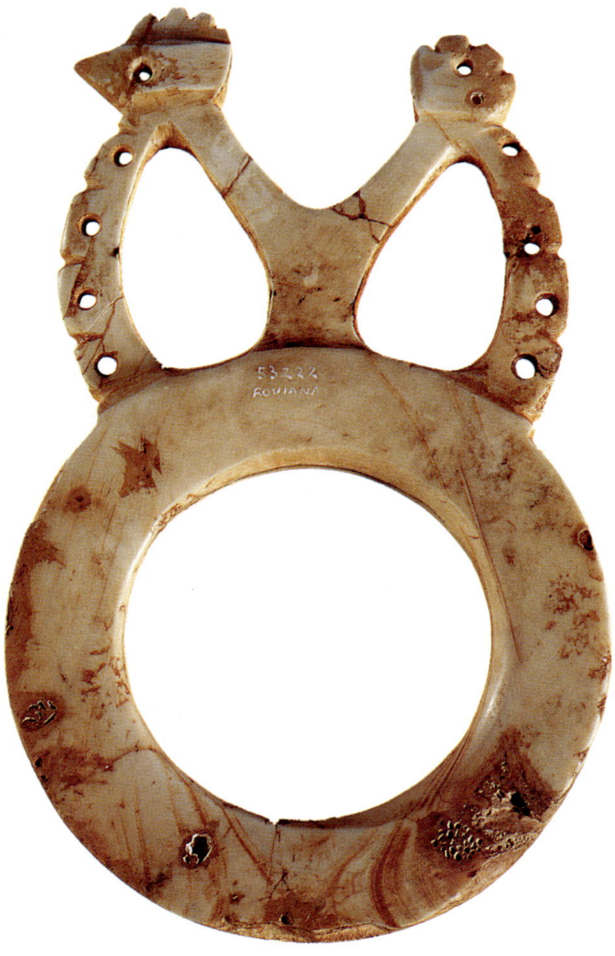

BUKOLO, CLAM SHELL ORNAMENT, ROVIANA, NEW GEORGIA, SOLOMON ISLANDS

Tridacna clam shell rings with complicated decorative projections may be worn as arm rings, but as high-value prestige objects they were also used in other contexts, as decoration and as exchange valuables. This one has been cut from ancient fossil clam shell with its characteristic discolouration but the workmanship is quite modern. *Length 18.5 cm.*

AM 53222. Purchased from Mr Mariano Kelesi 1989.

opposite: CLAM SHELL CARVING, CHOISEUL, SOLOMON ISLANDS

Various forms of rings cut out of giant clam shell are commonly recognised as items of ornament, currency, wealth and personal prestige throughout the Solomon Islands. Consequently, the motif of shell rings occurs through much of the art, whether rendered in wood-carvings, shell inlay work, or actual clam shell such as the *barava*—clam shell carvings placed on mortuary shrines. This carving combines elements of ornamental clam shell rings and *barava* in a prestige object. *Length 17 cm, width 9 cm.*

AM 26425. Presented by Sir William Goodfellow 1940.

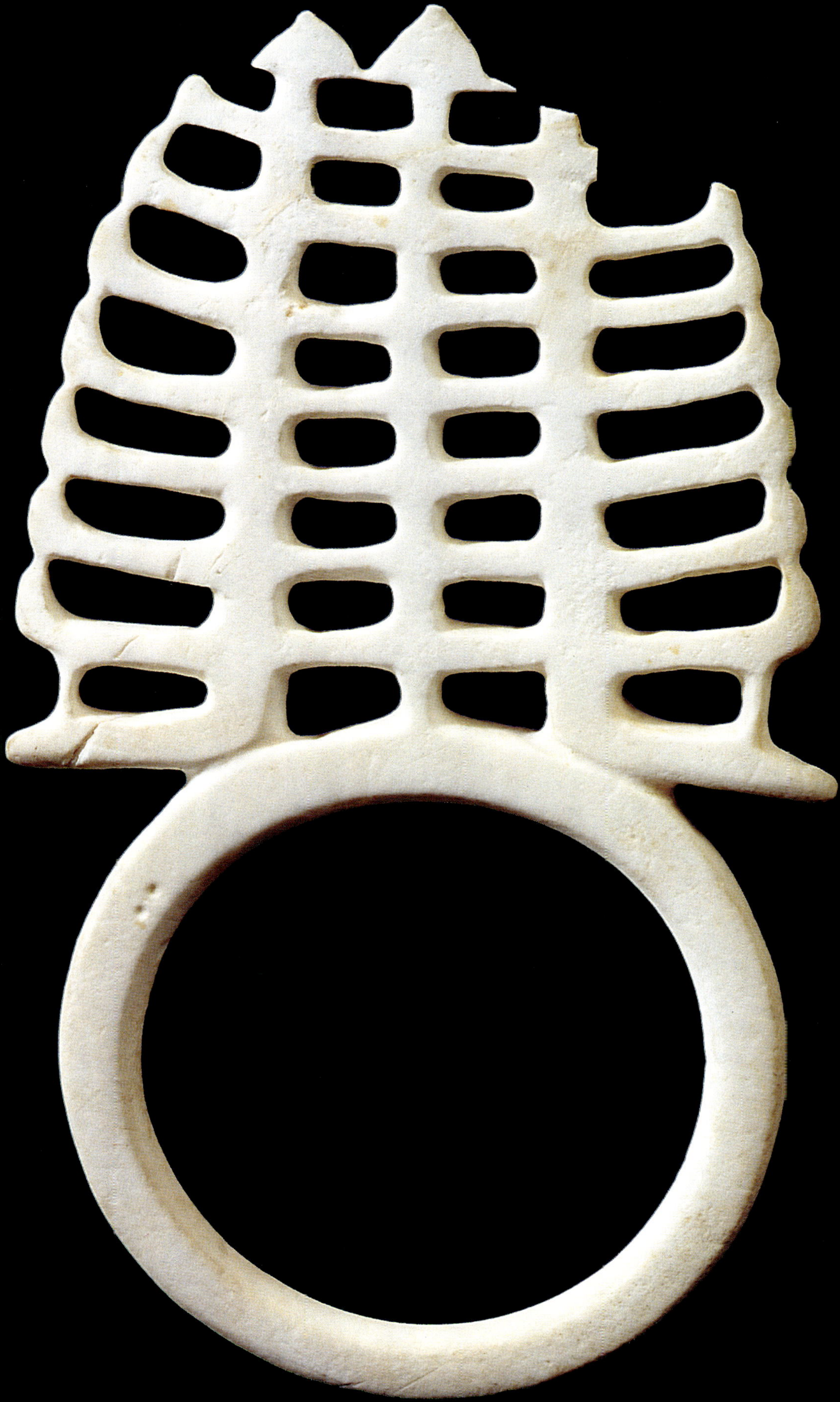

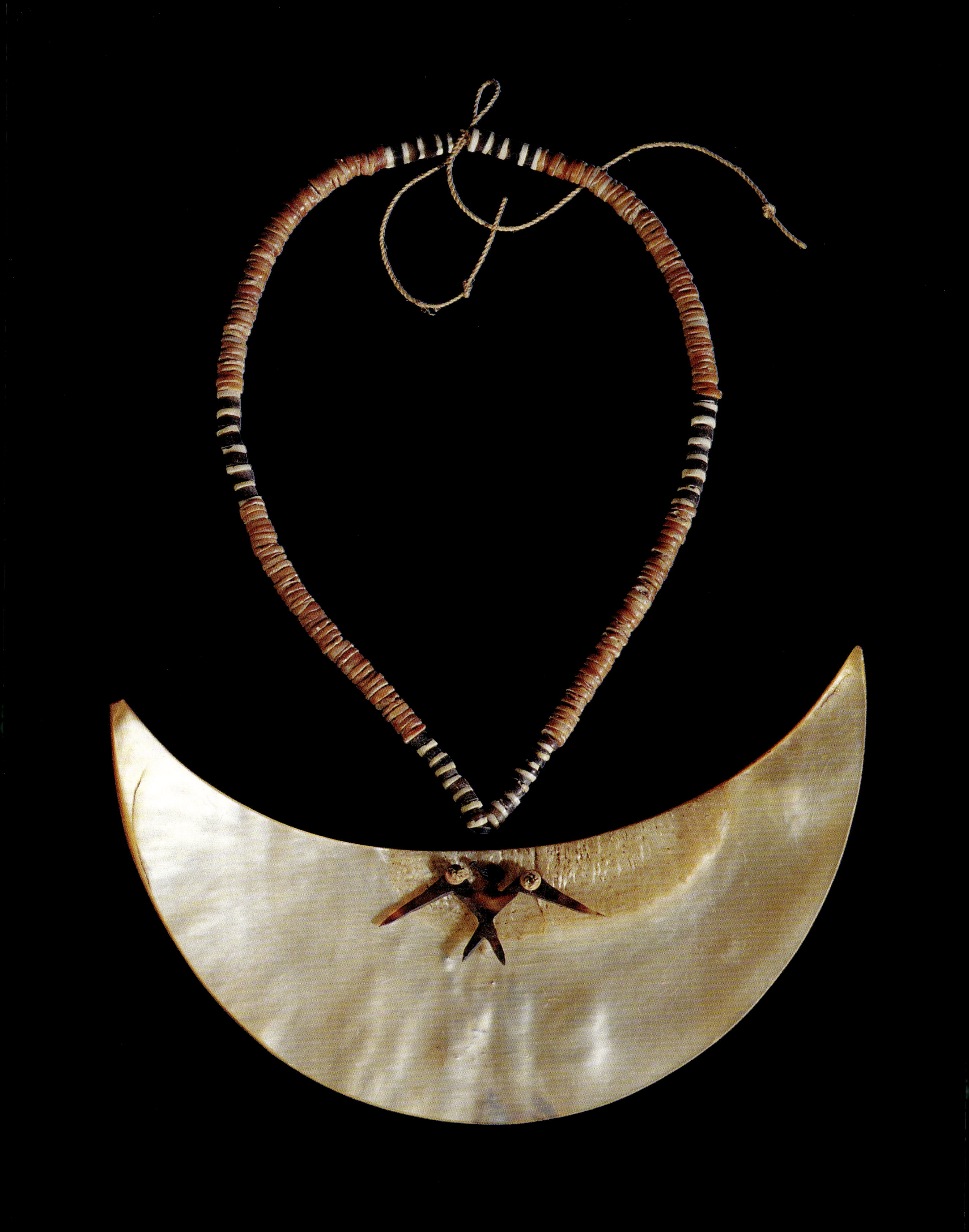

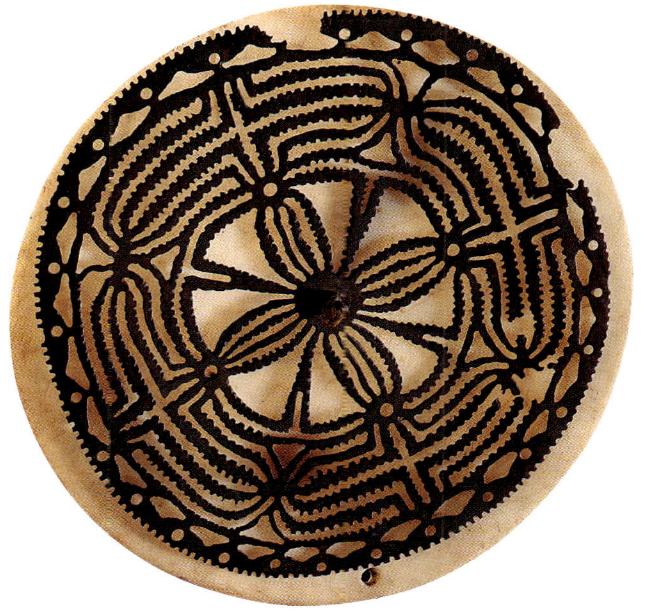

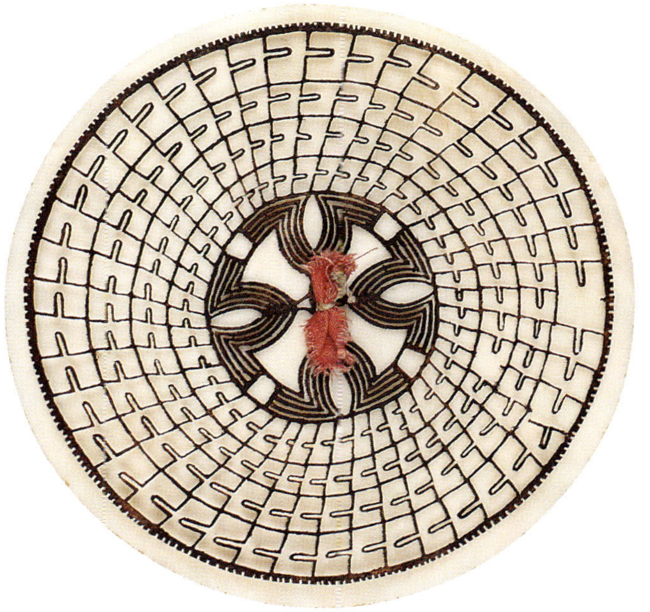

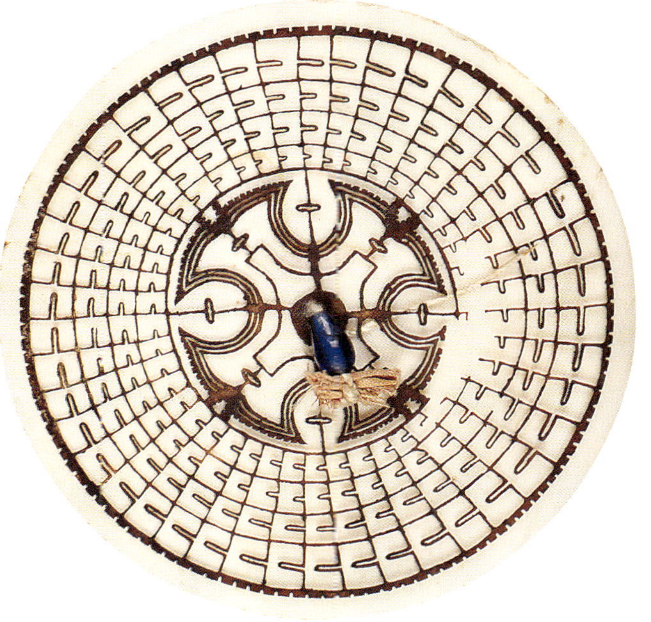

Kapkap, Forehead Ornaments, Solomon Islands

Variations on the *kapkap* form are made and worn quite widely in the Solomon Islands and coastal New Guinea but those from the Solomons are distinguished by the fineness of their turtle shell fretwork overlay. Most Solomon Islands *kapkaps* have their white backing disc sawn and polished from *Tridacna* clam shell, but in other areas large white curved *Melo* or *Cymbium* shells are used. Malaita was a major centre for their manufacture in the southern Solomon Islands and from there they were traded widely. *Kapkaps* made in the north-western islands of New Georgia and Choiseul often feature a small anthropomorphic figure in the centre of the fretwork. Men wore a *kapkap* in battle and at festivals as a symbol of their wealth. from top: *Diameter 13 cm; diameter 12 cm; diameter 11 cm.*

from top: *AM 19401. (From Malaita.) Presented by Mr George Smith 1933.*
AM 35532.1. (From Simbo Island.) Presented by Dr E. G. Sayers 1959.
AM 4688. Presented by Rev. W. A. Sinclair 1930.

opposite: *Dafe*, Pearl Shell Breast Ornament, Southern Malaita, Solomon Islands

Made in the late twentieth century, this *dafe* maintains all the features of old traditional forms. A small frigate bird motif carved in turtle shell is attached to the polished, gold-lip pearl shell crescent, which is worn suspended around a man's neck by the cord of shell money discs. This cord of shell money was probably made at Auki, a small island off the south-west coast of Malaita, which has long been the centre of currency making by women, who cut, drill and polish the red *Spondylus* shells. *Length 59 cm.*

AM 53229. Purchased from Mr Mariano Kelesi 1989.

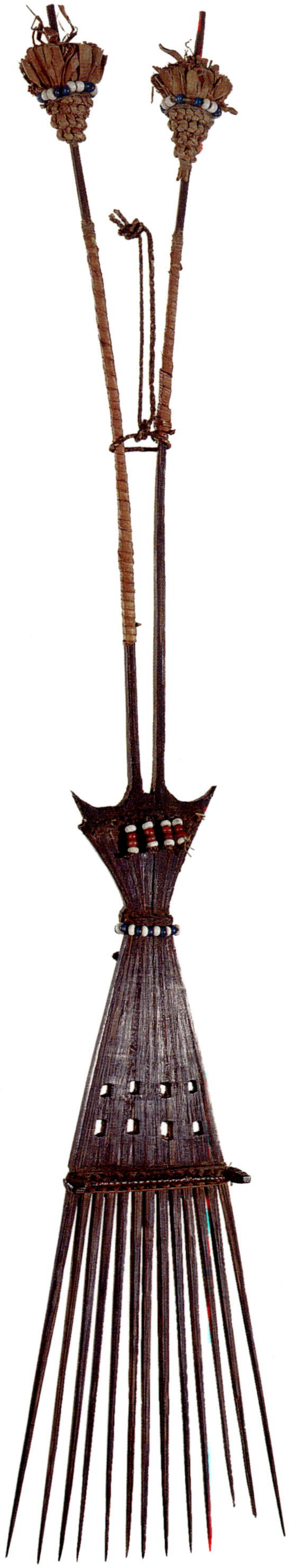

Comb, South-East Solomon Islands

This comb of palmwood is decorated with glass trade-beads. For everyday wear, men would sometimes add fresh flowers to the projections so that they swayed about with their movements. This form of comb is said to have originated on Ulawa but they were also made on other islands of the south-east Solomons. Most are decorated with *Nautilus* shell inlay but many were also decorated with other materials. *Length 44.5 cm, width 8 cm.*

AM 9072. Purchased from Rev. Archdeacon Comins 1918.

opposite left: ***Wari Hau*****, Baton With Knob of Iron Pyrites South Malaita, Solomon Islands**

These batons were made by the Areare people at the south-west end of Malaita and consist of a knob of iron pyrites that is covered with fine plaiting and lashed to the wooden handle with strips of cane. The handle is inlaid with *Nautilus* shell. They were worn suspended from a cord around the neck and hung down on the wearer's back with the knob uppermost. As a strictly ceremonial baton, their wearing was said to have been limited to those men authorised to claim payment for an execution. However, other earlier accounts suggest that they were worn more widely by men at ceremonial dancing. This one was collected in 1878. *Length 40 cm.*

AM 36374. Presented by Miss D. M. Darrack 1961.

opposite right: **Arm Bands, Northern Solomon Islands**

Arm bands like these, plaited in various patterns from red and black natural-coloured vines and yellow orchid fibre, are made by women in the northern Solomon Islands, including Bougainville and Buka. Very similar ones are made in the Admiralty Islands to the north-west, but without the red colour. Arm bands are worn by men, women and children, usually on the upper arm, as general decoration; but more elaborate examples are made for ceremonial occasions, such as girls emerging from seclusion or widows during their mourning. top: *Height 8.5 cm.* bottom: *Height 8 cm.*

top: *AM 279. Melanesian Mission Collection.*
bottom: *AM 48013.2. Presented by Mr Tucker 1977*

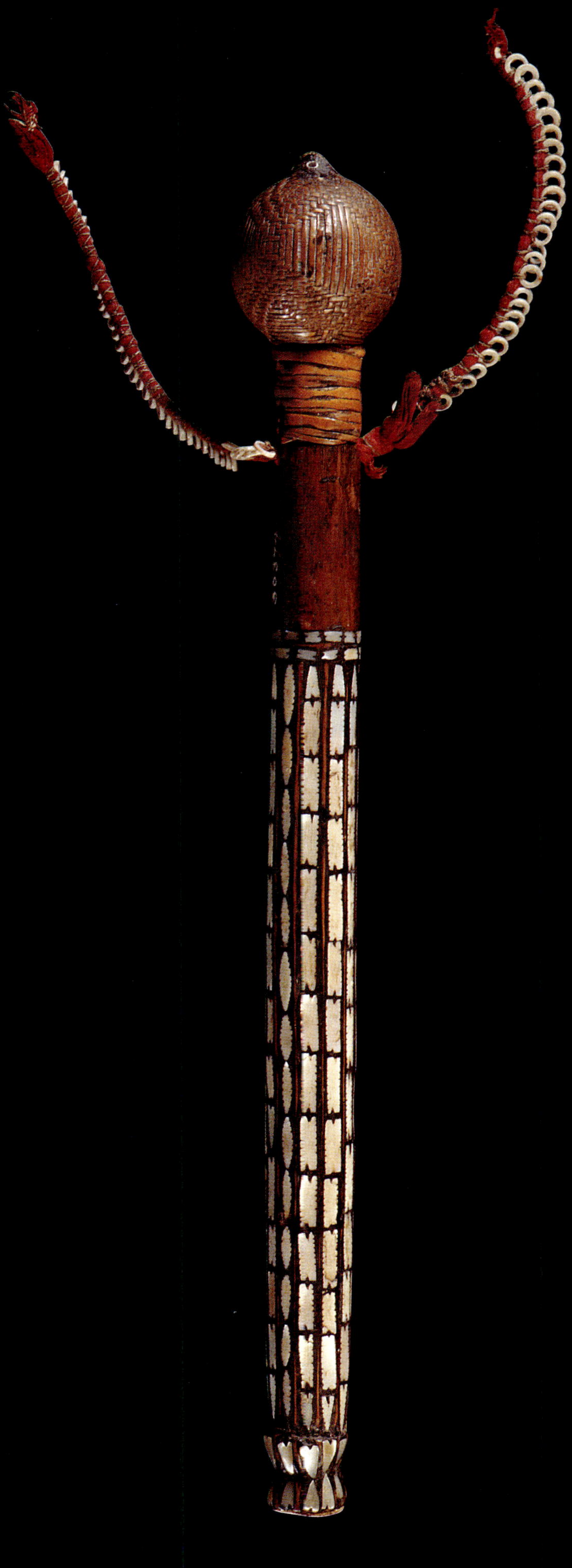
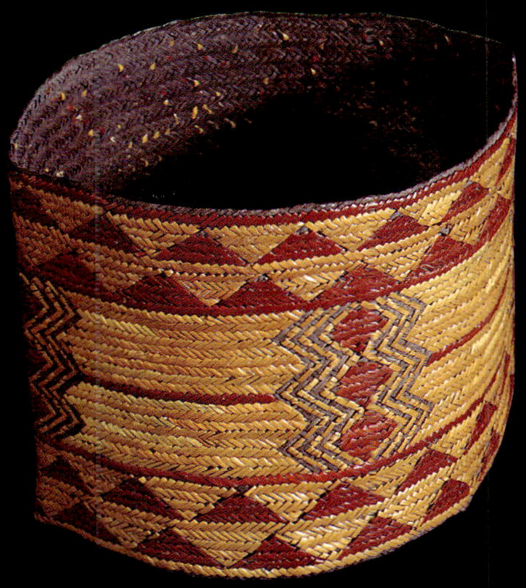
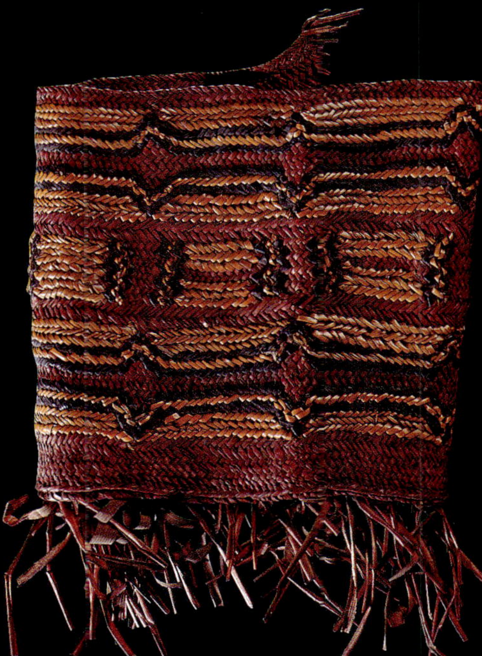

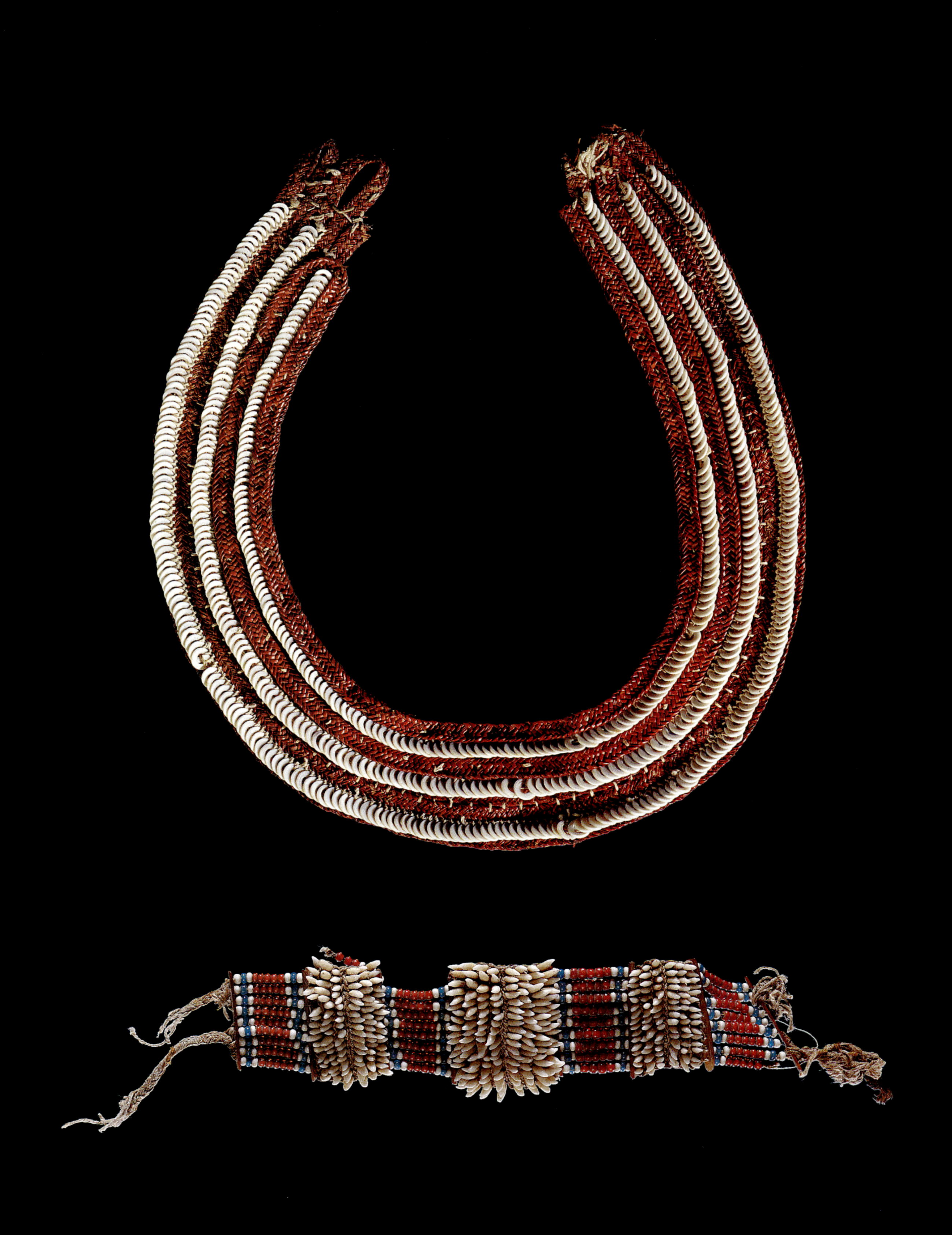

Necklace, Ruhuhaku, Musiminoi Village, Siwai district, Bougainville

This unusual and delicate little necklace has been constructed with red and white glass trade-beads strung in a careful pattern between teeth of the sail fish. An imported, commercially made, pearl shell shirt button has been incorporated to form a toggle, happily adopted because of the high traditional value accorded to pearl shell as a material of wealth. The Reverend Harry Voyce was a Methodist missionary stationed in Bougainville during the 1920s and 1930s, when he amassed a large and well-documented collection of local artefacts. *Length 30 cm.*

AM 20211. Rev. A. H. Voyce Collection. Presented by Sir William Goodfellow 1934.

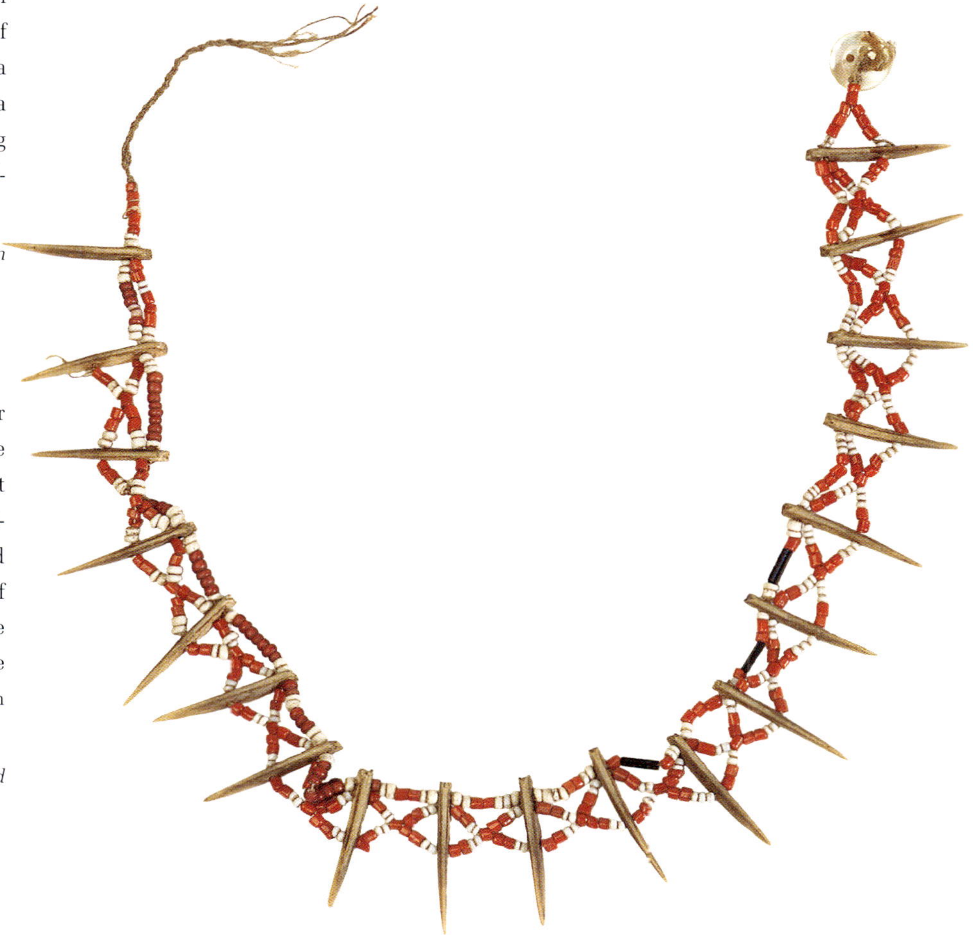

Ear plugs, San Cristobal, Solomon Islands

In many areas of the Solomon Islands, men pierced their earlobes, then gradually extended the lobe so that it became a large open loop. Several different types of ornament might be worn in these extended lobes. These large wooden plugs from San Cristobal have been decorated with a red seed or trade bead at the centre and concentric patterns of *Nautilus* shell insets, all inlaid into *Farinarium* resin. If the lobe became extended further, the owner could increase the diameter of his ear plug by wrapping it in leaf strips. from left: *Diameter 8.5 cm; diameter 10 cm.*

from left: *AM 15140. James Edge-Partington Collection. Presented by Dr Thomson Wilson Leys Memorial 1924.*
No. 601. Melanesian Mission Collection.

opposite top: Necklet, possibly Florida, Solomon Islands

Small, drilled shell discs have been attached to a plaited, red-dyed fibre necklet, probably worn as part of a larger ensemble. The shell discs have been drilled and polished in a way that differentiates them from usual shell money discs, indicating that they have been designed to serve as jewellery rather than currency. *Length 52.5 cm.*

AM 36275. Presented by Mr G. V. Binet 1961.

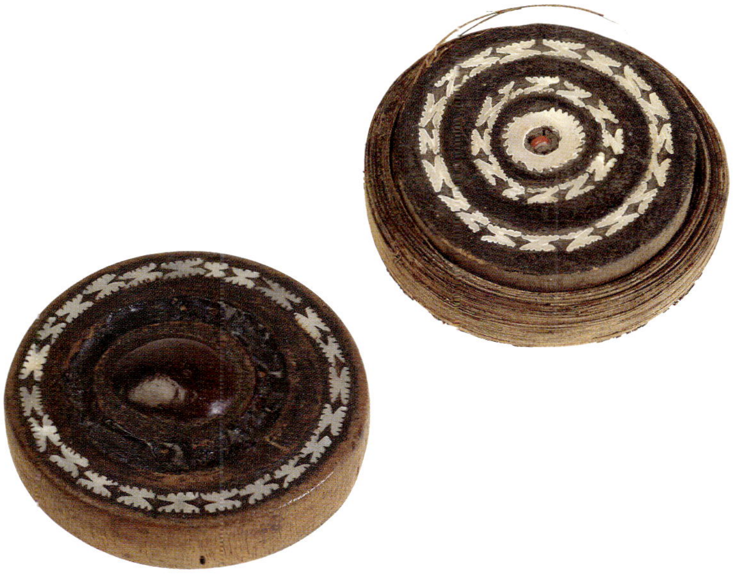

opposite bottom: Armlet, Solomon Islands

Red, white and blue glass trade-beads have been strung on native cord separated by clusters of porpoise teeth to form this striking armlet. Glass trade-beads offered Solomon Islanders the opportunity to enjoy a greater range of bright colours and their craftspeople took full advantage. *Length 15 cm, width 4.5 cm.*

AM 55333.

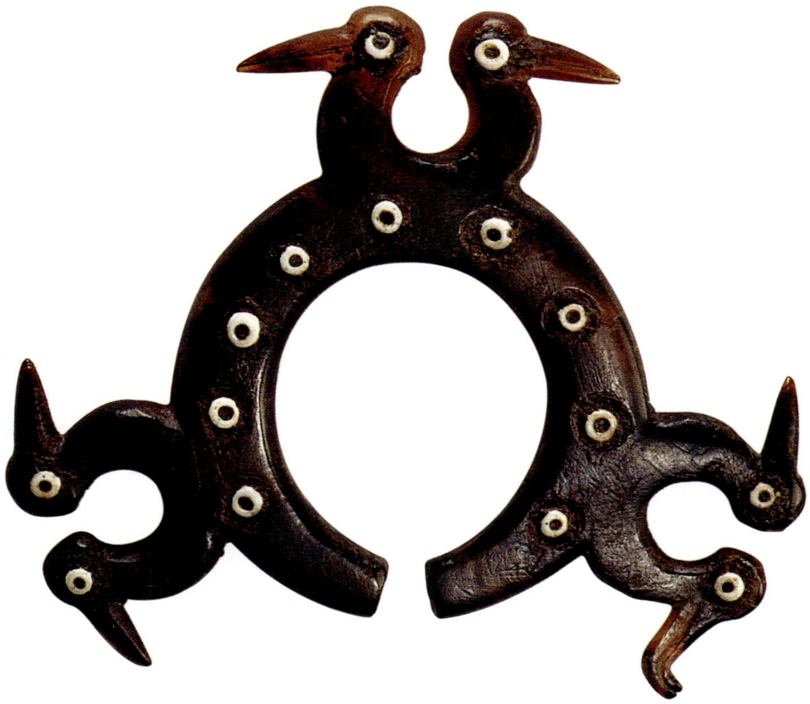

Turtle Shell Nose Ornaments, Solomon Islands

A variety of ornaments, especially those made of light turtle shell, might be worn through the perforated septum of the nose by both men and women in different areas. The wings and heads of frigate birds are the main motif in these examples. from top: *Length 5 cm; length 6.5 cm.*

from top: *AM 32392.2. Presented by Rev. C. Palmer 1951. AM 32392.1. Presented by Rev. C. Palmer 1951.*

opposite top: **Necklace, Guadalcanal, Solomon Islands**

In this necklace, flying fox teeth, individually drilled, have been attached to a fibre backing in sections, which are separated at regular intervals by three short strings of red, white and blue glass trade-beads. In composing these necklaces, the craftswomen always paid careful attention to the mathematics and geometry of the bead arrangements, thereby ensuring that the resulting patterns were consistent throughout the ornament. *Length 60 cm.*

AM 15112. James Edge-Partington Collection. Presented by Dr Thomson Wilson Leys Memorial 1924.

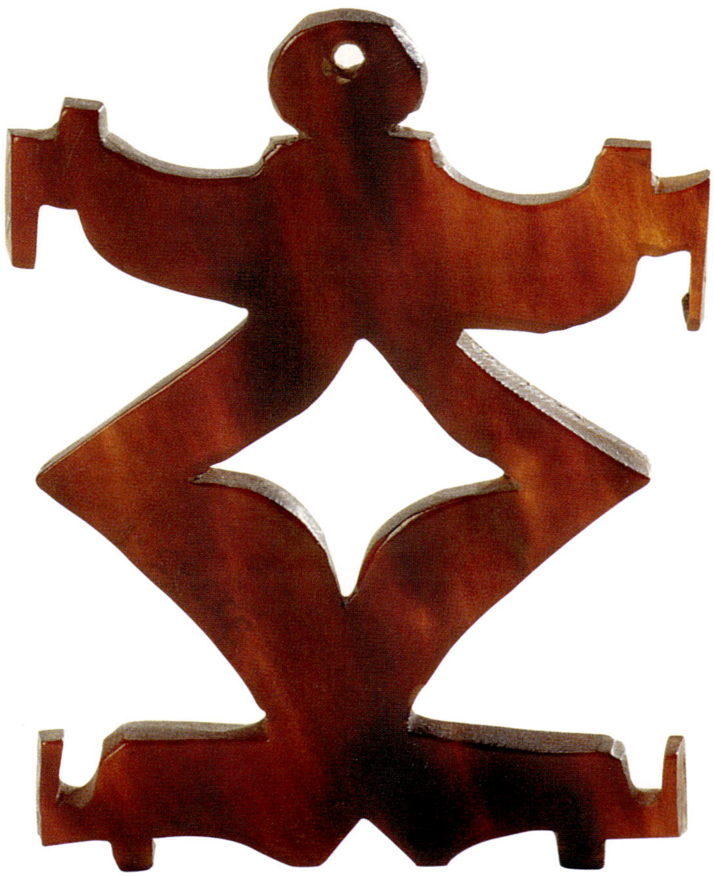

opposite bottom: **Clam Shell Neck Pendant, Probably New Georgia Islands, Solomon Islands**

Small clam shell neck pendants like this suspended on a flat plaited cord of red-dyed fibre echo the more complex, open-cut forms of *barava* clam shell plaques. *Barava* designs featured frontal ancestor figures and embodied their ancestral power. They were placed in front of little shrine huts holding the skulls of the ancestors and sometimes taken out in the headhunting canoes. This *barava*-shaped pendant conveys ancestral power to the personal level of its wearer. *Length 4.5 cm, width 7.8 cm.*

No. 218. Melanesian Mission Collection.

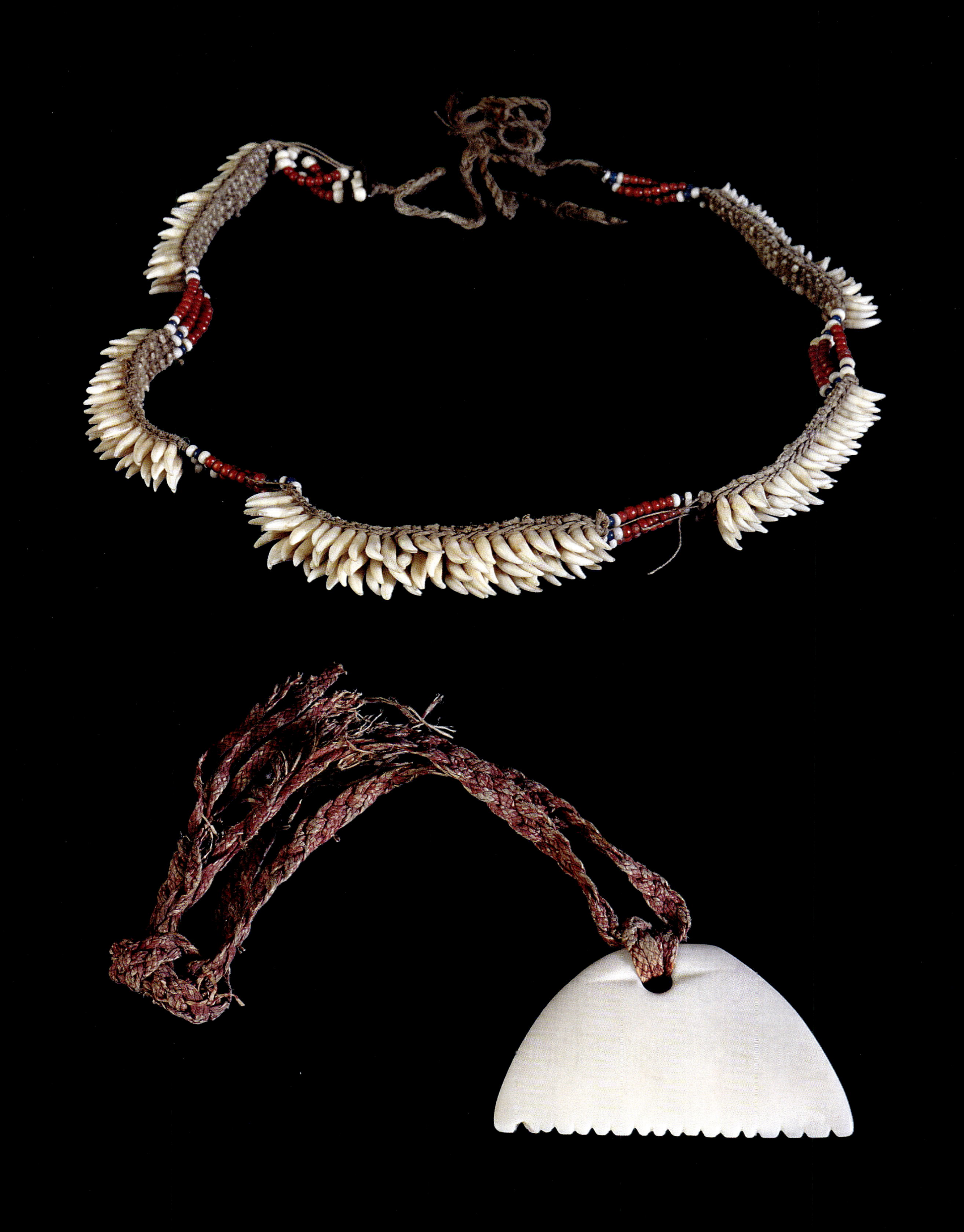

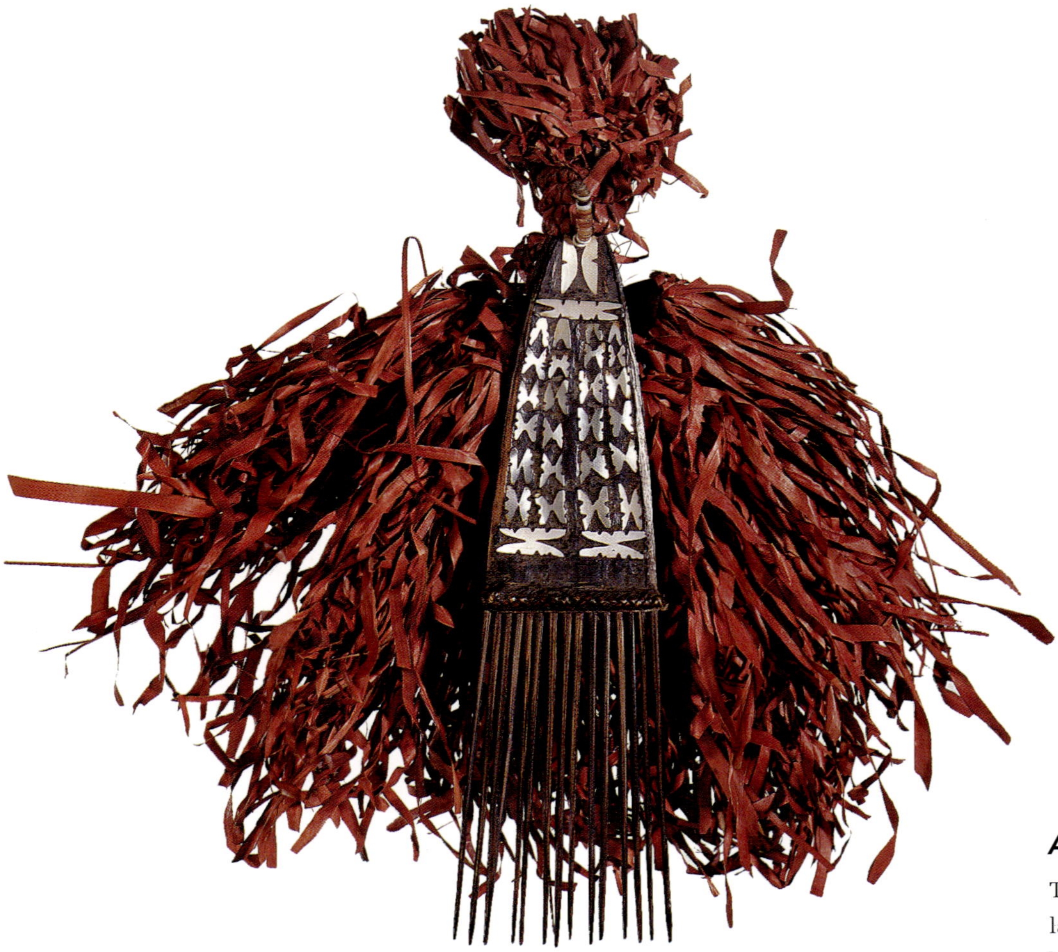

Arapa, Comb, Ulawa, Solomon Islands

The palmwood teeth of this comb have been lashed together on a crossbar, then coated with black paste made from crushed *Parinarium* nuts. Patterned shell pieces cut from *Nautilus* shells have then been inlaid into the body of the comb. This type of comb decorated with the red tassels cut from the dyed leaves of the fan palm was part of the standard regalia worn by young boys undergoing their puberty initiation into the bonito cult. The same red-dyed streamers were used to decorate the prow and stern of bonito canoes when the initiates were taken out to catch their first bonito. *Length 25 cm, width 6 cm.*

AM 32278. Presented by Rev. C. Palmer 1951.

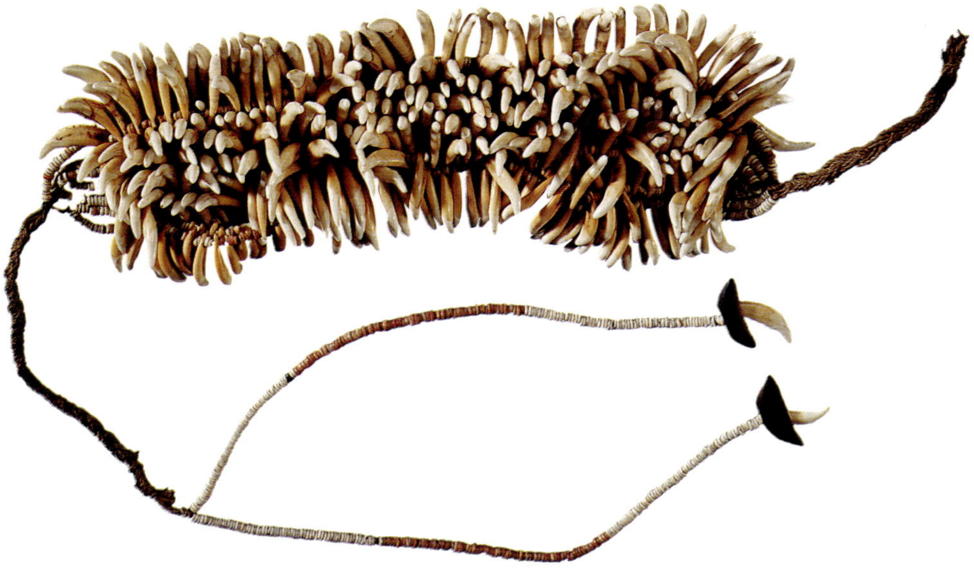

Necklace of Dog Teeth, Probably San Cristobal, Solomon Islands

Dog teeth represent considerable wealth in many of the cultures of the Solomon Islands. These have been threaded on strings of red and white shell money discs, adding even further value to the ornament. Both men and women could wear this ornament and it could also be used as currency for certain transactions, especially bride price. *Length 28 cm, width 11.5 cm.*

AM 13168. Purchased from Mrs Porter 1919.

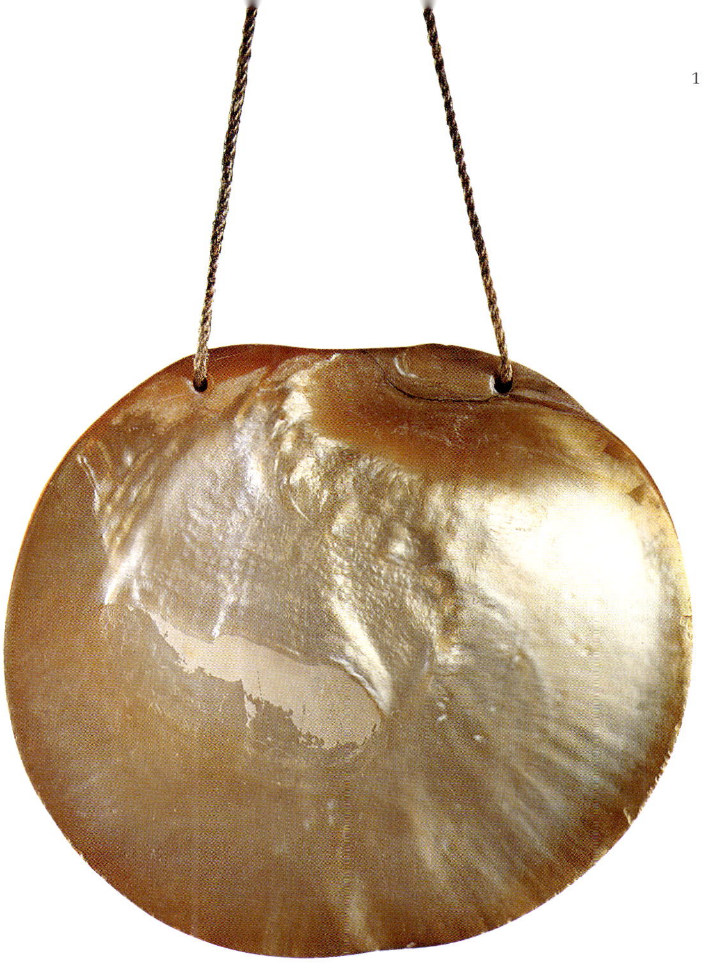

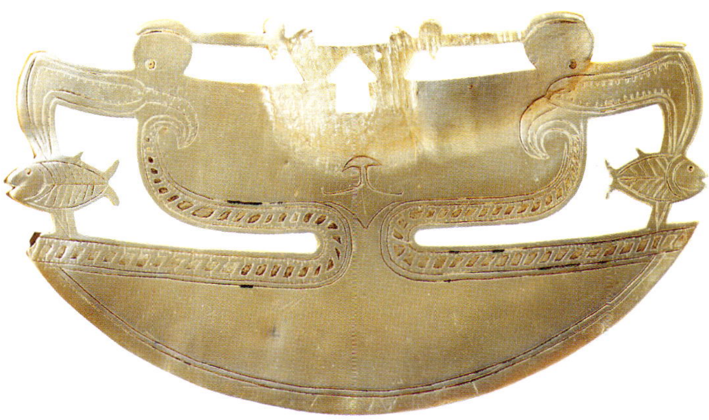

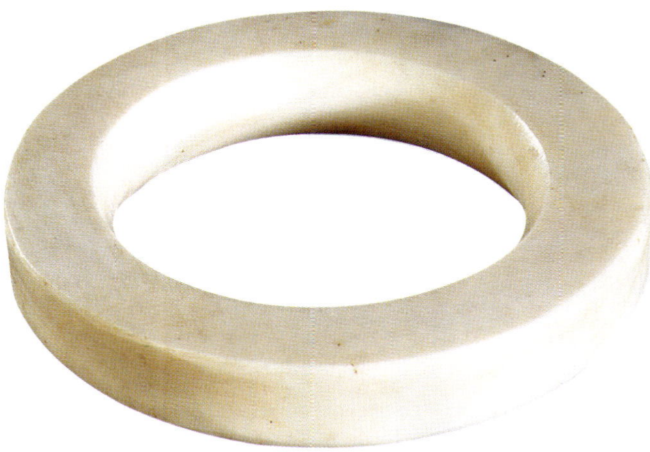

Gold Lip Pearl Shell Neck Pendant, Solomon Islands

Unfortunately Archdeacon Comins did not record where in the Solomon Islands he obtained this beautiful, polished, pearl shell pendant and its absence of embellishment offers no further clues. Pearl shell was highly valued for its aesthetic qualities across the Pacific, although in the Solomons it was more commonly shaped into a crescent form. *Length 16.5 cm, width 17 cm.*

AM 9027. Purchased from Rev. Archdeacon R. B. Comins, Melanesian Mission 1918.

Pearl Shell Breast Pendant, New Georgia, Solomon Islands

The British artefact collector, James Edge-Partington, who obtained this pendant during his own Pacific travels in the late nineteenth century, wrote that men of New Georgia also hung this breast pendant in the stern of their canoe as a charm to ensure fair weather. As usual for these pendants, fish and frigate birds are the main motifs. *Length 17.5 cm, width 10 cm.*

AM 15228. James Edge-Partington Collection. Presented by Dr Thomson Wilson Leys Memorial 1924.

***Hokata*, Clam Shell Arm Ring, Vella Lavella, Solomon Islands**

Vella Lavella was one of the main manufacturing places for arm rings cut from the shell of *Tridacna*, the giant clam. The manufacturing process differed in some areas. Either a piece of thick shell from the hinge of the clam was broken off by hitting with stones, then a perforation was chipped through with flints or other stones. Or the shape was cut out with a strip of abrasive fibre on a bow. Final polishing was achieved with pumice or sand, or abrasives made from shark skins. One ring could take six months of intermittent work. Arm rings were also used as currency. *Diameter 10.7 cm, height 1.8 cm.*

AM 47636.4. Purchased from Mr A. M. Bensley 1976.

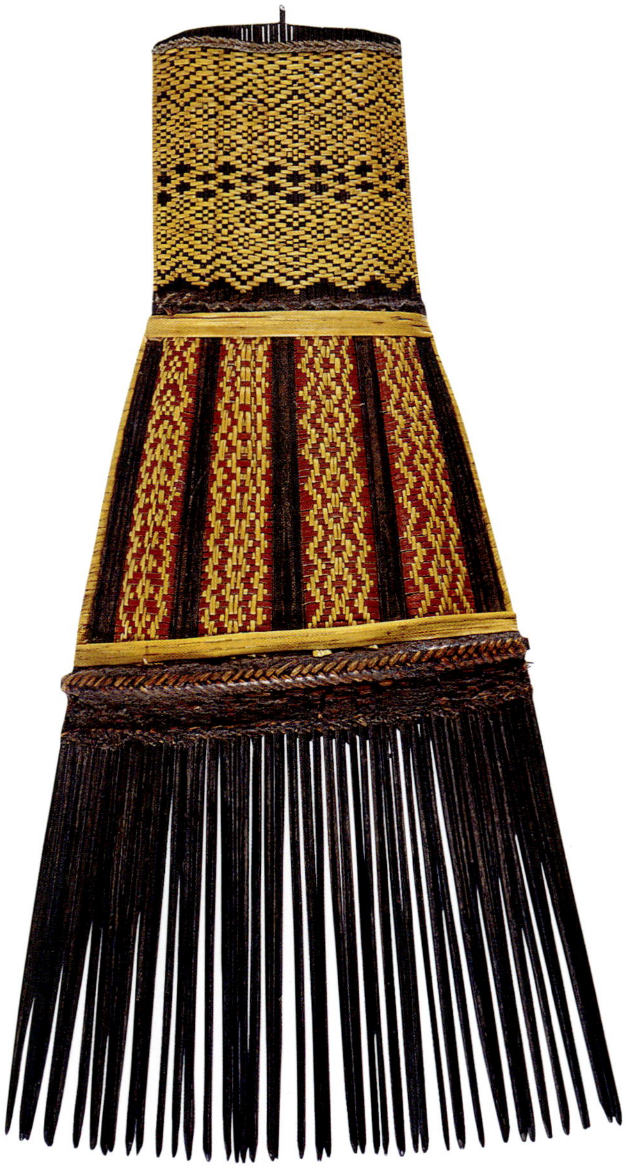

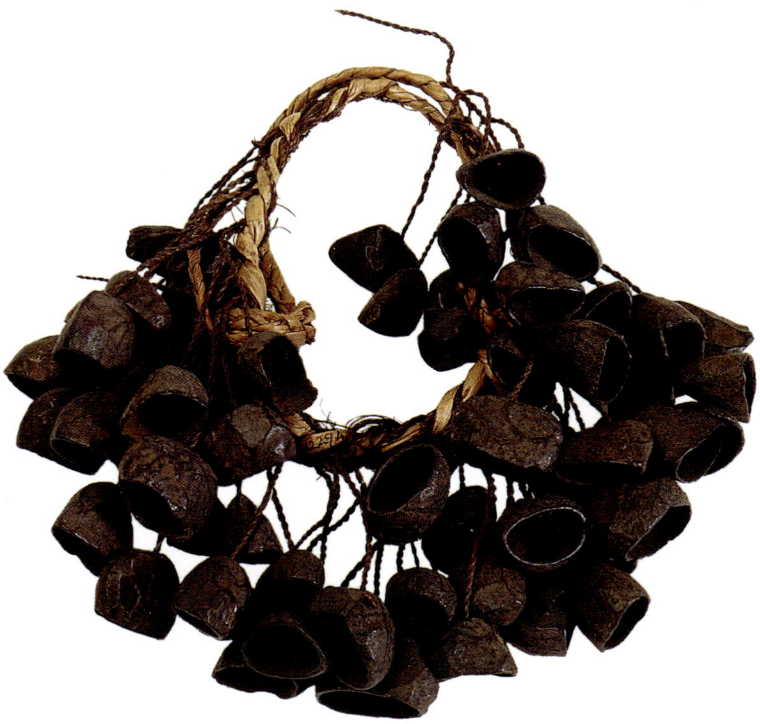

***Faa*, Comb, Malaita, Solomon Islands**

Teeth made from split sections of the core of tree ferns have been fixed together with a decorative plaiting of red and yellow strips. The yellow is vascular tissue of orchid vine and the red is waxy tissue of coconut palm dyed red with an extract of *Morinda* root. These combs are made by the East Kwaio hill people of Malaita Island, from where they are traded down to the coast and onward to other areas of the Solomons. They are usually worn only by men, along with ear sticks plaited from the same materials. *Length 14 cm.*

AM 32349. Presented by Rev. C. Palmer 1951.

Leg Rattle, Florida Island, Solomon Islands

Probably worn just below the knee by a male dancer, this rattle makes a loud staccato sound matching the rhythm of the dancer's movements. To make the rattle, *Pangium edule* seeds have been cut off and strung on a plaited fibre band. These hard brown seeds are used throughout Melanesia as rattles, often attached to clothing, ornaments, weapons and portable dance drums. *Length 22.5 cm, width 20.5 cm.*

AM 12294. Purchased from Mr E. Danneford 1898.

opposite: ***Laoniasi*, Necklet, Fiu, Malaita, Solomon Islands**

Strung on native cord with red *Spondylus* shell money discs, these clam shell discs have been engraved with varied designs mostly representing frigate birds. Similar single clam shell discs might also be worn around the neck, when they were usually called *ulute*. Whether singly or as a necklace, these seem to have been worn only by men, especially on certain ceremonial occasions. *Length 75 cm.*

AM 18386. Presented by Mr A. T. Pycroft 1932.

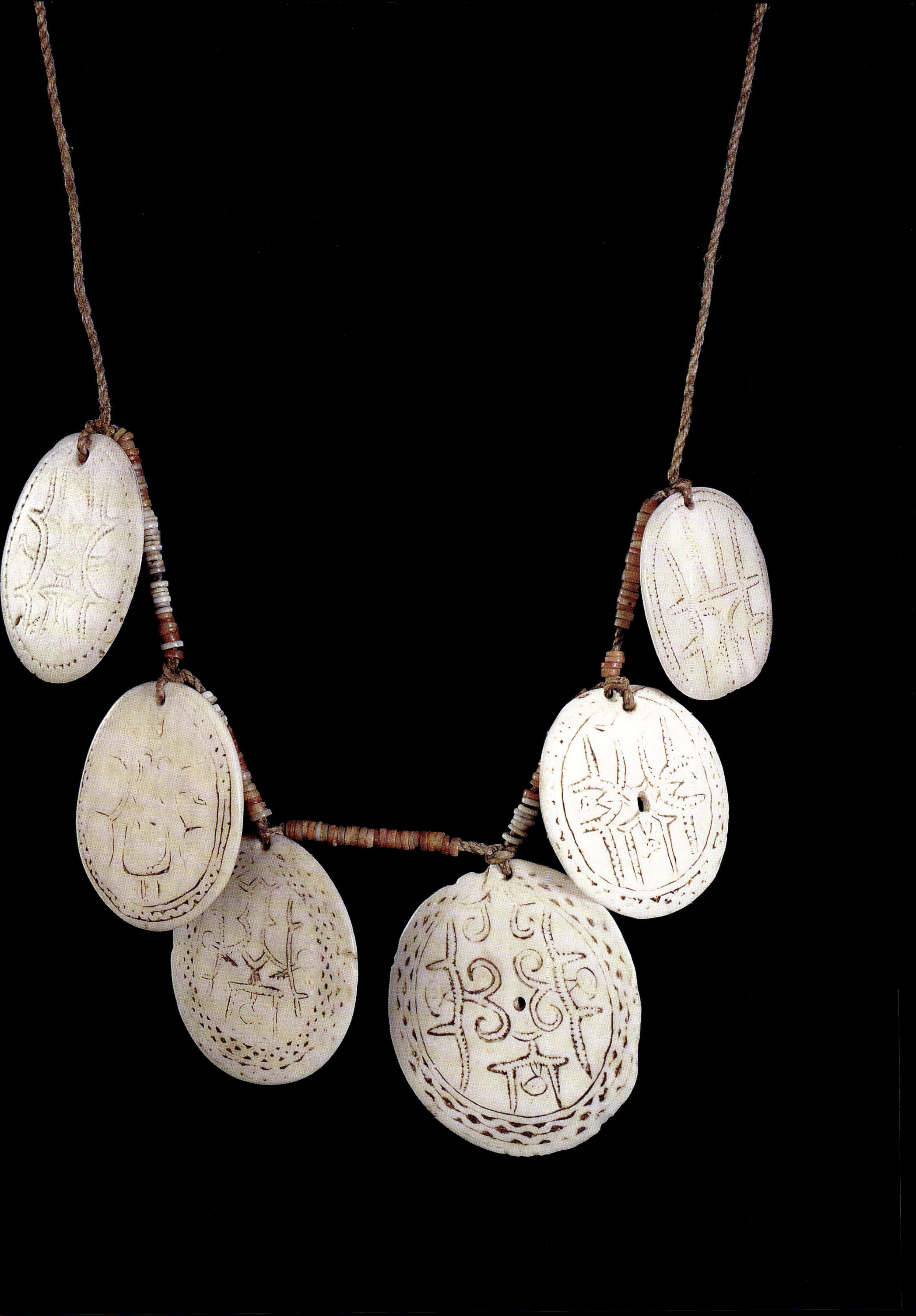

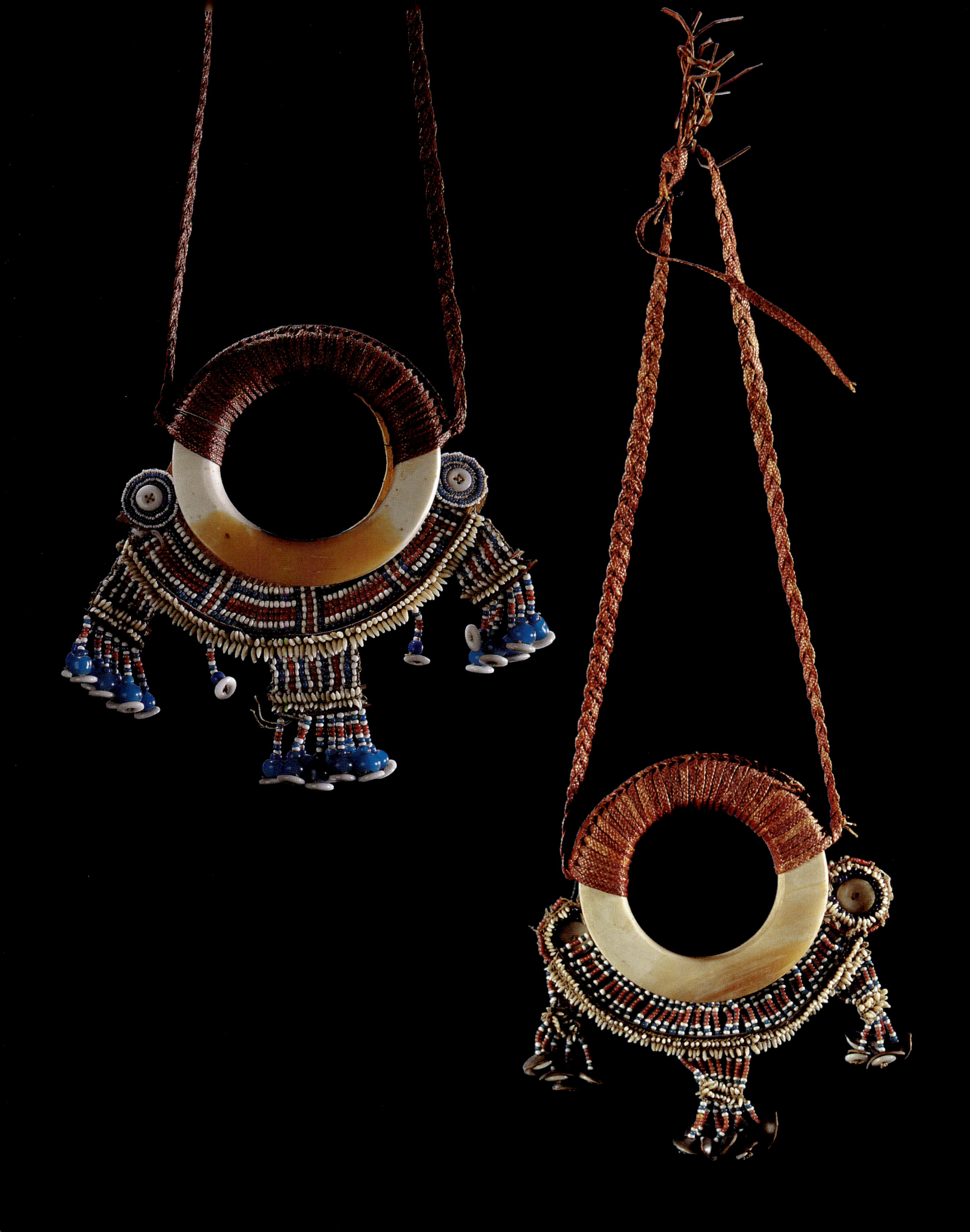

Kassia Clam-Shell Arm Ring, Choiseul, Solomon Islands

Poata and *mbokolo* are general words for clam-shell arm rings in the western Solomon Islands but each type had its very specific name, such as *kassia* for this one with a ridge running around the outside. Several early accounts describe the damage that such arm rings could do to an opponent when grappling in hand-to-hand combat. *Diameter 9.5 cm, height 3.7 cm.*

AM 15222.1. James Edge-Partington Collection. Presented by Dr Thomson Wilson Leys Memorial 1924.

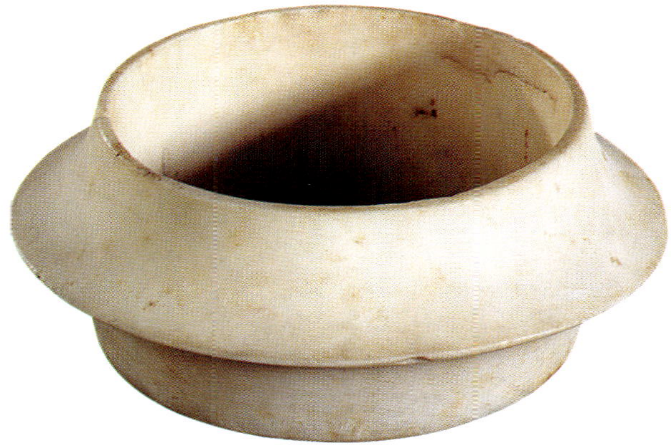

Poata, Clam Shell Arm Ring, Western Solomon Islands

Sadly, the unnamed missionary worker who obtained this magnificent clam shell arm ring did not record the exact locality from where it came, nor is there now any information on the transaction between the missionary and the Solomon Islander owner. Such a valuable prestige object must have belonged to an important person and would only have changed hands for a special reason. *Diameter 10.3 cm, height 5 cm.*

451/180 Melanesian Mission Collection.

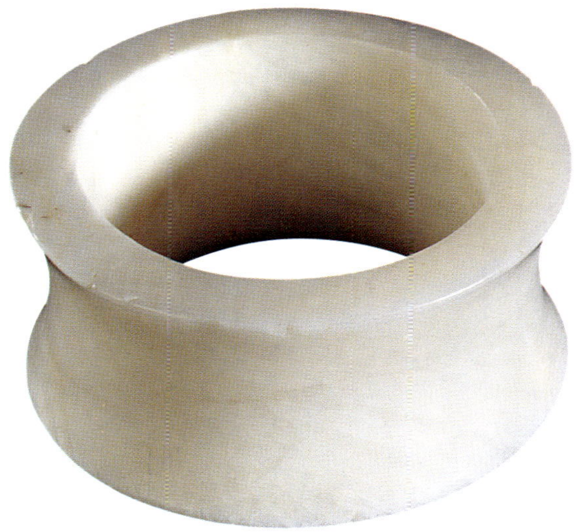

opposite: *Bakiha* Breast Ornaments, Vella Lavella, Solomon Islands

Embodying the higher powers of the ancestors and worn only by men of chiefly rank as a marker of their authority, the *bakiha* breast ornament combined items of currency and value into a display of wealth and influence. *Bakiha* also applies to the ring as a separate item, cut from fossil giant clam shell (*Tridacna gigas*) with its characteristic yellow stain, which in its plain form serves as shell money In the ornament form, the *bakiha* is backed with turtle shell and embellished with attachments of shell money beads, glass trade-beads, imported shirt buttons and teeth of opossums, porpoises and dogs, many of which feature in different contexts as money. This form of breast ornament is worn quite widely in the western Solomon Islands of New Georgia and Vella Lavella where it is also known as a *tarkola*. from left: *Length (with cord) 99 cm; length (with cord) 80 cm.*

from left: *AM 47649. Purchased from Mr A.M. Bensley 1976.*
AM 16409. Owned by Chief Ingova of Roviana Lagoon, collected by Admiral Davis of HMS Royalist *1892–93. James Edge-Partington Collection. Presented by Dr Thomson Wilson Leys Memorial 1924.*

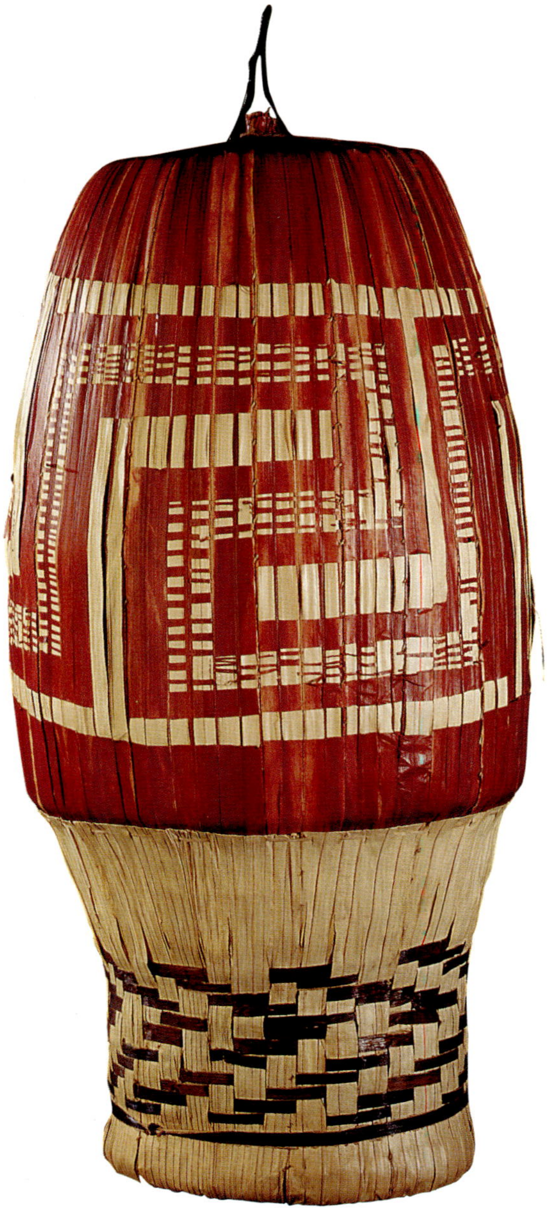

Upi, Initiation Hat, Teop Village, North Bougainville

All adolescent boys in villages on the north coast of Bougainville wear *upi* hats to hide and protect their growing hair. *Upi* boys have to obey special restrictions, especially any contact with women, for several years as part of their initiation into manhood. Made of the dried and bleached leaves of a small fan-palm stitched over a thin bamboo frame, the *upi* for everyday wear is usually left plain. Important ceremonies are held when the boys take on the *upi*, when some of the restrictions on *upi* wearers are lifted, and when the *upi* itself is removed. For the second ceremony, the boys wear a special *upi* such as this one, ornamented with elaborate patterns cut into palm leaves that have been dyed red in a secret process known only to the mountain people of the interior. *Length 42 cm, circumference 64 cm.*

AM 4588.2. Rev. A. H. Voyce Collection. Presented by Sir William Goodfellow 1934.

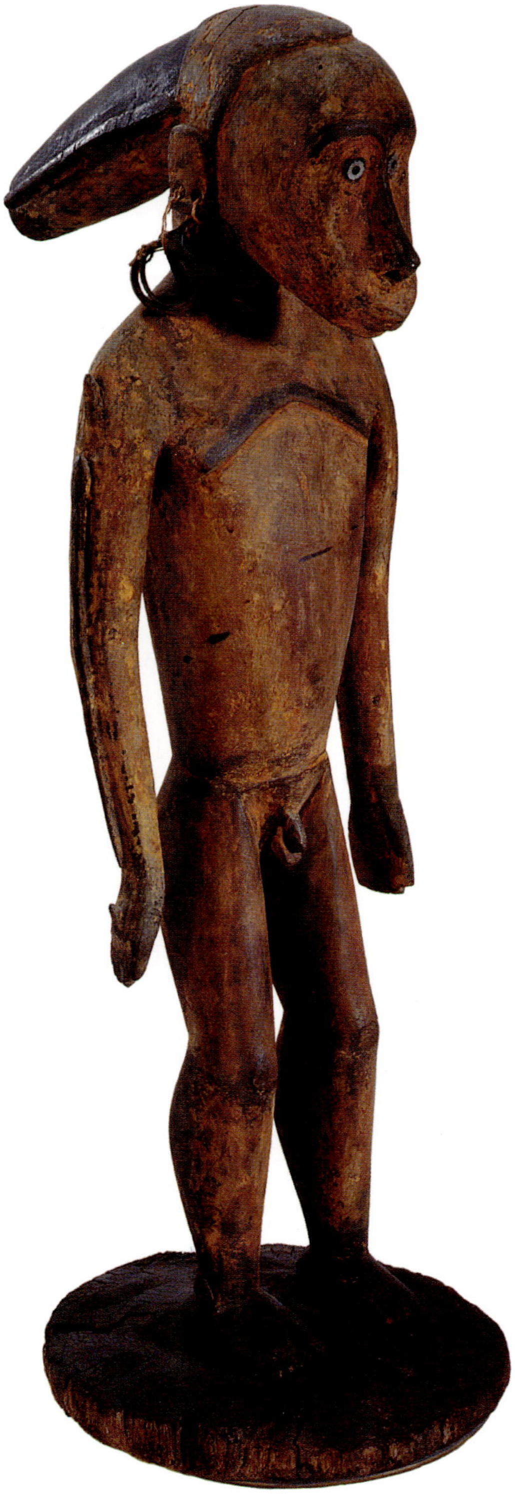

Munge-Dukna, Santa Cruz Islands

Carved figures in the Pacific are often decorated with the jewellery and adornment worn by living people. This *munge-dukna* household image of a man's guardian deity wears turtle shell rings in its ears and is depicted with the elongated *abe* hairstyle restricted to men of rank and influence in the community. *Length 67 cm, width 18 cm.*

AM 52442. Melanesian Mission Collection.

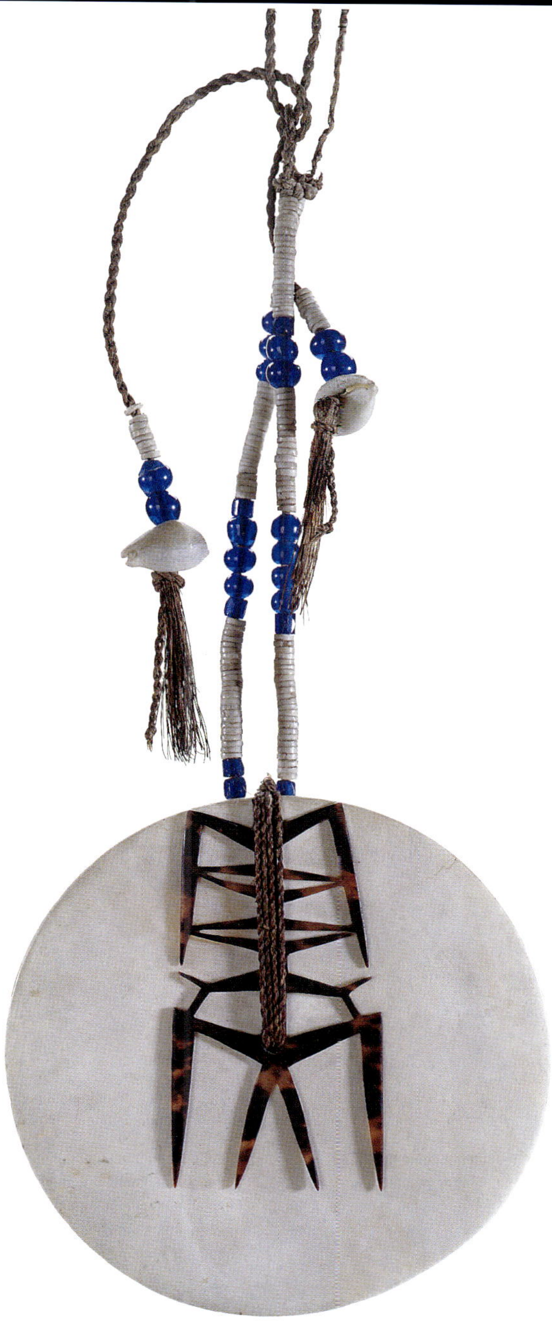

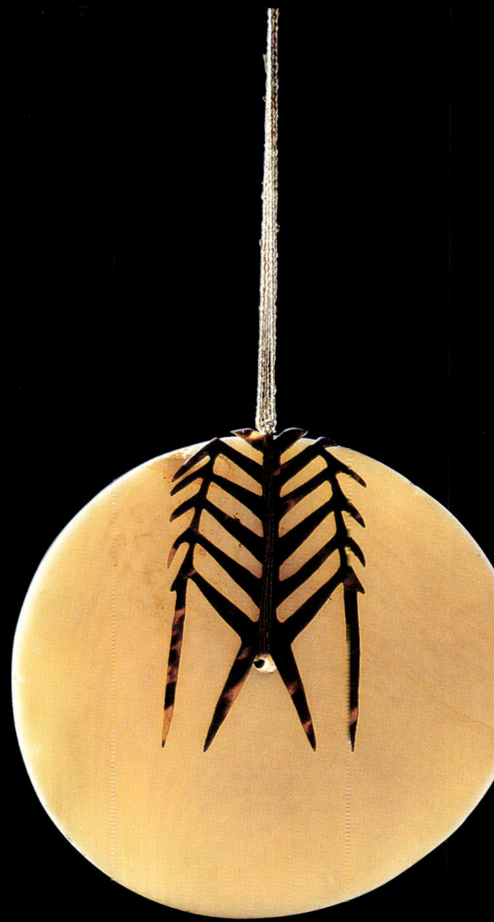

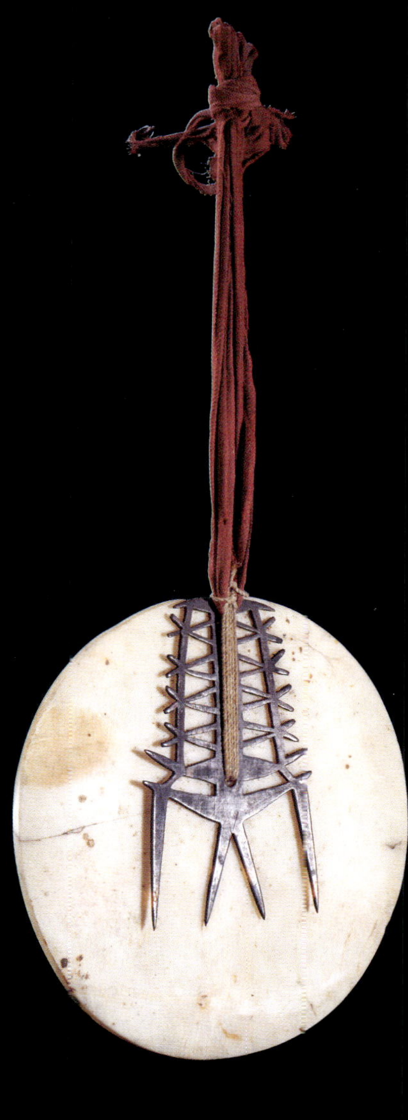

***Tema*, Breast Pendants, Santa Cruz Islands**

Important men wear white clam shell *tema* discs on their chest for ceremonies and formerly also for fighting. Nowadays, *tema* are worn along with a full set of other shell and feather ornaments by young men in the *nelo* dance, which celebrates their attaining of maturity Interpretations vary as to what is depicted by the turtle shell overlay but most see it as a frigate bird, sometimes with abstract fish or dolphins above. Archaeological excavations in the Santa Cruz area have demonstrated that the large *Tridacna* discs have been made there for almost 3000 years. clockwise from top left: *Diameter 15 cm; diameter 13 cm; diameter 17 cm.*

clockwise from top left: *AM 7317. Presented by Mr F. Crossley Mappin 1925.*
AM 18131. Presented by Miss E. Burgess and Mrs Ford Wilson 1932.
AM 20292.2. Purchased from Mr J. O'Neill 1934.

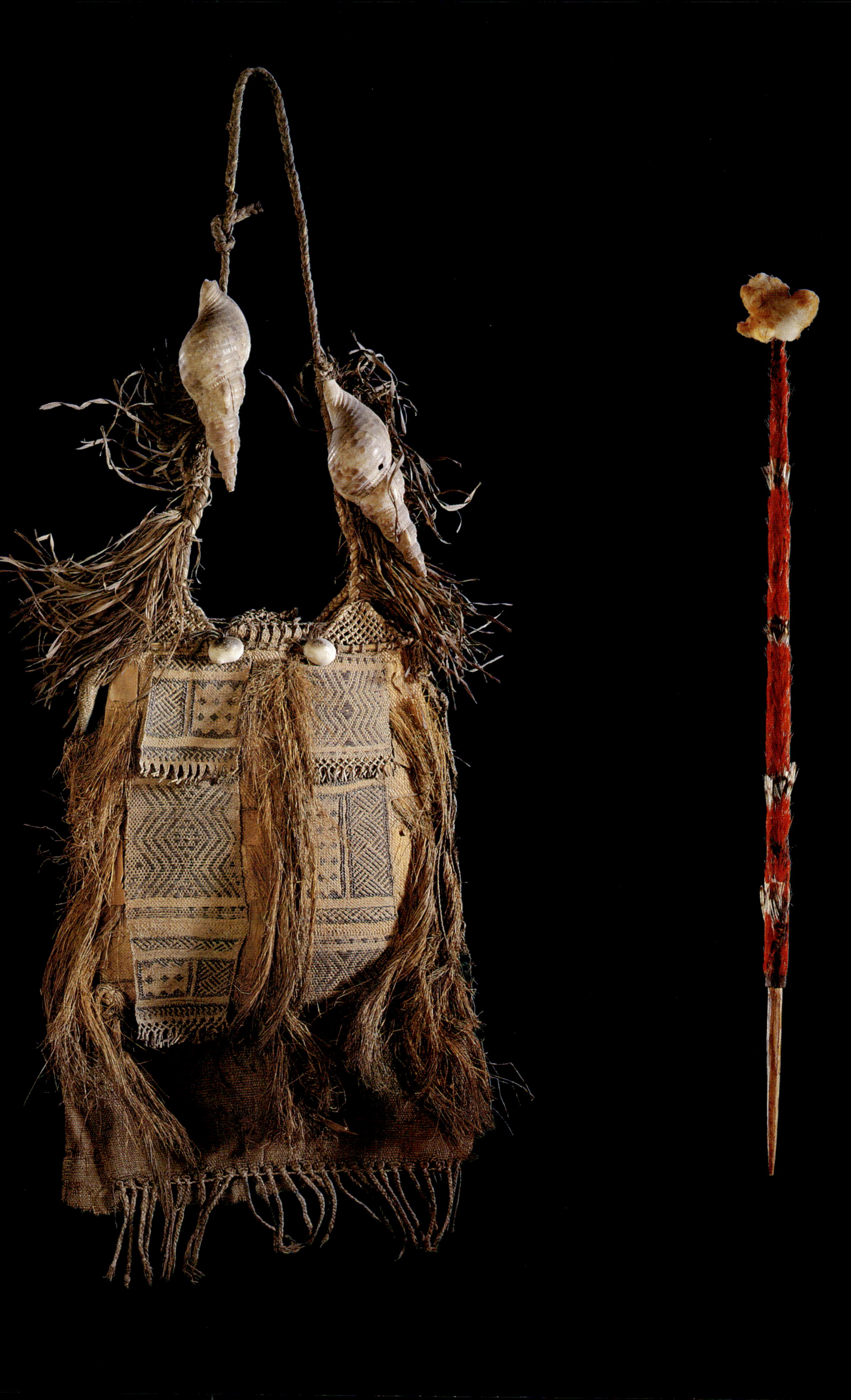

Loin Block, Big Bay, North-eastern Espiritu Santo, Vanuatu

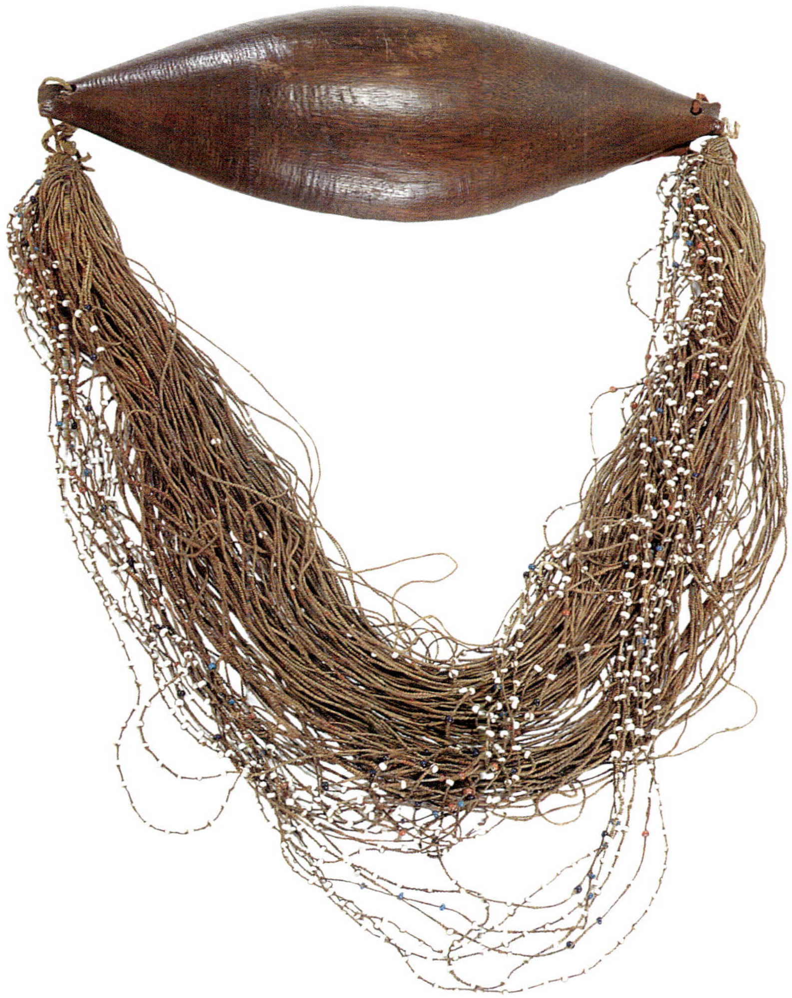

This curious piece of costume was worn by men over their pandanus loin cloths. The ovoid wooden shape was held with a string around the waist so that it rested horizontally at the rear above the buttocks. The loop of fibre strings ornamented with glass beads and shell discs hung down as a bundle in front over the man's pubic mat. Some accounts claim that it was used as a seat when the wearer sat on damp ground, but its original purpose is probably obscured by a long history of development. *Length 29 cm, width 11.5 cm.*

AM 3996. James Edge-Partington Collection. Presented by Dr Thomson Wilson Leys Memorial 1924.

Armlet, Tanna, Vanuatu

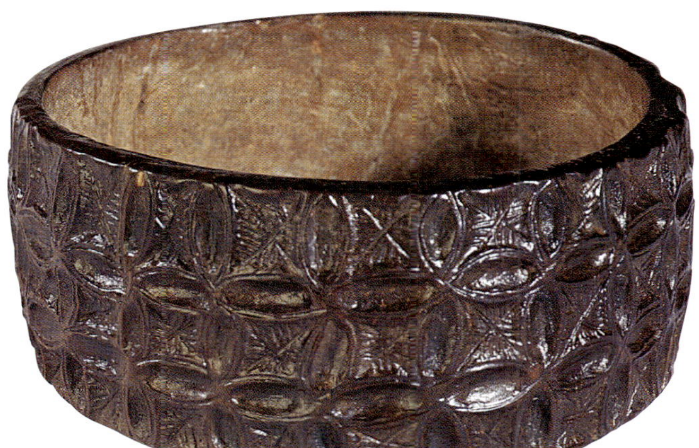

Cut from a coconut shell, this armlet features the same carved design often seen on the butt of fighting clubs from Tanna and Erromango. The pattern has been considered as derived from plant forms but it is also very reminiscent of tapa barkcloth designs common in Fiji, Tonga and Samoa. Many men on Tanna used to wear these armlets on their upper arm, often as many as six. Apart from their ornamental role, these armlets were also used to hold a man's plaited fibre sling, which he used to throw stones and spears. *Diameter 9.5 cm, height 4 cm.*

AM 31503. W. O. Oldman Collection 1948.

opposite left: Bag for Betel-Chewing Gear, Santa Cruz Islands

Small bags for carrying their betel chewing equipment and supplies were worn by Santa Cruz men on their upper arm and shoulder. Some of these bags were made of textiles woven by men from banana fibres on the local back-strap loom. Others were plaited by hand from fibres both plain and dyed. This unusual bag combines woven and plaited panels. It has been coloured with orange turmeric powder and decorated with shells, all combining to make an ornament as well as a functional bag. *Length 63 cm, width 23 cm.*

AM 14391. Purchased from Miss Isaacs 1925.

opposite right: *Noveapu*, Feather Head-Ornament, Santa Cruz Islands

Red feather money made from the feathers of small honey-eaters (*Myzomela cardinalis*) is the basis of a complex trading and monetary system linking the islands of Utupua, Vanikoro, Reef Islands, Duff Islands and Santa Cruz. The same red feathers are prominent on this head ornament, worn especially by young men in the *nelo* dancing, when they appear in full shell and feather ceremonial dress. *Length 36 cm.*

AM 46854. Presented by Dr Geoffrey Blake-Palmer 1975.

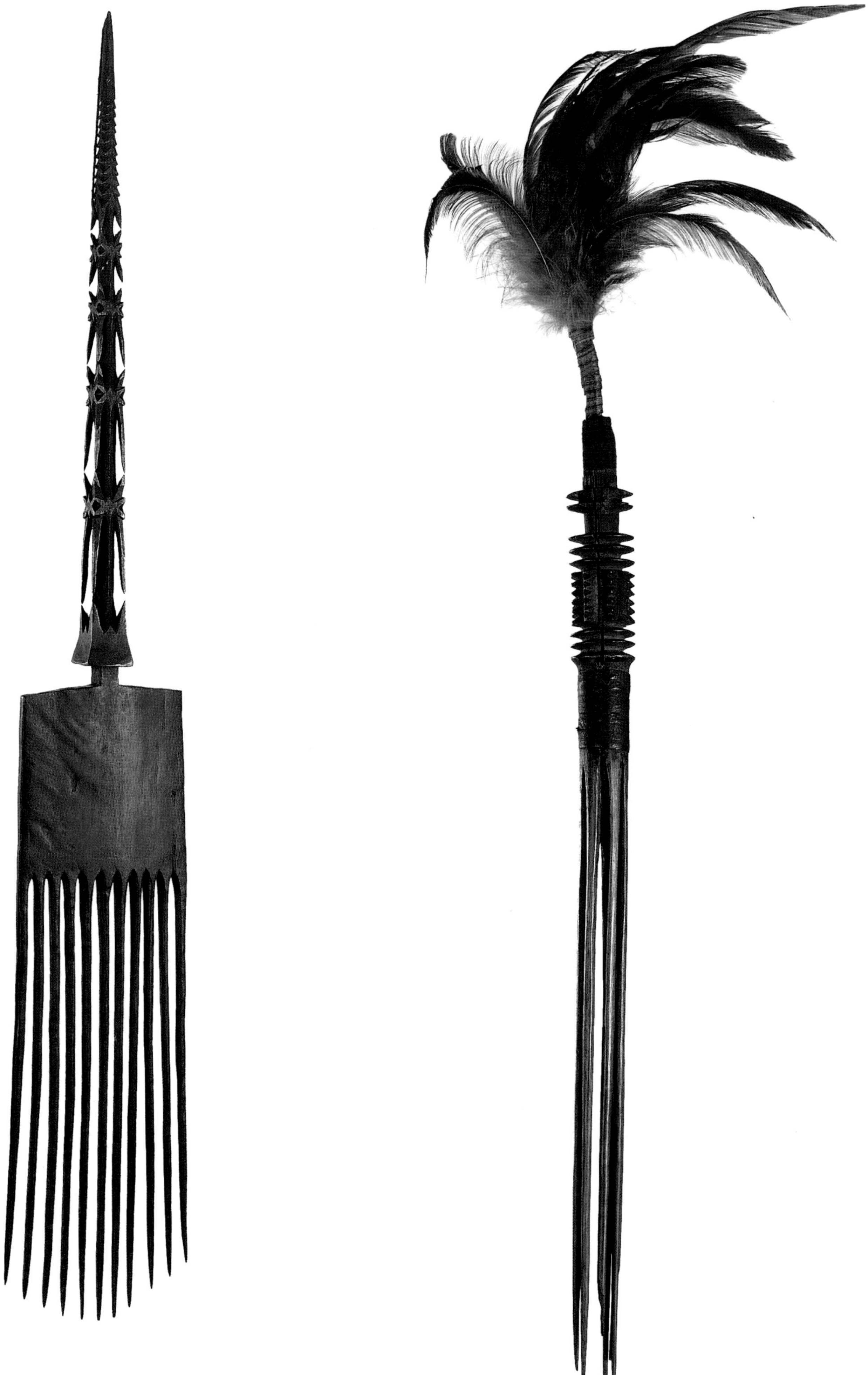

PEARL SHELL NECK PENDANT, TANNA, VANUATU

Pearl shell pendants of this form were quite widespread among various islands of Vanuatu. Exactly the same pendant made in numbers on the island of Mer (Murray) in Torres Strait are said to have first been made by a man from Tanna who was shipwrecked on Mer in the later nineteenth century. From then on, the people of Mer have copied his original design, which they interpret as representing the larval form of an ant-lion with its huge jaws, waiting for an ant to fall into its trap. On Mer, it is worn by both men and women. *Length 11.8 cm, width 2.8 cm.*

AM 14969. James Edge-Partington Collection. Presented by Dr Thomson Wilson Leys Memorial 1924

opposite left: **COMB, EFATE, VANUATU**

Carved out of one piece of hardwood, the decorative spike on this comb replicates the ornate barbed spears formerly made on Efate. Combs from Efate are now quite rare in museum collections, probably because the cultures of this island have been strongly affected by European settlement and influence. Traditionally, men of Efate let their hair grow long and often dyed it yellow, wearing it tied up in a high shock decorated with a comb. As European-influenced short hairstyles became popular, the manufacture and use of decorative combs declined drastically. *Length 50.5 cm, width 5 cm.*

AM 14993. James Edge-Partington Collection. Presented by Dr Thomson Wilson Leys Memorial 1924.

opposite right: **COMB, EFATE, VANUATU**

As with most of the combs made on Efate, this has been carved from one piece of hardwood and features a decorative spike with projecting discs, some notching, and a plume of waving feathers. Like other Pacific so-called combs, this is clearly a decorative ornament rather than a functional comb, even more obviously here where the long teeth are arranged in a circle, designed to slide into the man's thick hairdo and to hold in place as an ornament. Different types of combs may have been related to a man's status in the hierarchy of chiefly titles in traditional Efate society, but these correspondences are now unclear. *Length 54 cm, width 2 cm.*

AM 15044. James Edge-Partington Collection. Presented by Dr Thomson Wilson Leys Memorial 1924.

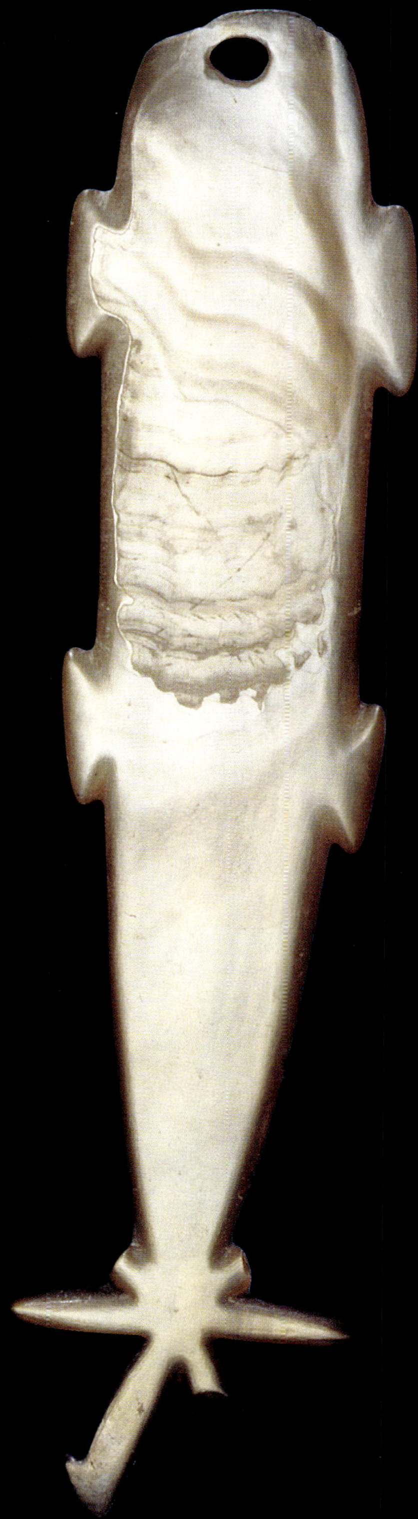

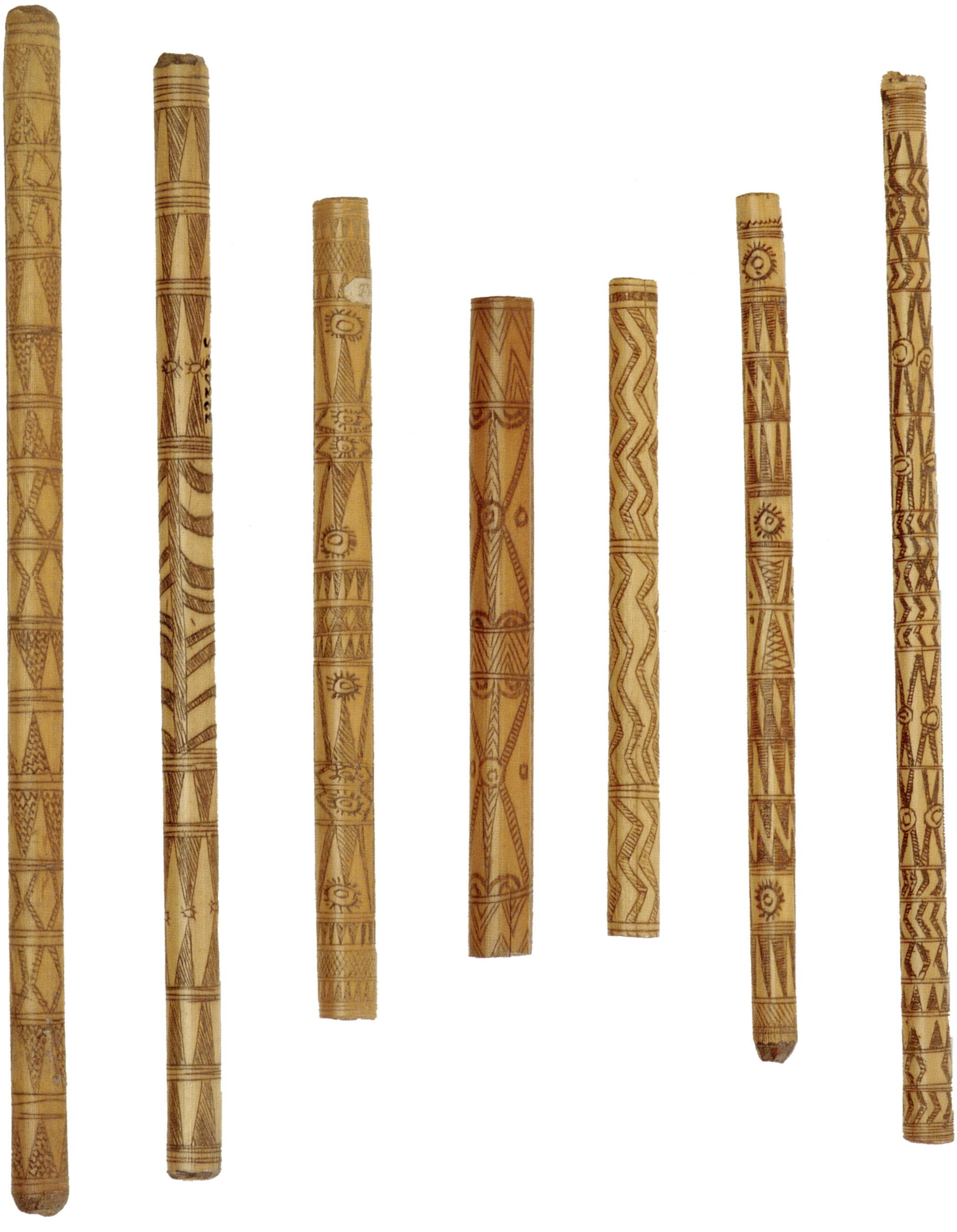

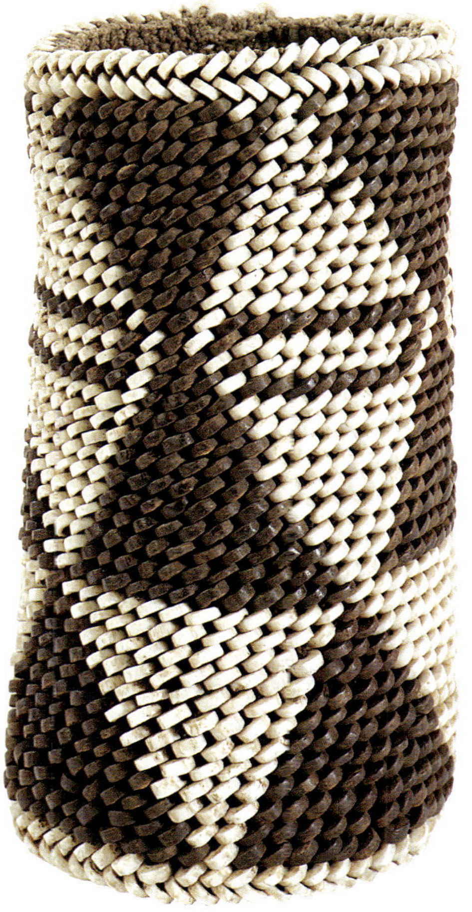

Pen, Arm Bands, Vanuatu

Traditional individually drilled discs of white shell and black coconut shell and coconut wood have been worked on to a plaited fibre foundation of native bark string to make these armbands. The technique attaches the discs in a characteristic sloping arrangement. Arm bands exactly like these collected on Ambrym in 1949 were said to indicate a man's acquisition of a special ritual that was not associated with the local graded system. In the complex trading systems that linked Ambrym, Malekula and nearby islands, 'copyrights' to new rituals could be purchased from trading partners. from top: *Height 18.5 cm; height 12.5 cm.*

from top: *AM 31586. W. O. Oldman Collection 1948.*
AM 31590. W. O. Oldman Collection 1948.

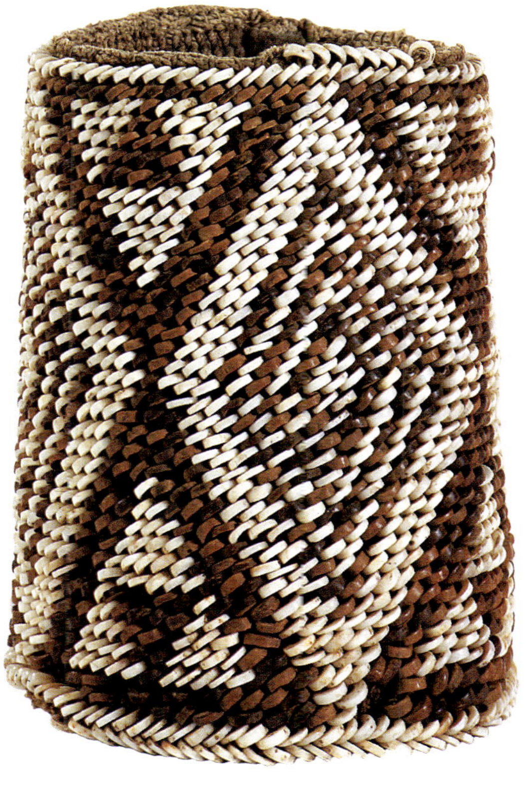

opposite: **Ear sticks, northern Vanuatu**

Formerly worn widely through men's and women's pierced earlobes in northern Vanuatu, especially the Banks Islands, Ambae and Maewo, these beautiful delicately incised ear ornaments have now completely disappeared from use. Sections of designs were incised and smoke-blackened on long lengths of reeds or sedges, which were then cut to the desired lengths. Most individuals had both earlobes pierced as a religious protection in preparation for entering the afterworld, but normally only one ear stick was worn at a time. The designs are derived from *suque* graded society symbols and represent sea life, fish, plants, and spirit figures. from left: *Length 18.8 cm; length 17.6 cm; length 12.7 cm; length 10.3 cm; length 10.1 cm; length 13.4 cm; length 16.5 cm.*

from left: *AM 4849. Presented by Mrs Tuke 1930.*
AM 32343.5 Presented by Rev. C. Palmer 1951.
AM 32343.11 Presented by Rev. C. Palmer 1951.
AM 32343.1 Presented by Rev. C. Palmer 1951.
AM 12525. Presented by Hon. E. Mitchelson 1910.
AM 4533. Presented by Miss White 1929.
AM 32320.8. Presented by Rev. C. Palmer 1951.

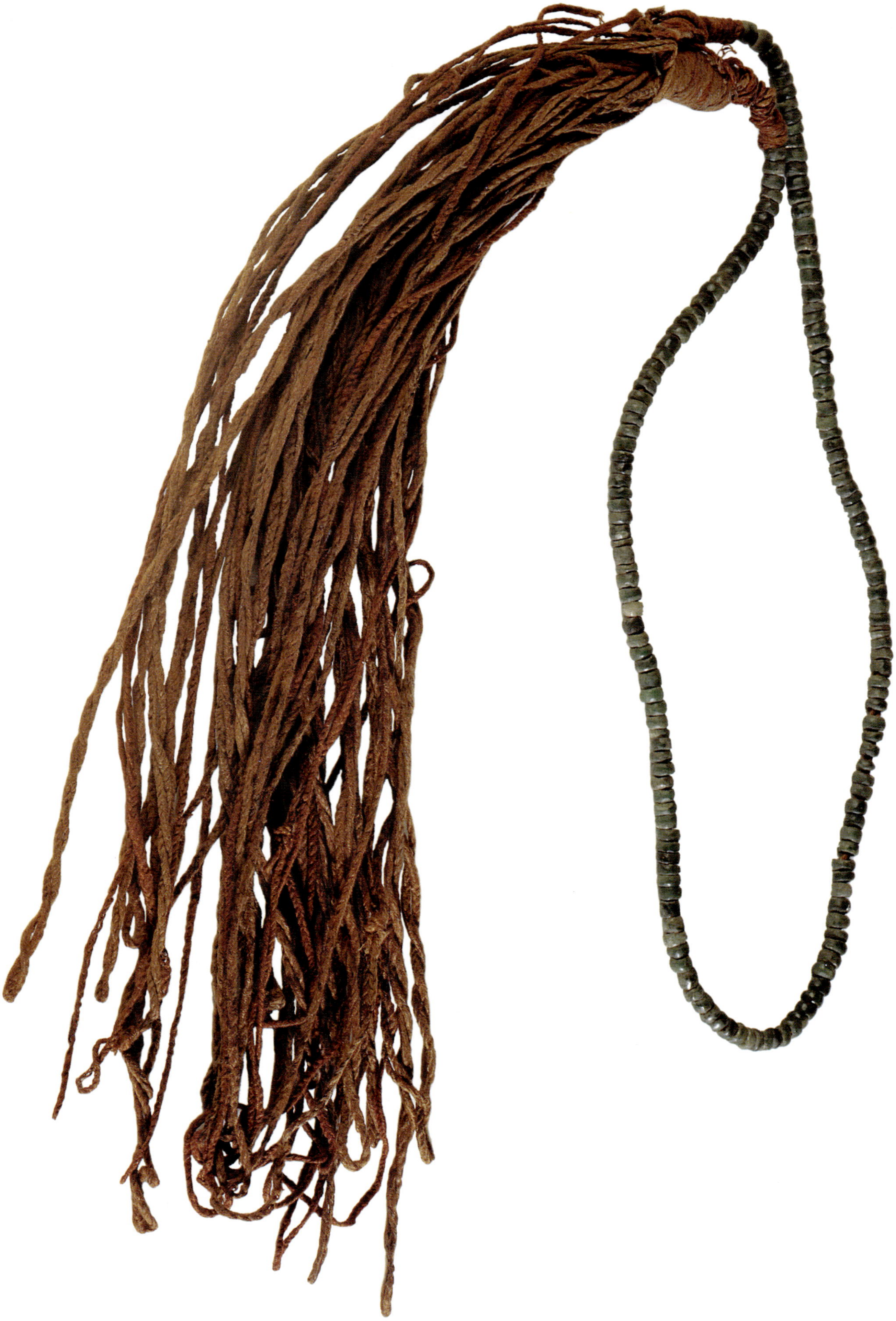

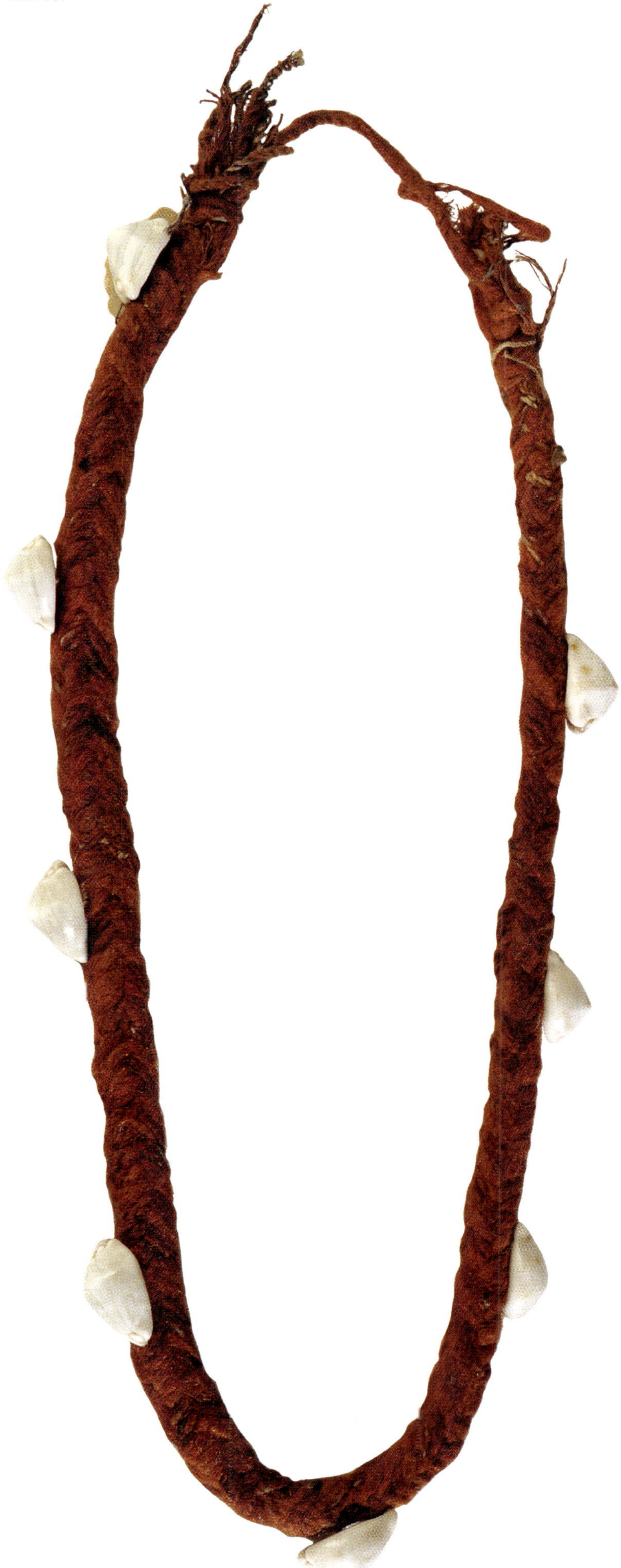

MAN'S BELT, UVEA, LOYALTY ISLANDS NEW CALEDONIA

Young men wore these belts low on their hips with a separate penis wrapper ending in a long cloth tassel. The belt is made of flying-fox fur plaited with invisible banana fibre to give it strength. Cowrie shells are attached at intervals to produce an ornamental item of high value that also emphasises the virility and masculinity of a man in his prime. *Length 72 cm.*

AM 15017. James Edge-Partington Collection. Presented by Dr Thomson Wilson Leys Memorial 1924.

opposite: ***MECIWE*, NECKLACE LOYALTY ISLANDS, NEW CALEDONIA**

This rare necklace consists of beads of serpentine with attached skeins of plaited reddish hair from the flying fox (*Pteropus*). The brightest coloured hair was stripped from the animal and plaited with banana fibre to give it strength. Each bead of serpentine has been separately shaped and drilled; this number of beads represents the work of several generations. These necklaces were among the most prestigious and highly valued possessions of the wives of chiefs. *Length 91 cm.*

AM 13163. Purchased from Mr J. W. Hadfield 1919.

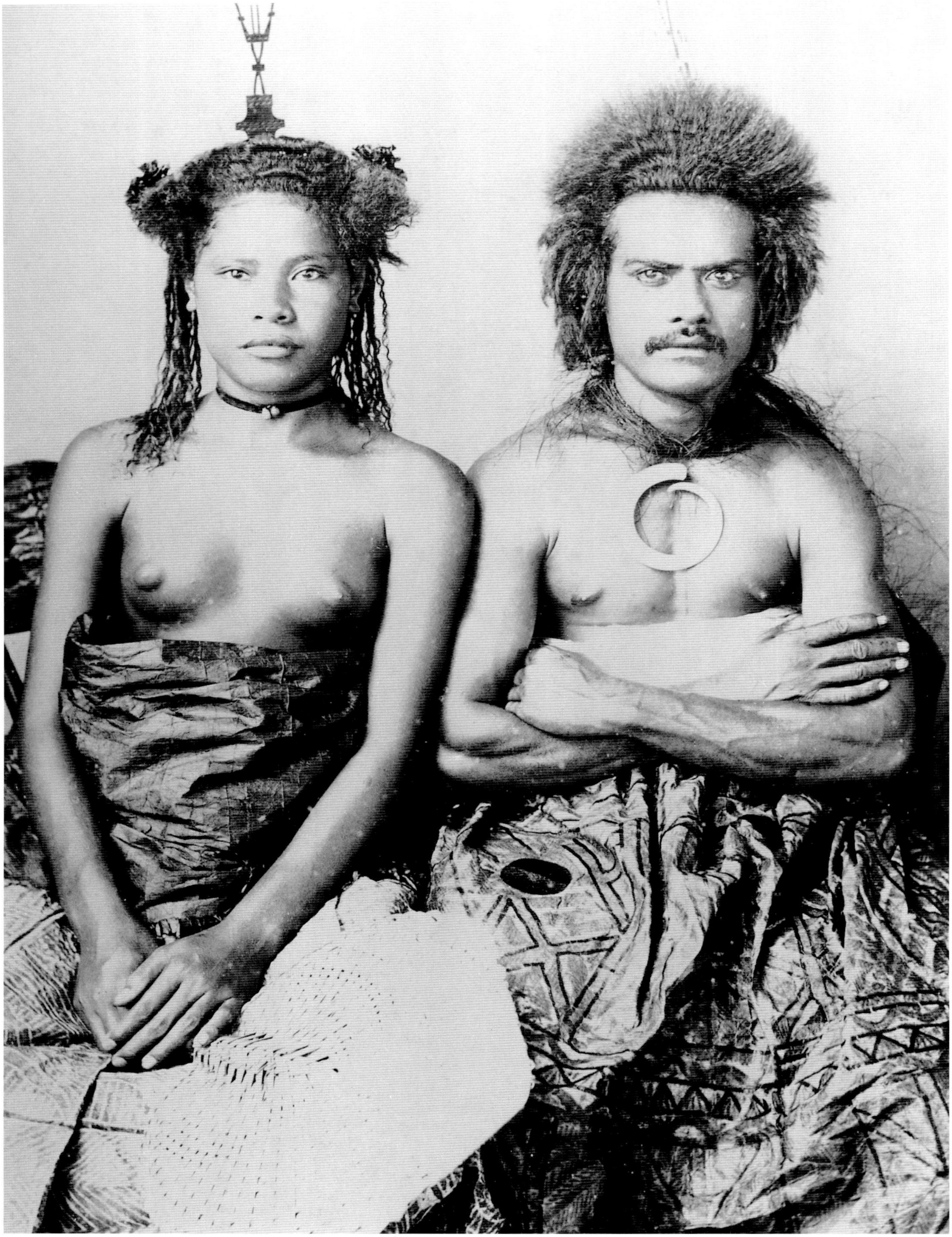

CHAPTER FOUR

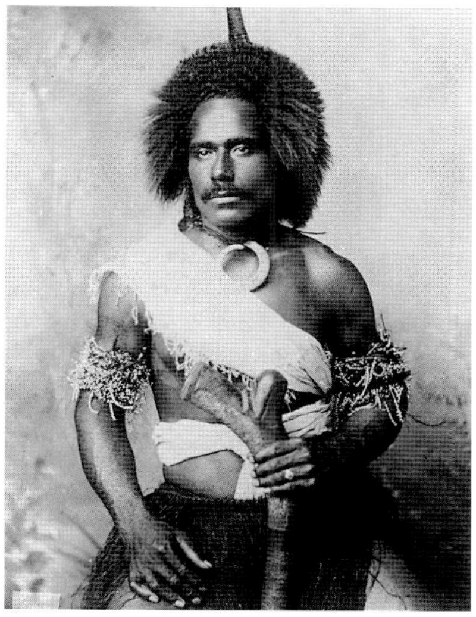

Warrior With Club, Fiji, 1890s

This young Fijian man posing in a photographer's studio in Suva has probably been dressed especially for the photo session. He wears an ornamental comb in his hair and a sash of fine white masi *barkcloth across his chest. His arm bands are composed of many strings of horse-hair threaded at intervals with imported glass trade beads. This combination of introduced horsehair and trade beads became popular with Fijian men as a decoration both for their own bodies and for their war clubs, and was often wound around a favourite weapon. The finely plaited strings of the suspension cord for his circular boar-tusk pendant or* batinivuaka *are also strung with tiny glass beads. This cord holds his* batinivuaka *tight at the base of his neck in the approved traditional manner, rather than flopping against his chest as is so often seen nowadays.*

Photo: Thomas Andrew, Alexander Turnbull Library, Wellington 98292-1/2, Reference Number PA7-01-07-2

opposite: **A Young Couple of high rank, Tonga, 1880s**

With their traditional hairstyles, this young couple pose in barkcloth garments that have been patterned by rubbing over stitched leaf kupesi *tablets. Around her waist the woman has added a rare piece of Tongan dark tapa, or* ngatu'uli, *of the type exchanged between bride and groom at their wedding. Complementing their wedding outfits, they both wear decorative combs in their hair. Around their necks, the groom has a valuable curled boar-tusk ornament, while the woman wears a tight black neck band holding a pair of tiny cowrie shells symbolic of fertility.*

Photo: Burton Brothers, Auckland Museum

POLYNESIA

FIJI, TONGA, SAMOA, NIUE, COOK ISLANDS, AUSTRAL ISLANDS AND SOCIETY ISLANDS, MARQUESAS ISLANDS, EASTER ISLAND, HAWAI'I, POLYNESIAN OUTLIERS

POLYNESIA GENERALLY REFERS to those island groups situated within the often-cited 'Polynesian triangle' whose outer extremes are demarcated by Hawai'i in the north, Rapanui (Easter Island) in the east and Aotearoa (New Zealand) in the south-west. Included here however are the Polynesian outliers, those islands settled by Polynesian peoples situated in island Melanesia. Fiji, although it straddles Polynesia and Melanesia, is also included here in Polynesia because of its geographic proximity, but more importantly its social and historical links to this area, especially with the islands of western Polynesia.

A wide range of island types is to be found within this region from the high volcanic islands of the Society, Hawaiian, Marquesan and Samoan islands, to the low-lying coral atolls of the Tokelau, Tuamotu and Tuvalu islands. The range of island types exists even within island groups such as Fiji, Tonga and the Cooks, with their mix of volcanic, raised coral and limestone islands, as well as coral islands the highest points of which are only a matter of metres above sea level.

Polynesia makes up the largest geographical sub-division of the Pacific region. Though general cultural concepts and the expression of these have evolved in different ways, there remains a cultural, artistic and linguistic homogeneity indicative of a shared Polynesian culture that developed about 3000 years ago in the 'cradle of Polynesia' that is Fiji, Tonga and Samoa. After the settlement of eastern Polynesia, inter-island contact continued to be important for economic, political and social reasons. The complex exchange system that developed between Fiji, Tonga and Samoa prior to European contact is a good example. For the highly stratified society of Tonga, it was vital to establish and maintain chiefly marriage alliances with Samoa and Fiji. It was through these ties that valued items such as ocean-going canoes, red parrot feathers, decorated barkcloth, sandalwood, whale teeth, and fine mats were exchanged between the three groups.

Within the highly stratified societies of Polynesia, such as Hawai'i and Tonga, scarce materials were valuable, hence boar tusks, whale ivory and red feathers were reserved for the chiefly. However, generally materials were valued because they encapsulated cultural ideas about fecundity, prestige and aptitude, and though difficult to obtain they were available to anybody with the physical skills, trading acumen and social networks to acquire them.

The Polynesian concept of *mana* extends to the idea that personal possessions may represent an individual, and further, that *mana* is absolutely inherent in body material such as hair, teeth and bones. Consequently, by wearing ornaments that incorporate these materials one may take on the *mana* of a fallen enemy or carry that of a revered ancestor or beloved elder, or they can be worn as tokens of affection for a treasured child or respected sister.

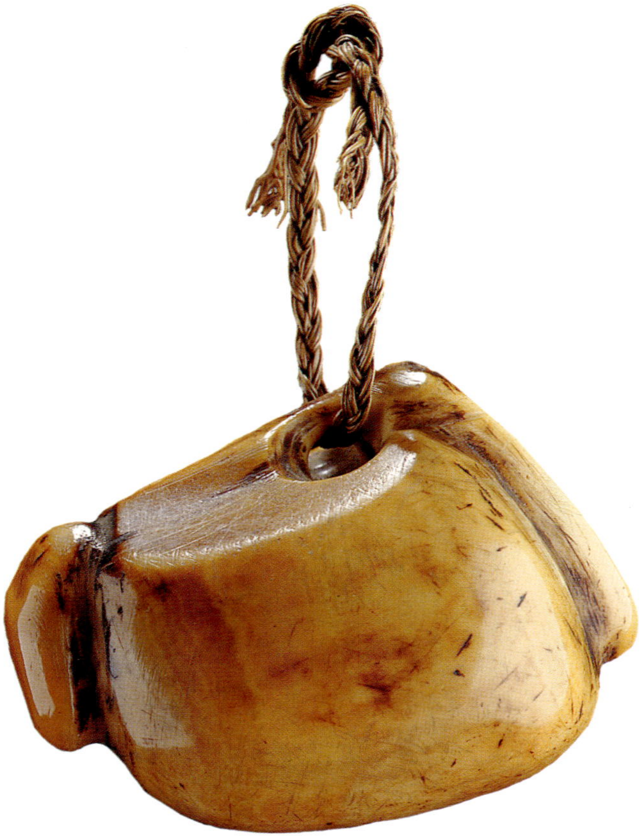

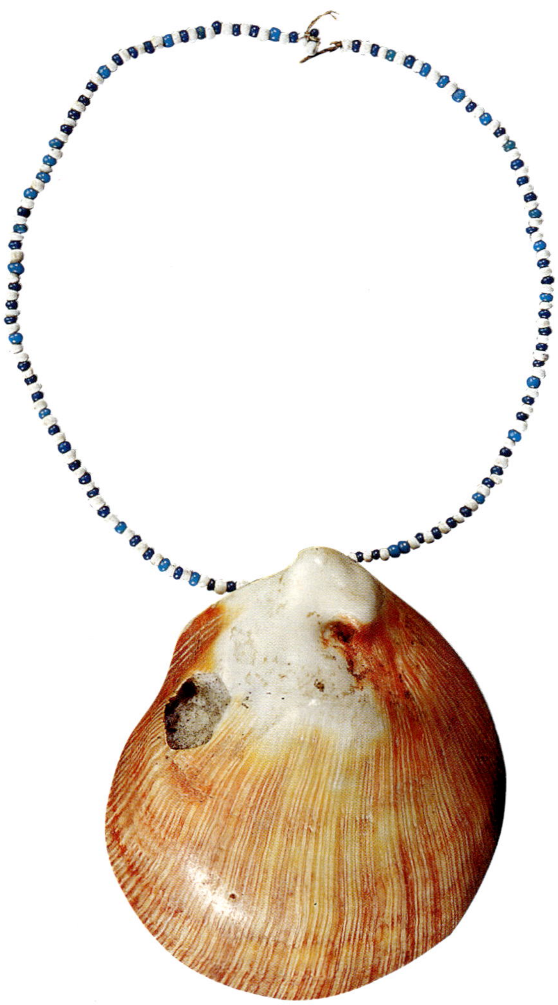

PENDANT, FIJI

The special significance of such pendants is unknown, but because they appear to indicate female genitalia, one theory is that they may be intended as female fertility symbols. Made of sperm whale ivory, a highly prestigious material, these pendants are relatively rare and exhibit the touch of a deft and sure carver's hand. For these reasons they must have been items of great value and import. *Length 4 cm, width 3 cm.*

AM 31568. W. O. Oldman Collection 1948.

***SOVUI*, NECK PENDANT OF *SPONDYLUS* SHELL, FIJI**

Like the cowrie shell, the *Spondylus* shell was the preserve of those of chiefly status. The *sovui* was worn like the pig tusk pendant at the base of the neck. Both of these types of neck ornament often had glass trade-beads strung on their fibre ties. Due to long use, the orange and yellow ribs on the outer surface of this ancient example have been almost worn smooth. *Length of shell 8.5 cm, width 8.3 cm.*

AM 13558. Presented by J. B. Turner Collection 1925.

opposite: ***SISI*, NECKLACE OF SPERM WHALE TEETH VANUA LEVU, FIJI**

Whale teeth, obtained primarily through trade exchanges with Tonga, were rare and therefore very prestigious. Necklaces of graduated whole whale teeth such as this example were some of the most valued items in Fiji. Single, whole, presentation whale teeth, *tabua*, are still highly valued today and maintain ritual significance in contemporary ceremonial exchanges. Smoked *tabua* were the most highly prized treasures, valued for their rich patina. *Length of longest tooth 9.5 cm.*

AM 31896. W. O. Oldman Collection 1948.

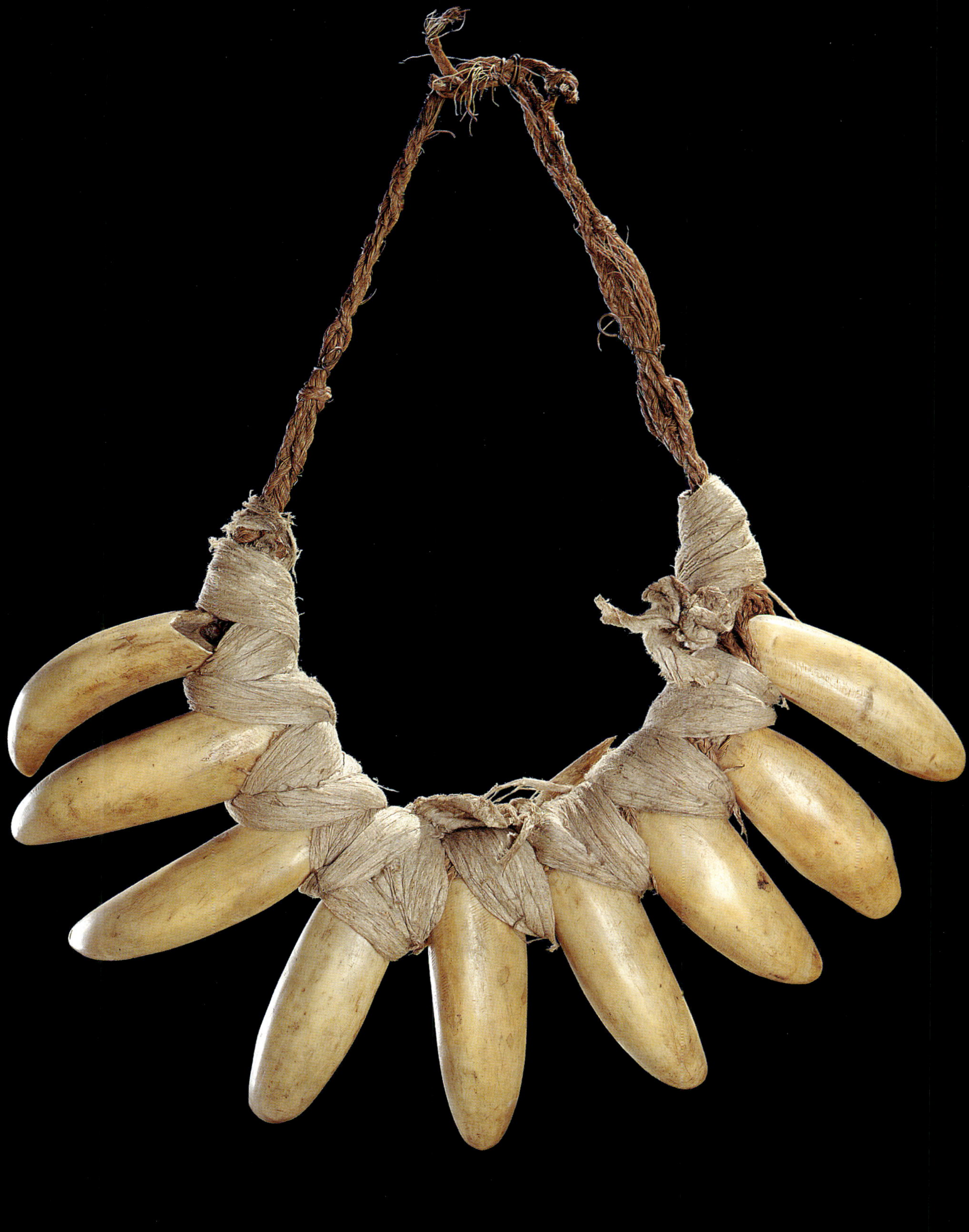

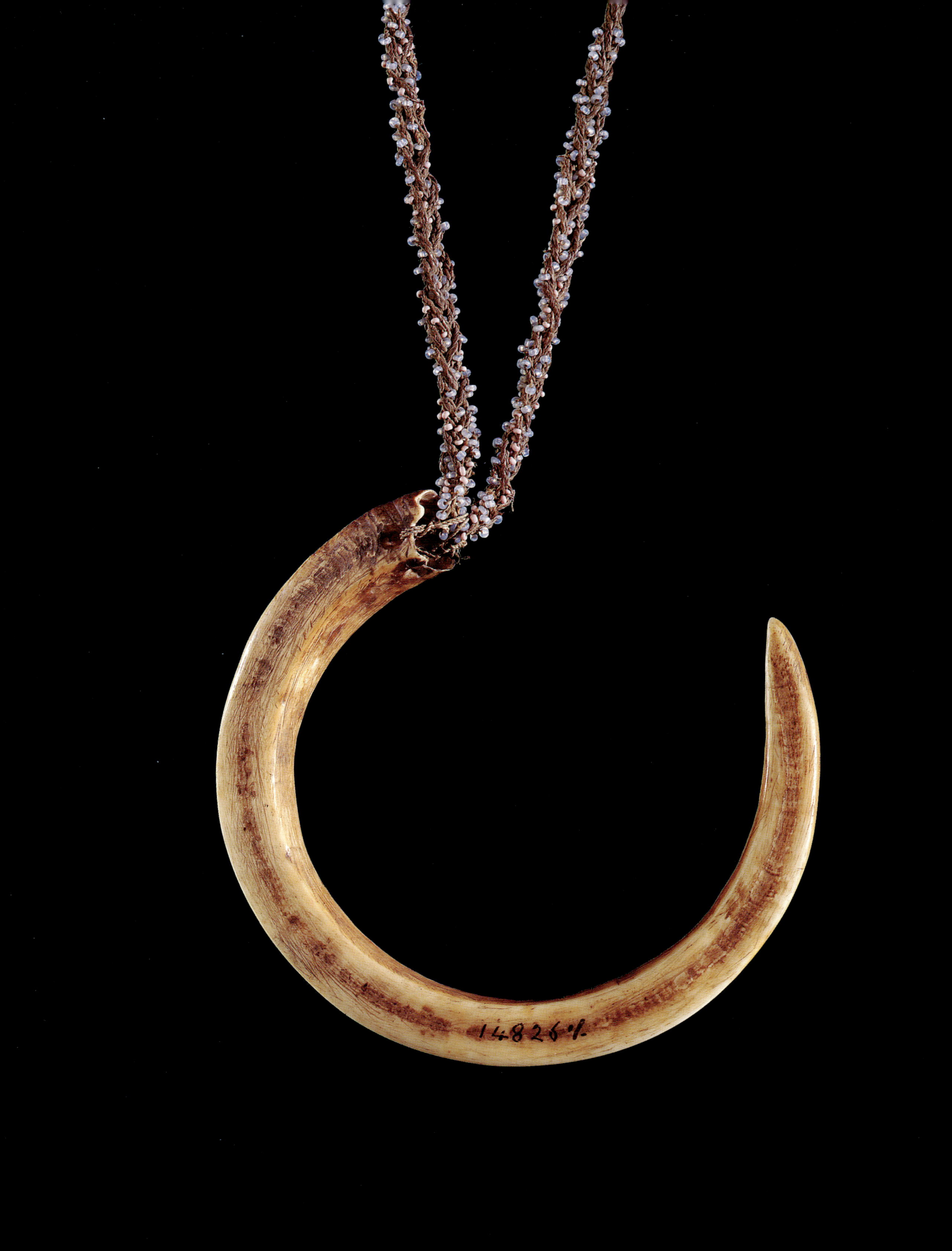

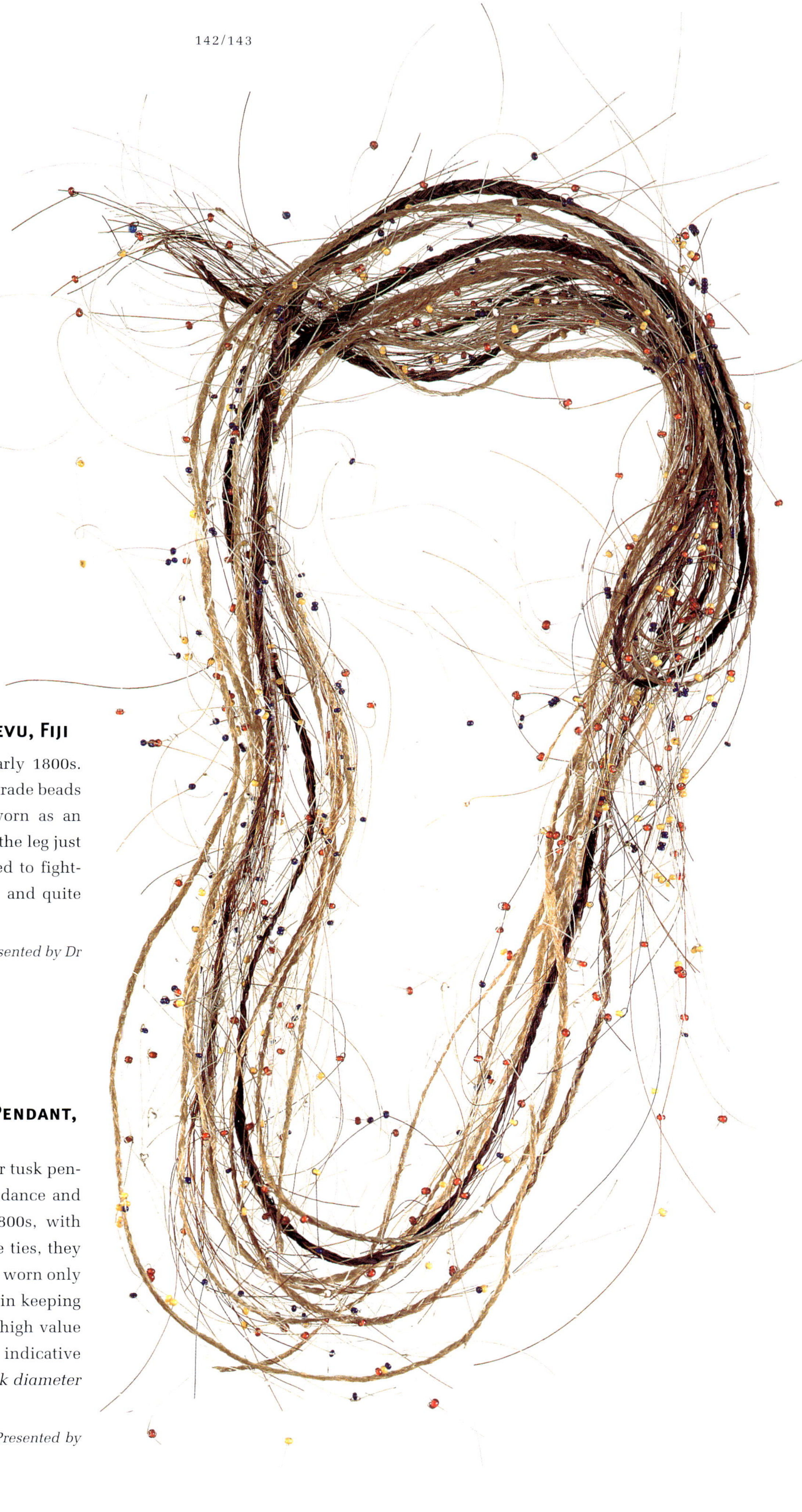

Ornament of Horse Hair, Vanua Levu, Fiji

Horses were introduced into Fiji in the early 1800s. Horsehair strung with introduced coloured trade beads as a prestige material soon came to be worn as an adornment, as arm bands as well as around the leg just below the knee. Horsehair was also attached to fighting clubs and incorporated into fly whisks and quite elaborate wigs. *Length 28 cm, width 11 cm.*

AM 14884. James Edge-Partington Collection. Presented by Dr Thomson Wilson Leys Memorial 1924.

opposite: *Batinivuaka*, Pig Tusk Neck Pendant, Fiji

Worn tight at the base of the neck, these boar tusk pendants were an integral part of ceremonial, dance and war attire. In the late 1700s and early 1800s, with introduced glass beads attached to the fibre ties, they served as symbols of chiefly status and were worn only by those of recognised rank. This would be in keeping with the rest of the Pacific, where pigs are high value items and simply donning a boar tusk was indicative of one's wealth, strength and influence. *Tusk diameter 12.5 cm.*

AM 14826.1. James Edge-Partington Collection. Presented by Dr Thomson Wilson Leys Memorial 1924.

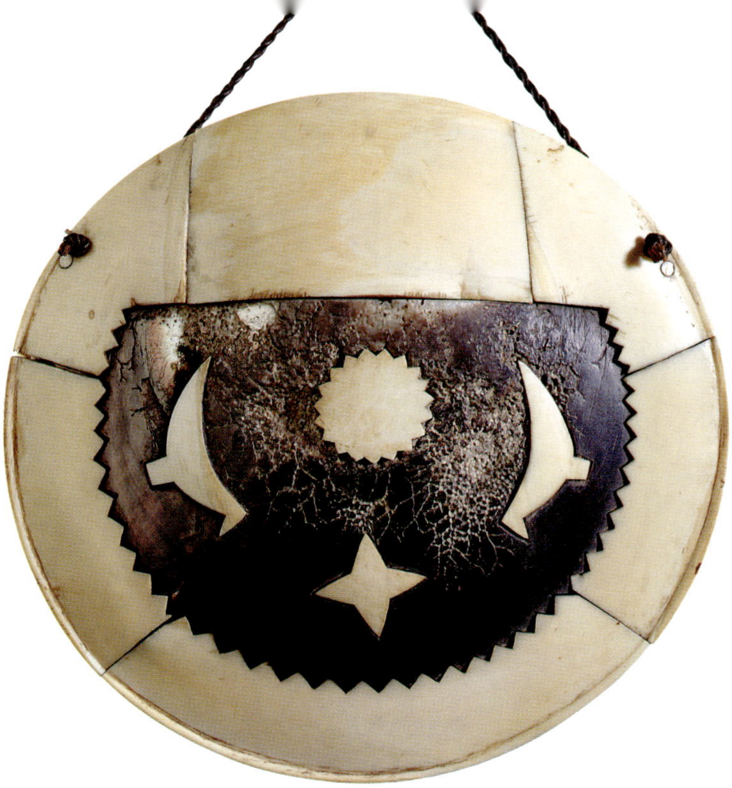

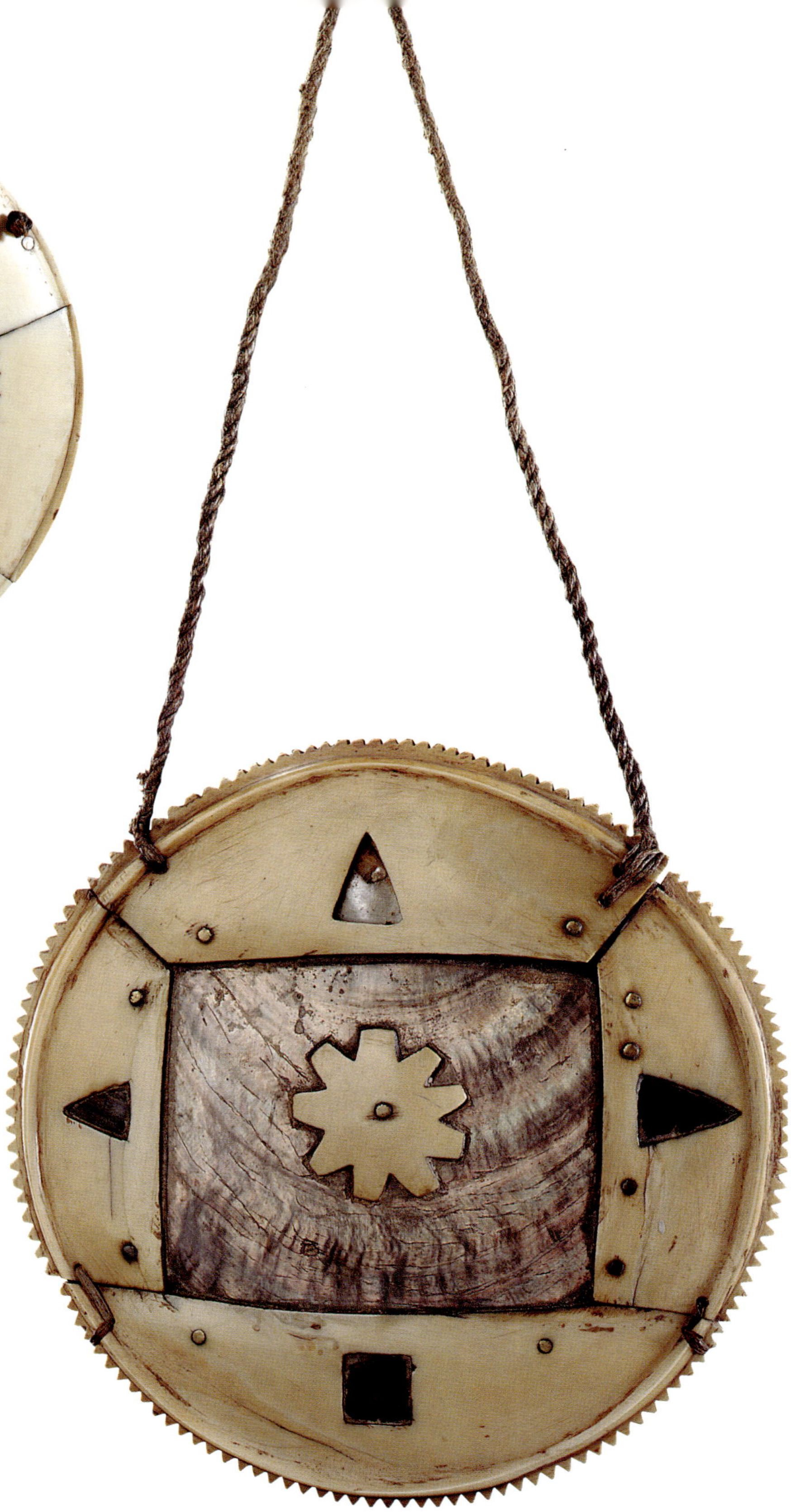

Civavonovono, Chief's Breastplate, Fiji

These *civavonovono*, said to have been made by Tongan and Samoan craftsmen for Fijian chiefs, have evolved from the large whalebone breastplates seen in Tonga by James Cook and his company. They were worn suspended from the neck, and a cord also ran across the back of the breastplate so they could be held rigid against the body during dancing and in combat. As a lone ornament, *civa*, or polished pearl shell, symbolised chiefly status; and in the 1800s its symbolism was enhanced when whale teeth plates were attached to encase the pearl shell. above: *Length 24 cm, width 25.6 cm;* above right: *Length 21 cm, width 21.7 cm.*

above: *AM 31498. W. O. Oldman 1948.*
above right: *AM 31497. W. O. Oldman 1948.*

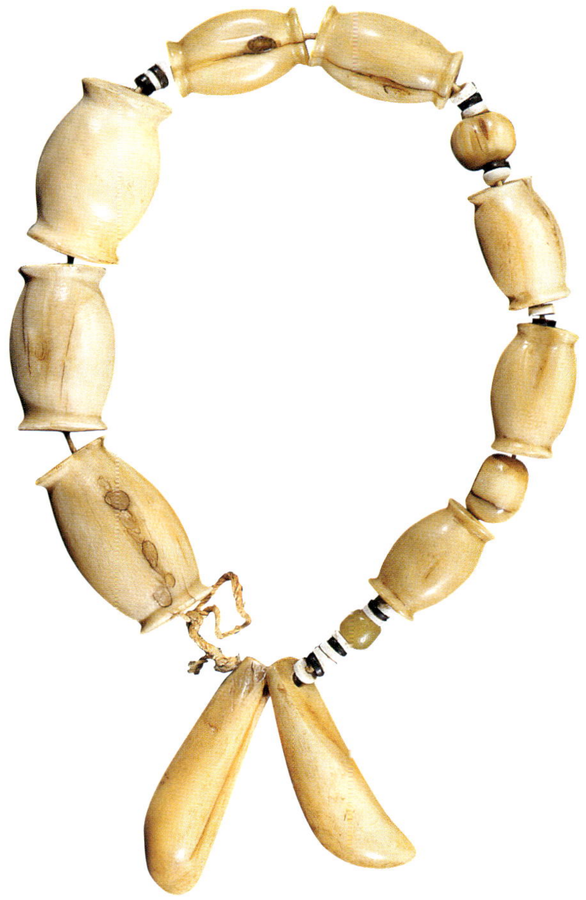

Necklace, Fiji

An undertaking during *iloloku*, mourning rituals, was the piercing and enlargement of one or both earlobes to take *saunidaliga*, ornamental ear plugs. It was believed that to avoid dire and degrading trials in the after-world it was necessary for everybody to have their ears pierced. Consisting of eight ear ornaments of sperm whale teeth, this necklace is also strung with shell discs, a glass bead, two ivory beads and two small unworked sperm whale teeth. *Length 35 cm.*

AM 14835. James Edge-Partington Collection. Presented by Dr Thomson Wilson Leys Memorial 1924.

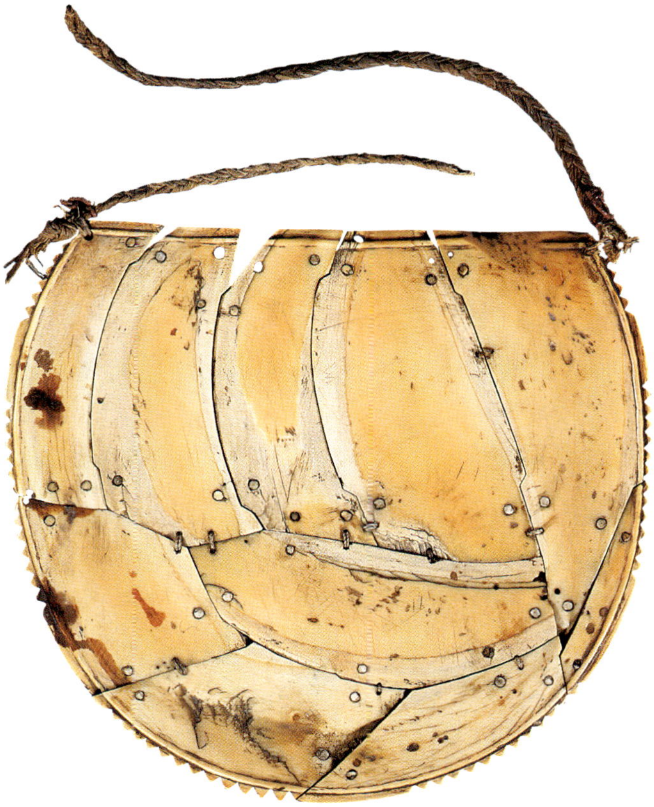

Civatabua, Sperm Whale Teeth Breastplate, Fiji

Whale teeth were the most highly prized of possessions in Fiji in the eighteenth and nineteenth centuries, so much so that it was forbidden for a commoner to own whale ivory. *Civatabua* were believed to confer invulnerability in war by virtue of their symbolic power. And certainly, in long-range combat they did offer physical protection in the form of armour against the Fijian bow and arrow. To achieve the rich patina so esteemed in Fiji the whale teeth are oiled then smoked over a smoky fire of sugar cane kindling. *Length 24.5 cm, width 28 cm.*

AM 31496. W. O. Oldman Collection 1948.

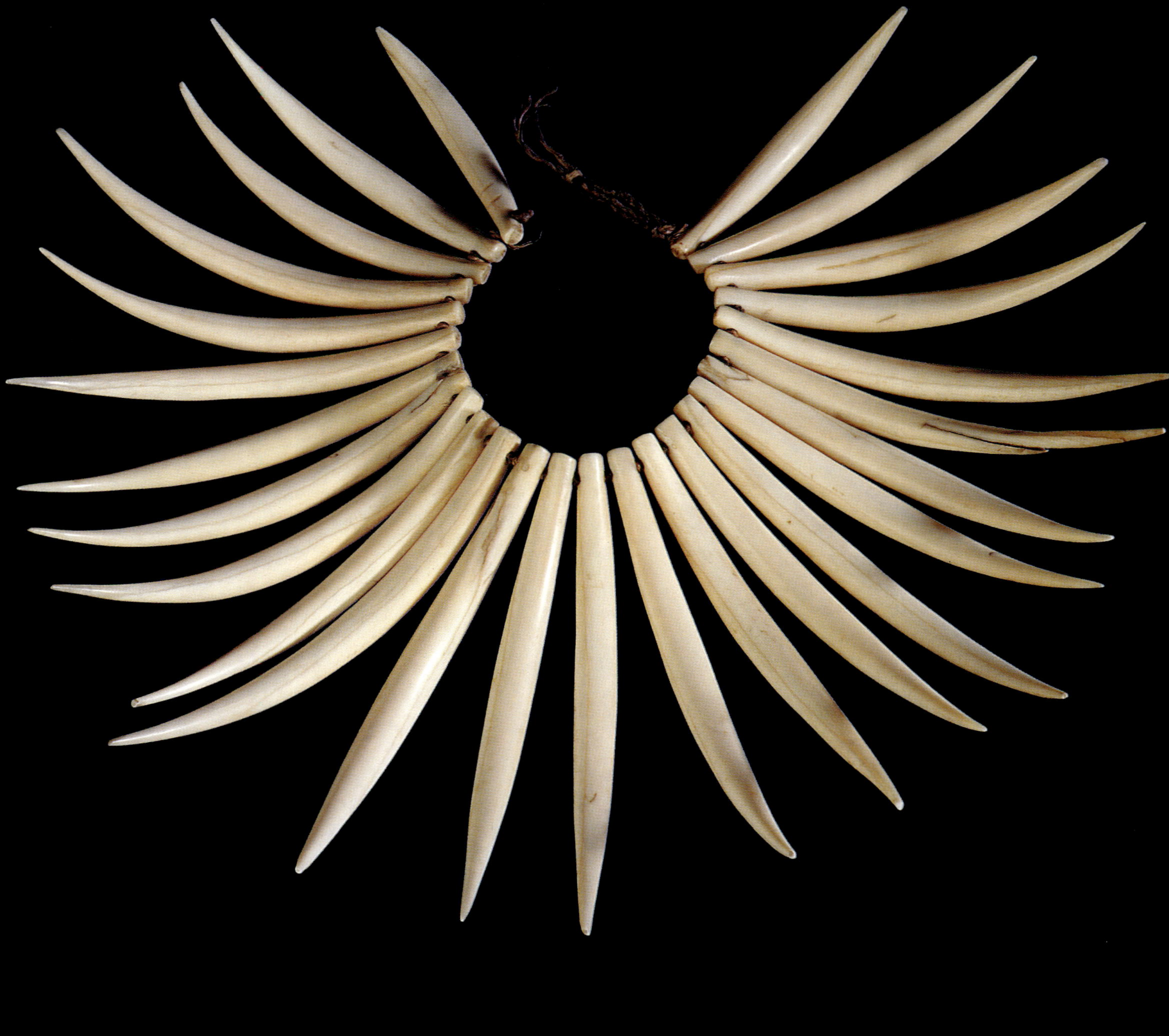

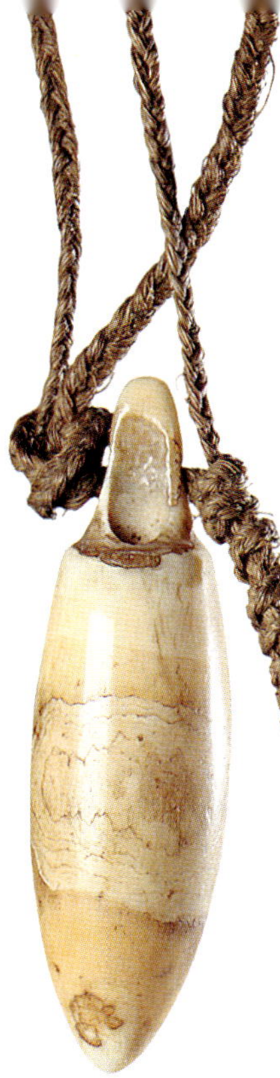

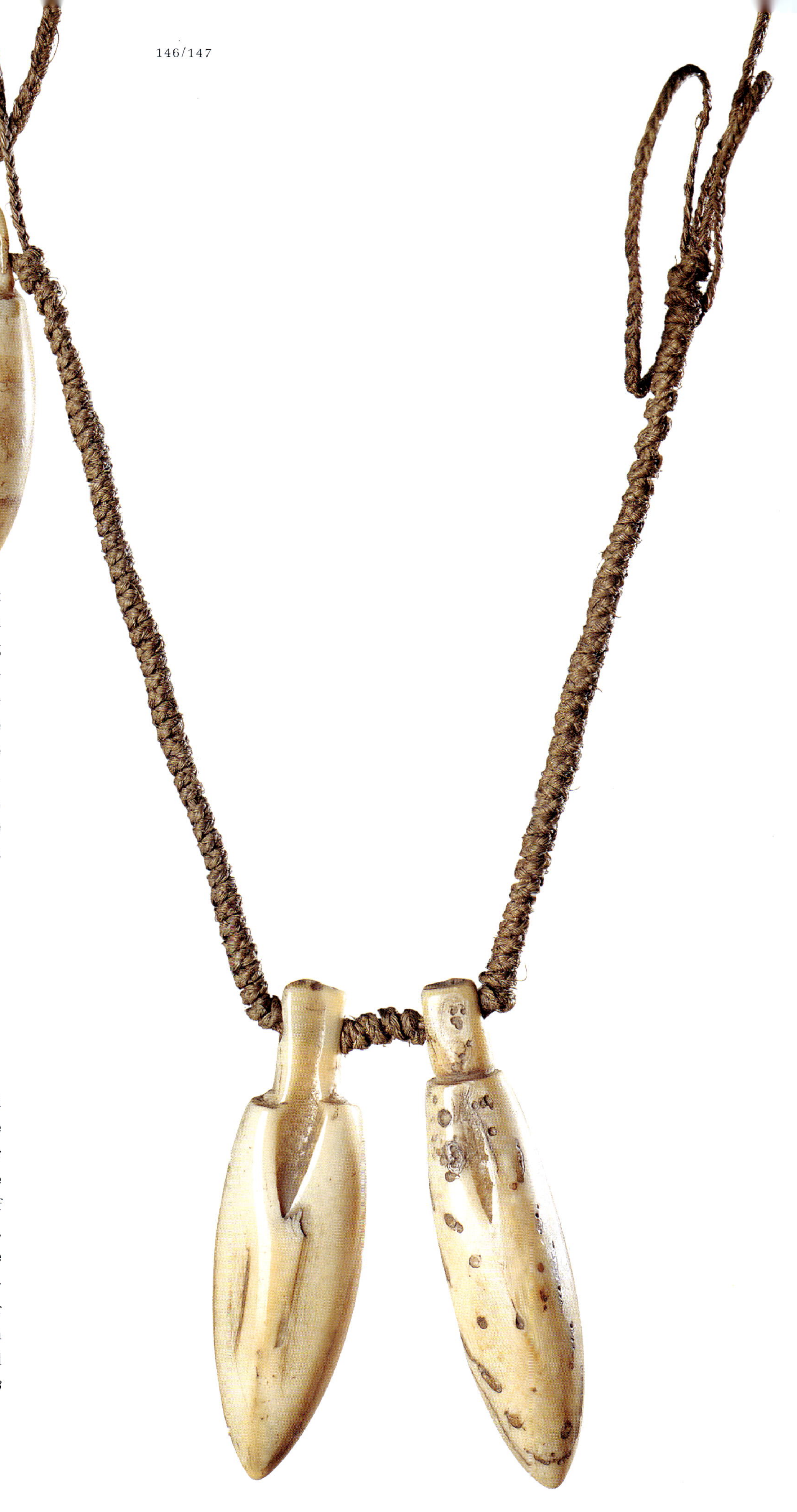

***Sika*, Dart Heads, Tonga**

Made of valuable sperm whale ivory, these dart heads were attached to long slender wooden shafts and used in the competitive dart throwing game of *sika mama'o*. This was the Tongan version of a widespread Pacific game. As commoners were prohibited from possessing prestige items such as whale teeth, these dart heads are most likely to have belonged to a person of rank. Like many other Tongan small ivory carvings, including a range of small female figures, these *sika* heads have been worn as ornaments in a necklace. *Longest one 11.7 cm.*

AM 31563. W. O. Oldman Collection 1948.

opposite: ***Wasekaseka* or *Waseisei*, Whale Teeth Necklace, Fiji**

Whale teeth were highly valued in Tonga, Fiji and Samoa and were therefore reserved for those of chiefly status. Evolved from the stubbier *vuasagale* necklace of complete teeth during the early 1800s, many 'sabre-toothed' necklaces of long split teeth were made and worn in Tonga, Fiji and Samoa, as whale teeth became more plentiful with the advent of European commercial whaling in these waters. This *wasekaseka* or *waseisei* exudes an aggressive elegance through the very dramatic, almost exaggerated, upward curve of its graduated 'teeth'. *Longest tooth 18 cm.*

AM 13346. Presented by J. B. Turner Collection 1925.

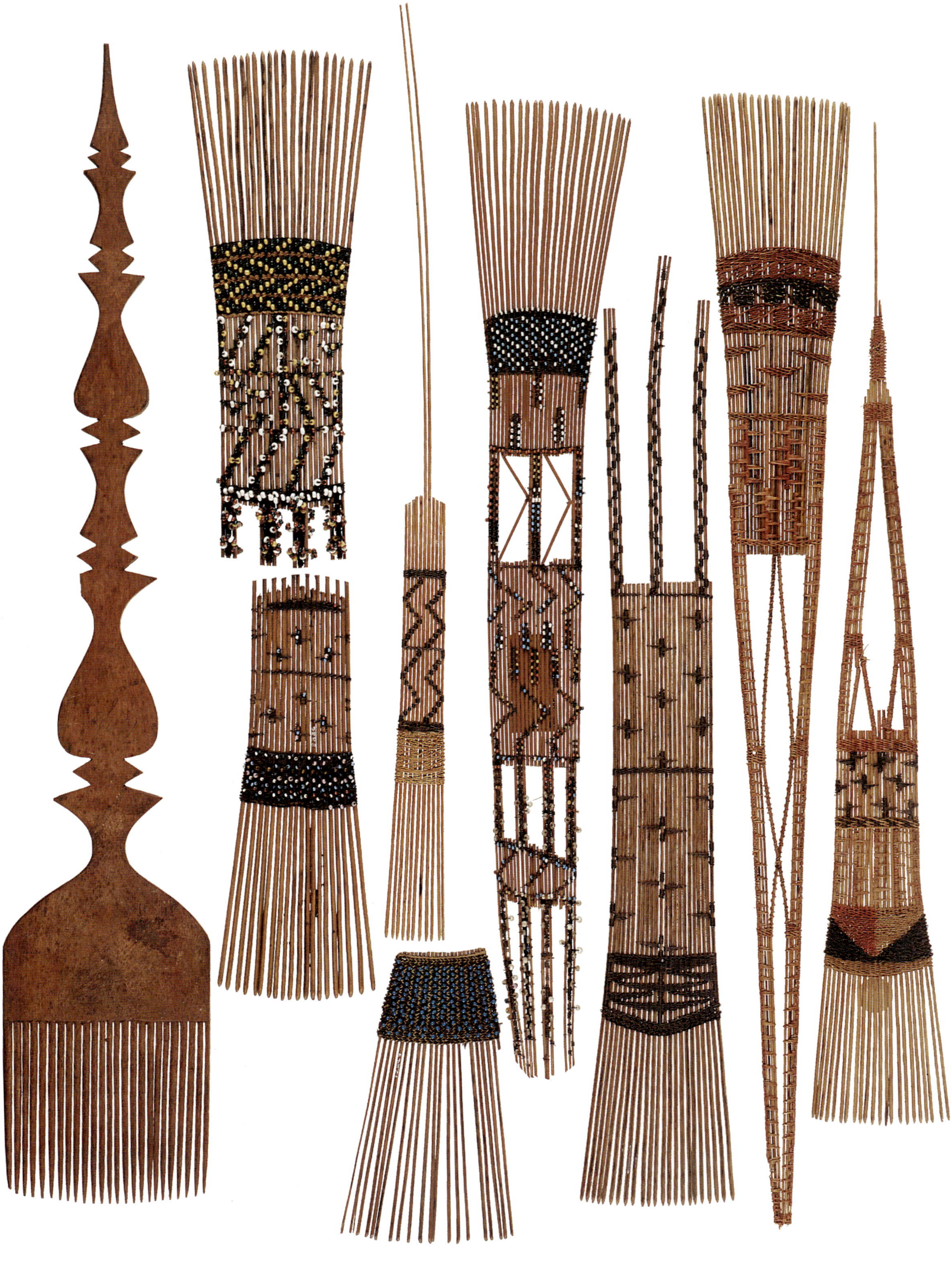

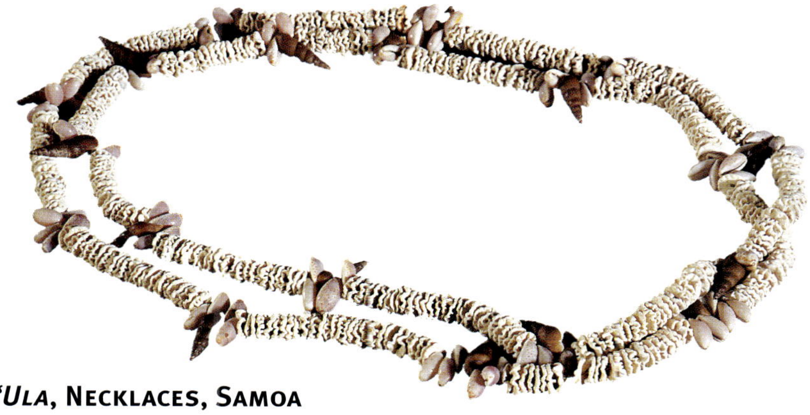

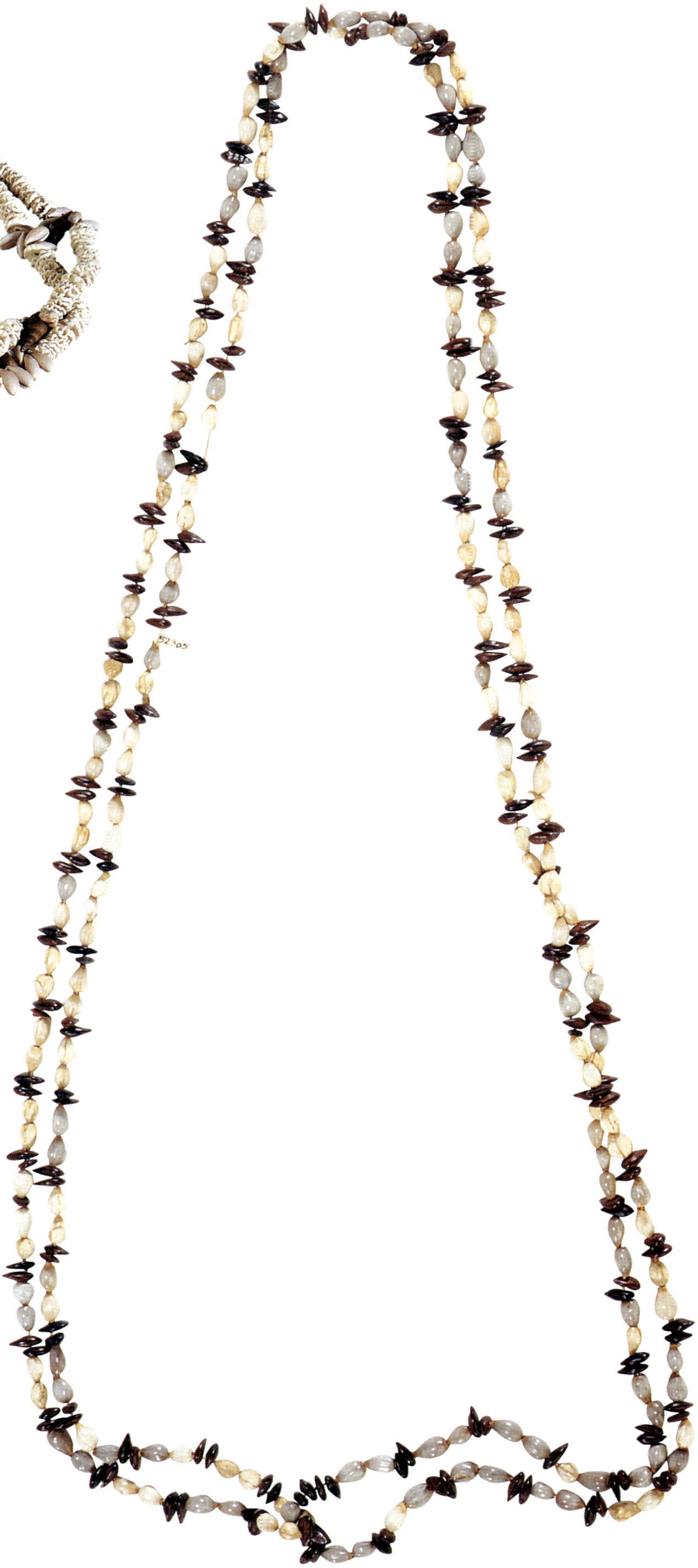

'ULA, NECKLACES, SAMOA

Modern necklaces in Samoa are composed of an extensive range of natural materials from the surrounding environment. The combinations of materials produce an infinite variety of necklaces from the lush, scented, colourful and less durable, such as those of fresh leaves and flowers, to the less colourful, non-scented but more durable necklaces of pods, seeds, shell, coral and ivory. Necklaces such as those shown here continue to be worn during festive occasions, feasts and gatherings, and are offered as gifts of welcome or farewell for family and friends. Necklaces of paper-wrapped candies are now popular gifts to departing friends at airports, to be distributed later to the children at home. above: *Length 130 cm;* right: *length 172 cm.*

above: *AM 52305.2. Purchased from Struan Ensor 1986.*
right: *AM 52305.1. Purchased from Struan Ensor 1986.*

opposite: ***HELU*, COMBS, TONGA**

Indicative of rank, *helu* were designed more as decorative ornaments for the head than for utilitarian purposes. Midribs of coconut fronds have been scraped clean of the attached leaf and bound together with fine strands of sennit fibre. Elaborate designs were achieved with these simple materials, made even more effective since European contact by the incorporation of coloured glass beads. clockwise from left: *Length 49 cm; 21.5 cm; 39.3 cm, 41 cm; 40 cm; 47.5 cm; 42.7 cm; 12.4 cm; 18 cm.*

clockwise from left: *AM 12853. Presented by Mrs J. Reid 1916; AM 14723.10. James Edge-Partington Collection. Presented by Dr Thomson Wilson Leys Memorial 1924; AM 41328.; AM 11745. Presented by Captain Laverlock 1880; AM 14723.2. James Edge-Partington Collection. Presented by Dr Thomson Wilson Leys Memorial 1924; AM 22208.1. Presented by G. Graham 1935; AM 22208.2. Presented by G. Graham 1935; AM 8836. Purchased from Mr Steele 1917; AM 12849 Presented by Mrs J. Reid 1916.*

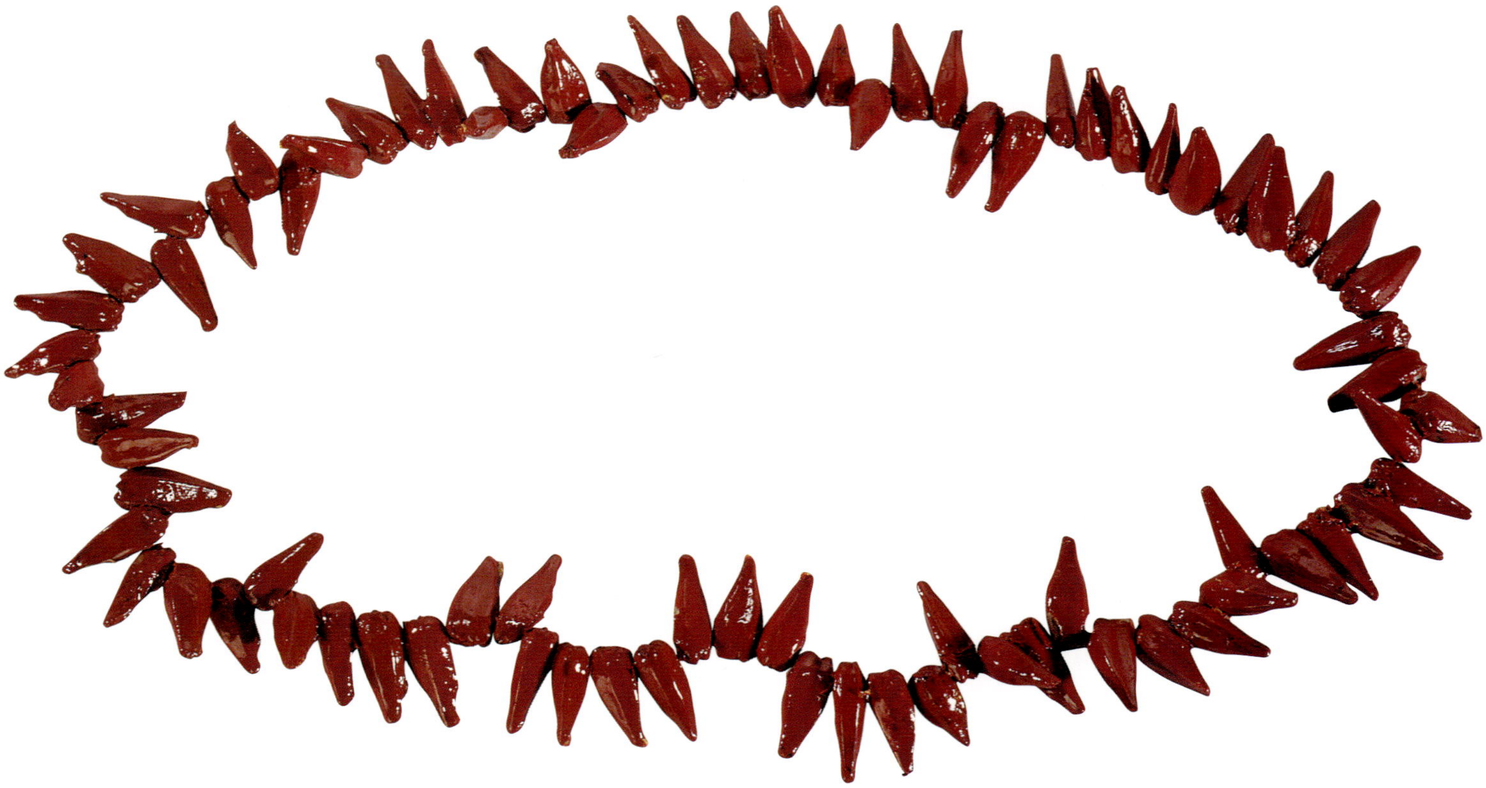

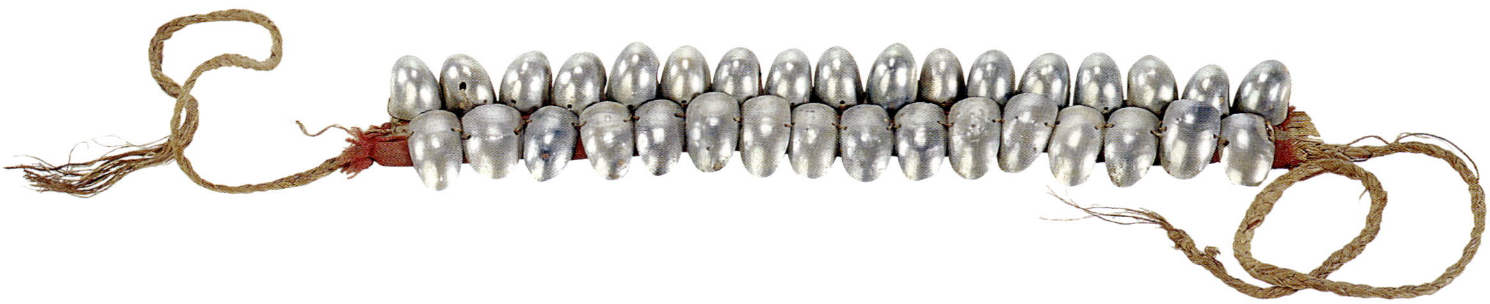

***'Ula fala*, Necklace of Pandanus Keys, Upolu, Samoa**

Worn primarily by *tulafale* or talking chiefs, *'ula fala* may today be worn by any persons of status. They are made from pandanus fruit keys, which range in colour from yellow to red. Today the keys are usually painted a dark red, *'ula*, perhaps enhancing the prestige of these necklaces by linking them to Polynesian regard for the colour red, which carries connotations of sacredness, high rank and value. *Length 118 cm.*

AM 55208. Presented by M. Pendergrast 1996.

***Pale fuiono*, Head Band, Samoa**

Pale fuiono are a part of the *tuiga*, which is a composite ceremonial head-dress. This is dismantled after use, and the individual elements carefully stored until needed again. This *pale fuiono* has two rows of polished *Nautilus* shell segments sewn on to a backing of cotton-covered pandanus strips, with attached plaited ties. *Nautilus* shell was imported from Tonga and was consequently rare and highly valued. Formerly, only appointed ceremonial village maidens, *taupou*, and high chiefs' sons, *manaia*, could wear the *tuiga* during important occasions. Today, these restrictions are much less rigid and many people wear modern versions of the *tuiga* for entertainments. *Length 26 cm, width 5 cm.*

AM 31596. W. O. Oldman Collection 1948.

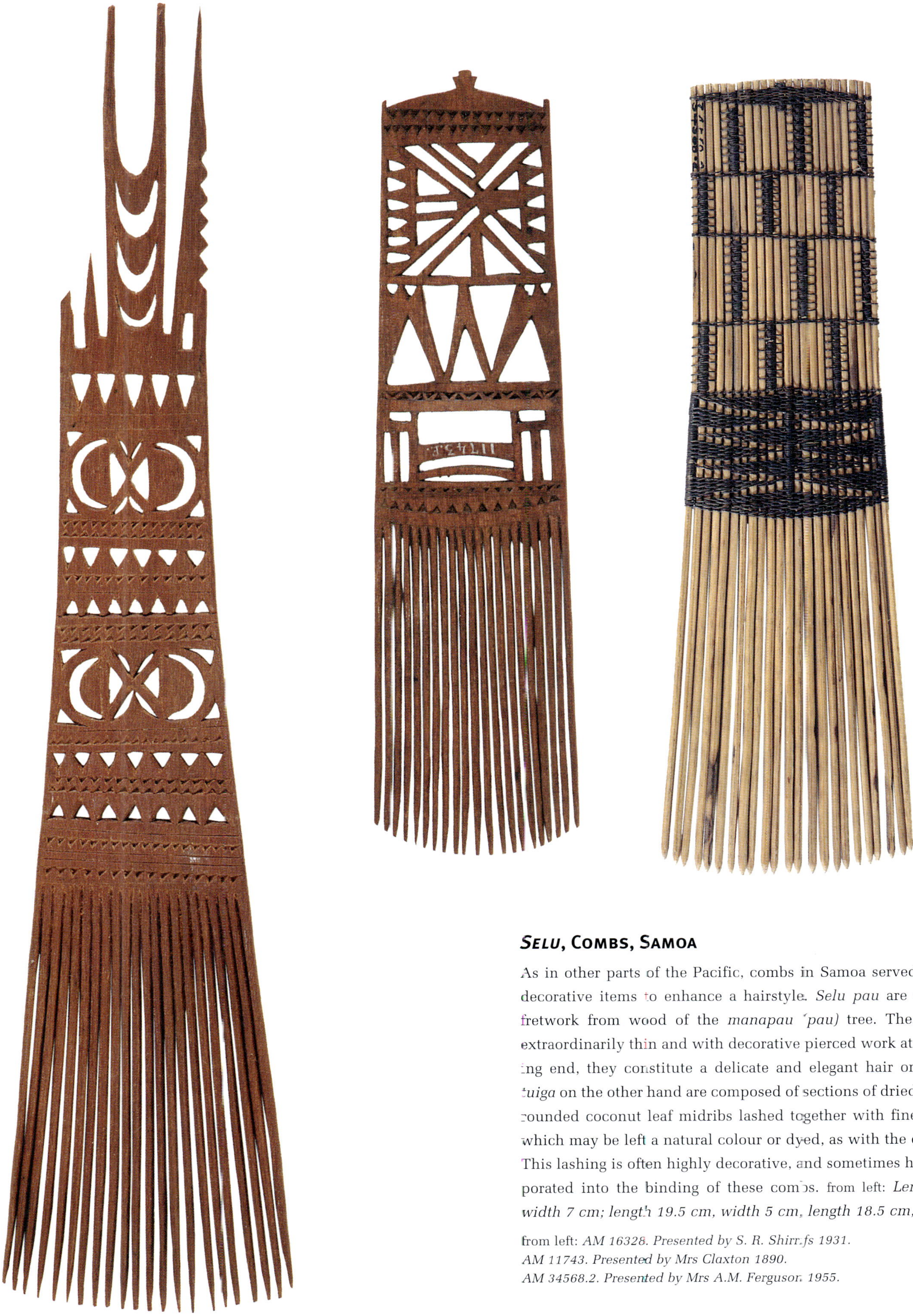

Selu, Combs, Samoa

As in other parts of the Pacific, combs in Samoa served primarily as decorative items to enhance a hairstyle. *Selu pau* are combs cut in fretwork from wood of the *manapau (pau)* tree. These combs are extraordinarily thin and with decorative pierced work at the outstanding end, they constitute a delicate and elegant hair ornament. *Selu tuiga* on the other hand are composed of sections of dried, cleaned and rounded coconut leaf midribs lashed together with fine sennit fibre, which may be left a natural colour or dyed, as with the example here. This lashing is often highly decorative, and sometimes hair was incorporated into the binding of these combs. from left: *Length 30.5 cm, width 7 cm; length 19.5 cm, width 5 cm, length 18.5 cm, width 6 cm.*

from left: *AM 16328. Presented by S. R. Shirrefs 1931.*
AM 11743. Presented by Mrs Claxton 1890.
AM 34568.2. Presented by Mrs A.M. Ferguson 1955.

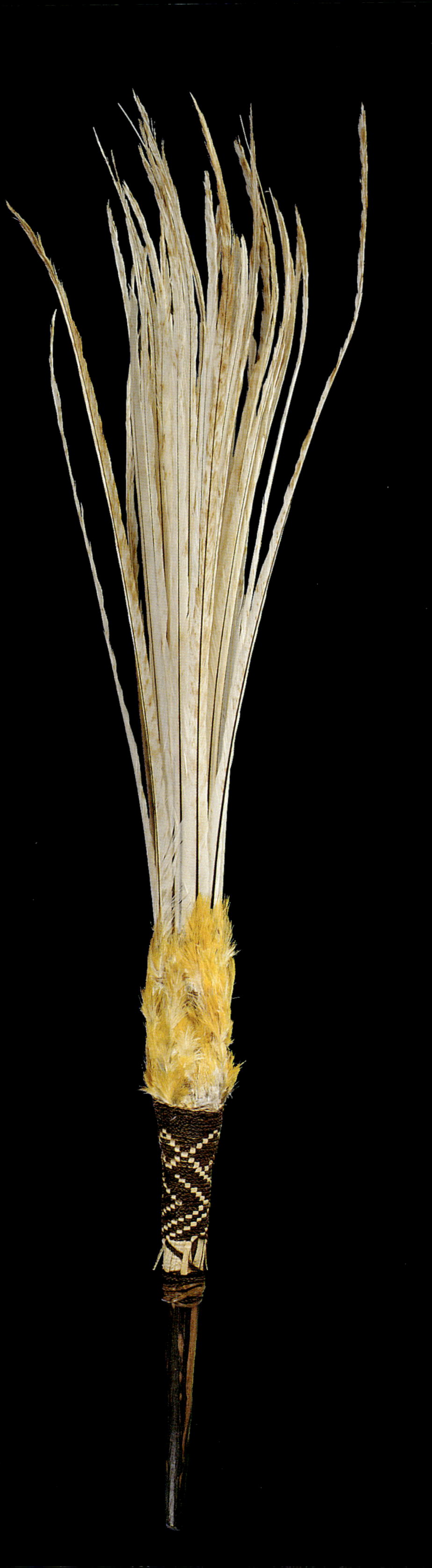

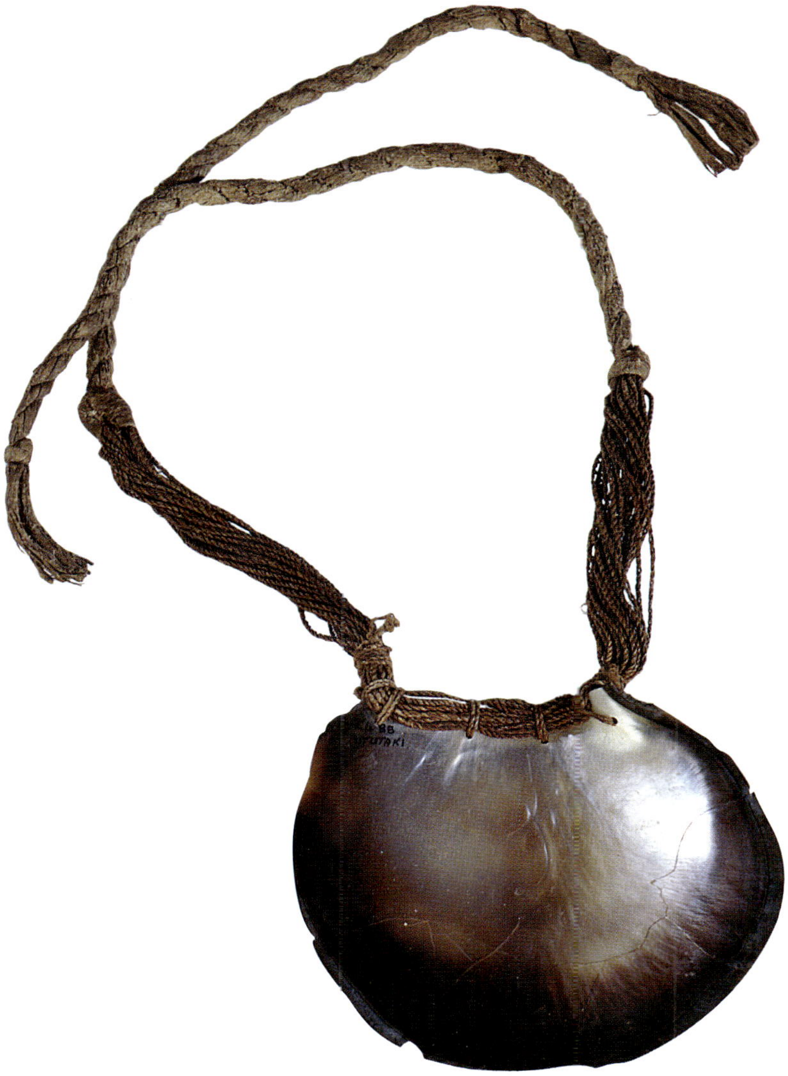

Tiha, Breast Plate, Aitutaki, Cook Islands

James Cook noted in 1777 that breastplates similar to this were the only ornaments he observed being worn at the time of his visit to Mangaia. Cook also mentions that the shells were attached to ties of loosely twisted human hair. Pearl shells did not occur in the waters of the southern Cook Islands group, and therefore had to be obtained from the northern atolls, either by trade or as gifts. As high value items because of the scarcity of their material, these pearl shell breastplates were the property of men and women of rank. *Length 6 cm, width 8 cm.*

AM 14488. James Edge-Partington Collection. Presented by Dr Thomson Wilson Leys Memorial 1924.

Rei, Neck Ornament, Cook Islands

Thought traditionally to have been produced in Atiu, *rei* were generally made of whale ivory. However there are a few examples such as this made of *taumanu* wood. Many writers have referred to the phallic nature of these ornaments, which are reminiscent of small ivory carvings seen attached to necklaces of hair and ivory ornaments variously localised to Mangaia, or to Rurutu or Tupuaʻi in the Austral Islands. This is perhaps indicative of the historic links and frequent travel between the southern Cooks group and the Austral Islands. *Width 11 cm.*

AM 38952. W. O. Oldman Collection 1948.

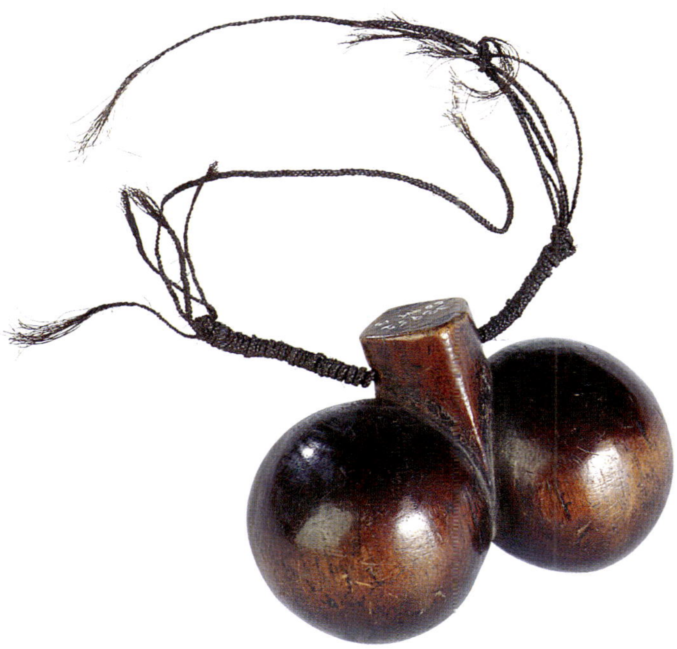

opposite: *Pala Hega*, Head Ornament, Niue

The tall white feathers are taken from the white-tailed Tropic bird, *tuaki* or *tavake*, which, with their colourful bills and long central tail streamers, are a spectacular sight wheeling around the islands of the Pacific. The yellow feathers are from the *kulukulu* dove. *Pala* refers to a feather head-dress, and *hega* is a lory with scarlet feathers on its throat and belly. This *pala hega* is without red feathers, but like the Hawaiian *ʻahu ʻula*, feather cloaks, their names retain the reference to the sacred Polynesian colour of red, even without the presence of red. *Length 87 cm.*

AM 16859. Presented by H. G. Cornwall 1931.

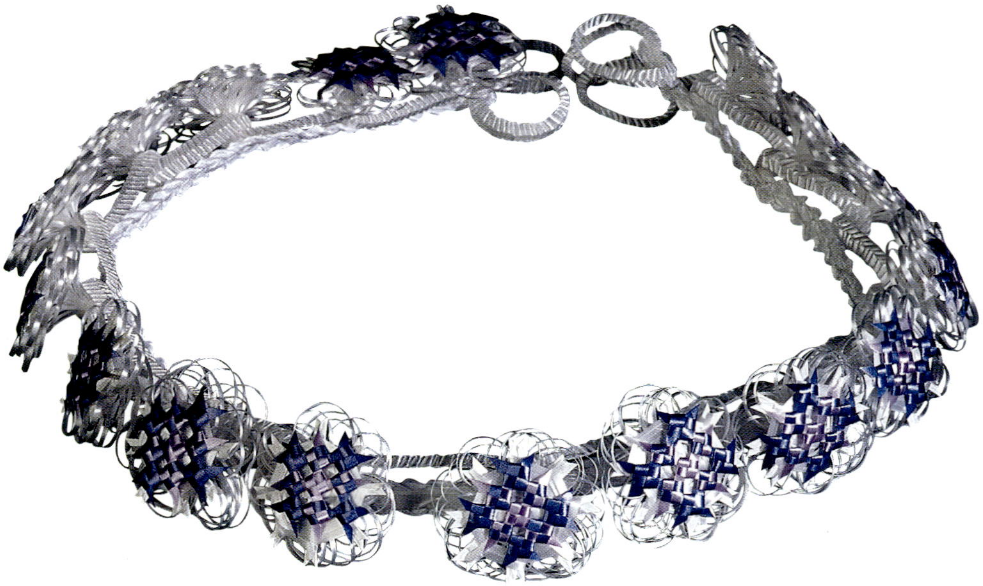

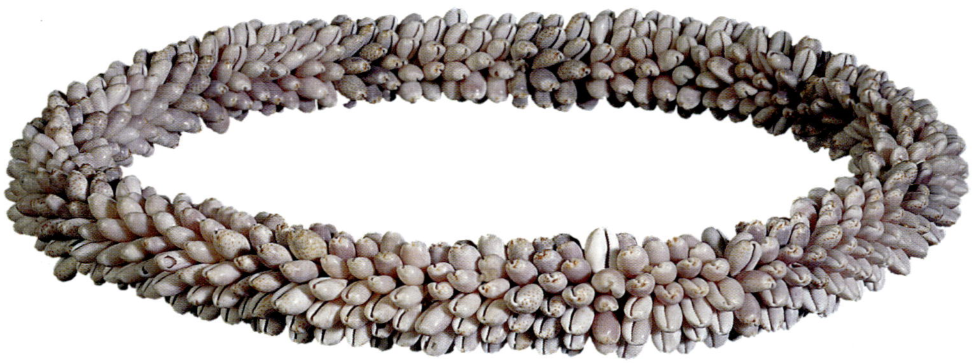

Belt, Mangaia, Cook Islands

Florets of blue, mauve and white ribbon have been mounted on a plaited band of fine white plastic. Cook Islands decorative bands, sashes and belts were previously of tapa cloth or plaited from *rauhara*, *pandanus* and *hau*, hibiscus. Made by Mama Kaa Toka in 1995, this contemporary piece in new materials still exhibits the forms and construction technique that have long been practised in Cook Islands weaving and plaiting. *Length 68 cm.*

AM 55111. Purchased from Mama Kaa Toka 1995.

***Hei*, Necklace, Cook Islands**

Hei is the general term used to refer to a neck ornament with a series of elements strung on a fibre cord to be worn around the neck. These may be composed of leaves, flowers, seeds, pandanus fruit keys, land snail shells and seashells. The *hei* is perhaps the most common and universal item of adornment in Polynesia, less formal and exclusive, by virtue of its material, so that they may be enjoyed by men, women and children, the high born and the commoner. *Length 52 cm.*

AM 46611.1. Bequest of Mrs Eva George 1974.

opposite: **Hat Band, Rarotonga, Cook Islands**

Hats do not have a long history in Polynesia. Traditionally, garlands of scented leaves and flowers, sun visors and sun or rain capes were a common part of everyday dress, and fishing hats were essential for protection from the glaring sun on the sea. Contact with other cultures has led to the creation and use of the range of hats evident in the Pacific today. Perhaps the earliest and most common introduced new form is the 'Panama' hat made from the young leaf of the coconut palm. Colourful and intricate shell hatbands were developed by Pacific Islanders to add interest to the European style hats of the Pacific. *Circumference 60 cm.*

AM 47210. Presented by Mrs O. Nevill 1975.

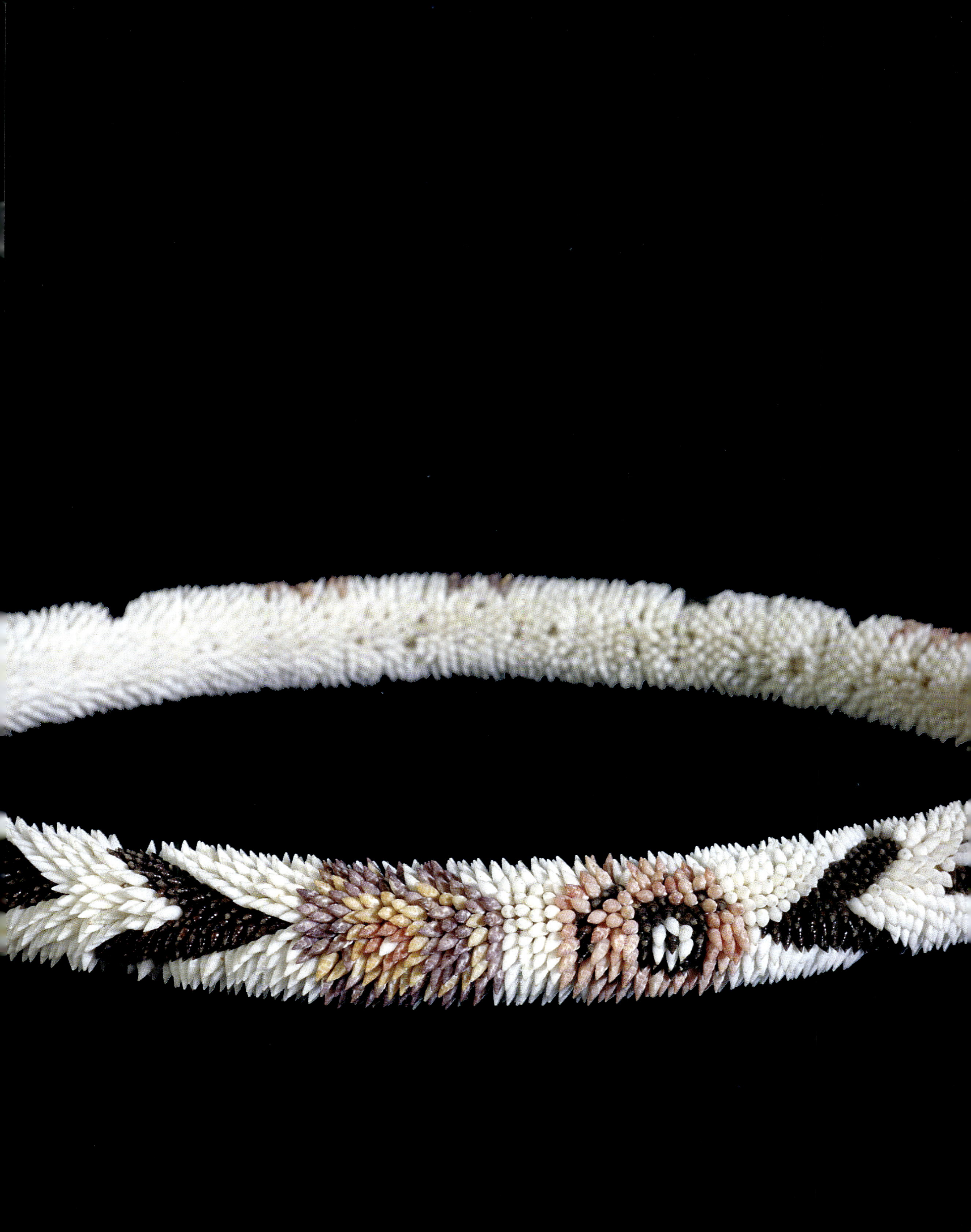

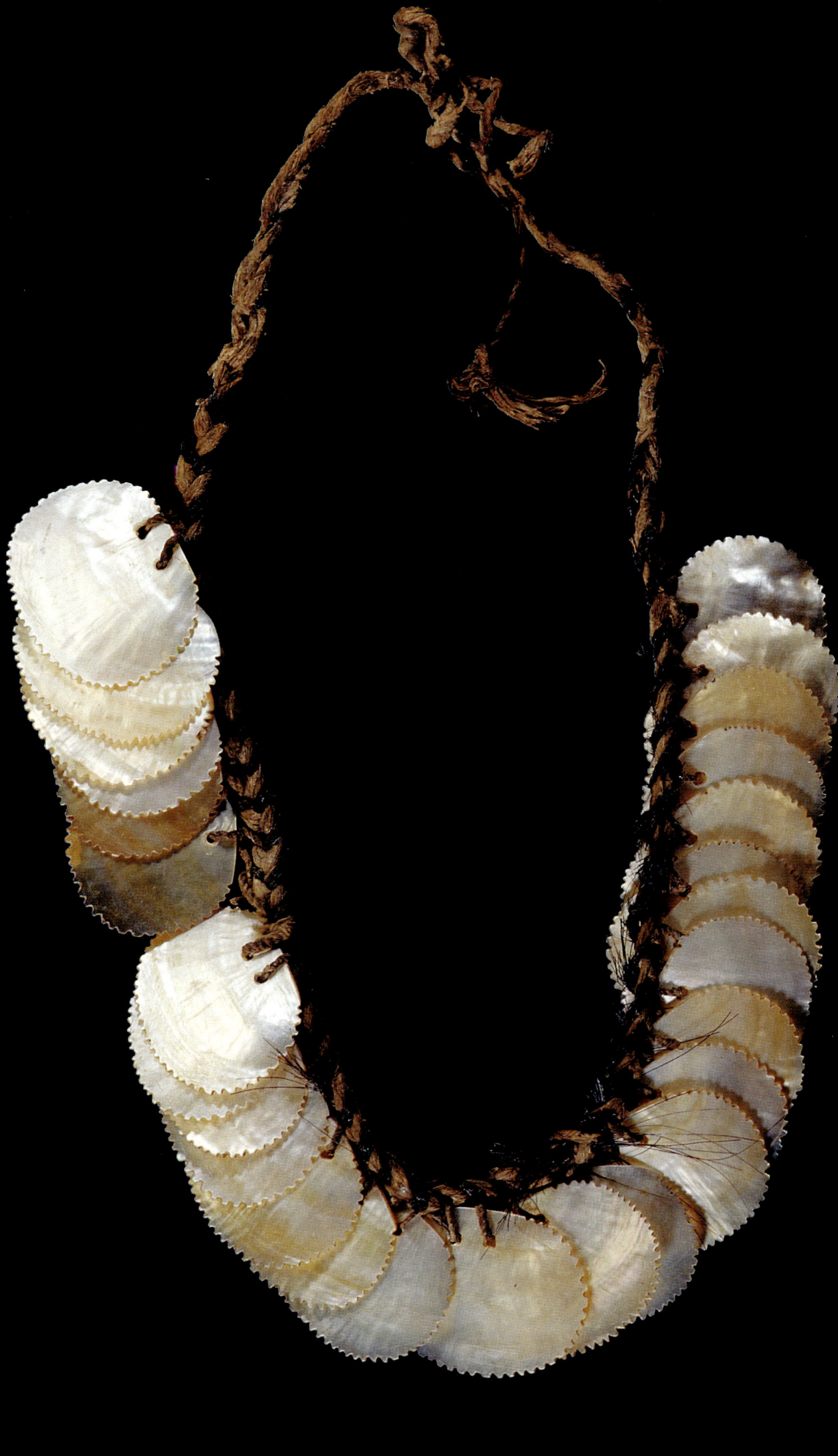

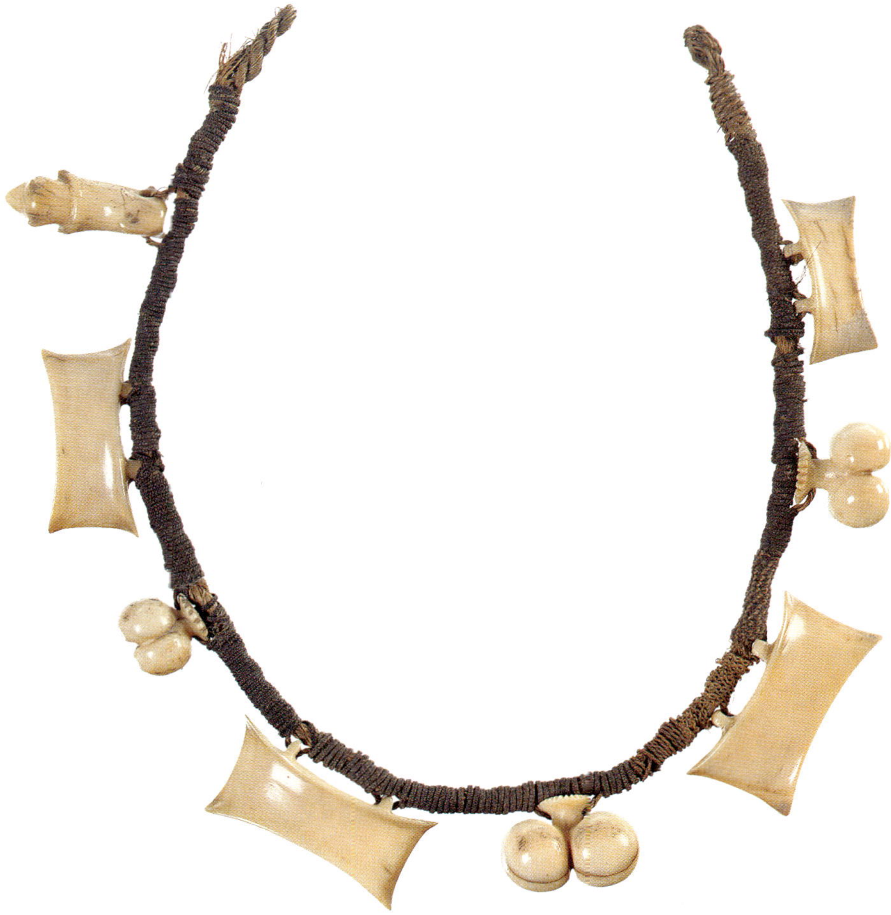

Necklace of Ivory Ornaments, Rurutu, Austral Islands

Though prestigious by the nature of the material from which they are made and hence reserved for those of chiefly status, necklaces of ivory and human hair are generally not uncommon in the islands of Polynesia. However, with its attached symbols of power rendered in ivory, this particular style of neck ornament is very rare. The carved symbols representing 'chief's seats', 'testicles' and 'pig', by their connotations would apparently refer to the influence enjoyed by the wearer over power and fecundity. *Length 45 cm.*

AM 31491. W. O. Oldman Collection 1948.

Taumi, Gorget, Tahiti, Society Islands

Tahitian military leaders and leading warriors wore these breast ornaments in battle. As has been suggested by some writers, they may have acted as shields during close hand-to-hand combat. However, *taumi* were employed primarily to signal the aristocratic status of the wearer and, like other insignia of rank around the Pacific, could be taken as booty from the battlefield. Being prestige items, gorgets were presented as tribute to ruling *ali'i*, high chiefs, and were included among the gifts presented during ceremonial events such as investiture ceremonies. Early accounts suggest that the dog hair and pearl shell incorporated into *taumi* may have been obtained through trade networks with the Tuamotu Archipelago. *Length 57 cm, width 56 cm.*

AM 31544. W. O. Oldman Collection 1948.

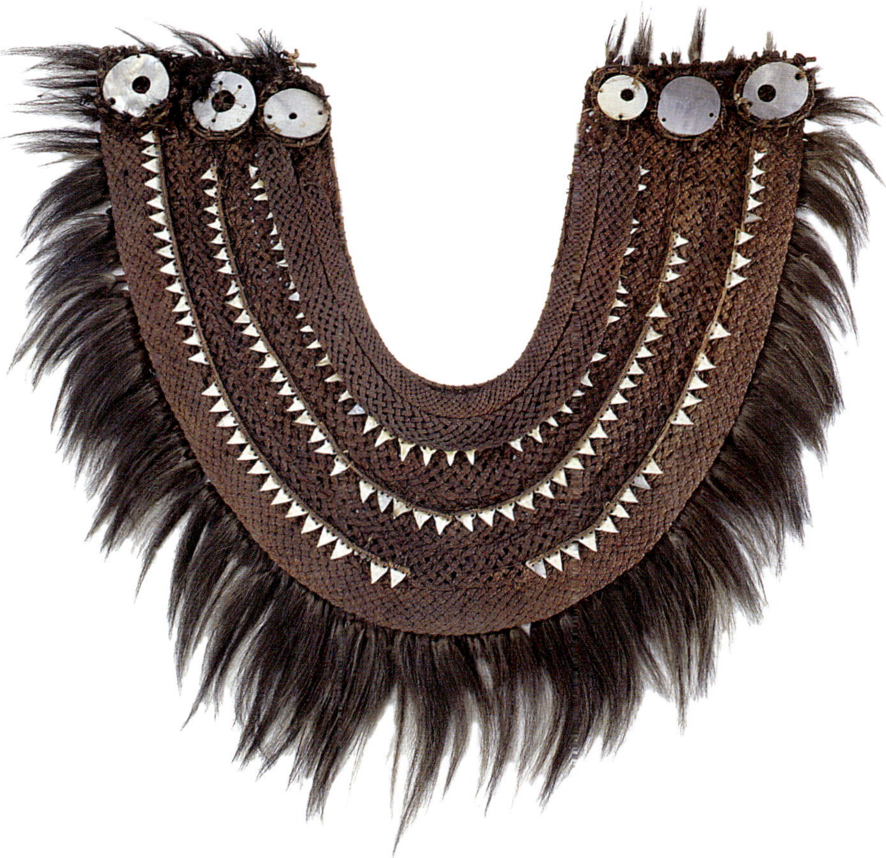

opposite: Necklace, Society Islands/Austral Islands

Necklaces of pearl oyster shell such as this are very rare. The shells have been scraped and cleaned to enhance the iridescent beauty of the material. The edges of the 27 discs are serrated and two suspension holes have been perforated along their upper edge. As a valuable material, either whole pieces or segments of pearl oyster shell were also incorporated into other prestige items, the most significant of these being the Tahitian *heva*, mourning costume and the chiefly flywhisks of the Austral Islands. *Length 42.5 cm.*

AM 52252.

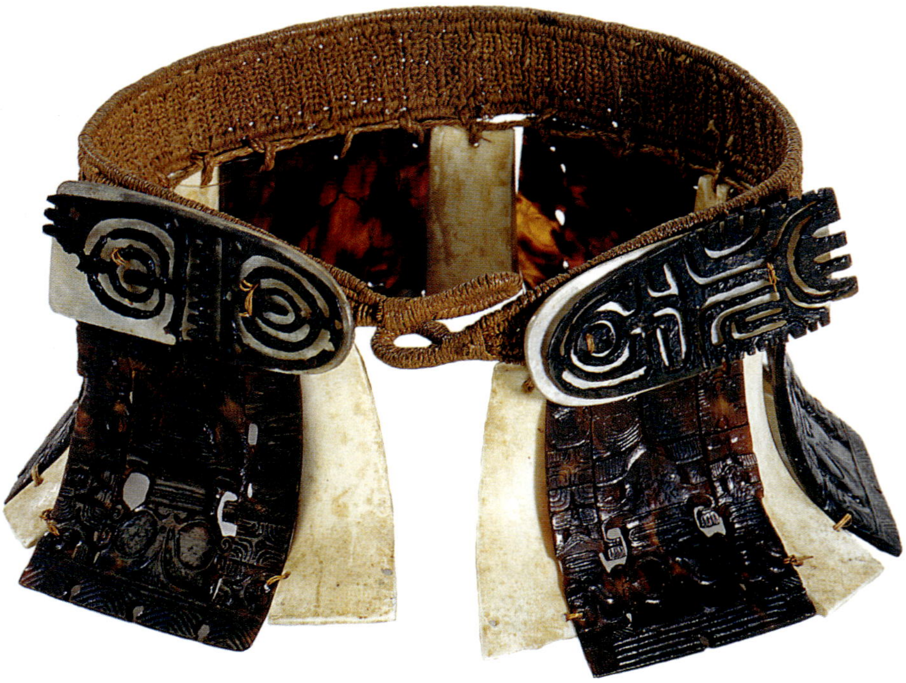

Pa'e kaha, Crown, Marquesas Islands

Made by *tuhuna*, master craftsmen, the *pa'e kaha* consists of *Triton* shell and turtle shell plates attached to a woven band of sennit fibre. Pearl shell discs overlaid with turtle shell, reminiscent of Melanesian *kapkaps*, were attached to the outside of the sennit band. These crowns are said to be properly worn with the shell plates flaring down the forehead and over the eyes, actually presenting the *tiki* figures upside down. The preserve of men and women of rank, crowns were paid for with pigs, never land. This was because if a woman were to walk on the land exchanged for a *pa'e kaha* it would be equivalent to her stepping over the head of the owner of the *pa'e kaha*, one of the greatest insults in Polynesia. *Length 45 cm, height 9 cm.*

AM 19005.2. Purchased 1933.

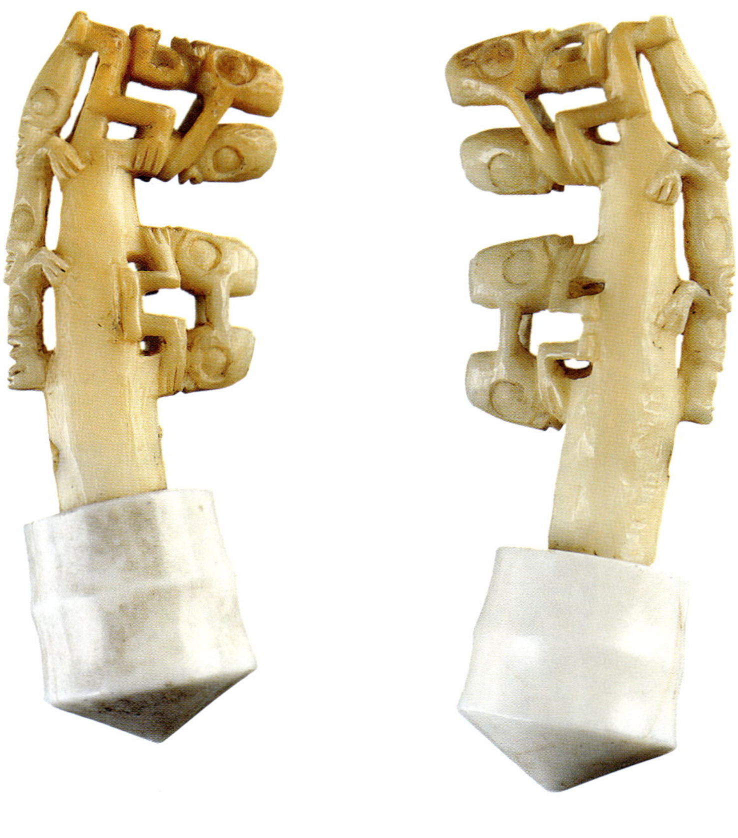

Taiana, Ear Plugs, Marquesas Islands

Used exclusively by women, these highly valued family heirlooms were inherited through the female line. Contrary to modern day practices, *taiana* were worn with the carved lengths projecting backwards from behind the earlobe and stopped with a shell cap at the front of the earlobe. Delicately carved from whale ivory, this pair of *taiana* exhibits typical eastern Polynesian carving elements, especially the bent-knee stance, hands on the stomach, and typical Marquesan *tiki* detail of large eyes and full, slightly open mouth carved in relief. *Length 5.8 cm, width 2.5 cm.*

AM 23666.2. Presented by E. E. Vaile 1938.

opposite: *Peue 'ei*, Porpoise Teeth Head-dress, Marquesas Islands

This elegant example is composed of porpoise teeth and glass beads bound with sennit fibre. Women wore these head-dresses by threading white tapa through the end loops to act as tie cords. It is said that without the glass trade-beads, fish vertebrae would have been used in their stead. By the time the Bayard Dominick Expedition visited the Marquesas Islands in 1920, these head-dresses were no longer being made. *Length 50 cm.*

AM 16764. Purchased 1931.

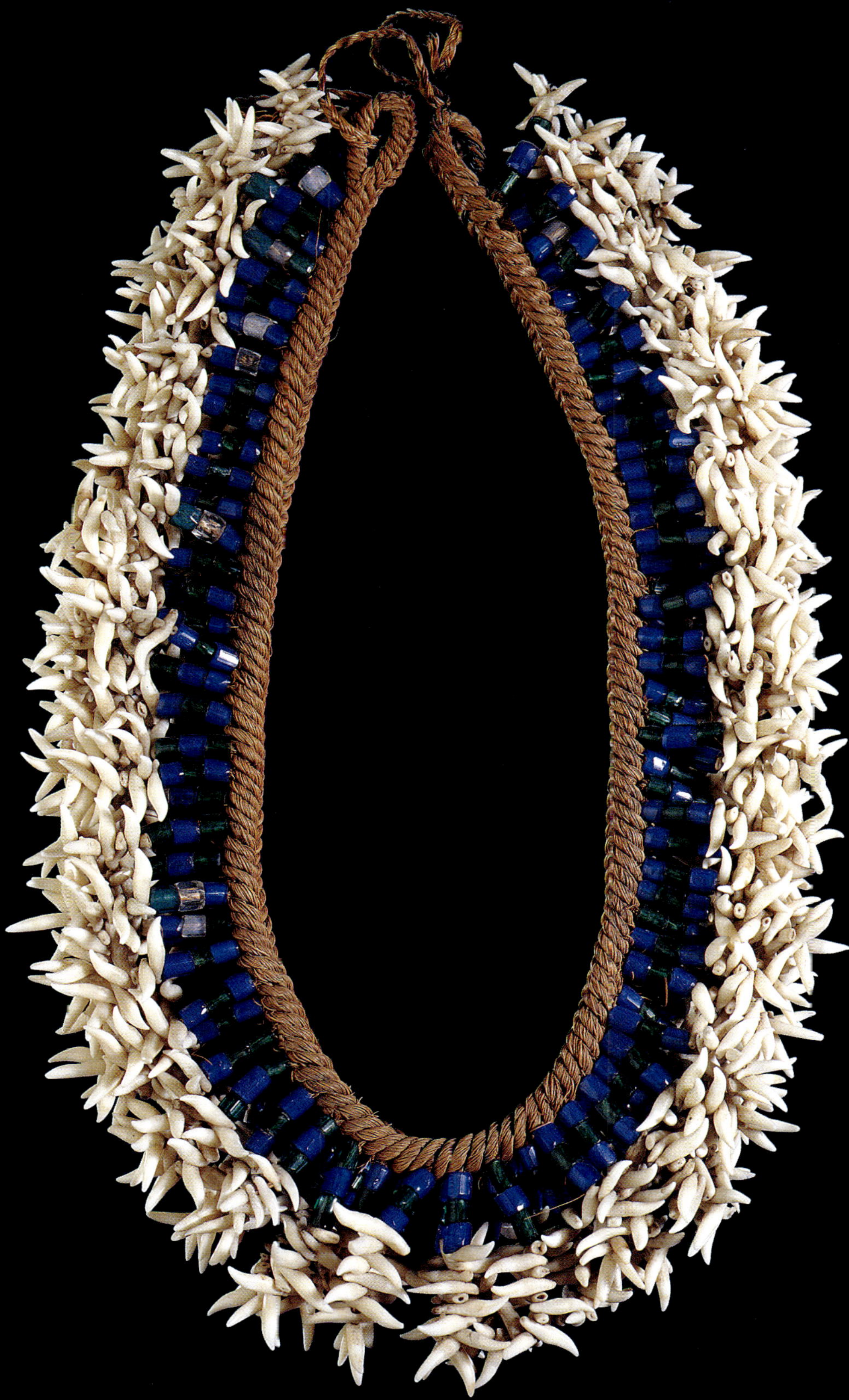

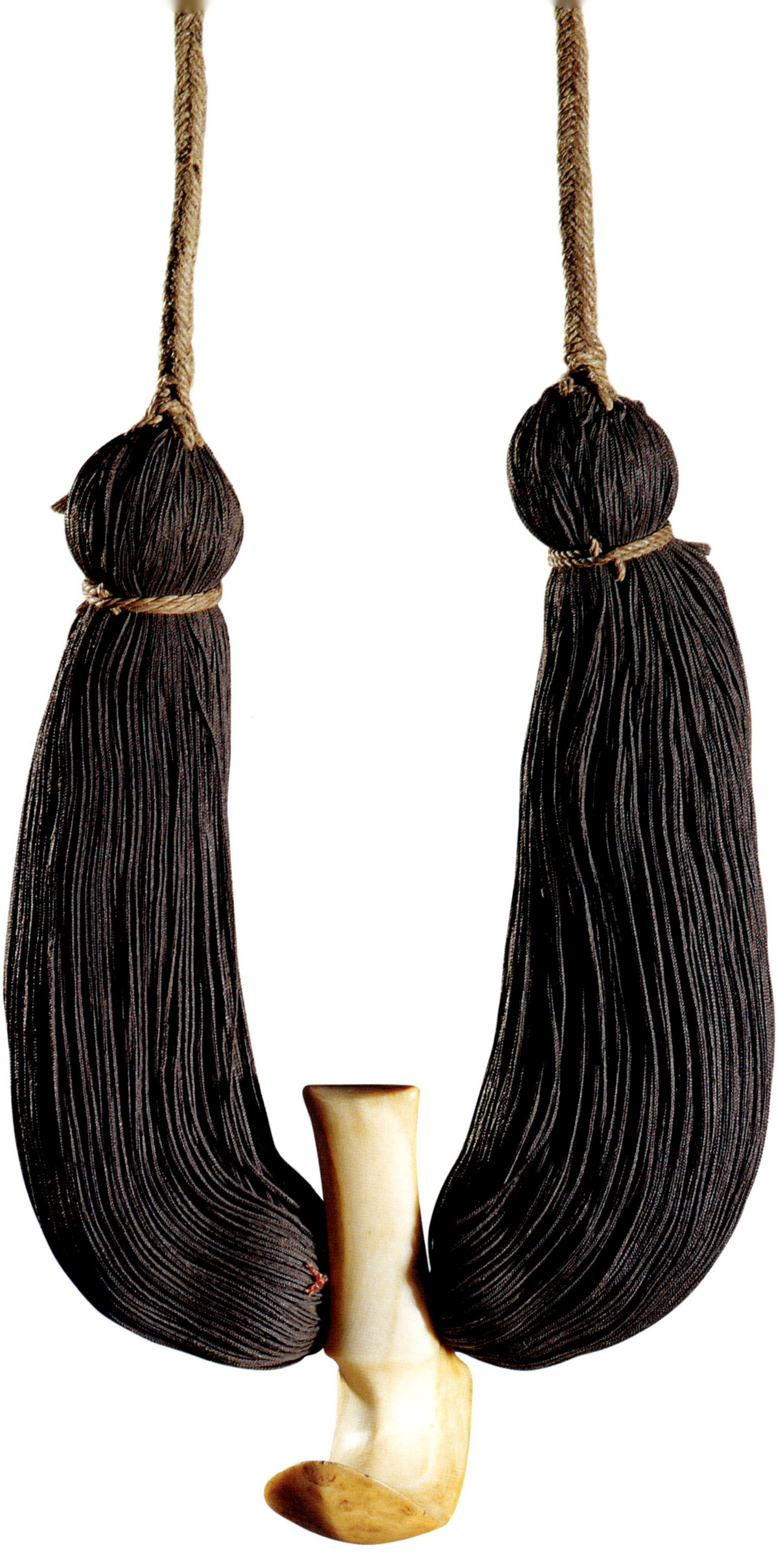

Lei niho Palaoa, Ivory Neck Ornament, Hawai'i

Sculpted from whale ivory, this dynamic hook form is suspended from bundles of very finely plaited human hair. Taken from the head, considered by Polynesians the most sacred part of the body, human hair is an embodiment of personal *mana*, and therefore the wearing of human hair at once affirms and increases one's *mana*. Through both its material and its pure form, within such a stratified society as Hawai'i this type of pendant encapsulated the status, *mana* and regenerative power of its chiefly wearer. *Length 79 cm.*

AM 14537. James Edge-Partington Collection. Presented by Dr Thomson Wilson Leys Memorial 1924.

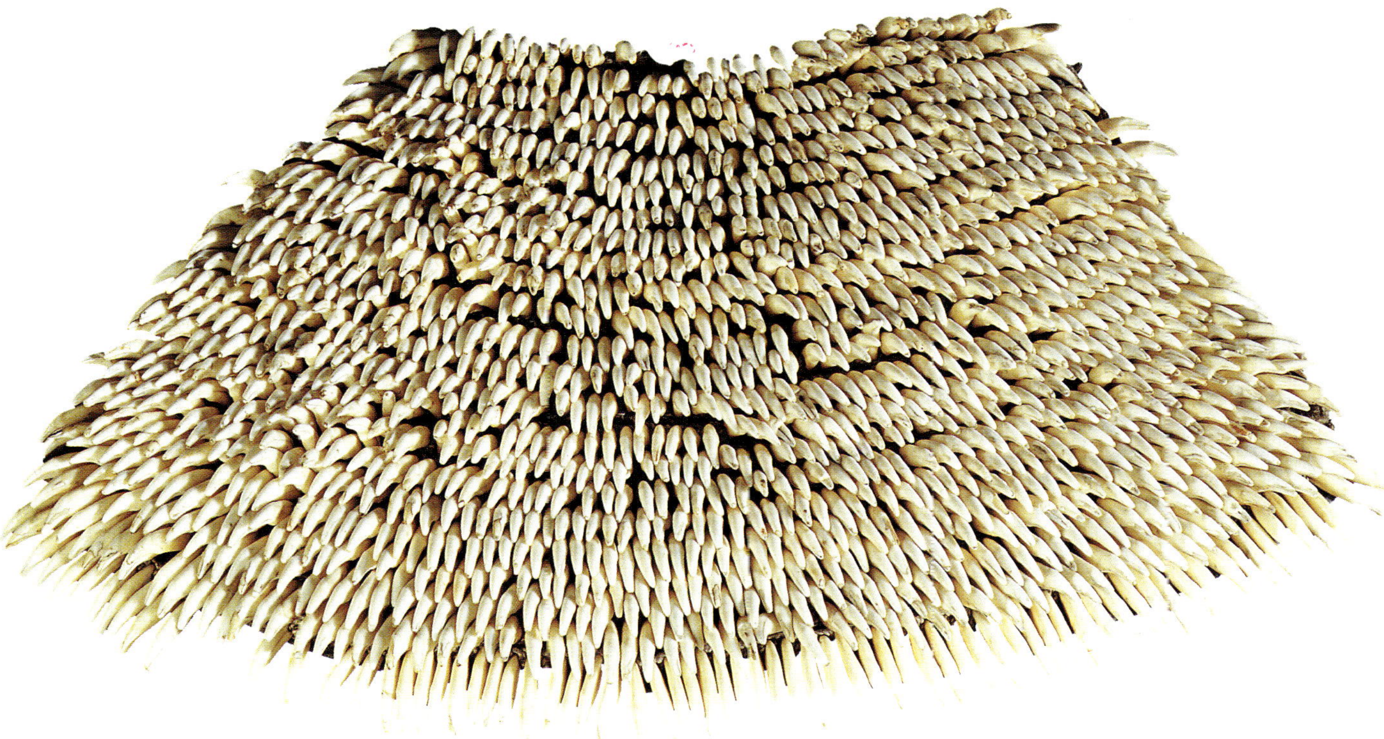

Kupe'e Niho 'Ilio, Dog Teeth Leg Ornament, Hawai'i

Often referred to as 'leg rattles', *kupe'e niho 'ilio* were worn by male dancers tied around the leg above the calf muscle. Each canine tooth is attached through a drilled suspension hole, and one can imagine the teeth rhythmically beating together during dance performances. They were usually worn one on each leg. *Circumference at top 49 cm, length 32 cm.*

AM 31474. W. O. Oldman Collection 1948.

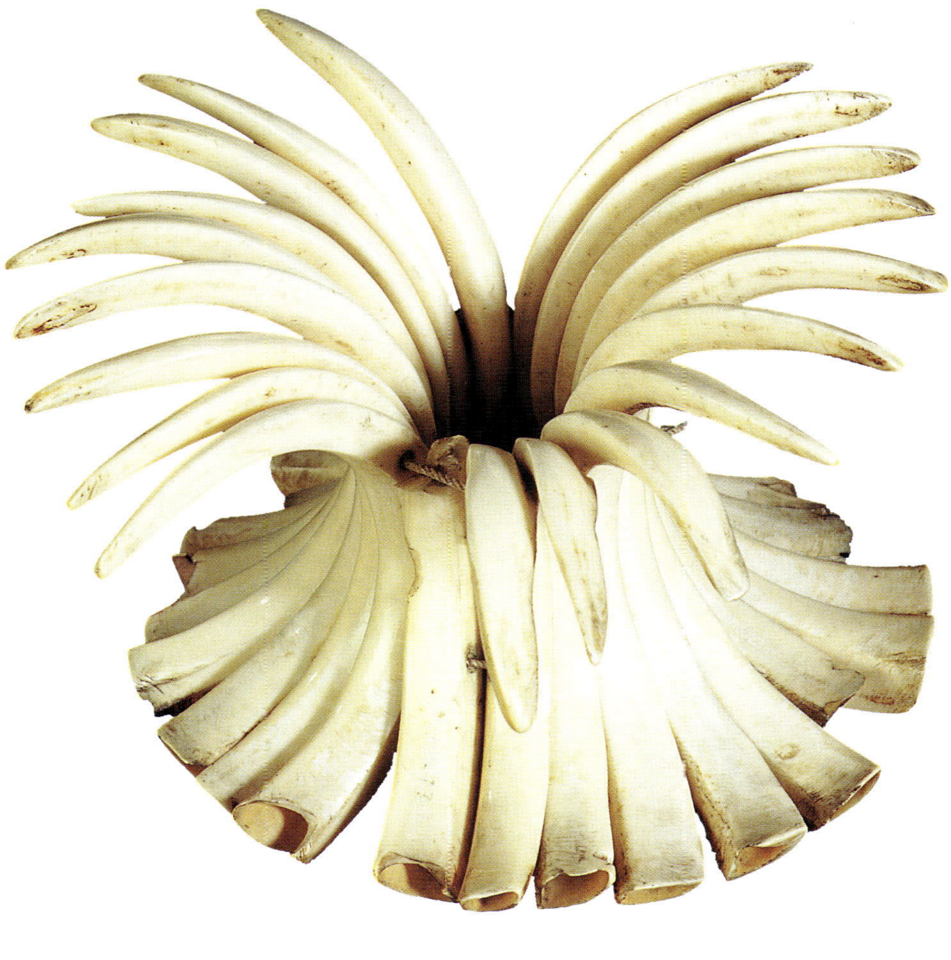

Kupe'e Ho'okalakala, Boar Tusk Bracelet, Hawai'i

Throughout Polynesia, ownership of pigs is an indicator of high social standing, and consequently ornaments of pigs' tusks are symbolic of the wearer's social class. *Kupe'e ho'okalakala*, or spiked bracelets, are usually said to have been worn exclusively by women, though both men and women are known to have worn them during ritual performances of *hula* dance. Traditionally the tusks are threaded together with a very strong fibre cord obtained from the *olona* shrub. The fibre ties in this example have been reinforced with copper wire. *Length 15 cm, width 11 cm.*

AM 31473. W. O. Oldman Collection 1948.

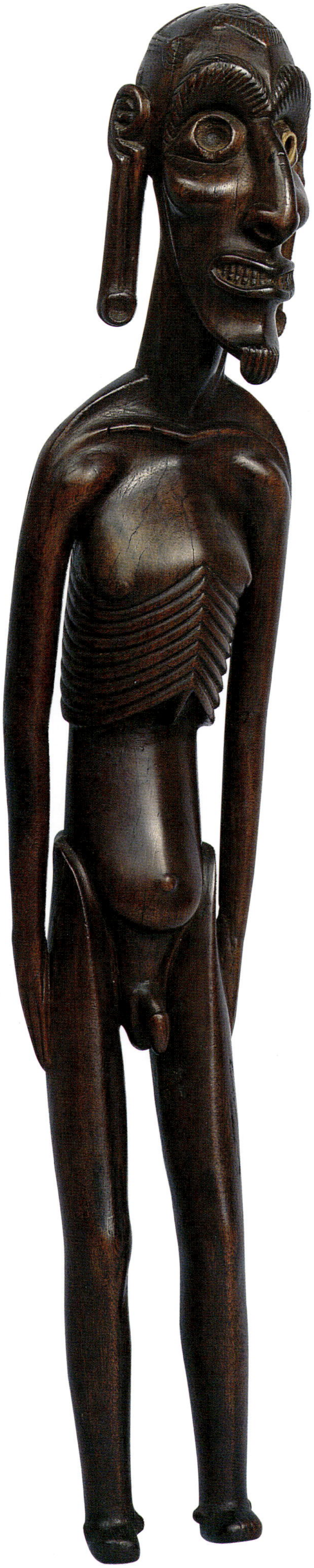

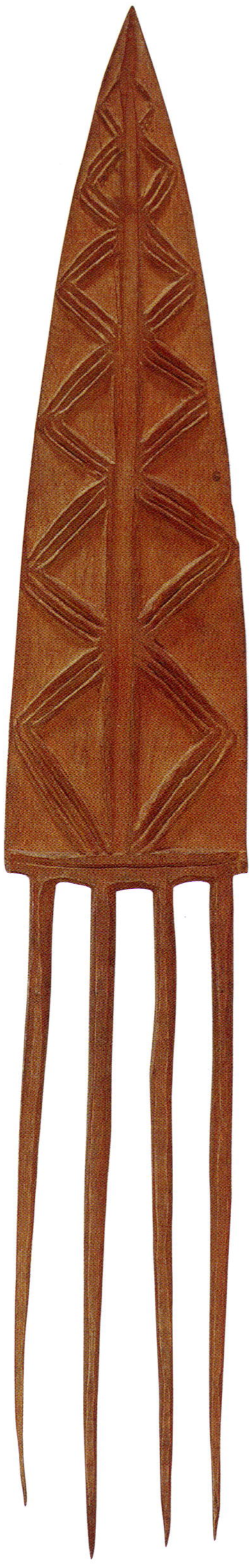

Moai Kavakava, Ancestor Figure, Easter Island.

According to Easter Island tradition, the legendary hero Tu-ko-ihu carved the first wooden figures called *moai kavakava* after he had seen two sleeping spirits who looked like skeletons. *Moai kavakava* figures, always male, were held up to the sky in rituals dedicated to the gods, especially rituals connected with harvest. On festive occasions, a man might wear all his wooden images suspended on a cord around his neck through a lug in the back of the figure. Some *moai kavakava* figures have glyphs of the Easter Island script carved on their heads. *Length 45.5 cm, width 8.5 cm.*

AM 2751. James Edge-Partington Collection. Presented by Dr Thomson Wilson Leys Memorial 1924.

Comb, Anuta, Solomon Islands

Anuta is a tiny remote eastern outlier of the Solomon Islands with a very small population of Polynesian descent. This four-pronged comb has been carved out of one piece of wood by a craftsman of Anuta, which is also famous for its well-shaped ocean-going canoes. As with most Polynesians, a man's head is extremely *tapu* and his comb also takes on some of that sacred power. The carved motif reflects ancestral patterns carved on Anutan house posts. *Length 32.5 cm, width 5 cm.*

AM 14918. James Edge-Partington Collection. Presented by Dr Thomson Wilson Leys Memorial 1924.

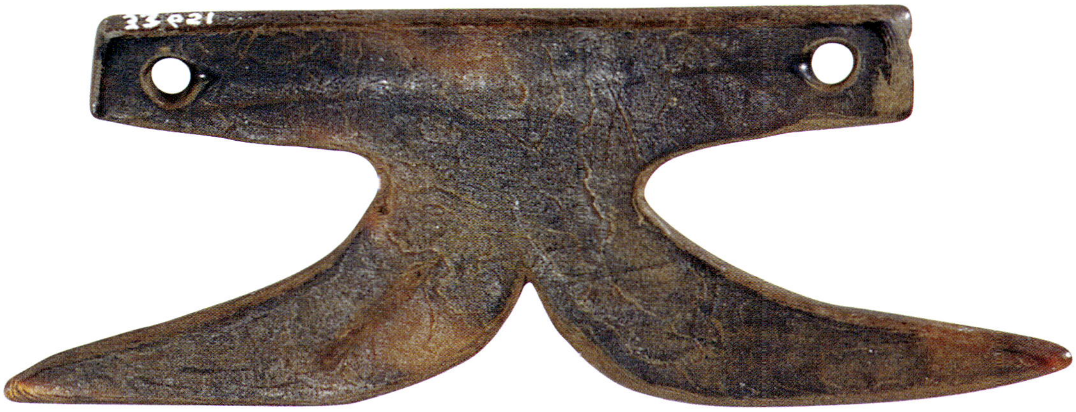

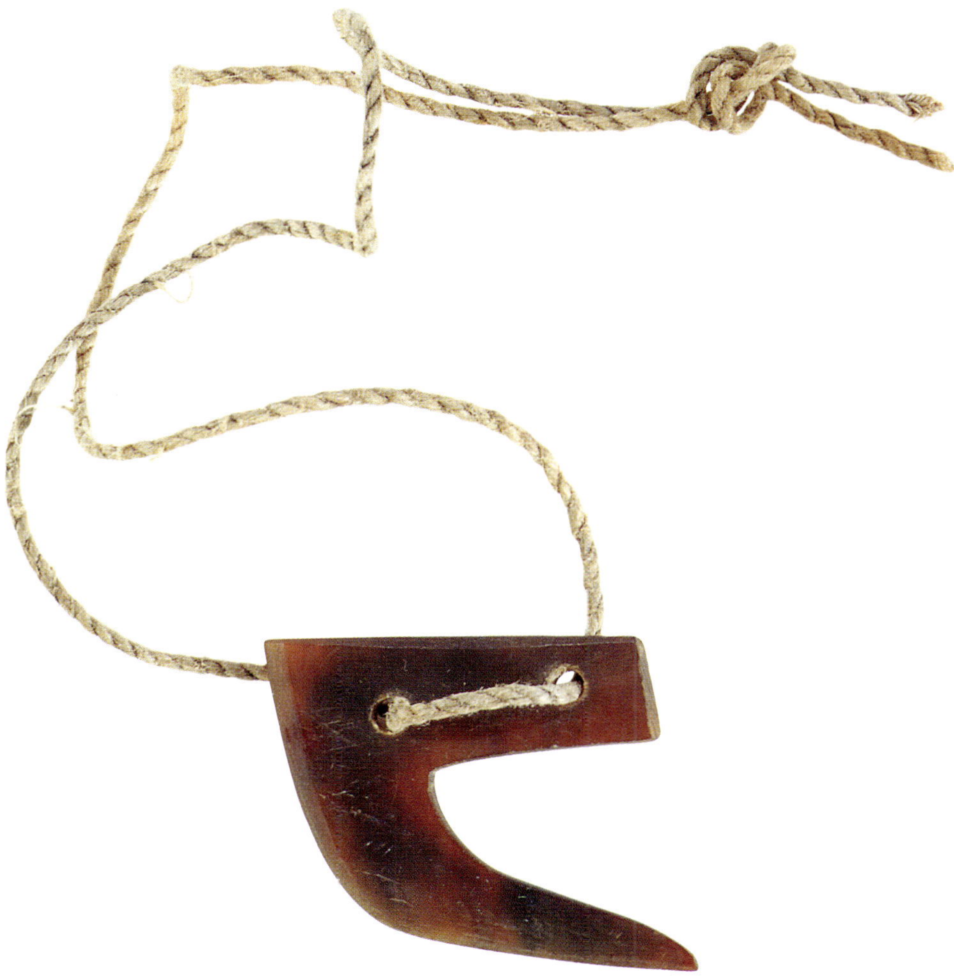

Fishhook Point Neck Ornaments, Tikopia, Solomon Islands

Women of the tiny Polynesian outlier of Tikopia often wore turtle shell fishhook points as part of their jewellery, usually as a single pendant on a cord around the neck or as a necklace with several attached to the neck cord. Occasionally they might also be worn on a cord around the wrist. above: length 3.3 cm, *width 8 cm;* left: *length 5 cm, width 3.5 cm.*

above: *AM 33651 Presented by Lieutenant Commander J. D. O'Neill 1953.*
left: *AM 33647.1. Presented by Lieutenant Commander J. D. O'Neill 1953.*

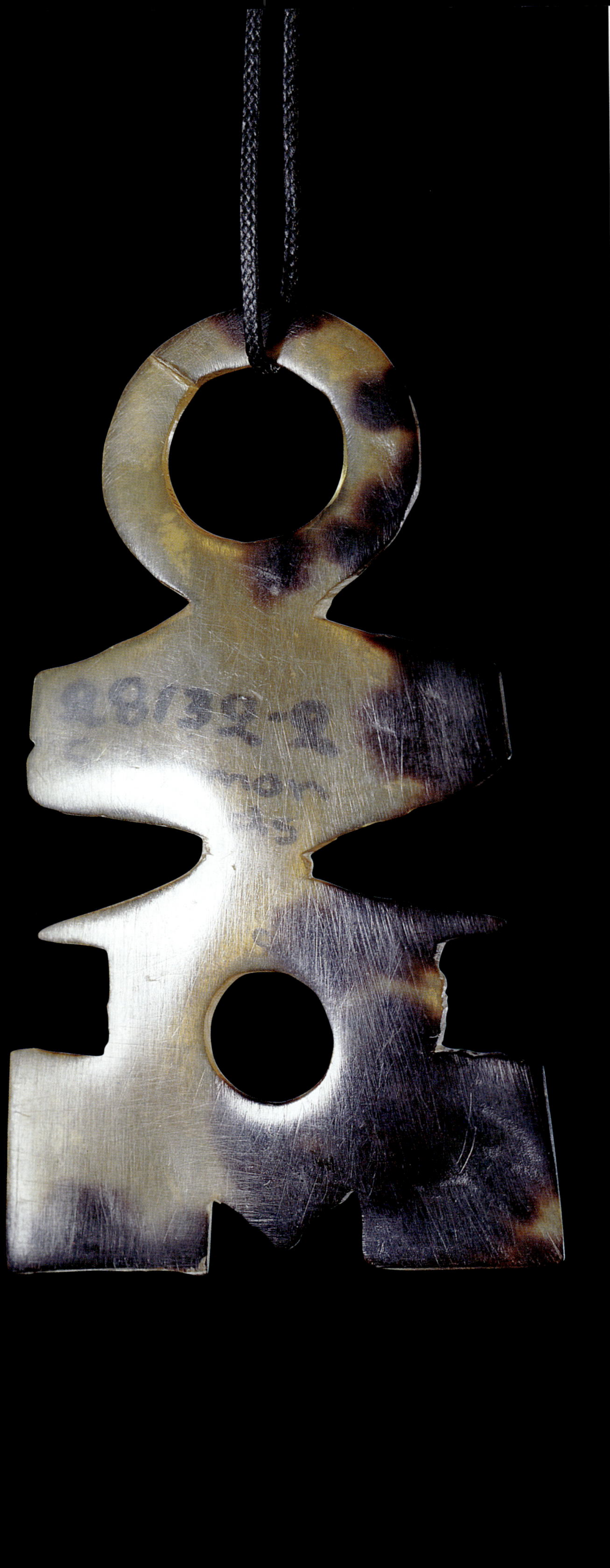

Asana Maka Lua, Nose Ornament, Ontong Java Atoll, Solomon Islands

Ontong Java is one of the atolls in the outer Solomon Islands populated by people of Polynesian descent. Young boys of the chiefly class had the wings of their noses pierced by a slow painful process as part of the *sana* ceremonies marking their initiation into manhood. Thereafter at special dances, these men wore a pair of these turtle shell ornaments clipped through their nose perforations. Smaller turtle shell pendants of the same anthropomorphic shape were also worn as ear ornaments and these continued in use long after the nose pendants became obsolete. *Length 6.5 cm, width 4.3 cm.*

AM 28132.2. Presented by Cyril Belshaw 1946.

opposite: *Avi* or *Matanipara*, Breast Pendant, Tikopia, Solomon Islands

Still showing traces of the turmeric that has rubbed off from the body of its owner, this simple plain pendant has been cut from a local shell, usually *Conus* or *Tridacna* giant clam, and highly polished. It is suspended on a neck cord of native fibre string. Smaller versions called *matanipara* are worn on the wrist or ankle. This is probably one of the most widespread forms of basic Pacific breast pendant, shaped out of locally available shells. *Diameter 7.5 cm.*

AM 33966.1. Presented by Lieutenant Commander J. D. O'Neill 1953.

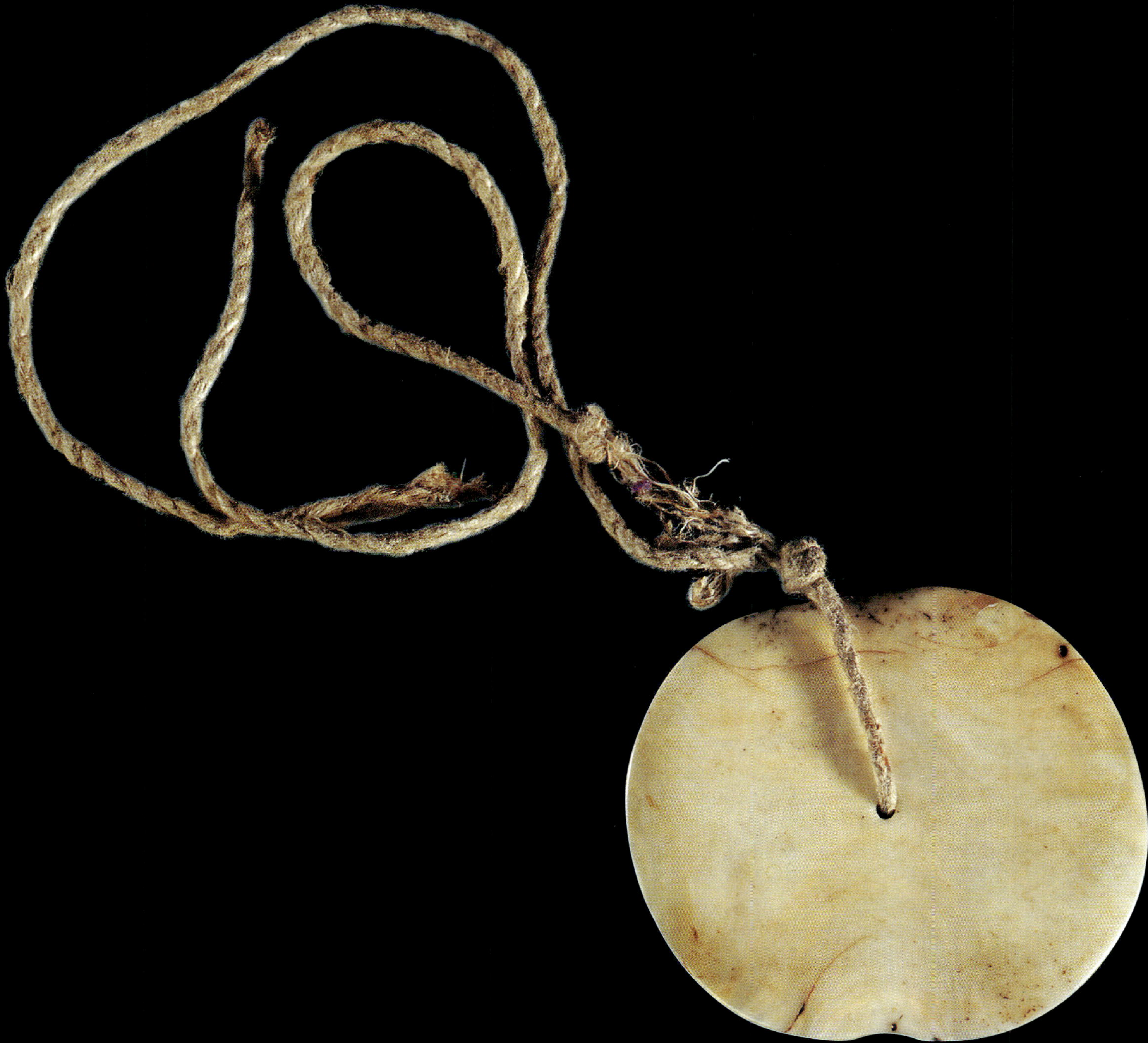

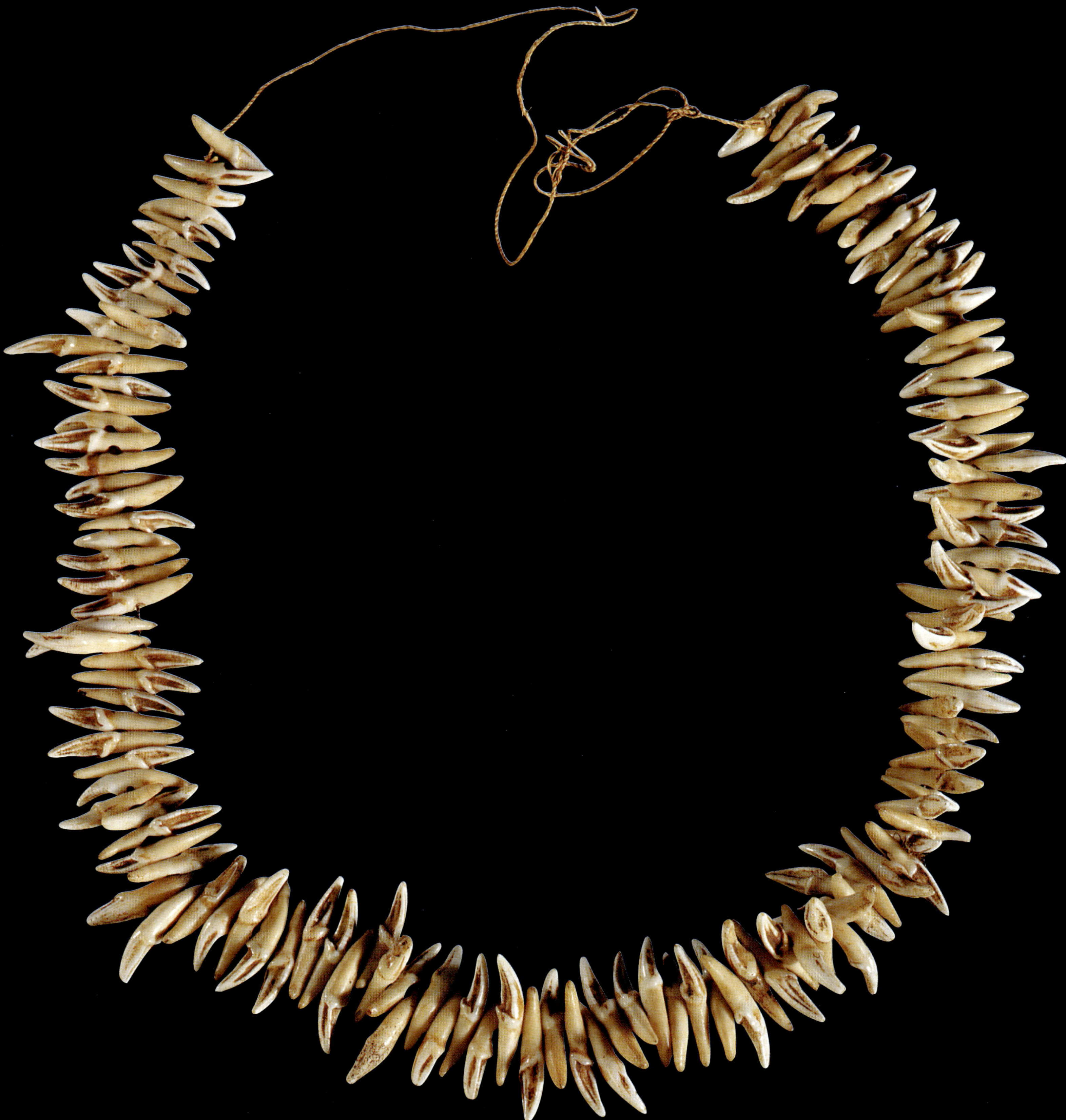

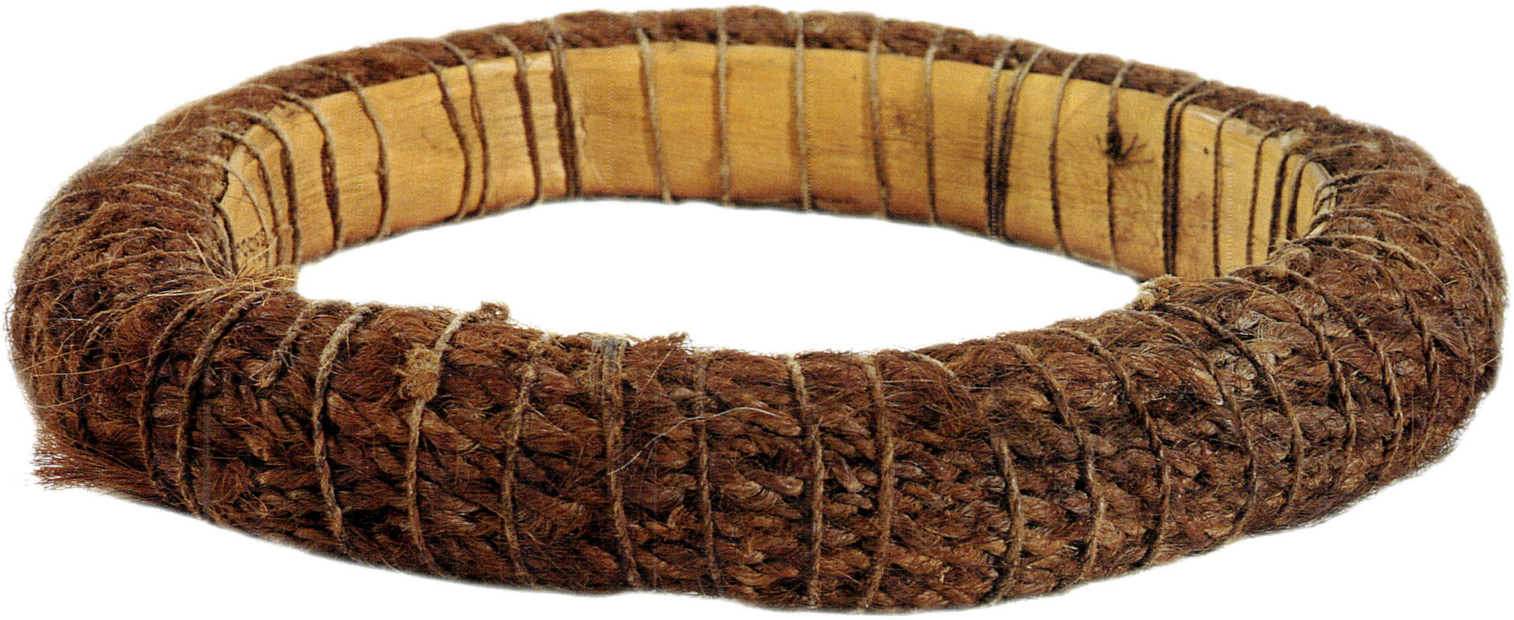

opposite: ***Tu'u*, Necklace of Flying Fox Teeth, Rennell Island, Solomon Islands**

In much of the Solomon Islands, flying fox teeth form an important component of indigenous currency, but on the Polynesian outlier of Rennell, as with other Polynesian cultures, there was no traditional use of currency items. Here the teeth are purely for personal decoration. The old Polynesian religion of Rennell was replaced by Christianity as late as 1938 and much of the original culture still remains strong. *Length 22 cm.*

AM 26454.1. Presented by Miss Clara Waterston 1942.

***Fau Rauuru*, Head-dress of Hair, Tikopia, Solomon Islands**

Before European contact it was the men in Polynesia who wore their hair long, and the women that kept theirs closely cropped. The head is considered *tapu* (sacred), therefore anything associated with it is treated with care and respect. One of the most important mourning rituals of Tikopia was the cutting of a man's hair during the funeral rites of a close relative. This hair was gathered up, rolled, then coiled and attached to a pandanus foundation by female relatives, and worn by them during special public or ceremonial occasions. *Diameter 22 cm.*

AM 33652. Presented by Lieutenant-Commander J. F. A. O'Neill 1953.

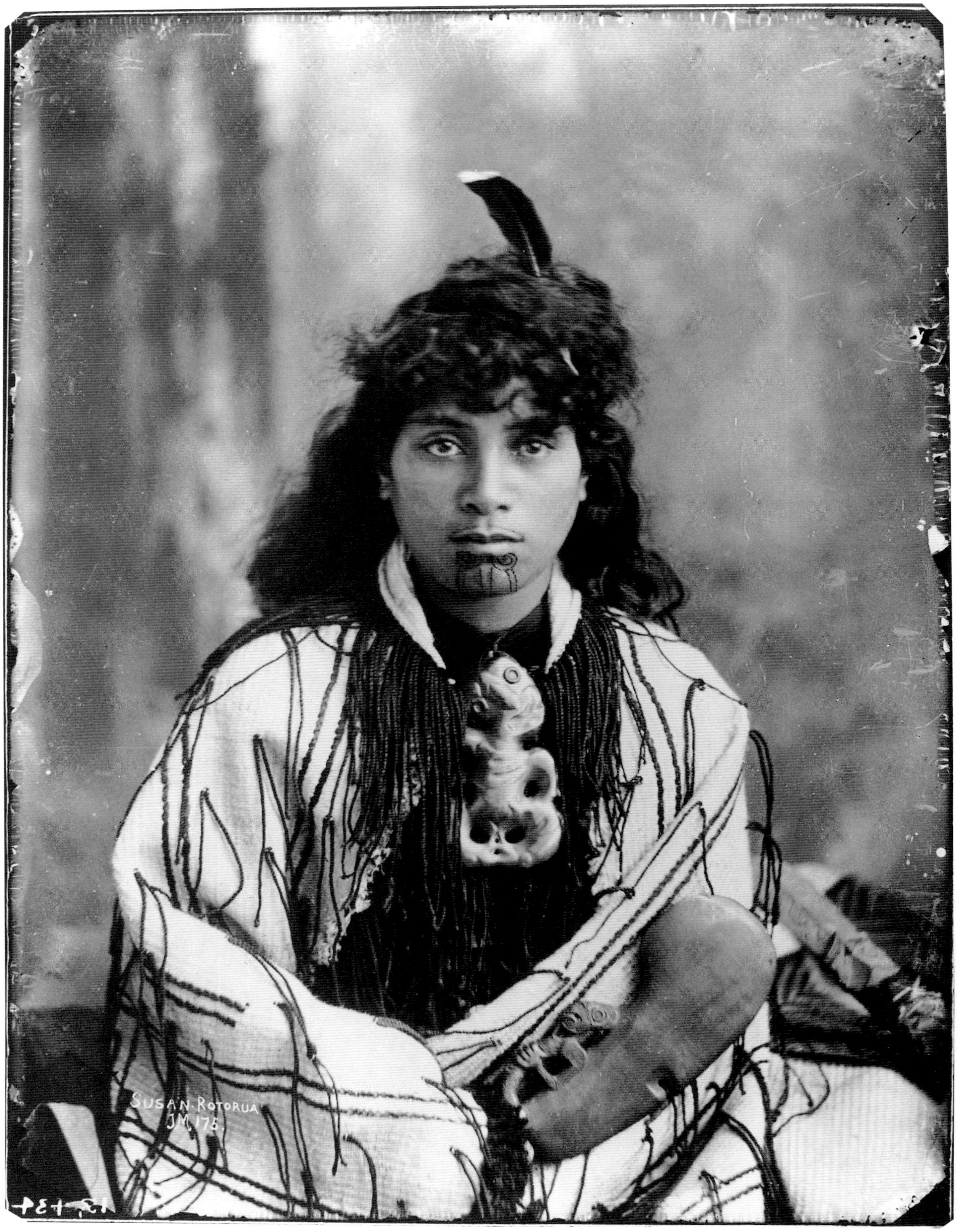
SUSAN·ROTORUA
JM 175

CHAPTER FIVE

AOTEAROA / NEW ZEALAND

WHEN THE EASTERN Polynesian ancestors of the New Zealand Maori people arrived in New Zealand about 800 to 1,000 years ago, they encountered a land mass very different from the small tropical islands of their homeland. The islands of New Zealand are large continental fragments with a wide range of rock types and many different environments. Their climate is temperate to cold, with marked seasonal differences. New Zealand forests contained a wide variety of large trees suitable for building and carving canoes and houses. Both of the two main islands contain large areas at some distance from the sea but well endowed with rivers and lakes. These new environments and the large range of resources provided challenges and opportunities for Maori culture as it developed in New Zealand far beyond its eastern Polynesian foundation.

All Maori throughout the country spoke the same Polynesian language, though with some minor dialectical variations. Society was organised everywhere along the same lines, with major tribal groups or *iwi* tracing their links through common descent from crew members of the original migration canoes. Within *iwi*, smaller subtribal groups or *hapu* were the corporate bodies of society, owning land and villages and acting together in warfare, agriculture and ceremonial affairs. All society was arranged hierarchically by birth and descent into a class of *rangatira* of noble birth and a larger lower class of commoners. Below these were war captives who lived as slaves but did not form a hereditary class. These classes of society could be distinguished by the quality and value of their weapons, costume and ornament, although at times of war and large building projects, *rangatira* and commoners worked together.

At an early archaic stage of Maori cultural development, trade routes moved argillite stone for adzes and ornaments from quarry sources in Southland and Nelson to all parts of the country. Later, after its discovery in south Westland and inland Otago, jade became more popular for woodworking tools and especially for ornaments in the classic period of Maori culture. New jade cutting skills were learnt so that previously woodcarved forms of figures could also be rendered in precious jade, creating heirloom ornaments that lasted for centuries. Bone, mammal teeth and shell were also used for ornaments, but jade was and still is the most favoured.

Both men and women wore ornaments appropriate to their rank but men tended to be more decorated, with their long hair wound up in a topknot held by a comb and with ear ornaments of jade or shark teeth. Male tattoo was also more prominent than female, covering the face and showing on buttocks and thighs. In addition to these permanent ornaments and body markings, men and women often temporarily coloured their faces and bodies with red ochre and other coloured pigments, especially blue and yellow, sometimes in complicated patterns or as a total cover over themselves and their clothing. Jade ornaments, many newly made and some old family heirlooms, are still treasured and worn by Maori people today, expressing their identity and their continuing adherence to Maori values.

left: **'Susan, Rotorua', New Zealand, about 1900**

This young Maori woman is one of the guides who led tourists through the thermal areas at Rotorua. On her lips and chin she displays the typical tattoo patterns of the time. For her photograph by this commercial photographer, she wears a huia feather in her hair and a woven flax korowai *cloak with a European-style dress underneath. Solely for effect, she carries a short wooden weapon called a* wahaika, *previously used by male warriors. Suspended on a flax cord around her neck is a beautiful, extremely large* hei-tiki *ancestral pendant of the rare Bay of Plenty style. This was probably an ancient heirloom belonging to her own family.*

Photo: Josiah Martin, Auckland Museum

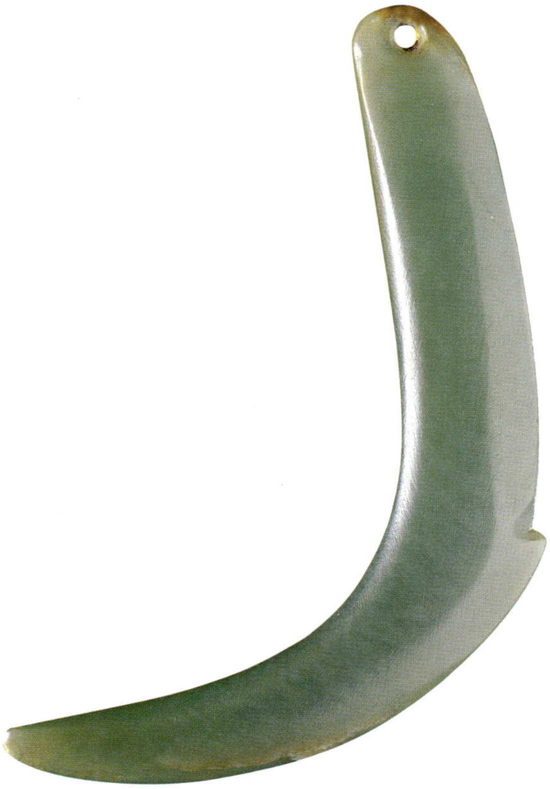

Jade Pendant in Fishhook Form, Near Kaikohe, North Auckland, New Zealand

In many Pacific cultures, fishhooks were worn as neck pendants. In some of the Oceanic cultures it was a complete hook, in others a part of a hook—either the point or the shank—and in yet others a pendant in stylised fishhook form had evolved. For Maori, the *hei-matau* pendant had reached the furthest in stylisation. This rare nephrite pendant retains more of the original fishhook form but has achieved a remarkable abstract sculptural quality. *Length 7.2 cm.*

AM 3053. Presented by Mrs E. E. Goodhue 1961.

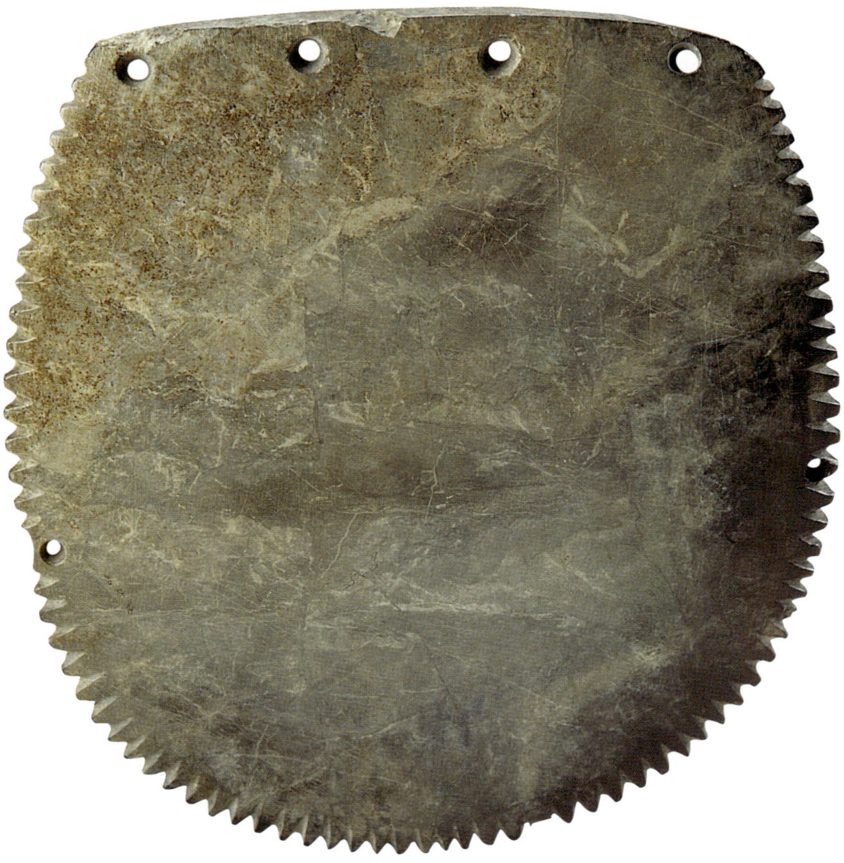

Serpentine Disc Breast Pendant, Motueka, Nelson District, New Zealand

Reminiscent of similar notched whalebone and ivory pectoral discs from elsewhere in the Pacific, the large archaic Maori disc pendants are all carved from stone. Another serpentine pectoral disc from Banks Peninsula has two raised fish carved in relief, while another has an abstract branched figure in relief. All share the notched edges and several suspension holes across the top where, according to old Polynesian fashion, an elaborate multiple braided neck cord of flax would have been attached. Uniquely, this pectoral pendant also has a small hole drilled on each side, probably for tying feathers to enhance the decorative effect. *Length 16.4 cm.*

AM 3417. Purchased from E. B. Williams Trustees 1971.

opposite: *Hei-tiki*, Jade Breast Pendant, Whangarei, North Auckland, New Zealand

Hei-tiki are the most characteristic and most highly valued of all Maori personal ornaments and heirlooms. They represent a female or sexless human figure with head tilted to one side, and many have their own personal name. The most common form has its hands placed symmetrically on the hips. This particular *hei-tiki* is a perfect example of the rarer low relief form, with fine detailed facial features, projecting ears and one hand on its chest. Worn by men or women suspended from a flax neck cord with albatross bone toggle, some *hei-tiki* of this form are so old that the suspension hole has worn through from the action of the flax neck cord and a new hole has had to be drilled. Some are so ancient that they have two or three replacement holes. *Length 13.2 cm.*

AM 19026.1. Purchased from A. Brodie 1933.

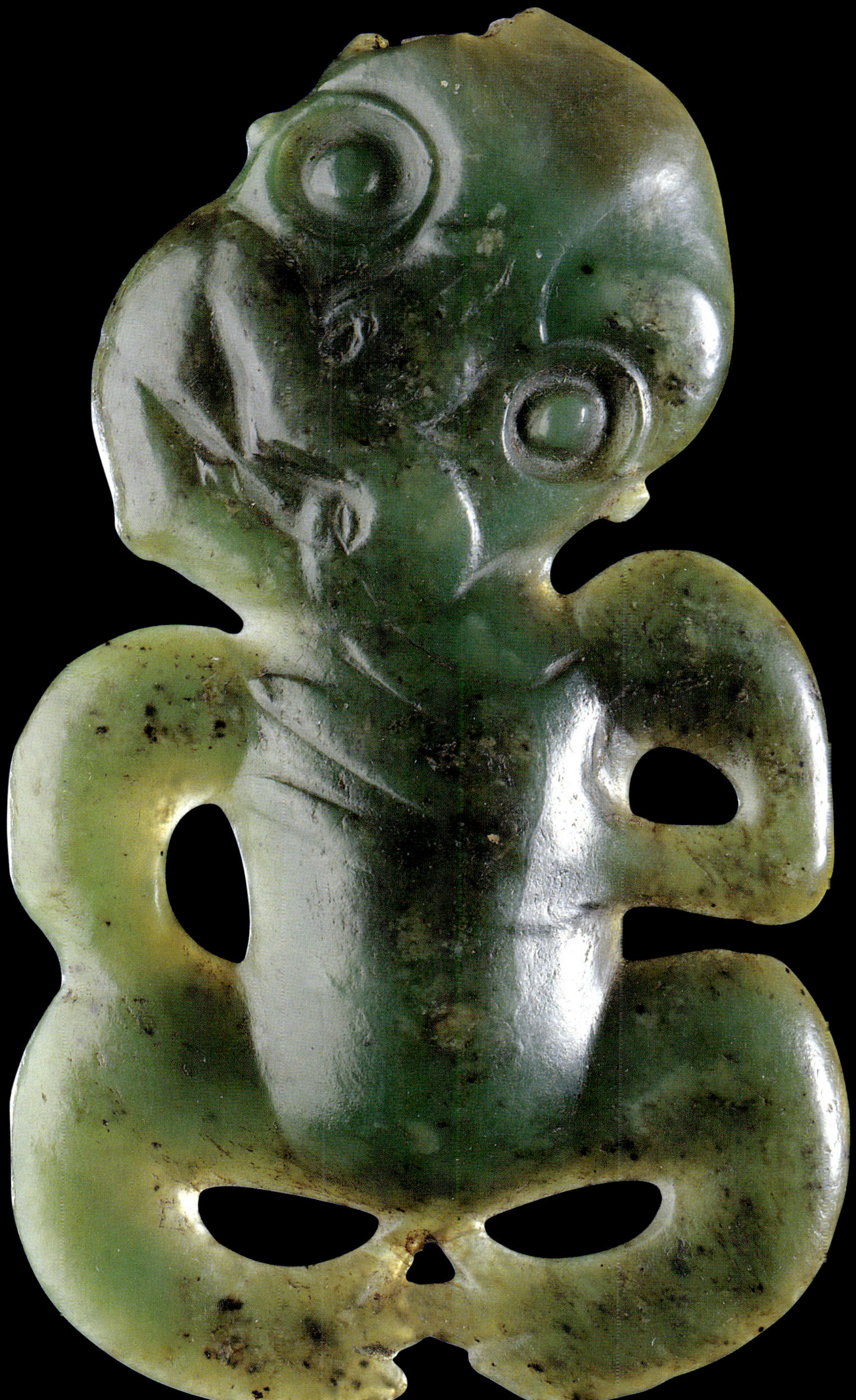

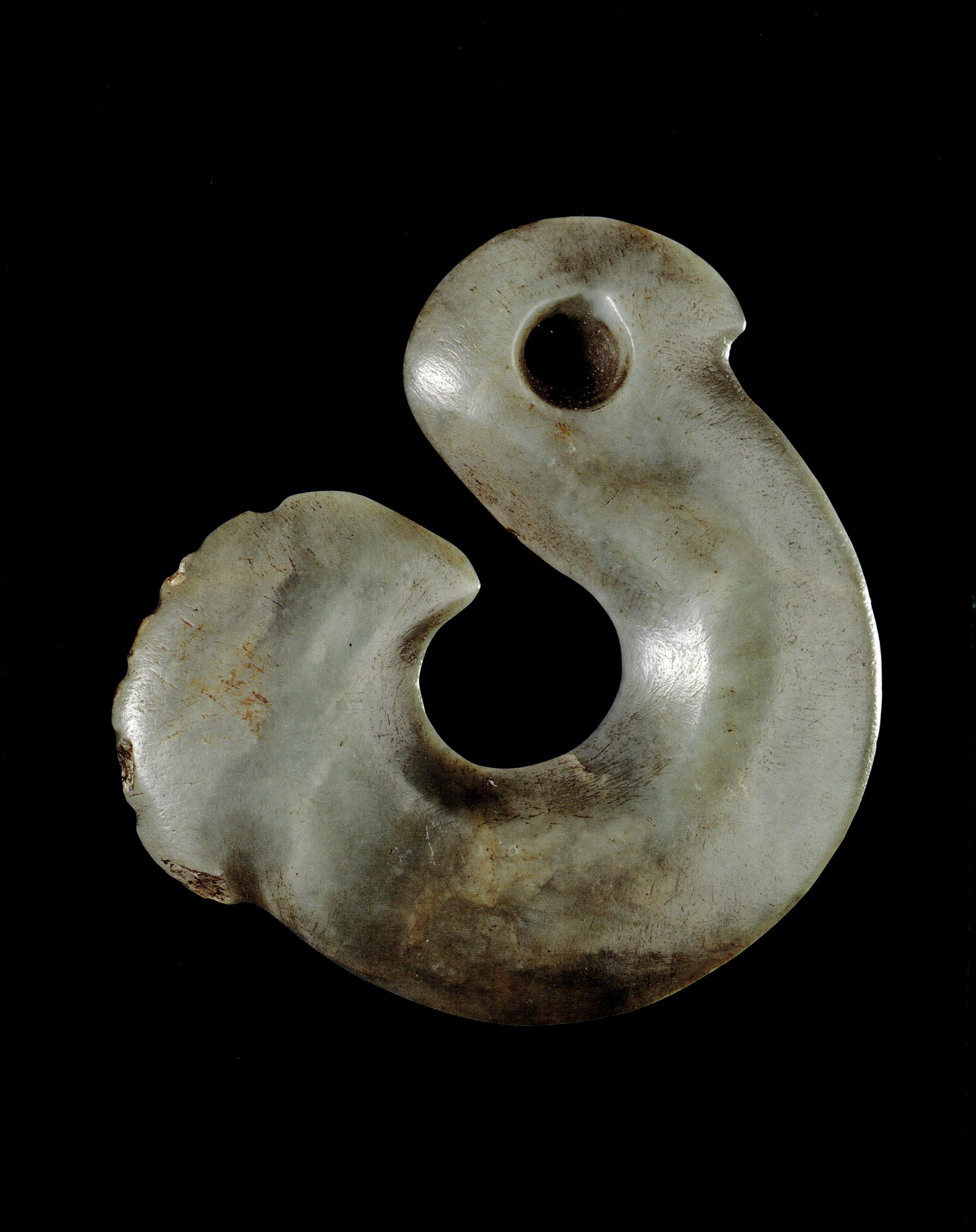

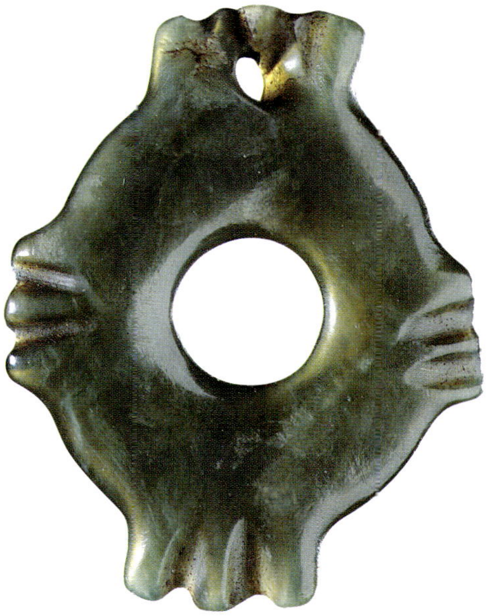

PORIA KAKA, JADE PENDANT, NEW ZEALAND

To encourage wild kaka parrots to approach their snares, Maori hunters kept pet kaka tethered by a leg ring of bone or jade. In time, these parrot leg rings were considered as ornaments to be worn as either breast or ear pendants. More elaborate examples in jade were produced solely as ornaments. *Length 3.8 cm.*

AM 5521. Presented by Mr A. Frater 1912.

IMITATION WHALE TOOTH NECK PENDANT, RAOUL ISLAND, KERMADEC ISLANDS, NEW ZEALAND

Carved out of whalebone in the modified form of an archaic Maori whale tooth pendant, this unique ornament was recovered from an archaeological site dated to the fourteenth century in the Kermadec Islands, which lie half-way between New Zealand and Tonga. New Zealand obsidian has been found at Raoul Island, indicating that early Polynesian voyagers travelled back from New Zealand in this period of extensive Polynesian interisland movement. Comparable imitation whale tooth pendants were popular among early New Zealand Maori at this period, carved out of whalebone or moa bird bone. *Length 5.9 cm.*

AR 7454. Auckland Museum 1978.

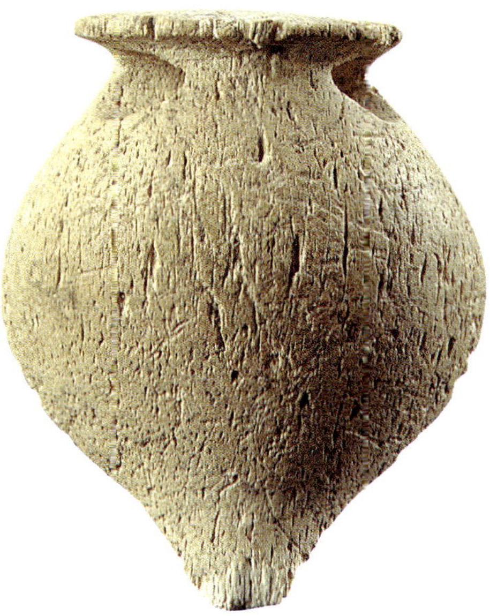

opposite: **HEI-MATAU, JADE BREAST PENDANT, NEW ZEALAND**

This sculptural jade pendant worn suspended from one end of the curve, is abstracted from the shape of a fishhook or *matau*. It possibly refers to the fabulous fishhook of the demigod Maui with which he fished up the North Island of New Zealand, still called Te Ika a Maui, The Fish of Maui. A *hei-matau* is regarded as a symbol of special knowledge relating to the activities of gods, ancestors and the supernatural world, to be worn only by *tohunga*, ritual experts well versed in such esoteric knowledge. *Length 6.1 cm.*

AM 31903. W. O. Oldman Collection 1948.

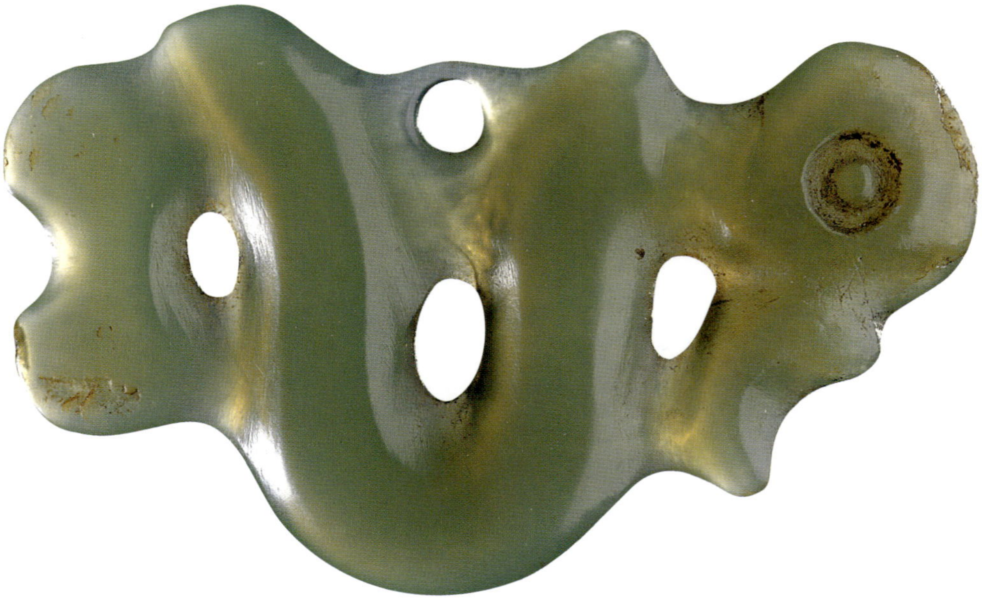

MANAIA, JADE BREAST PENDANT, WAIOMIO VALLEY, NORTH AUCKLAND, NEW ZEALAND

Called a *manaia* because it echoes the sinuous profile manaia figure of woodcarving, this small pendant has been ground and polished out of nephrite jade. This highly valued variety of jade is known as *inanga* to the Maori because of its pale colour and translucence similar to the small inanga whitebait fish delicacy. In woodcarvings, *manaia* figures are regarded as spiritual protectors for the frontal ancestral *tiki* figures. *Manaia* figures in jade are probably the rarest form of Maori jade pendant and seem to have become concentrated in the far north of the North Island after being traded hand to hand from southern districts. *Length 5.2 cm.*

AM 34759. Presented by The Misses Stewart 1956.

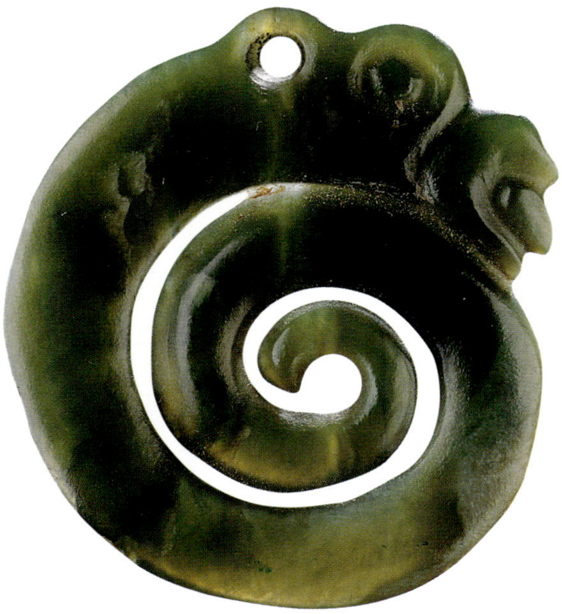

KOROPEPE, JADE EAR OR BREAST PENDANT, NEW ZEALAND

Sometimes said to represent an eel, *koropepe* pendants seem to be a relatively modern form; no ancient examples are known, although the spiral is a major motif of all Maori art. Many are also made out of bowenite, called *tangiwai* by Maori; this is a softer mineral than nephrite and is much easier to carve, and consequently is often chosen by more recent and less patient stone workers in preference to the harder nephrite. For similar reasons, many others are carved out of bone. *Length 4.8 cm.*

AM 7150. Presented by Mr H. E. Vaile 1925.

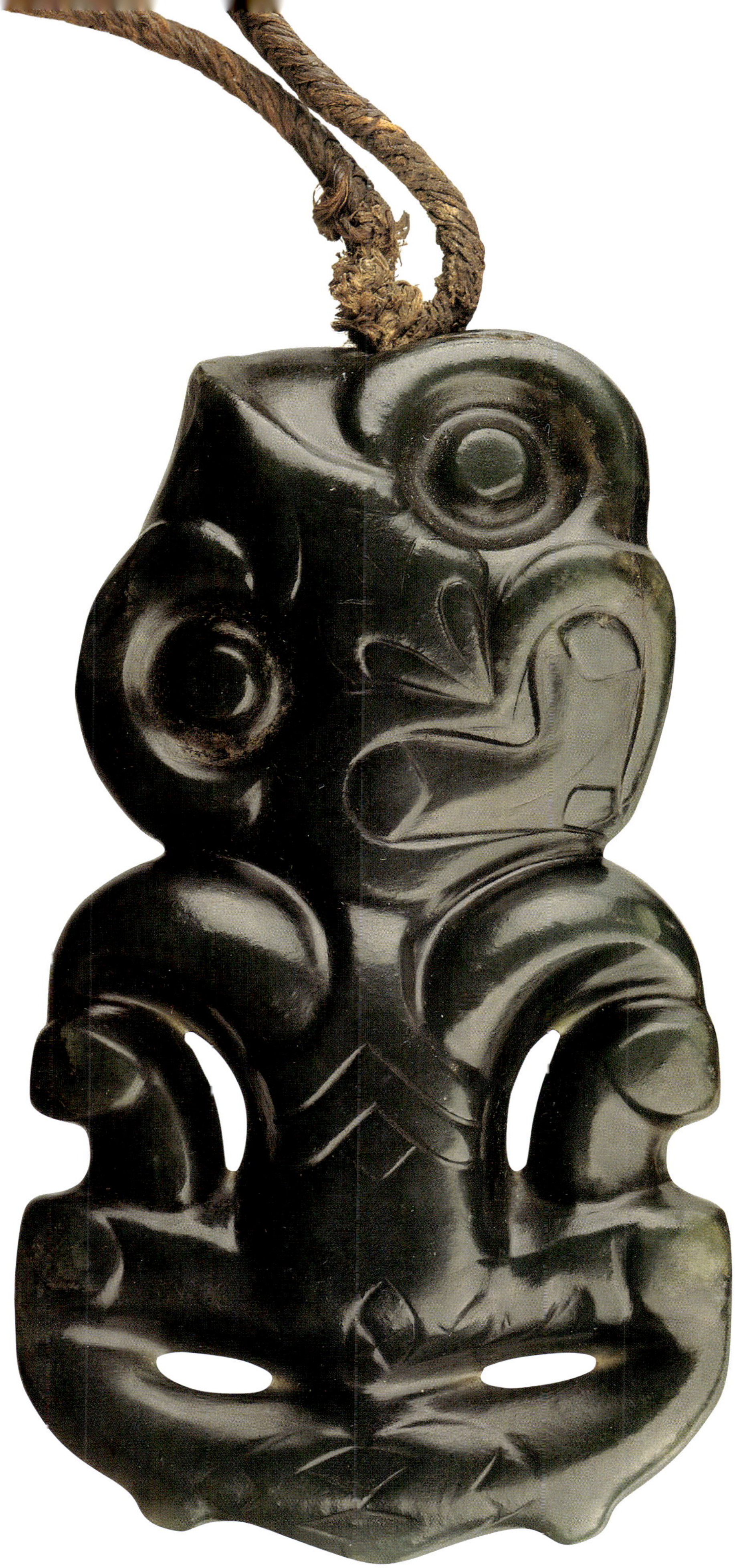

HEI-TIKI, JADE BREAST PENDANT, NEW ZEALAND

With its tilted peaked head and large eyes matching the woodcarving style of the Taranaki district in the west of the North Island, this large *hei-tiki* of deep green *kawakawa* nephrite is of the more common type with its hands placed symmetrically on the hips. It probably originally had inlaid eyes of *paua* (abalone) shell ring, which were often replaced with red sealing wax in post-European times. This *hei-tiki* was obtained by Lieutenant Matthew Flinders of Australian coastal mapping fame, somewhere off the coast of New Zealand in 1797. It is one of the few old *hei-tiki* that has retained its original plaited-flax neck suspension cord. *Length 15.6 cm.*

AM 5587. Purchased from Mrs Palmer 1912.

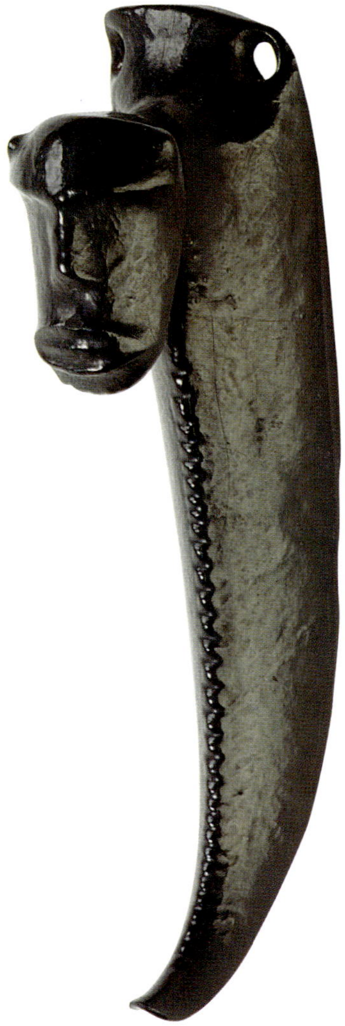

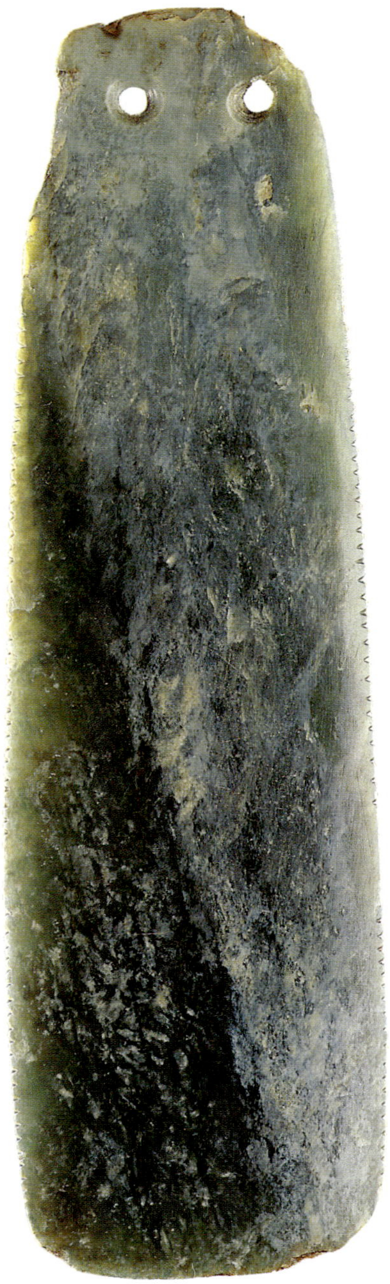

Serpentine Breast Pendant, Waitotara, New Zealand

Found at Waitotara just north of Whanganui in the early 1870s, this delicately carved serpentine pendant features an early Polynesian style of face and an archaic form of notching on the chin and down the central rib. Its overall shape is developed as an imitation from the simple shaped whale tooth form of pendant that was brought to New Zealand from East Polynesia by the first settlers at least 800 years ago. Serpentine pendants generally date from early in the Maori occupation of New Zealand, around the thirteenth to fourteenth centuries. With its two suspension holes and tapered shape, this ornament may prefigure later *rei puta* breast pendants made out of a sperm whale tooth that were popular in the eighteenth century. In a masterly touch, the craftsman has grooved the rear of the delicate upturned lower point, which is reminiscent of the more prominent lower curve on a Hawaiian *lei niho palaoa* whale tooth pendant. *Length 10.2 cm.*

AM 5063. Presented by Miss Morrison 1927.

Breast Pendant in the Form of an Adze, New Zealand

Light, thin, jade breast pendants in the form of a woodworking adze blade were especially popular in the North Auckland district. They usually have two suspension holes to take a neck cord with a complicated lashing pattern. Fine notching along the edges continues an archaic Maori decorative motif that is sometimes said to serve as a genealogical reckoning. Maori people called this variety of jade *kahurangi* because of its resemblance to clouds floating in the heavens. *Length 15.6 cm.*

AM 10307A. Presented by Mr H. E. Vaile 1925.

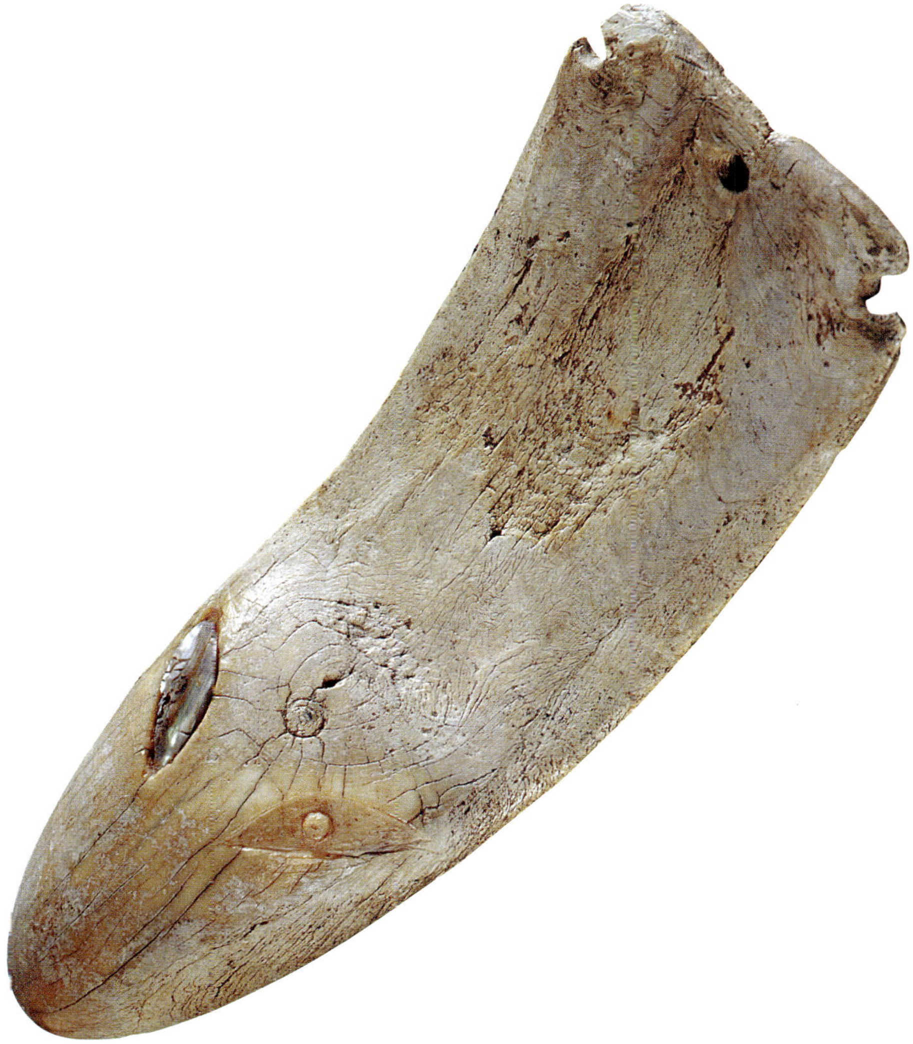

Rei puta, Breast Pendant, New Zealand

A sperm whale tooth has been cut down and polished to produce the characteristic shape of a *rei puta*. Vestigial slanting eyes, often with black inlay, are all that remain of a stylised face at the lower end. *Rei puta* were popular ornaments among North Island Maori during the eighteenth century, as seen by Captain Cook's expeditions, but by the early nineteenth century they had gone out of fashion. The form is clearly derived from earlier archaic whale ivory pendants, and indeed intermediate evolutionary examples are known, ranging from one with a full figure and repeating chevron arms to several South Island examples with a complete face at the lower end. *Length 17 cm, width 6 cm.*

AM 2938. Presented by Hon. W. Stewart 1928.

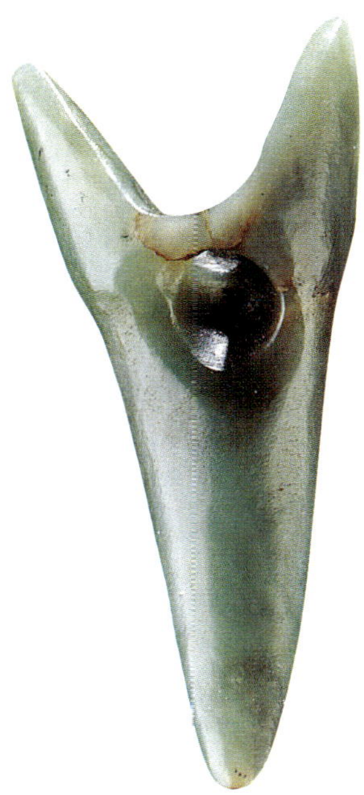

Jade Pendant in Imitation of a Shark Tooth, New Zealand

Maori men and women often wore a real shark tooth, recent or fossil, as an ornament in their earlobe, embellished in post-European times with red sealing wax moulded over the root of the tooth and trailing black cotton ribbons. Sometimes, to create an ornament of higher value, a replica of a shark tooth was carved out of nephrite jade to be worn either as an ear ornament or drilled for suspension as a neck pendant. *Length 4.5 cm.*

AM 580. Purchased from Mr Danneford 1895.

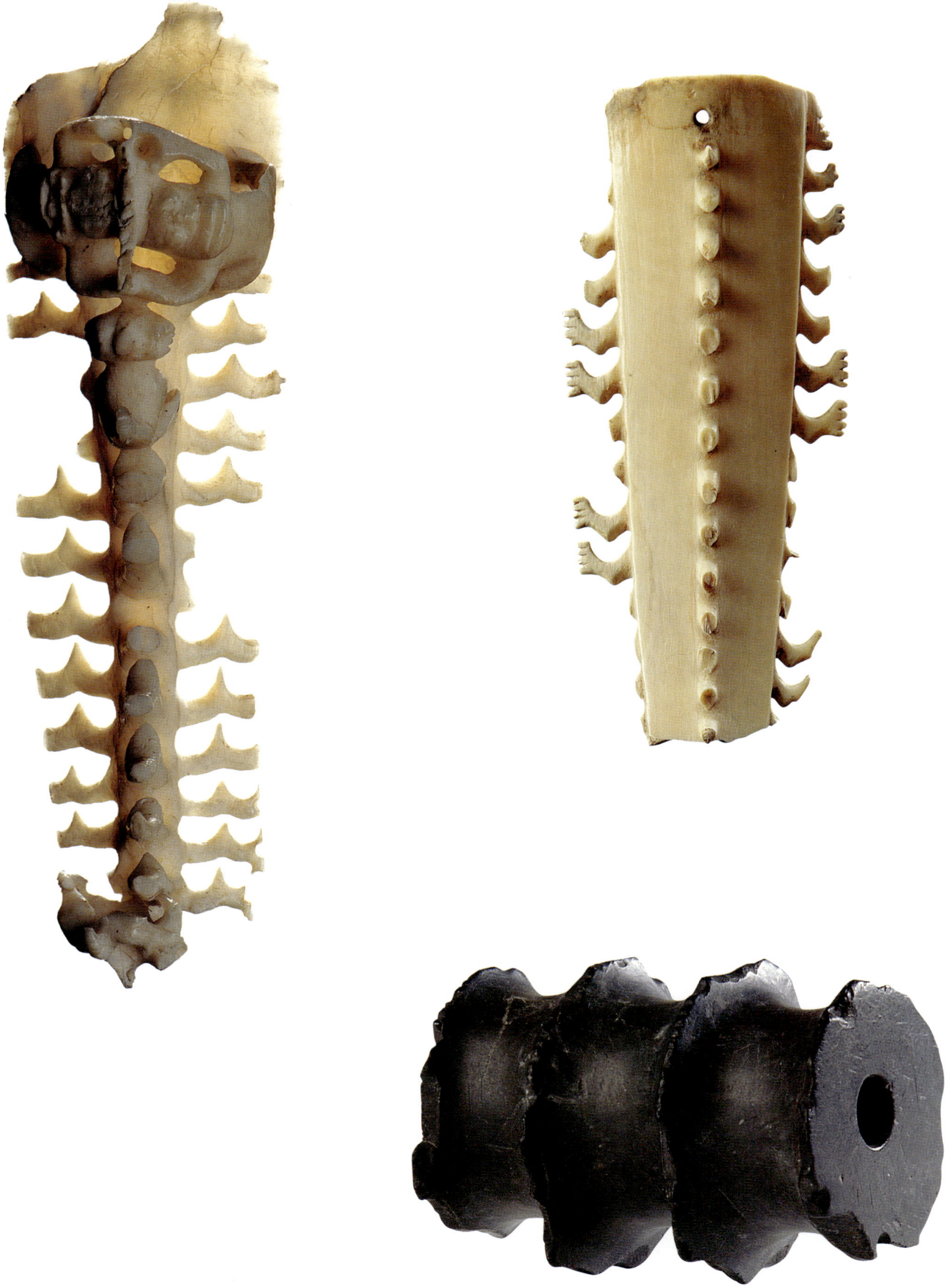

opposite, clockwise from top left:

Rei niho, Chevroned Breast Pendant, Whangamumu, North Auckland, New Zealand

In 1895, storm erosion of an ancient Maori living area in sand dunes beside Whangamumu Harbour exposed this archaic breast pendant carved from a sperm whale tooth. The form, with crouching figures back to back and arms raised, relates to early Eastern Polynesian art, suggesting that it was probably carved in the thirteenth or fourteenth century AD by Maori whose art styles still retained strong echoes of their tropical Polynesian origins. The chevron shapes are derived from stylised human arms and legs, and are characteristic of many archaic Maori bone artefacts. *Length 12.8 cm.*

AM 21859. Presented by Mrs Lushington 1935.

Chevroned Breast Pendant, Coromandel Peninsula, New Zealand

Estimated to date from the fourteenth to the sixteenth centuries, chevroned pendants fashioned out of whale teeth or bone were made in several different forms. But they all share the archaic features of notching on edges and the chevrons, which are stylised arms or legs. This unusual one has been carved from a sperm whale tooth, cut flat to remove the curve of the tooth. Other chevroned pendants were made as a mirror image pair, perhaps representing a stylised profile animal with many legs, to be worn lashed flat at the top so that their curves diverged at the lower end. Chevroned pendants are some of the most intricate of fine Maori ornament carving. *Length 11.3 cm.*

AM 20015. Presented by Robert A. Laidlaw 1934.

Serpentine Reel Ornament, Parengarenga Harbour, North Auckland, New Zealand

Reel neck ornaments of stone, bone, ivory and fossil shell were worn by archaic Maori as necklaces or as single pendants during the fourteenth and fifteenth centuries. Stone reels are usually found as single pendants, such as this one carved from black serpentine with grey veining. It is one of the largest Maori reel ornaments known and weighs 190 grams—quite heavy to hang around one's neck. Traces of notching survive on the damaged edges of its four sharp and pronounced ridges. *Length 7 cm.*

AM 30819. Presented by Mr A.H. Watt 1949.

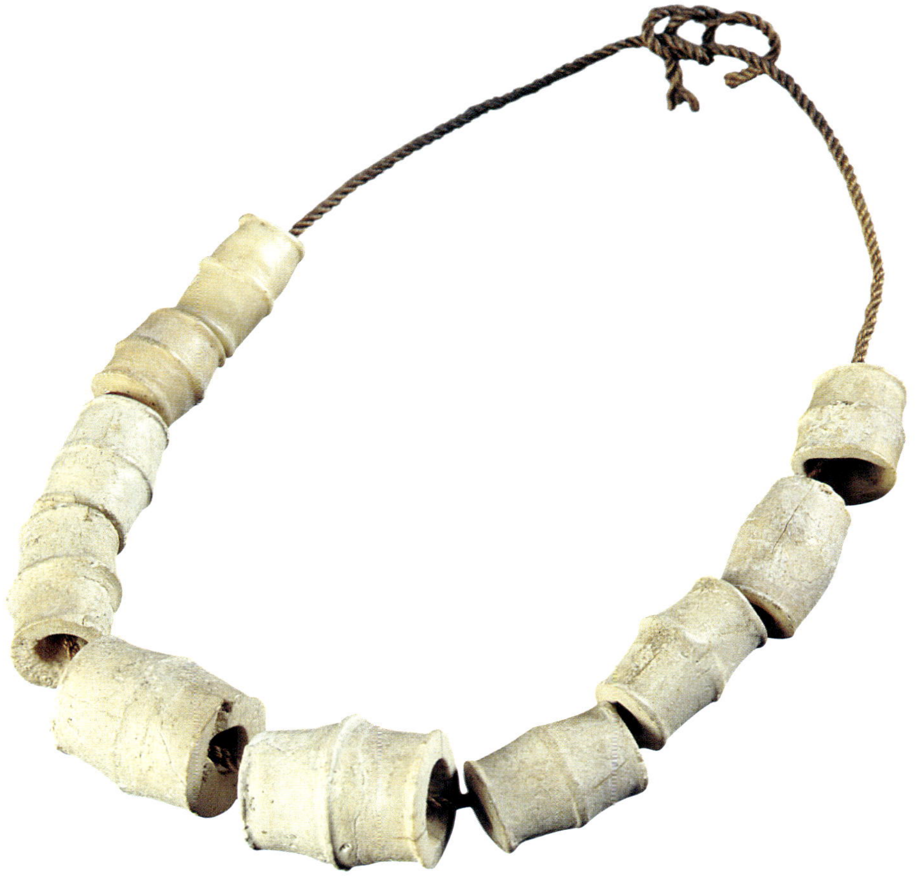

Necklace of Ten Ivory Reels, Mercury Bay, Coromandel Peninsula, New Zealand

Many of the people at the famous late thirteenth century moa hunter site of Wairau Bar near Blenheim in the South Island were buried wearing their bone, stone or ivory reel necklaces. Archaic Maori necklaces were obviously one of the most popular types of body ornament in these times, having been found at many other early sites. The elements of this Mercury Bay necklace have each been carved with terminal ridges and one central ridge. Some reel necklaces supported a central pendant of a whale tooth or its imitation in bone or stone. *Length of maximum reel 2.4 cm.*

AM 6049. Presented by Mr L.S. Birdwill 1916.

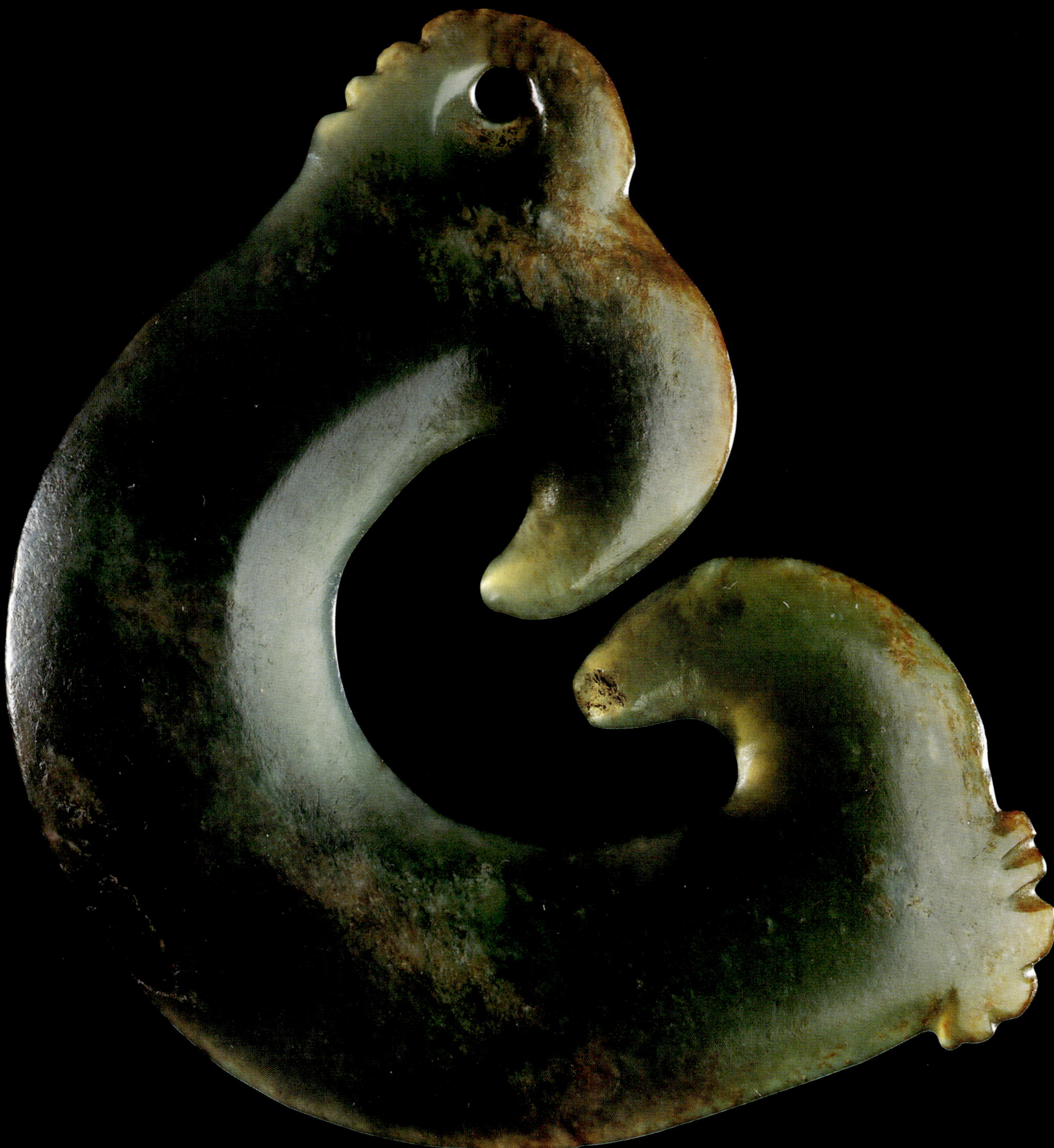

right: ***WHAKAKAIPIKO*, KINKED EAR-PENDANT, MAHURANGI HEADS, NORTH AUCKLAND, NEW ZEALAND**

The most common form of Maori ear-pendant, usually called a *kuru*, is a straight, often bulbous, piece of polished nephrite or bowenite, with a suspension hole at one end. These were worn by men and women, usually in one ear only. Kinked ear-pendants like this one are very rare compared to *kuru* and are hardly ever seen now except in old museum collections. It has been suggested that the *whakakaipiko* is derived from a stylised bird form. This highly polished example has been cut from the *kawakawa* variety of nephrite, so named because of its resemblance to the deep green colour of *kawakawa* leaves. *Length 10.3 cm.*

AM 5599. Purchased from Mr Edward Spencer 1912.

far right: ***KAPEU*, CURVED JADE EAR-PENDANT, NEW ZEALAND**

After the straight *kuru* type of ear pendant, the most common are those with a curve at the end, called a *kapeu*. This one carved out of beautiful pale *inanga* jade bears the personal name of *Parekarangi*. Many Maori treasures—including personal ornaments, weapons, houses and canoes—had their own personal name, thereby maintaining a connection with the famous ancestors who had created or owned them. Named treasures, *taonga*, are remembered in songs and legends, even long after they have been lost. *Length 14.7 cm.*

AM 2540. Presented by Mr D. Macfarlane 1928.

opposite: ***HEI-MATAU*, JADE BREAST PENDANT, NEW ZEALAND**

The name *hei-matau* means a fishhook designed to be suspended around the neck. In this example, the abstracted fishhook form has been elaborated further by transforming the end with the suspension hole into a *manaia* type of profile head, which also suggests a bird's head. The other end has been crafted as a mirror image. This variety of jade was called *totoweka* by the Maori, meaning the blood of the weka bird, which refers to the red patches on the green jade. *Length 8.2 cm.*

AM 19256. Purchased from Mrs Walsh 1933

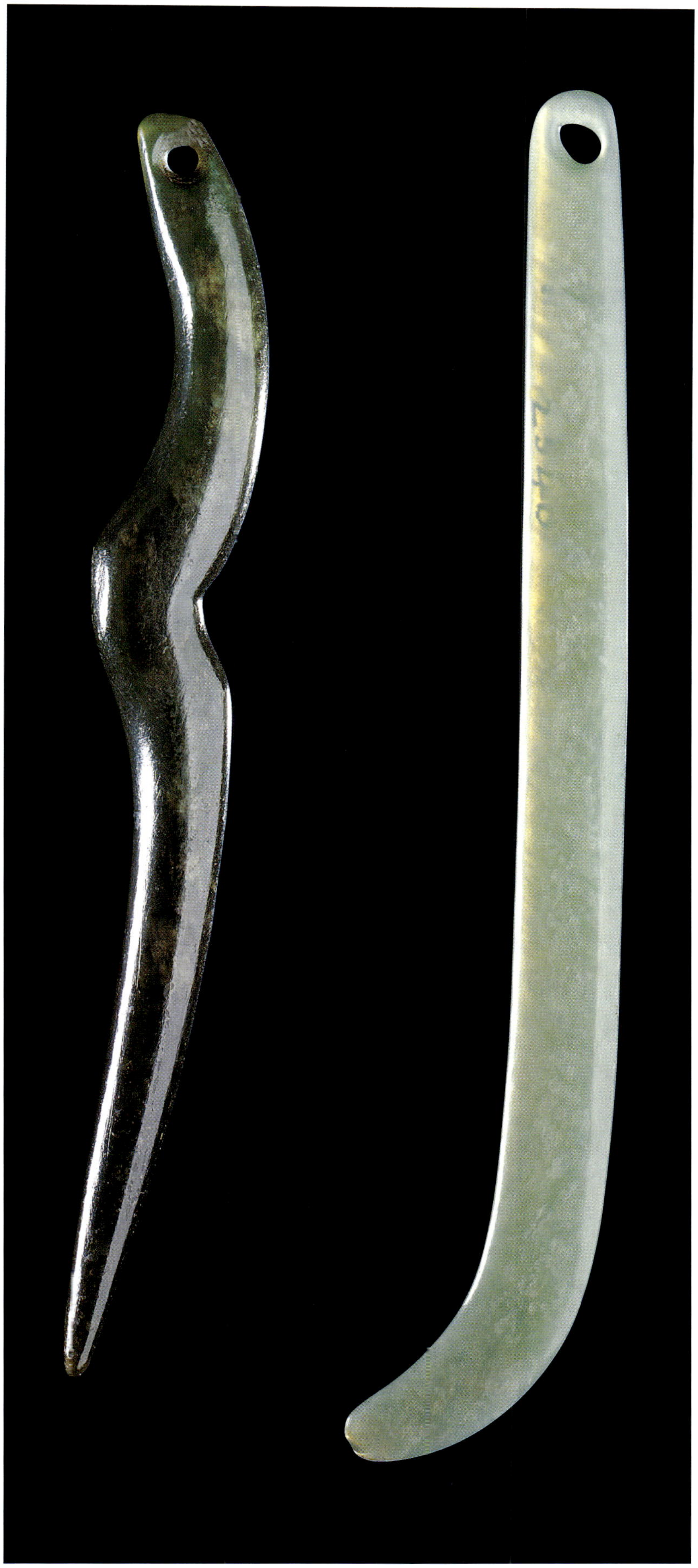

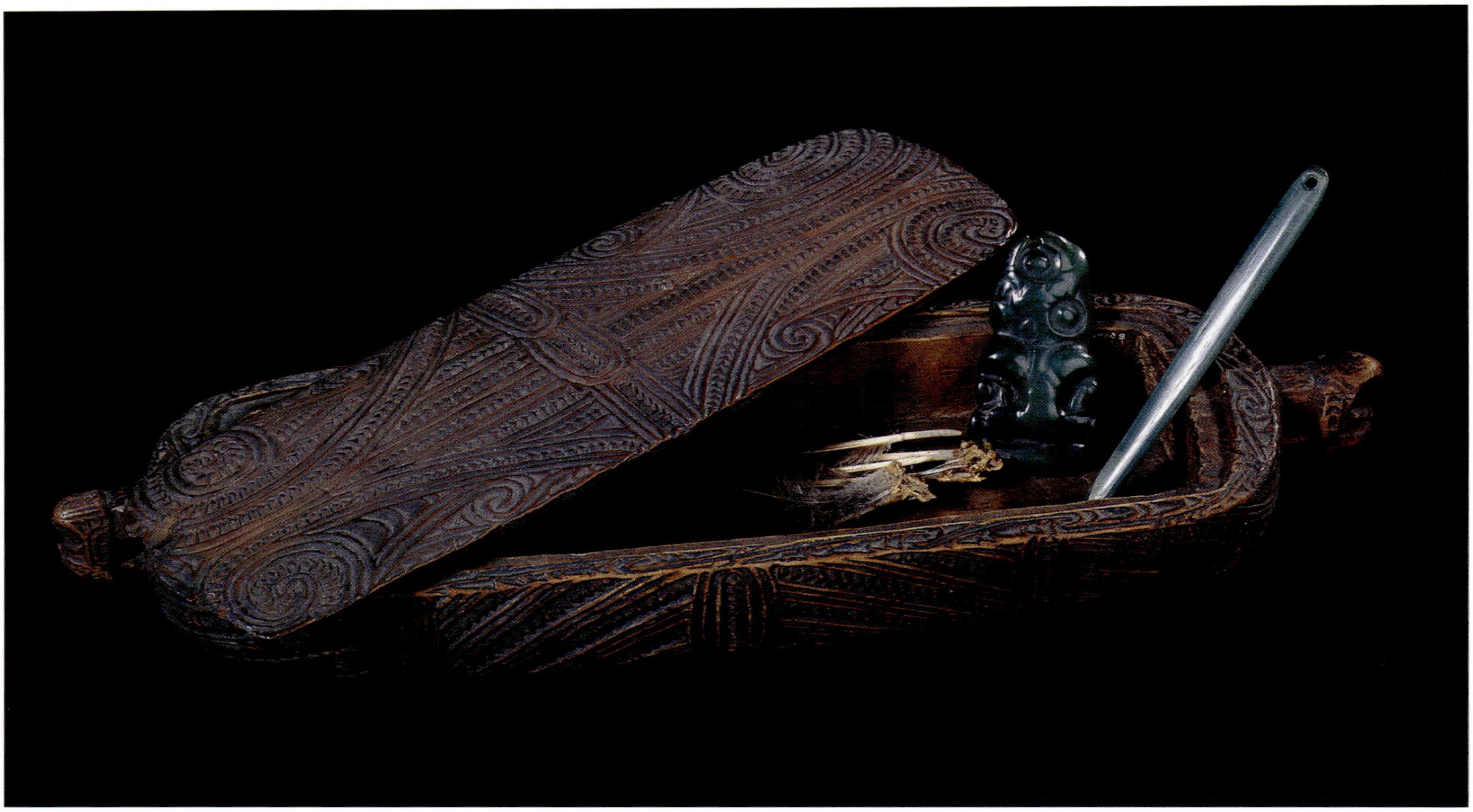

Wakahuia, Treasure Box, East Coast, New Zealand

Treasure boxes called *wakahuia*, meaning canoe-shaped, or *papahou*, meaning flat and rectangular, were carved by men out of totara and kauri timber to hold their personal treasures of jade ornaments, combs and feathers. Since most of these ornaments were worn about the extremely *tapu* head of a chiefly person, his treasure box and its contents were especially sacred and dangerous to commoners. It was hung by cords from the interior rafters of the chief's house, being carved underneath where the designs could be seen. *Length 39 cm.*

AM 16398. James Edge-Partington Collection. Presented by Dr Thomson Wilson Leys Memorial 1924.

Heru, Combs, New Zealand

Maori combs were constructed either by carving out the complete comb from one solid piece of whalebone or wood, or by binding together individual wooden teeth. An archaeological series of one-piece combs from the Kauri Point site in the Bay of Plenty dating from the mid-sixteenth to the mid-eighteenth centuries shows a gradual change in the anthropomorphic designs on the combs from notched and spiked geometric forms to rounded curvilinear forms. This later form was in fashion when the first Europeans arrived. Men wore their hair long, tied up in a topknot and held in place with a decorative comb. clockwise from top left: *Length 12 cm, width 5.5 cm; length 13 cm, width 5 cm; length 16.5 cm, width 10.3 cm; length 16 cm, width 5.5 cm.*

clockwise from top left: *AM 366. Lake Taupo. Purchased from Mr Eric Craig 1892.*
AM 16393. James Edge-Partington Collection. Presented by Dr Thomson Wilson Leys Memorial 1924.
AM 32026. Waverley, Taranaki. Purchased from Mrs Stiechan 1951.
AM 17189. Purchased from McKenna's auction 1932.

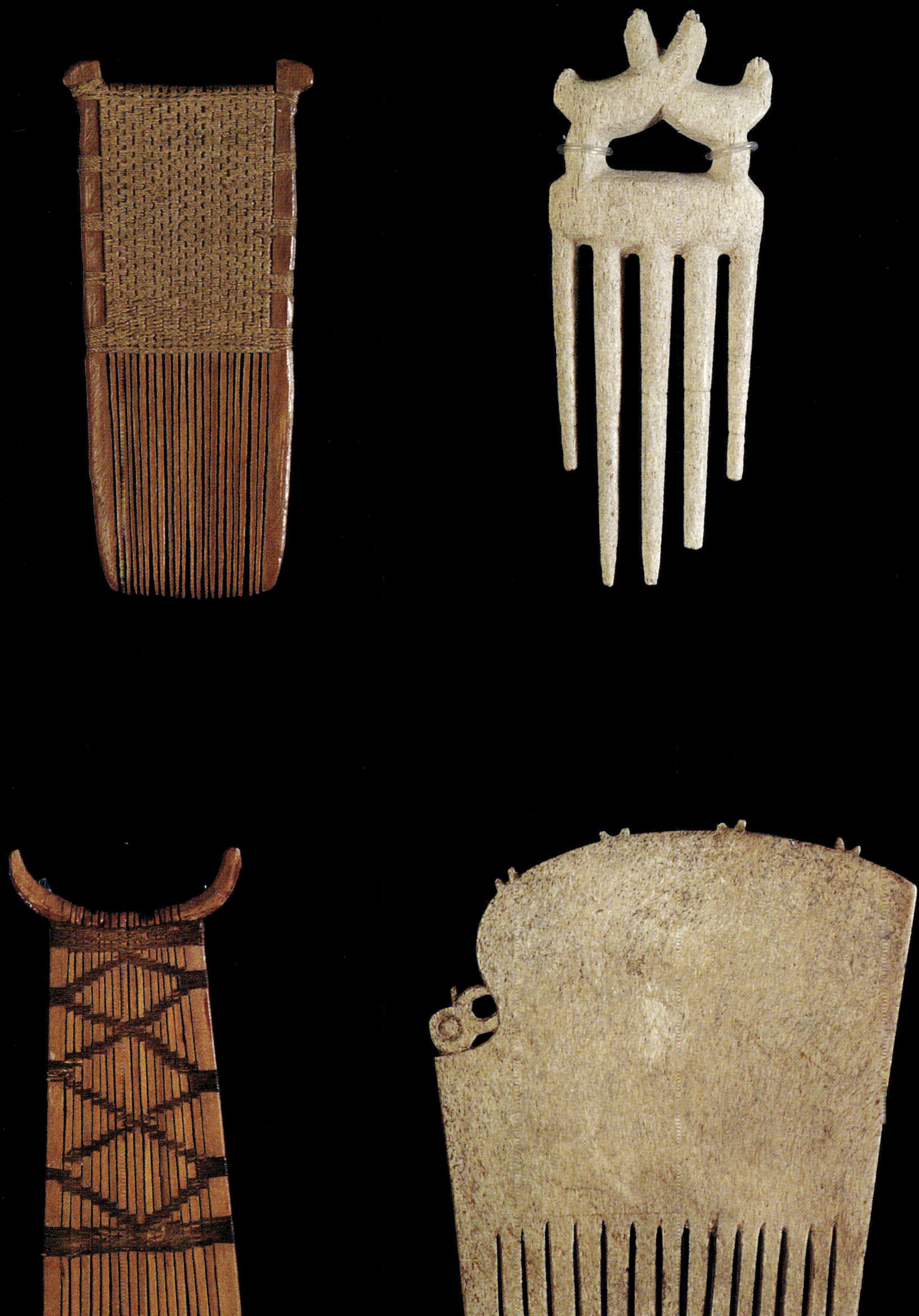

A NOTE ON THE COLLECTIONS

The collections of Pacific jewellery and related artefacts now in the Auckland Museum have come from a wide variety of sources over many years since the founding of the museum in 1852. There are now several hundred jewellery items in Auckland Museum and further pieces are constantly being added to the collection.

Many have come from interested individuals who have generously presented items to the museum. Their contribution is acknowledged in the captions along with the year in which the item was presented to the museum. Other pieces have been purchased for the collection, either privately or at auction. Where known, the name of the vendor and the year of purchase are given in the caption.

Several important ethnographic collectors are represented in the Auckland Museum jewellery collections. One of the most significant is James Edge-Partington, an English authority on the material culture of the Pacific. He travelled through Australia, New Zealand and the Pacific between 1879 and 1881, and much of his collection was obtained in the course of these travels. After his return to England, he continued to collect Pacific artefacts that became available there, including items collected by A.C. Haddon in New Guinea and Torres Strait and material derived from the London Missionary Society Collection. In 1924, his collection of approximately 2,500 items was purchased in England by Mrs Selwyn Upton and Mr W. Cecil Leys, and presented by them to Auckland Museum in memory of their late father Dr T. W. Leys who had a long and distinguished association with Auckland Museum.

Another famous collector was William O. Oldman who never travelled to the Pacific but assembled his personal collection of Pacific artefacts in England while making his living as a London dealer in ethnographica. In 1948 he sold his Pacific collection to the New Zealand Government, which distributed it among the main New Zealand museums. One important collector and scholar of Pacific cultures who spent all of his working life in the Pacific was Harry Maude, who presented the majority of this museum's Kiribati collection in 1985. He first went to work in the then Gilbert Islands group in 1929 as a cadet in the British Colonial Service, accompanied by his wife, Honor Courtney Maude.

Several other collectors whose names occur among the Auckland Museum jewellery collections are important for their connections, their dates and the areas that they reached. Some of these are Russell Bond (Unevangelised Fields missionary in Dutch West New Guinea in the 1950s), Ralph Bulmer and Bruce Biggs (University of Auckland anthropologists in the New Guinea highlands in 1959/1960), Rev. George Brown (pioneer Wesleyan Methodist missionary in New Britain in the 1870s), Rev. Archdeacon R. B. Comins (Melanesian Mission missionary in Vanuatu and the Solomon Islands in the 1890s), Mr. Tucker (Methodist Mission official who presented items collected by Rev. A. H. Scriven, missionary in the Trobriand Islands 1912 to 1930), J. B. Turner (businessman in

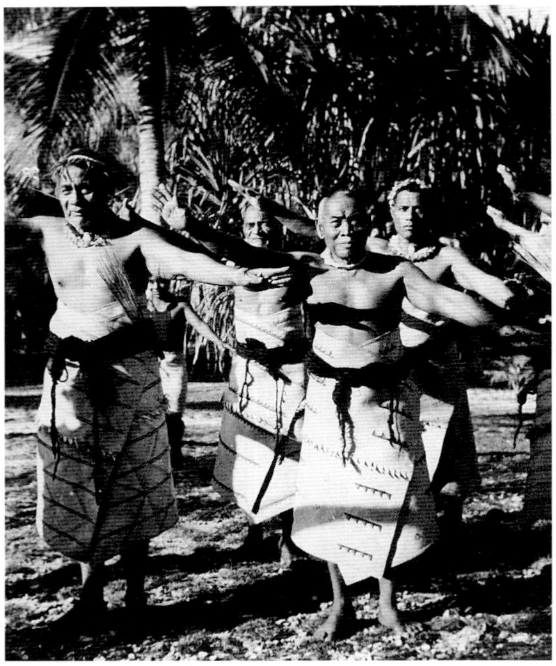

MALE DANCERS, TARAWA, KIRIBATI 1939

Song and dance continue to be very significant art forms in Kiribati today. These male dancers wear the finely woven pandanus dress mat, be. *Human hair belts,* nuota, *secure the mats around their waists; often the decorative elements within the mats are achieved using human hair also. Headbands of leaves and flowers are simple and constructed quite quickly, and may be discarded soon after use. However two of the dancers wear* nta, *spondylus shell pendants, which are valuable family heirlooms.*

Photo: O.M. Turbot, Auckland Museum C48025

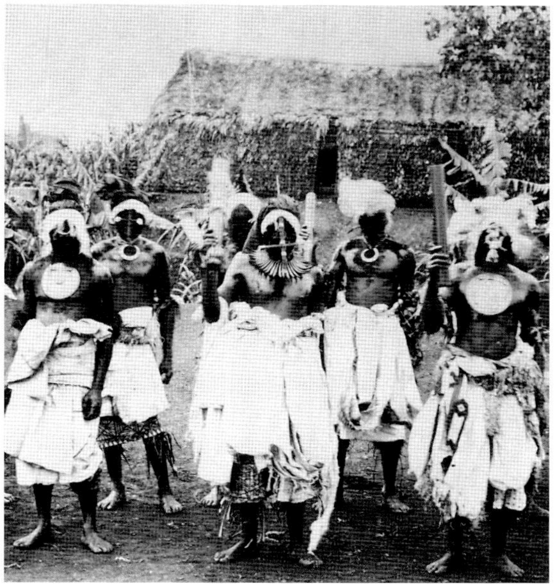

Fan and bamboo *meke* dance, Wainibuka, Viti Levu, Fiji, 1881

For their meke *dance with large palm leaf fans and bamboo tube beaters, these Fijian men wear a variety of shell and ivory breastplates, tusks and necklaces of split sperm whale teeth. Their faces are blackened with charcoal and their bodies are coated with scented coconut oil. Their clothing consists of brown or white tapa barkcloth turbans and copious drapes of white tapa around their waists worn over freehand painted tapa wrap-arounds.*

Photo: From Ansdell 1882 Plate 37

Fiji in the 1880s to 1920s), Rev. A. H. Voyce (Methodist missionary in Bougainville from 1920s to 1930s), James Adams Wilkes (colonial official in early post-German New Guinea).

Many of the other collectors and donors are now just names in the museum files with no information about what they were doing in these areas or how or why they obtained these objects. Collectors such as R. Recknagel and G. Stuart in German New Guinea in the 1880s must have experienced some amazing adventures, but their only record now are their names attached to their collections. Nevertheless, the contribution of all of these people is acknowledged and appreciated by the museum and its public.

As with most museum collections of artefacts, the records of where items were collected are often vague and unreliable. Even where the locality of collection has been carefully recorded, this does not always mean that the item was made there. This is especially true for such portable artefacts as jewellery that was traded and exchanged around the islands by the islanders themselves and by European settlers and travellers. This uncertainty is sometimes reflected in the captions in this book where the stated origin may not be the place where the jewellery was actually collected or may be an origin attributed to an unlocalised item by the authors on the basis of comparison.

For dates of manufacture, the records are even more vague. Obviously the item was made before the recorded date of acquisition by the museum, but for almost all the items that is the only definite date available. Shell and stone jewellery can last for a reasonably long time in a village situation, while archaeological finds may be hundreds of years old. Other pieces have been held in private collections for many years before coming to the museum. Except for the rare early pieces whose age is discussed in the captions, most of the items illustrated in this book were probably made at some time after the first decades of the nineteenth century at the earliest.

Most of the archival and recent field photographs included to illustrate the wearing of Pacific jewellery in its original cultural contexts have been selected from the photographic collections of Auckland Museum, except where noted in the captions. Significant earlier Pacific photographers represented here are Thomas Andrew (traveller and later professional photographer based in Samoa in the later nineteenth century), John Watt Beattie (Tasmanian professional who made an extended trip through Melanesia on the *Southern Cross* mission ship in 1906), Russell Bond (Unevangelised Fields missionary in Dutch West New Guinea in the 1950s), Mrs A. Grace-Jones (missionary in Papua New Guinea from 1961 to 1963), Josiah Martin (Auckland professional in the later nineteenth century), Percy Money (Australian missionary in Collingwood Bay between 1901 and 1911), James Adams Wilkes (colonial official in early post-German New Guinea), and Alexander Wollaston and Cecil Boden Kloss (explorers in Dutch West New Guinea in 1912).

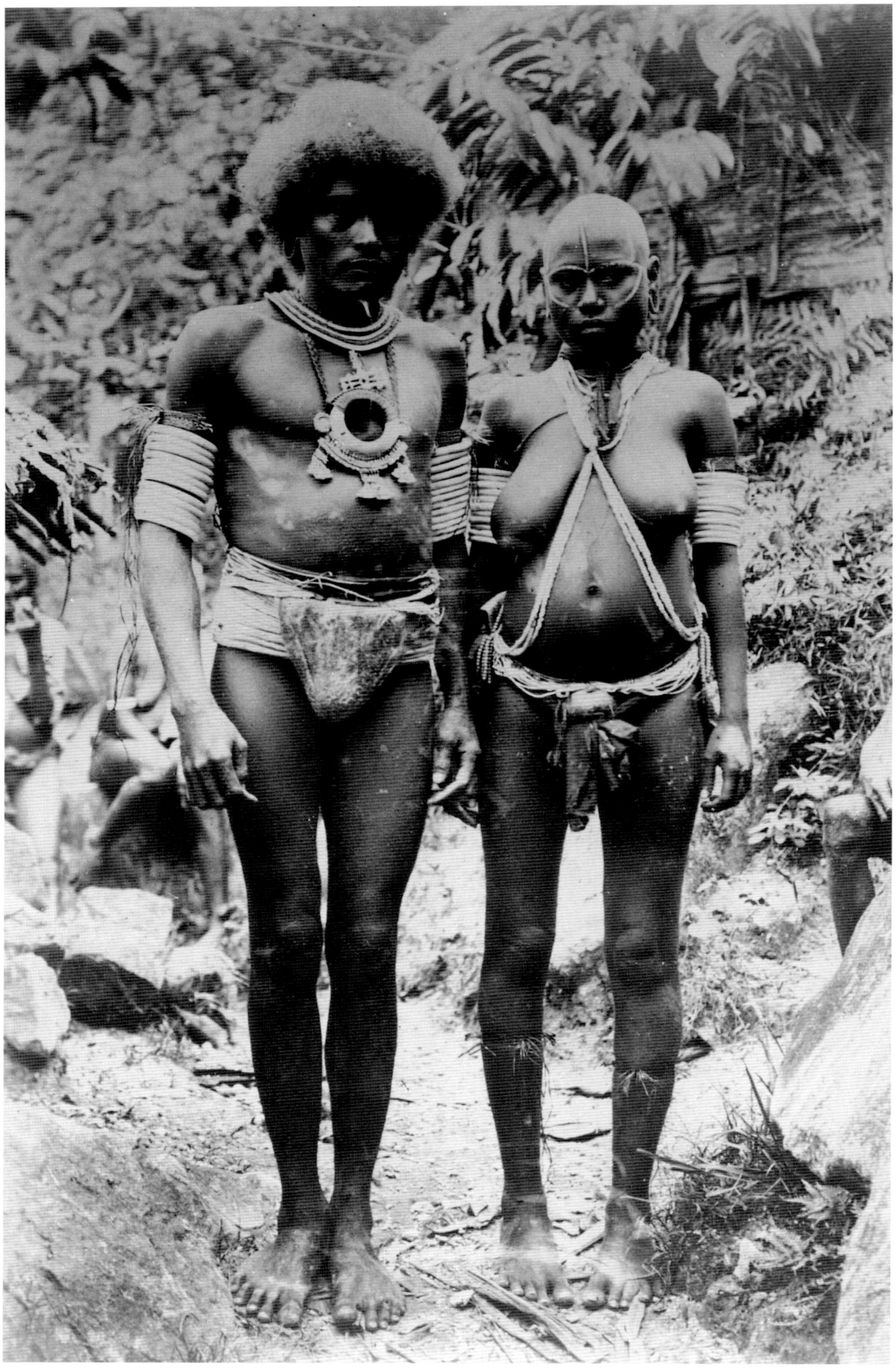

Nake and his bride Tali, Solomon Islands, c. 1900

Probably photographed at New Georgia or Vella Lavella, both Nake and his wife Tali from Simbo are wearing breechclouts of plain tapa barkcloth. Their clam shell armrings represent considerable wealth from both of their families, paraded for the wedding ceremonies. On his chest, Nake wears a chief's breast ornament consisting of a clam shell ring decorated with opossum teeth, called a bakiha *at New Georgia or* tarkola *at Vella Lavella.*

Photo: Alexander Turnbull Library, Wellington F111265-1//2

BIBLIOGRAPHY

Alkire, William H. *An Introduction to the Peoples and Cultures of Micronesia.* Addison-Wesley Modular Publications, Module 18, 1972

Ansdell, Gerrard. *A Trip to the Highlands of Viti Levu being a description of photographic views taken in the Fiji Islands during the dry season of 1881.* Blair Ansdell, London, 1882

Bodrogi, Tibor. *Art in North-east New Guinea.* Hungarian Academy of Sciences, Budapest, 1961

Bonnemaison, Joel, Christian Kaufmann, Kirk Huffman and Darrell Tryon. *Arts of Vanuatu.* Crawford House, Bathurst 1996

Buck, Peter H. 'Arts and Crafts of Hawai'i', *Bernice P. Bishop Museum Special Publication* 45. Bishop Museum Press, Honolulu, Hawai'i, 1957

Buck, Peter H. 'Arts and Craft of the Cook Islands', *Bernice P. Bishop Museum Bulletin 179.* Honolulu, Hawai'i, 1944

Buck, Peter H. 'Samoan Material Culture', *Bernice P. Bishop Museum Bulletin 75.* Honolulu, Hawai'i, 1930

Buck, Peter H. 'The Material Culture of the Cook Islands (Aitutaki), *Memoirs of the Board of Maori Ethnological Research, Volume I.* New Plymouth, New Zealand, 1927

Clunie, Fergus. *Yalo i Viti: Shades of Fiji: A Fiji Museum Catalogue.* Fiji Museum, Suva, 1986

Edmundson, Anna and Chris Boylan. *Adorned: Traditional Jewellery and Body Decoration from Australia and the Pacific.* University of Sydney, Sydney, 1999

Firth, Raymond. *We, The Tikopia. A Sociological Study of Kinship in Primitive Polynesia.* Allen and Unwin. London, 1961

Heermann, Ingrid and Ulrich Menter. *Schmuck der Südsee: Ornament und Symbol.* Prestel-Verlag, Munich, 1990

Kirch, Patrick Vinton. *On the Road of the Winds: An Archaeological History of the Pacific Islands before European Contact.* University of California Press, Berkeley, 2000

Koch, Gerd. *The Material Culture of Kiribati.* English translation by Guy Slatter. The Institute of Pacific Studies of the University of the South Pacific. Suva, Fiji, 1986

Linton, Ralph. 'The Material Culture of the Marquesas Islands', *Memoirs of the Bernice P. Bishop Museum Volume VIII, No. 5.* Honolulu, Hawai'i, 1923

Neich, Roger. A Semiological Analysis of Self-Decoration in Mount Hagen, New Guinea. In I. Rossi and contributors: *The Logic of Culture. Advances in Structural Theory and Method.* Bergin, South Hadley, Massachusetts, 1982

Neich, Roger. *Pounamu: Maori Jade of New Zealand.* Auckland Museum/ David Bateman, Auckland, 1997

Newton, Douglas. *Arts of the South Seas: Island South-east Asia, Melanesia, Polynesia, Micronesia.* Prestel Munich, 1999

Ohnemus, Sylvia. *An Ethnology of the Admiralty Islanders: The Alfred Bühler Collection, Museum der Kulturen, Basel.* University of Hawai'i Press, Honolulu, 1998

Parkinson, Richard. *Thirty Years in the South Seas: Land, and People, Customs and Traditions in the Bismarck Archipelago and on the German Solomon Islands.* Crawford House, Bathurst, 1999

Phelps, Steven. *Art and Artefacts of the Pacific, Africa and the Americas.* The James Hooper Collection. Hutchinson, London, 1975

Prickett, Nigel. *Nga Tohu Tawhito: Early Maori Ornaments.* Auckland Museum/ David Bateman, Auckland, 1999

Quiggan, A. Hingston. *A Survey of Primitive Money: The Beginnings of Currency.* Methuen, London, 1949

St Cartmail, Keith. *The Art of Tonga.* Craig Potton Publishing, Nelson, New Zealand, 1997

Sinclair, James. *Wigmen of Papua.* Jacaranda, Brisbane

Smith, S. Percy. *Niue: The Island and Its People.* University of the South Pacific, Suva, 1983

Specht, Jim and John Fields. *Frank Hurley in Papua: Photographs of the 1920–1923 Expeditions.* Australian Museum Trust, Sydney, 1984

Speiser, Felix. *Ethnology of Vanuatu: An early twentieth century study.* Crawford House, Bathurst, 1990

Strathern, Andrew and Marilyn Strathern. *Self-Decoration in Mount Hagen.* Duckworth, London, 1971

Waite, Deborah. *Art of the Solomon Islands from the collection of the Barbier-Müller Museum.* Musée Barbier-Müller, Geneva, 1983

Waite, Deborah. *Artefacts from the Solomon Islands in the Julius L. Brenchley Collection.* British Museum Publications, London, 1987

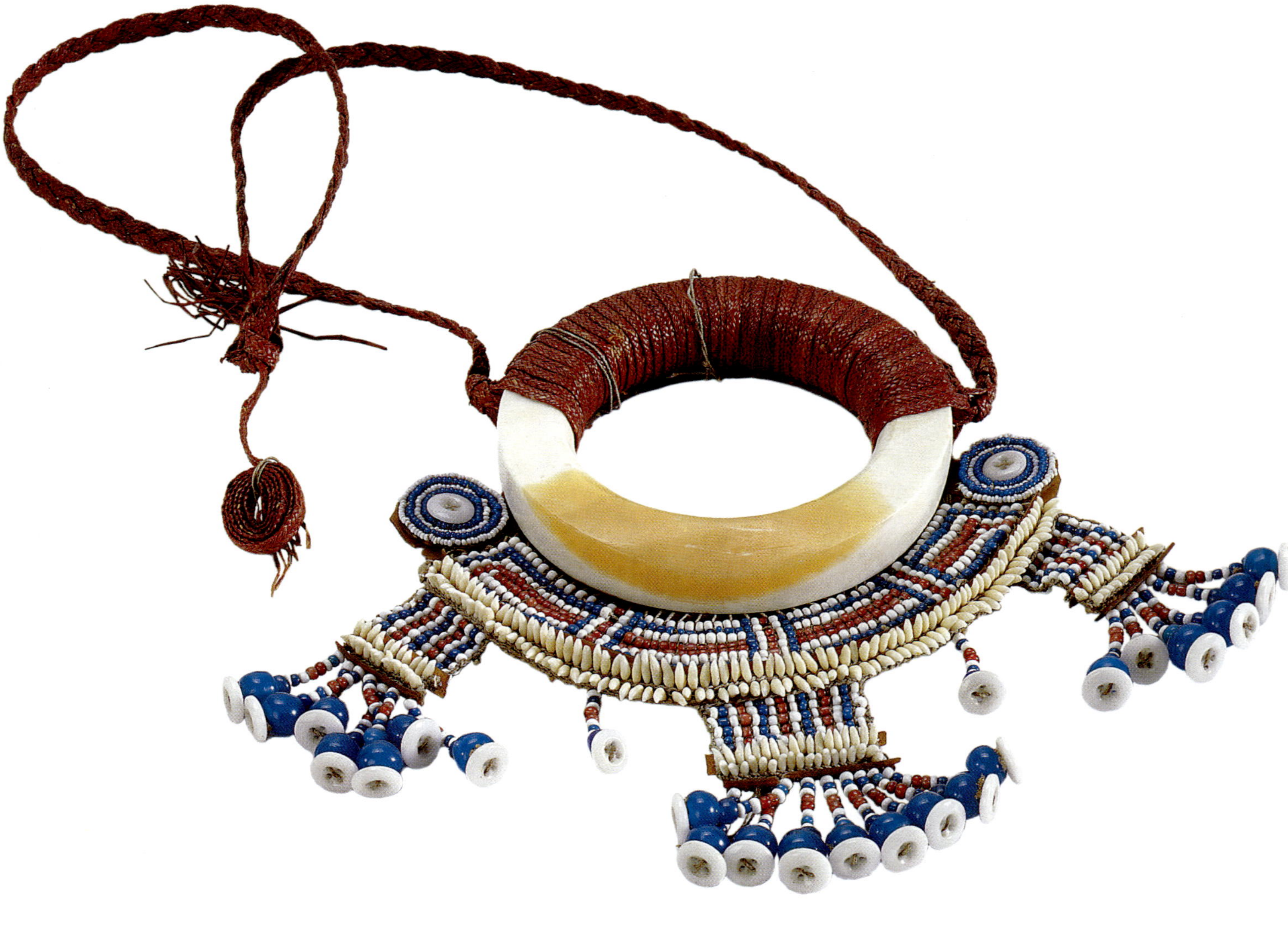

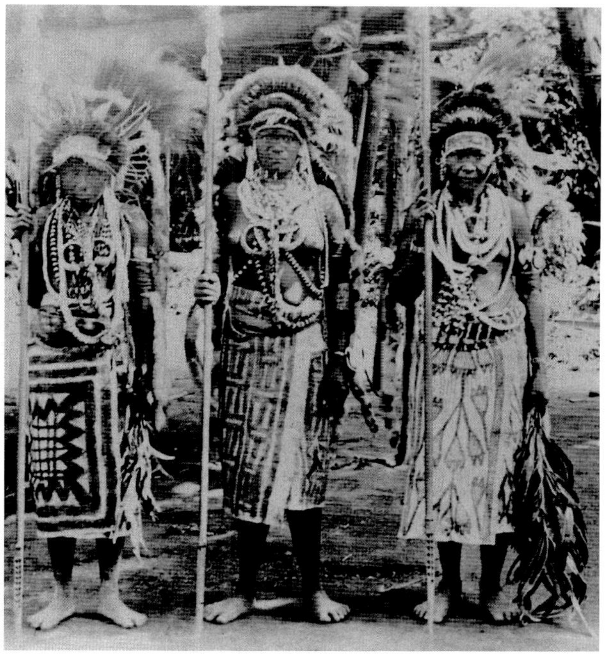

ONJOB WOMEN WEARING MEN'S FIGHTING REGALIA, WANIGELA AREA, COLLINGWOOD BAY, ORO PROVINCE, PAPUA NEW GUINEA, BETWEEN 1901 AND 1911

Percy Money, the local missionary who took this photograph, described a unique custom practised by the women of the Onjob people when a chief had died. After the funeral is finished, the women of the tribe dress in their husbands' war costumes of plumes and ornaments to perform a ceremonial dance armed with the men's spears. This also becomes an occasion for the women to display the wealth of their husbands in the form of their shell and teeth ornaments.

Photo: Percy Money, Auckland Museum 97/53

opposite: ***BAKIHA* BREAST ORNAMENT, VELLA LAVELLA, SOLOMON ISLANDS**

Embodying the higher powers of the ancestors and worn only by men of chiefly rank as a marker of their authority, the bakiha *breast ornament combined items of currency and value into a display of wealth and influence. This form of breast ornament is worn quite widely in the western Solomon Islands of Vella Lavella and New Georgia.*

AM 47649. Purchased from Mr A.M. Bensley 1975.

INDEX

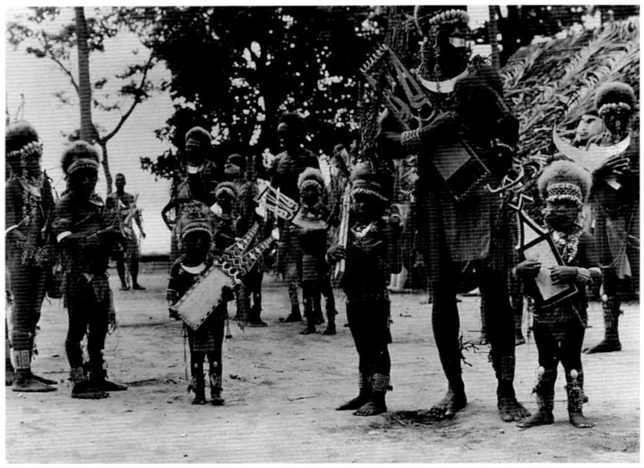

Young initiates into the bonito cult, Santa Ana, Solomon Islands, 1943

These boys are dressed in full ceremonial costume of shell and animal teeth valuables for the final stage of their initiation into the bonito cult. The older boy in front wears a nose ornament called tamono-arafa *cut from pearl shell. Each initiate carries a wooden shield carved with designs based on frigate bird motifs. The unusually wide range of ages among the initiates reflects the fact that this initiation ceremony in 1943 had been delayed for many years and was also expected to be the last ever held.*

Photo: Merrill Moore, Auckland Museum C20812